Praise for The Ninefold Way of Avalon

"This book is a deepening of the previous works, *Avalon Within* and *The Mythic Moons of Avalon*, for those who feel called to dedicate themselves to a particular path embedded within Avalonian tradition and lore...The scholarship, the dedication, and the love that brought this book out into the world by Jhenah Telyndru is second to none."

—JOANNA VAN DER HOEVEN, AUTHOR OF *THE BOOK OF HEDGE DRUIDRY* AND *THE PATH OF THE HEDGE WITCH*

"Jhenah Telyndru embodies the true work of the priestess as she reveals what must be shared, veils what must be sought through mystery, and creates new magickal models with deep roots. In *The Ninefold Way of Avalon*, she weaves threads of poetry, academia, and magickal service, revealing hidden gems of history and lore while sharing treasures only found from direct practice to create a ninefold vision of magickal training and community."

—CHRISTOPHER PENCZAK, CO-FOUNDER OF THE TEMPLE OF WITCHCRAFT TRADITION AND BESTSELLING AUTHOR OF *THE TEMPLE OF WITCHCRAFT* SERIES

"An intriguing and enlightening look at the often-confusing subject of Avalon, exploring nearly a millennia of myths, stories, and beliefs that surround the mysterious Isle of Apples and weaving a modern living practice from the evidence of the past. The book offers not only some clarity on the wider subject but guidance for those who want to actively engage with this place and all that it represents, making it an invaluable resource."

—MORGAN DAIMLER, AUTHOR OF *IRISH PAGANISM*

"In this fantastic and accessible work, Telyndru slowly peels away the shroud of mystery surrounding the mystical shores of Avalon...I cannot imagine a better resource for those wishing to immerse themselves in the waters of Avalon."

—MHARA STARLING, AUTHOR OF *WELSH WITCHCRAFT*

T0352886

THE NINEFOLD WAY OF

AVALON

© Sharone Marraccini

About the Author

Jhenah Telyndru (New York) holds an MA in Celtic Studies from the University of Wales, Trinity St. David, and has a bachelor's degree in archaeology. She founded the Sisterhood of Avalon in 1995, and serves as the Academic Dean of the Avalonian Thealogical Seminary. Jhenah hosts residential training retreats around North America and the UK, presents internationally at conferences and festivals, teaches online workshops and immersion programs, and facilitates pilgrimages to sacred sites in the British Isles and Ireland through Mythic Seeker Tours. A priestess in the Avalonian Tradition for almost 35 years, Jhenah has been following a Pagan path since 1986. Visit her at www.ynysafallon.com and www.sisterhoodofavalon.org.

THE NINEFOLD WAY OF
AVALON

Walking the Path of the Priestess

JHENAH TELYNDRU

Llewellyn Publications
Woodbury, Minnesota

First Edition
First Printing, 2023

Book layout by R. Brasington
Cover art by Lauren Blake
Cover design by Shannon McKuhen
Editing by Laura Kurtz
Interior Art by Llewellyn Art Department

Llewellyn Publications is a registered trademark of Llewellyn Worldwide Ltd.

Library of Congress Cataloging-in-Publication Data (Pending)
ISBN: 978-0-7387-6496-2

Llewellyn Worldwide Ltd. does not participate in, endorse, or have any authority or responsibility concerning private business transactions between our authors and the public.

All mail addressed to the author is forwarded but the publisher cannot, unless specifically instructed by the author, give out an address or phone number.

Any internet references contained in this work are current at publication time, but the publisher cannot guarantee that a specific location will continue to be maintained. Please refer to the publisher's website for links to authors' websites and other sources.

Llewellyn Publications
A Division of Llewellyn Worldwide Ltd.
2143 Wooddale Drive
Woodbury, MN 55125-2989
www.llewellyn.com

Printed in the United States of America

CONTENTS

ACKNOWLEDGMENTS

While the process of writing a book often feels like a solitary endeavor, it has been my experience that it is only made possible through the support, encouragement, and understanding of others. This book was a particularly difficult one to birth, in part because of life circumstances during the time of the COVID-19 pandemic, but also because of how much this work has taken residence in my heart. I have been working on and with aspects of this book for almost three decades, and what you hold in your hands is just a portion of all of the words I've written for this book in that time. Some of those words will make their way between other covers, while I have evolved away from others—and sifting between them was no easy task.

I have had many midwives assisting me with this birth, some more directly than others, but I am grateful for all of the beautiful support I've received. I would first like to acknowledge my gratitude to the Sisterhood of Avalon and all of my Sisters. I am especially thankful for the women of the Council of Nine and the SOA Board of Trustees, past and present, both for their support of me during this process and for their incredible dedication to the maintenance and flourishing of our community.

Special thanks go out to Sisters Kelly Woo and Kate Brunner for sharing their artistic gifts: Kelly for patiently working with me to manifest the Nine Path Symbols, and Kate for masterfully rendering the cosmological map of the Avalonian Tradition in a way my chicken-scratch never could.

I am grateful for the expertise of Kitos Digiovanni, PhD, whose independent translation of the Metz Inscription (chapter 4) from Latin was of enormous assistance. Thanks also to Morgan Daimler and Katherine O'Meara Reynolds for their assistance with the Modern and Old Irish spellings for druidess, prophetess, and poetess.

Yet again I find myself at a loss for the words needed to adequately thank my amazing editor Elysia Gallo for her brilliant mind, clarity of vision, and patient support in getting this book birthed and sent out into the world. Thank you a millionfold for believing in this work and in me. Thank you as well to the rest of the incredible publishing team at Llewellyn Worldwide, especially my copy editor, Laura Kurtz.

I am grateful as well for the incredible circle of friends who have blessed my life in so many ways—who support and uplift me, who encourage and hear me, who understand and are patient with me, who arrange sleepovers with our children so that I can meet deadlines, who make sure that I eat and sleep, and who are truly reflections of the Divine in the world. Thank you especially to Judy, Lori, Tiffany, and Morgaine.

And last but not least, I am grateful to my children, who have grown up in a home with a crazy writer/chaos gremlin for a mother and yet have still managed to become the most grounded, loving, compassionate, and understanding beings I know. They have been so patient and understanding of my process; as they begin to transform into adults before my eyes, they have also been a cherished source of support and my biggest team of cheerleaders. Thank you for the privilege of being your mother. I love you both!

INTRODUCTION

Three Chains Which Uphold the Vessel of Sovereignty:
Service to Self, through Wholeness remembered;
Service to Community, through Skills reclaimed;
Service to the Divine, through Connection renewed.
—J. TELYNDRU

From the moment I first became aware of Avalon, I have endeavored to find her. First, in the pages of literature, later through the discipline of academia, and always, humbly, through the promptings of spirit. I have searched for Avalon in the echoes of myth—through the vessel of the landscape, in moon-drenched orchards, and in collective women-song. I have sought her out in lonely library stacks, between the yellowed pages of out-of-print treasures, and in the late-night illumination of digitized journals. I have journeyed through more subtle realms … stepping over thresholds, passing over nine waves, and learning to kindle a fire in the hearth of my heart.

Along this journey, I have witnessed Avalon as shapeshifter. Here, a paradise: ripe with fruit … rich with grain and grapes and honey. There, a college of Druidesses … a cloister of priestesses, greatly knowledgeable in mathematics and astronomy … mistresses in the arts of music, of healing, of alchemy. Flying forth from their island home as flocks of black-feathered birds to places of learning, to fields of battle, to gather around fountains … some sweet with mead, others tinged with iron.

Sometimes she is a symbol of resistance … a symbol of hope, persisting: the resting place of Arthur, the once and future king. Sometimes he is healed—awaiting the moment of Britain's greatest need. Sometimes he is buried—his name etched upon a leaden cross. Always, he is in the keeping of She who is Born of the Sea: Morgen. His ally and enemy. His healer and sister. The Barge Queen who lays his wounded head upon her lap, and the first of Nine Sisters who lays his wounded body upon her golden bed.

Avalon's shapeshifting ability is both the result of and the reason for her longevity.

The Avalonian Stream of Tradition is the lineage of symbol, story, and Sisterhood that has traveled down the current of time to arrive here with us in the present and into our keeping. This stream is not a straightforward one, however; its path of flow has connected it to many adjacent teachings, filtered it through many unconscious constructs, and nourished more souls than we could ever dream of as it coursed along its way. There are many places where we can enter the Avalonian Stream of Tradition, many vessels from which to partake of her healing abundance. But no matter the form those vessels take or the construct of the shoreline, all connect to the same source and are fed by the same water—even as it winds its way through different cultural landscapes, even as it encounters different social perspectives over time.

From our vantage point today, the more of this stream we are able to see, the deeper we are able to immerse in it. The more we are aware of the history of its flow—the landscapes it has passed through, the makeup of its waters—the more we are able to reach back to touch the source of the stream and come into authentic relationship with She who awaits us there. This immersion can also reveal the tributaries and branches of the stream; the places where waters from other sources join and mix with it, as well as the places where rivulets have diverged from the main course—here, going its own way, flowing to a trickle before drying out … there, joining with larger and mightier rivers until it reaches the waters of the great ocean … flowing out beyond the Ninth Wave and passing, finally, out of our sight.

The challenge and charge of those who seek to walk the ways of the Avalonian Priestess is to become as whole a vessel as we can, in order to carry the waters of this particular stream—to allow it to induce transformation in our lives, and reawaken the Sovereignty of self that we have far too often deferred. It is only when we are able to fill the Vessel of the Self with these waters that we can be in service as a Cauldron Kindler, a Cup Bearer, or a Grail Maiden—both for ourselves and for others. We can then engage in priestess service that aims to catalyze and heal, inspire and protect, support and envision, remember and create, express and celebrate—bridging the space between the worlds to allow the creative essence of the Awen to flow through us—both in Sovereignty and in service.

The work that follows is a sharing of what this decades-long journey has taught me about the Holy Isle, as well as a reflection on the path of the Avalonian priestess as seen through the mirror of my own understanding—both in what it may have looked like in the past and in how it can manifest in the present. While there are many modern paths inspired by the lore and legends of Avalon, I can only speak for the Avalonian Tradition as I have written about it and as the Sisterhood of Avalon practices it.

To this end, the first half of this book will delve into the mythic currents of the Avalonian Stream of Tradition. Using history, legend, folk tradition, and comparative mythology, we will explore the symbolism underscoring these motifs as we work to pull aside the veil of mists that obscures the origin, purpose, and cultural context of the Island of Apples and those who dwell there. We will also investigate what is known about the roles of holy women in pre-Christian Celtic societies, and delve into the origins of the mysterious Nine Sisters of Avalon.

We will do this through an examination of the groups of nine women found in the traditions of many Celtic lands as well as in related cultures of Indo-European derivation.

In the second half of this book, the information we have gathered is used to inform a neoteric approach to a modern Avalonian Priestess Path, inspired by the energies of the Ninefold and the components of Avalon's Stream of Tradition. The Avalonian perspective that the word "priestess" is a verb—something we do rather than someone we are—also serves to move us beyond the modern Pagan limitations of what priestessing looks like. We all know the priestess-ceremonialist, the priestess-oracle, the priestess-healer. Let us also make space for expressing sacred service in ways that are in sovereign alignment with our skills, our divinely gifted passions, and our work in the world—let us come to know the priestess-creator, the priestess-scholar, the priestess-guardian, the priestess-caregiver, the priestess-mediator, and the priestess-advocate, to name just a few.

In support of this goal, a hands-on system of spiritual engagement is presented to assist in connecting with the Ninefold aspects of the self, experiencing the energetic currents of each of the Ninefold Paths firsthand, and fostering authentic connections with the Ninefold Guardians of the Holy Isle. Taken together, they reveal the threshold we must cross to embark upon a course of service to Avalon guided by the Ninefold Path of the Priestess.

My intention for this book is for it to be the resource I wish I had when I first embarked upon this marshy pathway—sometimes made of solid ground, sometimes hindered by brackish mud, and always obscured by the mists of time—with the faith that it would bring me, in truth, to Avalon. It is my greatest hope that others will find this work to be a good companion on their own journeys to the Holy Isle whether they are in search of well-researched historical and cultural information or desiring a guided approach to spiritual engagement with the Realms of Avalon. May this book be of assistance to all who wish to build a bridge into connection, understanding, and relationship with Ynys Afallon—the Blessed Isle of wisdom, abundance, and renewal that awaits us in the Annuvian waters beyond the Ninth Wave, and deep within our own hearts.

THE MATTER OF AVALON

When we consider her potential origins in a mysterious pre-Christian past, her development as a cornerstone of hope in Arthurian legend, her reflowering into consciousness during the Victorian period, and the inspiration she brings to the Neopagan movement of the present, it is clear that the Matter of Avalon is a potent energetic current. Not only has she withstood the passage of time, but she has both reflected and been amplified by it.

But what is the truth of Avalon? Was she a physical place, a literary setting, or part of the Brythonic Otherworld? An island of priestesses or a kingdom of fairy women? A place of healing, or an Island of the Dead? Part of an ancient Pagan belief system, or a magical piece of lore that has burned brightly in the imagination of storytellers for centuries?

It is the nature of the Otherworld to be able to hold seemingly opposing energies at the same time, and so perhaps Avalon is all these things—and none of them. We will never be able to say with any certainty where or even whether any iteration of Avalon ever existed in the physical world, but this doesn't make her cultural influence any less real or her symbolic meaning any less true. Certainly there are physical locations that have come to be associated with the Isle of Avalon, but which came first: the legend or the location?

First appearing in the written record during the early medieval period and elaborated upon for centuries afterward, it is easy to dismiss Avalon as a purely literary creation, a fantastical setting found only in legend without any historical relevance or archaeological proof of its existence. However, the truth of Avalon is much more complicated than that.

Along with an enormous corpus of tales that became interwoven with the lore of Arthur over time, Avalon has become inextricably connected with the story of that once and future king. It is likely that Avalon's appearance in Arthurian legend is what has preserved her memory for us, transmitting it through time and into our modern-day keeping. While this preservation was primarily accomplished through story tradition, Avalon as we have come to know her is informed by the commingling of several very authentic streams of tradition. These streams flow through history as well as mythology, and are fed both by what has been recorded by chroniclers as well as what has been transmitted through folklore and cultural belief.

Whatever or wherever Avalon may once have been, her ability to inspire has transcended any physical location, exceeded any cultural time frame, and moved beyond any political borders to touch people around the world—and has done so for centuries. Perhaps, then, the power of Avalon is not in where she lies but in what she represents, as well as the mythic memories that have been transmitted as part of her narrative flow.

Convergence

To understand the whole of Avalon, we must tease out several interweaving streams of tradition that have converged to inform the essence of what we recognize today as Avalon. These streams of tradition include:

Traditions of Otherworldly Islands

Traditions of Ninefold Sisterhoods

Traditions of Vessels of Sovereignty

As these comingling streams passed through different cultural landscapes over the course of time, the nature and appearance of their flow shifted in response to the sociocultural environments through which they journeyed. As a result of these shifts, Avalon's increasingly unified stream of tradition began to exhibit different characteristics as its waters both mirrored, and were changed by, the cultural dynamics that interacted with its flow. As its story evolved, each version of Avalon can be seen to take on a form that best reflected what was most needed of it in the context of each given time frame or cultural circumstance.

When retracing the story of Avalon, it is therefore helpful to look at the different iterations or interpretations of symbols, plotlines, or characters as not being strictly linear or hierarchal, a quality due in part to the convoluted nature and evolution of Arthurian Tradition. A known path of story evolution sees Welsh tales—which contain story elements preserved in oral tradition that potentially originated in the Continental Celtic mother culture—migrate to France. There, the tales eventually become refashioned and augmented with local traditions that may also have had origins in the same Celtic mother culture, but which evolved independently in a Gaulish and then Breton context. Breton culture itself arose from a wave of immigration in the sub-Roman period of Brythonic peoples from Cornwall and Wales to an area that is today called *Breizh* (Breton), *Bretagne* (French), or *Brittany*.

Eventually, these evolved stories returned to Britain, where they underwent further transformation. When rewriting these tales, some British authors seem to have removed French story details that were not culturally relevant (or politically acceptable) and replaced them with older, native Welsh narrative elements that arose from separate yet adjacent traditions. As you can see, the process as we understand it is a complicated matter.

It is because of processes like this, as well as the natural shifts in story that one would expect from a body of literature that has developed over the course of more than a thousand years, Avalon has taken different forms at different times. She has been an Otherworldly paradise, an island of semidivine women, a realm of enchantresses, and the dwelling place of a collective of learned women. In modern tales, particularly *The Mists of Avalon* and all its inspired works, she is often a temple-college of very mortal priestesses. And yet, the underlying essence of Avalon has been carried from form to form, even as the cultural understanding of—and relationship with—that essence has shifted over time.

In the same way that archaeologists are able to obtain insight into a society based on analyses of their material cultural remains, a society's story traditions serve as psychological artifacts that can reveal a great deal about the cultural zeitgeist of a particular place and time. The cultural information transmitted through the historical record and through the medium of literature both contain truths, for one is always a reflection of the other. This is certainly the case for Arthurian legends in general, and we will examine the specifics of it as it concerns the Island of Avalon in particular.

So let us begin our exploration of this evocative yet enigmatic place by examining the cultural ancestry and literary inheritances of the Holy Isle. This overview will demonstrate the ways in which the motifs of Otherworldly Islands, Ninefold Sisterhoods, and Vessels of Sovereignty have both formed and informed the Avalonian Stream of Tradition, ebbing and flowing into and out of it over time, while the motifs themselves continued to evolve and grow independently. This information, in turn, will be used to inform our own understanding of Avalon's magic and how we can best approach her shores as modern practitioners.

Concerning Oral Tradition

The earliest written accounts of Avalon may prove the most informative for our understanding of her nature. They serve as a bridge, of sorts, between the traditions that were organically connected to her and transmitted through the medium of orality—that is, the form and function of the Holy Isle as inherited and understood by the individuals who first wrote about her—and those which evolved out of her literary legacy. Where manuscripts of ink and vellum can be definitively dated with certain degree of accuracy, oral tradition is much more numinous, existing in a timeless space passed down through generations and across cultural boundaries.

Oral tradition is living tradition, its vitality renewed as it is carried forward on the breath of each person who shares the story. Unlike the static nature of the written word, the mutable nature of orality gives it a greater ability to remain relevant, allowing it to gradually shift in response to, and as a reflection of, the cultural context and societal challenges of those who share the tale. Ostensibly, stories that did not remain relevant would cease to be passed along, eventually falling out of memory.

When Welsh vernacular tales (tales in their native tongue) were written down for the first time during the medieval period, it is believed that they included story elements originated in the mythology of the Pagan Celtic Britons. While under Roman rule, Christianity had come to Britain by the end of the fourth century, although conversion was not complete until the seventh.

Generally speaking, most scholars believe that the stories of Y Mabinogi and other tales included in the same manuscripts were first written down in the eleventh or twelfth centuries. It is thought that members of the Welsh nobility at the time hired scribes to preserve the cultural heritage of their people in response to their loss of independence to the English. There is, therefore, an assumption that these tales were faithfully recorded from orality, and were likely based on the recitation of professionals bards. Although not explicitly stated, some of the characters in these tales are believed to have once been Celtic British deities. This suggests that at least some components of these stories had been preserved in orality during the Christian period for at least four hundred years before they were written down. No matter how true to the oral tales the redactors of these stories may have been, the state of these tales at that given moment in time was clearly the result of centuries of cultural evolution.

Additionally, these stories from oral tradition continued to be transmitted orally even after they were written down and therefore continued to evolve independently of the literary record. We must remember that these manuscripts were limited in number and kept in the private collections of the nobility; they were expensive to produce and had to be copied by hand. And even if they weren't, the average person wasn't able to read. It is also likely that the tales that made it into writing represent just one version of any given story whose elements could differ regionally or over time. This means that more than one story tradition may have existed for any given tale.

Sometimes story variants show up independently in the literary record—whether contemporary to the first redactions or centuries down the line—while others may have been preserved through folk practices related to characters and events but lack direct reflections in the written record. Still others may have faded away before ever being recorded.

British folk practice and traditions that survived into the modern period may well have some ancient roots, but absent any contemporary sources to verify them (e.g., accounts of classical writers), we cannot prove any direct connection to ancient Pagan practices. Some traditions coming into being during the Christian period might nevertheless have a Pagan "feel" to them; rather than ancient survivors, they may instead be reflections of the needs of an agrarian people to be in right relationship with their land, seeking intercession, blessings, and healing.

All of this said, when it comes to the stories recorded out of orality during the medieval period in Wales and other Celtic lands, I feel it is important to emphasize that the tales that preserve strains of pre-Christian mythology should not be considered "corrupted" or "defective" in the forms we have received them. They are the result of an organic narrative evolution in response to cultural changes (such as the Roman occupation, the gradual conversion to Christianity, the waves of post-Roman invasions) and shifts in social needs (such as those accompanying the societal changes arising from moving away from the tribalism of the Iron Age and toward unified kingdoms with centralized leadership of the medieval period). Regardless of their evolutionary progress over time, these stories are still very much a part of Welsh heritage. The very fact that these stories actively remained in oral tradition and continued to be transmitted from generation to generation and then were deemed worthy of preservation in writing is proof of their continued relevance and cultural importance.

On Legends and Lore

The muse of History has three handmaids, very much younger than herself, the children of her maturity. They are called Hagiography, Folklore and Toponymy. They are all three necessary for the fulfillment of her task.[1]

—G. H. Doble

Generally speaking, mythology and folklore are important sources for understanding a culture because they are reflections of the societies that birthed and maintained them. These stories unconsciously provide windows into their culture of origin's belief system, their values, their view of the world, and their concept of their place within that world. Just

---

1   G. H. Doble, "Hagiography and Folklore (Read before the Society at a Meeting Held at Exeter College, Oxford, on November 11, 1942)," *Folklore* 54, no. 3 (1943): 321–333, https://doi.org/10.1080/0015587x.1943.9717685, 321.

because a story is considered a legend doesn't mean that it has no basis in fact or its contents are purely imaginary. In actuality, the details preserved in myths and legend reflect the sociocultural contexts from which they arose.

For example, we can learn a lot about medieval Welsh society when we read the tales of *Y Mabinogi*. A face-value reading of these stories from a modern perspective provides insight into many aspects of medieval Welsh culture, including laws and hierarchies, the rights and privileges of women, modes of dress and societal expectations, ethics and morality, trade and diplomatic relations with other nations, beliefs concerning magic and the Otherworld, and societal expectations.

We can delve deeper into the tales by analyzing them from the perspective of their contemporary audience; this reveals a cultural code that gives subtextual meaning to narrative details that would have been immediately understood by someone in medieval Wales, but lost on the modern reader. Reading the stories in this context permits us to understand the cultural significance of story elements such as the animals that appear, the fabrics people wear, the colors of their horses, the order in which characters are seated at a feast, the language forms that they use when speaking to each other, and so on. An even deeper understanding of these tales can be obtained by reading them in their original Middle Welsh, which reveals a great deal of linguistic nuance and creative wordplay simply lost in translation.

Some tales include allusions to contemporary political situations that someone in medieval Wales would easily recognize, but only an historian of medieval Wales would be able to catch today. Other stories contain references to historical events or personages distant to even the medieval writer, who may not have recognized them for what they are. Depending on the impact of these events and the amount of time the tales spent in orality, the presentation of these historical figures and situations in the narrative may have evolved in such a way that they have become characters with godlike powers (or who are literally identified as divinities), their homes have become magical lands, and their actions have become larger than life. This is a process mythologists call *euhemerism*, whereby accounts of historical events change over time to take on the qualities of myth.

Reverse euhemerism can also occur. Sometimes legends, especially those containing elements of the supernatural, are in fact remnants of sacred stories that have evolved over time to reduce the stature of the gods in keeping with cultural changes, e.g., those that accompanied the coming of Christianity. Although demoted in status, it is not unusual for these former divinities to nevertheless carry remnants of past attributes that attest to their divine heritage. In Welsh legends, for example, Brythonic deities often appear in the guise of Otherworldly queens, powerful magicians, giants, fairies and mermaids, sorceresses, and characters possessing supernatural powers such as prophecy, healing, and shapeshifting.

Another thing to take note of when reading these stories is the appearance of characters, settings, or plot points that appear to be out of place compared to the contemporary cultural context of the times in which they were written. There are several reasons this might occur. First, it can be because the tale is intentionally depicting a place or person existing outside the ordinary scheme of things—e.g., characters living in magical settlements below a lake or exhibiting the opposite from expected reaction to events, such as laughing at a funeral—in order to create a contrast with "the norm". Alternatively, these out of synch elements could be a mythic remnant of an older narrative stream that was preserved within the tale; which is to say, the story itself evolved but portions of it maintained characteristics of an earlier time period. An example of this is the subtextual matrilineal inheritance plotline in the Fourth Branch of *Y Mabinogi*—a form of inheritance through the mother-line that was not in practice during medieval Wales but nevertheless shows up in several Welsh tales written in this period.

Likewise, the legends concerning enclaves of holy or Otherworldly women from Celtic lands sometimes straddle these possibilities. Are these women—who often present as fay beings, witches, or enchantresses—what remains of cultural memories of ancient priestess orders that have entered the realms of legend in possession of supernatural powers through the process of euhemerism? Or were these groupings of magical women once collectives of goddesses, whose provenance over various aspects of living and dying became diminished over time, turning them into fairy women with mysterious powers?

In truth, we cannot be entirely sure of either possibility, nor can we fully account for instances of a third option—where new stories of fairy women come into being that are not the result of euhemerism or reverse euhemerism, instead arising from the influence of older fairy legends to become a literary motif. Thankfully, in some cases we are able to trace the evolution of stories and characters back along a particular stream of tradition, and many scholars have spent lifetimes outlining the literary heritages of many aspects of the lore of Celtic lands and related tales in Arthurian Tradition. However, much has been lost to us—in part because of the Celts' dedication to oral transmission of their sacred teachings and in part because of cultural shifts that may not have valued the transmission of stories that centered, for example, the roles of women, Pagan or otherwise.

Regardless of whether there is any direct historical basis for the events depicted in legends like the Four Branches, or in the stories of Avalon that are part of Arthurian Tradition, elements of historicity and cultural authenticity are embedded in these narratives. The end result is a body of literature that nevertheless serves as an invaluable resource for the transmission of native traditions and beliefs, some of which may be the cultural inheritors of pre-Christian British practices and mythology. Since there is very little direct information about these pre-Christian practices or beliefs, the information that we can glean indirectly from this literature becomes especially precious.

Arthurian Tradition

Any examination of Avalon must, by necessity, include a discussion of Arthurian Tradition. Just as the mortally wounded King Arthur was borne across the waters to be held in the keeping of the Holy Isle, so too has the memory of Avalon been carried forward to us, preserved in the stream of tradition that has formed, and been formed by, Arthurian legend.

Although authors from other nations have expanded upon the corpus of work concerning Arthur and his court, at its foundation, these tales remain "The Matter of Britain." Originating in the story traditions of the Brythonic Celtic peoples of Wales, Cornwall, Brittany, and the Old North, it passed into France by way of Breton *lais* and courtly poetry before spreading throughout Europe. Story elements that modern readers consider core to Arthurian Tradition—such as the Round Table, the Quest for the Grail, and the Sword in the Stone—are not present in the earliest tales; they were added by French and German writers and soon became accepted as part of Arthurian "canon."

The literary development of Arthurian legend over time is a reflection of the lands through which its stream of tradition has flowed, and its evolution is a mirror of sorts for the cultural history of Britain and medieval Europe. It is a complex matter that spans centuries and defies national borders, becoming an interweaving of various cultural influences.

Arthurian legends from different periods are infused with the politics of their day, as court poets and traveling minstrels used these tales to flatter their patrons or support the agendas of their kings. Part of the popularity of the Arthurian Tradition in the Celtic lands of Wales, Cornwall, and Brittany is the vision it presented: an imagined time when Britain was sovereign, formed by a loose confederation of kingdoms that were united under a High King who held the Saxon invasions at bay.

The story cycles of Arthurian Tradition combine within it strains of history and legend, mythology and religion, literature and oral tradition. They have grown from the seeds of their ancient origins to flourish in a continual renewal and reinterpretation, even into the modern day—still dynamic, still developing. Initially rooted in native sources, the fruits of the Arthurian Tradition being harvested today will, in turn, yield the seeds of a new crop that will be recalibrated to feed its future audience in new ways.

Libraries worth of books analyzing Arthurian legends have been written by scholars who have dedicated their lives to its study; occultists, psychologists, and religious people have found profundity in the symbolism embedded in the tales and authors have poured out their Awen or inspiration in service of creating new stories within the Arthurian realms. Taken together, these works have produced a vast corpus of literature that draws equally from deep wells of wisdom and high peaks of creativity.

Because of the vast catalog of symbols and motifs carried along the stream of Arthurian Tradition, only a few facets of the whole of the Arthurian jewel will be touched upon within this work. We will focus— by necessity and in support of our purpose—on the currents that carry the wisdoms of the Vessels of Sovereignty, the paradisiacal islands of the Otherworld, and the holy women who hold both in their keeping.

When researching Avalon and the women associated with her in Arthurian lore, there comes a point at which their appearances no longer serve as a chronicle of tradition but cross into a purely literary realm. When that happens, these accounts are less able to inform our understanding of Avalon's original nature and instead become more instructive about the perspectives held by the authors—and by extension, their contemporary societies—concerning the place of women and their power, the ramifications of their sexuality and sovereignty, and the belief in (and practice of) magic.

From his very first written mention to the full blooming of Arthurian literature and into today, Arthur was many things. Whether or not he was ever an historical personage, he was certainly a culture hero…a messianic figure who promised to return when Britain needed him the most, and someone who relied upon the magic of Avalon to keep him—and the promise of freedom and sovereignty he represented to so many—alive. In return, the tales of Arthur served to keep the memory of Avalon alive—and it is this memory that we will now explore.

Earliest Written Accounts of Avalon

The first recorded reference to Avalon appears in the *Historia Regum Britanniae* (*History of the Kings of Britain*), a Latin pseudohistory written by Geoffrey of Monmouth (c. 1095–c. 1155) in 1139. A cleric and scholar of Welsh or Welsh-Norman descent, his works were so instrumental in establishing Arthurian canon that the whole of the lore and its subsequent additions came to be classified as "pre-Galfridian" and "post-Galfridian," in reference to his name in Latin: Galfridus Monemutensis.

In his *Historia*, Geoffrey writes that Arthur's sword Caliburn had been forged on the *Insula Avallonis*, the Island of Avallon, the isle to which Arthur would later be taken to be cured of his mortal wounds after his last battle.

> And even the renowned king Arthur himself was mortally wounded; and being carried thence to the isle of Avallon to be cured of his wounds, he gave up the crown of Britain to his kinsman Constantine, the son of Cador, duke of Cornwall, in the five hundred and forty-second year of our Lord's incarnation.[2]

The *Historia* influenced a variety of historical accounts written in vernacular Welsh, first appearing in the thirteenth century, called *Brut y Brenhinedd* (*Chronicle of the Kings*). These histories were not direct translations of the Latin *Historia*; different versions included commentary and additional lore from Welsh bardic tradition but they stayed

---

2 John A. Giles, "British History by Geoffrey of Monmouth," in *Six Old English Chronicles* (London: Bohn, 1848), https://en.wikisource.org/wiki/Six_Old_English _Chronicles/Geoffrey%27s_British_History/Book_11.

fairly faithful to the source material. In the *Brut*, Geoffery's Insula Avallonis is called "Ynys Afallach" in Welsh, a name that has a complex etymology that we will consider in detail shortly.

Geoffrey's later work, the poetic *Vita Merlini* (*The Life of Merlin*) written in Latin c. 1150 CE, elaborates further on the Insula Avallonis, although here he calls it the Insula Pomorum—the Island of Apples. Its abundant nature causes him to compare it with the Fortunate Isle of classical tradition, and its description resonates strongly with similar island paradises found in the lore of other Celtic cultures.

> The island of apples which men call "The Fortunate Isle" gets its name from the fact that it produces all things of itself; the fields there have no need of the ploughs of the farmers and all cultivation is lacking except what nature provides. Of its own accord it produces grain and grapes, and apple trees grow in its woods from the close-clipped grass. The ground of its own accord produces everything instead of merely grass, and people live there a hundred years or more.[3]

Geoffrey goes on to tell us that this island paradise is ruled by nine women, who are both learned and possessed of great magics. One of the central currents in the Avalonian Stream of Tradition is its connection to the motif of the Ninefold Sisterhood, a concept we will explore in depth throughout this work.

> There nine sisters rule by a pleasing set of laws those who come to them from our country. She who is first of them is more skilled in the healing art and excels her sisters in the beauty of her person. Morgen is her name, and she has learned what useful properties all the herbs contain, so that she can cure sick bodies. She also knows an art by which to change her shape, and to cleave the

---

3 Geoffrey of Monmouth, "The Life of Merlin," trans. John Jay Parry, *Vita Merlini: The Life of Merlin* (Sacred Texts), accessed August 26, 2022, https://www.sacred-texts.com/neu/eng/vm/index.htm, lines 908–915.

air on new wings like Daedalus; when she wishes she is at Brest, Chartres, or Pavia, and when she wills she slips down from the air onto your shores. And men say that she has taught mathematics to her sisters, Moronoe, Mazoe, Gliten, Glitonea, Gliton, Tyronoe, Thitis, Thitis is best known for her zither.[4]

Although not explicitly called Avalon, it is clear that this island is identical with the Insula Avallonis of the *Historia*; Geoffrey here identifies the Island of Apples as the place to which Arthur was brought for healing after his last battle:

> Thither after the battle of Camlan we took the wounded Arthur, guided by Barinthus to whom the waters and the stars of heaven were well known. With him steering the ship we arrived there with the prince, and Morgen received us with fitting honour, and in her chamber she placed the king on a golden bed and with her own hand she uncovered his honourable wound and gazed at it for a long time. At length she said that health could be restored to him if he stayed with her for a long time and made use of her healing art. Rejoicing, therefore, we entrusted the king to her and returning spread our sails to the favouring winds.[5]

In this first in-depth narrative of Arthur's journey to Avalon for healing, it is Arthur's men who bring the wounded king to Morgen's island. This detail appears to be unique to the *Vita Merlini*, as all subsequent retellings of Arthur's journey to Avalon show him ferried there by powerful queens or Otherworldly women from the Holy Isle.

That said, it is from these very first descriptions of Avalon that all others proceed; Geoffrey's account establishes the main characteristics of Avalon: it is a place of self-sustaining abundance, those who dwell there enjoy long and healthy lives, it is ruled wisely by a sisterhood of

---

4 Geoffrey of Monmouth, "The Life of Merlin," lines 916–928.
5 Geoffrey of Monmouth, "The Life of Merlin," lines 929–940.

nine who possess extraordinary abilities, it is place where the sword of Arthur's kingship was forged, and it is the final destination of the mortally wounded Arthur so that he may be restored to health.

Classical Influences

It is worthwhile to pause for a moment to consider a bit of cultural context. Two of the earliest writers to mention Avalon in their works—Geoffrey of Monmouth and Gerald of Wales (whom we will discuss shortly)—were the products of a medieval classical education that greatly influenced both their perspectives on their subject matter and their views on the world itself.

In the early medieval period, a scholar and bishop (who was later canonized) named Isidore of Seville (560–636 CE) wrote one of the first encyclopedic compendiums of Western knowledge: a twenty-volume work entitled *Etymologiae* (*Etymologies*). In it, Isidore gathered, organized, and summarized a vast corpus of classical works, covering an enormous range of topics that included word origins, grammar, theology, geography, natural science, cosmology, culture, and medicine. *Etymologiae* was a popular textbook used in the education of the learned class in medieval times.

Himself a scholar (and at the end of his life, a bishop), Geoffrey of Monmouth would have received such an education, and its influence is apparent in his writings. For example, his description of the Island of Apples quoted above is believed to have been based on an entry from *Etymologiae*:

> The Fortunate Isles…produce all kinds of good things, as if they were happy and blessed with an abundance of fruit. Indeed, well-suited by their nature, they produce fruit from very precious trees; the ridges of their hills are spontaneously covered with grapevines; instead of weeds, harvest crops and garden herbs are common there. Hence the mistake of pagans and the poems by worldly po-

ets, who believed that these isles were Paradise because of the fertility of their soil. They are situated in the Ocean, against the left side of Mauretania, closest to where the sun sets…[6]

This entry, in turn, was likely informed by the works of classical writers such as Plutarch, who locates these islands in the Atlantic and describes them as being:

> two in number, separated by a very narrow strait; they are ten thousand furlongs distant from Africa, and are called the Islands of the Blest. They enjoy moderate rains at long intervals, and winds which for the most part are soft and precipitate dews, so that the islands not only have a rich soil which is excellent for plowing and planting, but also produce a natural fruit that is plentiful and wholesome enough to feed, without toil or trouble, a leisured folk.… Therefore a firm belief has made its way, even to the Barbarians, that here is the Elysian Field and the abode of the blessed, of which Homer sang.[7]

One wonders at the provenance of Geoffrey's further elaboration that the Fortunate Isle was ruled over by Nine Sisters who were learned in healing, science, and the arts. Chief among these sisters was Morgen, who received the wounded Arthur and promised to heal him. It is possible that Geoffrey may have recognized in Avalon an echo of the paradisiacal western islands of classical tradition, associated with the Garden of the Hesperides ("Daughters of Evening") famed for its golden apples. He may have also identified a sisterhood of well-educated women with the Nine Muses of Greco-Roman antiquity. Apollo, leader of the Muses in some myths, is also associated with Hyperborea ("Beyond the North Wind")—a paradisiacal island that some classical writers identified with

---

6   Stephen A. Barney et al., *The Etymologies of Isidore of Seville* (Cambridge, UK: Cambridge University Press, 2006), 294.

7   Plutarch and Bernadotte Perrin, "Sertorius," in *Plutarch's Lives* (Cambridge, MA: Harvard University Press, 1919), 8.

Britain and its people with the Gauls. Of the Hyperboreans, Pindar writes:

> Nor is the Muse a stranger to their lives, but everywhere are stirring to and fro dances of maidens and shrill noise of pipes: and binding golden bay-leaves in their hair they make them merry cheer. Nor pestilence nor wasting eld approach that hallowed race: they toil not neither do they fight, and dwell unharmed of cruel Nemesis.[8]

The presence of this potential influence doesn't mean that the idea of Avalon itself was crafted whole-cloth from the classical myths familiar to these writers without any connection to native British tradition. Instead, when considering these early accounts of Avalon, Celticist John Koch writes, "It is not impossible for the nexus of ideas that surface in the Latin of Geoffrey and Giraldus in the 12th century were already current in the vernacular some centuries earlier."[9] In fact, in addition to accounts of classical historians such as Strabo and Tacitus that predate these first medieval writings (and to which Geoffrey may have had access), early vernacular writing from Celtic lands also support the existence of native Celtic traditions concerning conclaves of women, as we shall see.

That said, Geoffrey is well known for interweaving classical accounts with Celtic traditions in his works.[10]

> [A]t the beginning of his History, Geoffrey stated categorically that Walter the Archdeacon presented him with a 'certain very ancient book written in the British language' and that he then proceeded to translate the book into plain, straight-forward Latin.

---

8 Pindar, "Pythian Ode X," in *The Extant Odes of Pindar*, trans. Ernest Myers (London: Macmillan and Co., 1874), 97.

9 John T. Koch, "Avalon," in *Celtic Culture: A Historical Encyclopedia* (Santa Barbara, CA: ABC-CLIO, 2006), 147.

10 Roger Sherman Loomis, *Wales and the Arthurian Legend* (Cardiff, UK: University of Wales Press, 1956), 155.

This source book is mentioned again casually [...] and then referred to [...] in the short epilogue which appears at the end of some versions of the History, with the variation that its antiquity is not stressed [...][.] The essential problem of Walter's very ancient book is that we do not possess it.[11]

When seeking to determine which aspects of Geoffrey's accounts of Avalon are drawn from Welsh sources, the dialog between Merlin and Thelgesin (the Latinized names of Myrddin and Taliesin) in the *Vita Merlini* are of particular interest. The descriptions of Avalon and Arthur's journey to the Insula Pomorum quoted above are taken from this dialog—the form of which, scholars believe, was influenced by *Ymddiddan Myrddin a Thalesin* (*Dialogue between Myrddin and Taliesin*), a prophetic work from Early Welsh literature included in the *Black Book of Carmarthen* (*Llyfr Du Caerfyrddin*) which likely predates Geoffrey. "Although this influence does not extend to content, we might regard the incorporation of the two prophets as something of a Welsh source marker, for the passage itself is rich in Welsh prophetic allusions found elsewhere."[12]

These Welsh inclusions can be seen in the prophetic wild man motif embodied in Myrddin Wyllt in the *Vita Merlini*, details of which are also clearly influenced by the poems "Yr Afallennau" ("The Appletrees") and "Yr Oianau" ("The Greetings"), both also found in the *Black Book of Carmarthen* (the manuscript itself is dated to the thirteenth century, but the poems themselves are likely of older provenance). In these poems, the Wild Man figure believed to be Myrddin has gone mad as a result of the Battle of Arfderydd, which saw Briton fight against Briton, resulting in many deaths. Suffering with the traumas

11 Geoffrey of Monmouth, *The History of the Kings of Britain*, trans. Lewis Thorpe (London: Penguin Classics, 2015), 14–15.

12 Victoria Flood, "Arthur's Return from Avalon: Geoffrey of Monmouth and the Development of the Legend" *Arthuriana* 25, no. 2 (2015): pp. 84–110, https://doi.org/10.1353/art.2015.0022, 87.

of war, Myrddin has taken refuge in the Coed Celyddon (Caledonian Forest).

There, he is hidden from the outside world though the magical properties of the apple trees, and with the power of foreknowledge bestowed upon him from his madness, he speaks his prophecies to piglets—an animal with strong Otherworld associations in Welsh tradition. The similarities between these poems and the *Vita Merlini* strongly suggest that regardless of any classical influences, Geoffrey is also drawing upon native Welsh sources, and his apparent understanding of the underlying Otherworldly meaning of symbols such as apples underscores his naming and description of Avalon.

Geoffrey's Influence

Inspired by Geoffrey, Anglo-Norman hagiographer Robert Wace (born c. 1115) wrote the *Roman de Brut (The Book of Brutus)*, a pseudohistory of British kings named after Brutus—a survivor of the Trojan war and legendary founder of Britain. Ostensibly a French translation of the *Historia Regum Britanniae*, the length of Wace's work was twice that of Geoffrey; it followed the *Historia's* general form but the narrative was interwoven with information from other sources, while adding his own imaginative details, and omitting portions that were particularly politically charged. Of particular note, Wace's *Brut* infuses the court of Arthur with elements of chivalry. It contains the first literary reference to the Round Table, and gives the first written account of the prophecy that Arthur would return from Avalon.

> So the chronicle speaks sooth, Arthur himself was wounded in his body to the death. He caused him to be borne to Avalon for the searching of his hurts. He is yet in Avalon, awaited of the Britons; for as they say and deem he will return from whence he went and live again. Master Wace, the writer of this book, cannot

add more to this matter of his end than was spoken by Merlin the prophet. Merlin said of Arthur—if I read aright—that his end should be hidden in doubtfulness. The prophet spoke truly. Men have ever doubted, and—as I am persuaded—will always doubt whether he liveth or is dead. Arthur bade that he should be carried to Avalon in this hope in the year 642 of the Incarnation.[13]

The original French uses the word *Bretun* for those awaiting Arthur, and at the time Wace was writing, the term could be used to refer to the Welsh, Bretons, or Cornish in equal measure, underscoring the importance of this belief to the Brythonic peoples who were struggling against the English and French under the rule of Henry II.[14] Wace's account is at odds with that of Geoffrey on the subject of Arthur's return, however—a plot point that factors greatly into the preservation of Avalon, in my opinion.

During his dialogue with Thelgesin in the *Vita Merlini*, Merlin details the renewed ferocity of the Saxons in their war against the Britons after Arthur's journey to Avalon. Thelgesin suggests that someone should take a fast ship to fetch the healed Arthur back so that he could re-establish the old order and drive the invaders out. Merlin disagrees that Arthur's return would restore peace and instead says the enemy will only be defeated through an alliance between the Scots, Welsh, Cornish, and Bretons. Scholars believe that the difference in the two accounts can be attributed to the prophecy of Arthur's return being of Breton (rather than Welsh) origin.

The *Roman de Brut* was greatly influential on subsequent Arthurian works in French, as well as on the first English language work concerning the story of King Arthur and his knights, a long-form poem called *Brut* or *The Chronicle of Britain*. Written c. 1190 by an English priest

---

13 Wace, *Arthurian Chronicles: Roman De Brut*, trans. Eugene Mason (Project Gutenberg, 2003), https://www.gutenberg.org/ebooks/10472.

14 Flood, "Arthur's Return," 96.

named Layamon, *Brut* includes this description of Arthur's journey to Avalon, wherein he is fetched by two elven maidens:

> *And I will fare to Avelon to the fairest of all maidens*
> *To Argente their Queen, an elf very fair,*
> *And she shall my wounds make all sound*
> *All whole me make with healing draughts,*
> *And afterwards I will come again to my kingdom*
> *And dwell with the Britons with mickle joy.*
> *Even with the words that came upon the sea*
> *A short boat sailing, moving amid the waves*
> *And two women were therein wounderously clad.*
> *And they took Arthur anon and bare him quickly*
> *And softly him adown laid and to glide forth gan they.*
> *Then was it comewhat Merlin said whilom*
> *That unmeasured sorrow should beat Arthur's forth faring.*
> *Britons believe yet that he is still in life*
> *And dwelleth in Avelon with the fairest of all elves,*
> *And every Briton looketh still when Arthur shall return.*[15]

Here, the inhabitants of Avalon are identified as elves, an Old English word of Germanic origin for supernatural beings and spirits of the land; in Britain, this word would slowly give way to the use of fay or fairy to refer to these Otherworldly folk. In place of Morgen, Layamon names Argente the Queen of Avalon, although some scholars speculate that this may have resulted from a scribal error for the name Margante, a form of Morgen.

Alternatively, others have argued that unlike Morgan—a male name in Welsh, which contributed to some confusion—Argante would have

---

15 Frederic Madden, *Layamon's Brut, Or Chronicle of Britain: A Poetical Semi-Saxon Paraphrase of the Brut of Wace. Now First Published from the Cottonian Manuscripts in the British Museum, Accompanied by a Literal Translation, Notes, and a Grammatical Glossary* (United Kingdom: Society of Antiquaries of London, 1847), 144–145.

been a properly Celtic women's name, and sounded enough like the perplexing original that Layamon may have intentionally chosen it.[16] Other writers have associated her with the Welsh goddess Arianrhod ("Silver Wheel") or Aranrhod (perhaps "Circular Mound"), who also ruled over an island kingdom. In subsequent Arthurian tales, however, Morgen or Morgan is almost always one of the black veiled women in the barge who brings the mortally wounded king to Avalon, even in the later tales when she has acted as his foe in the rest of the narrative.

Gesta Regum Britanniae (*Deeds of the Kings of Britain*) is another work that was strongly inspired by Geoffrey's *Historia Regum Britanniae*. Written in Latin during the mid-thirteenth century by a Breton monk named Guillaume de Rennes, it does not directly name Avalon, but describes the island to which Arthur is taken as a place where it is eternally the springtime—lush with all manners of flowers, and all who dwell there are youthful and whole. A beautiful, royal virgin attends to the wounded king, and aided by her maiden, brings Arthur to the palace of "regis Avallonis"—either the palace of King Avallo, or the palace of the king of Avalon—so that she can heal him. It is suggested in the narrative that Arthur's delay in returning to take up the fight against the Saxons is due to his love for Morgan, and that they dwell together in Avalon as a couple.[17] Morgan first becomes identified as Arthur's sister in Chrétien de Troyes's *Erec et Enide* (c. 1165), a plot point that mostly remains intact in the tradition from that point forward.

The Glastonbury Connection

Giraldus Cambrensis (c. 1146–c. 1223), also known as Gerald of Wales, is the author of *De Principis Instructione* (*On the Instruction of a Prince*)

---

16 Lucy Allen Paton, *Studies in the Fairy Mythology of Arthurian Romance* (Boston: The Athenaeum Press, 1903), 27.

17 John Rhys, *Studies in the Arthurian Legend* (Oxford, UK: Clarendon Press, 1891), 335.

and *Speculum Ecclesia* (*Mirror of the Church*). In them, he addresses some of the lore around the death of Arthur and the belief in his eventual return. Not only does his writing make a clear association between Avalon (which he calls Ynys Avallach) and Annwn, the Welsh Otherworld, but it is also the first written account to connect Avalon with Glastonbury. In *Speculum Ecclesiae*, he writes:

> And so, after Arthur had been mortally wounded there, his body was taken to the Isle of Avalon, which is now called Glastonbury, by a noble matron and kinswoman named Morgan; afterwards the remains were buried, according to her direction, in the holy burial-ground. As a result of this, the Britons and their poets have been concocting legends that a certain fantastic goddess, also called Morgan, carried off the body of Arthur to the Isle of Avalon for the healing of his wounds. When his wounds have healed, the strong and powerful king will return to rule the Britons (or so the Britons suppose), as he did before.[18]

This mention of bards describing Morgan as an Otherworldly goddess certainly suggests a pre-Christian origin for this aspect of the story, at least in Gerald's opinion, and seems to imply preexisting oral tradition as his source. In the later Welsh version of this work, found in Llanstephan MS.4 (c. 1400), Margan is called "a goddess of Annwfyn" (*Margan, dwywes o Annwfyn*), again reinforcing the connection between Avalon and the Otherworld.[19]

---

18 Gerald of Wales, "The Discovery of the Tomb of King Arthur from Speculum Ecclesiae," trans. John William Sutton, *The Tomb of King Arthur* | Robbins Library Digital Projects, The Camelot Project 2001, https://d.lib.rochester.edu/camelot/text/gerald-of-wales-arthurs-tomb.

19 Anonymous, "The Burial of Arthur | Claddedigaeth Arthur," trans. Georgia Henley, *Global Medieval Sourcebook*, accessed June 26, 2022, http://sourcebook.stanford.edu/text/burial-arthur.

Not only does Gerald of Wales connect Glastonbury with Avalon in his *De Principis Instructione*, he directly names Morgan as Arthur's healer and ruler of the island.

> What is now called Glastonbury was, in antiquity, called the Isle of Avalon; it is like an island because it is entirely hemmed in by swamps. [...] Morgan, a noble matron, mistress and patroness of those regions, and also King Arthur's kinswoman by blood, brought Arthur to the island now called Glastonbury for the healing of his wounds after the Battle of Camlann.[20]

Writing after the famous exhumation of Arthur and Guinevere's graves by the monks of Glastonbury Abbey in 1191, Gerald believed the account to be authentic, saying in his *De Principis Instructione*:

> Although legends had fabricated something fantastical about his demise (that he had not suffered death, and was conveyed, as if by a spirit, to a distant place), his body was discovered at Glastonbury, in our own times, hidden very deep in the earth in an oak-hollow, between two stone pyramids that were erected long ago in that holy place. The tomb was sealed up with astonishing tokens, like some sort of miracle. The body was then conveyed into the church with honor, and properly committed to a marble tomb. A lead cross was placed under the stone, not above as is usual in our times, but instead fastened to the underside. I have seen this cross, and have traced the engraved letters—not visible and facing outward, but rather turned inwardly toward the stone. It read: "Here lies entombed King Arthur, with Guenevere his second wife, on the Isle of Avalon."[21]

---

20 Gerald of Wales, "The Discovery of the Tomb of King Arthur from *Liber de Principis Instructione*," trans. John William Sutton, *The Tomb of King Arthur* | Robbins Library Digital Projects, The Camelot Project 2001, https://d.lib.rochester.edu /camelot/text/gerald-of-wales-arthurs-tomb.

21 Ibid.

The primary link between Glastonbury and Avalon, therefore, hinges on this discovery of Arthur's grave—a discovery that later scholars have found suspect for several reasons. Aside from the absence of conclusive archaeological evidence from twentieth-century excavations at the site and the belief (based on the Latin syntax and style of writing) that the now-lost lead cross was a twelfth-century forgery, scholars have identified two potential motivations for the monks to have perpetrated such an elaborate fraud: one financial, one political.

Believed to have been founded in the eighth century, Glastonbury Abbey is said to have arisen at the site of the first Christian church in Britain—an ancient wattle-and-daub structure tradition claims was built in the first century CE by Joseph of Arimathea. At its height, Glastonbury Abbey was the wealthiest and most powerful abbey in Britain, having amassed a trove of treasures and relics that, along with its mythic history, made it a popular pilgrimage site.

However, a massive fire in 1184 destroyed much of the abbey and its holdings, including the ancient church. Hurting for funds to support their effort to rebuild, the monks allegedly discovered the graves of Arthur and Guinevere in 1191, renewing interest in the site and attracting wealthy benefactors. The abbey was rebuilt, and Arthur and Guinevere were reburied in a splendid tomb in front of the church's high altar. Sadly, nothing remains of this tomb; everything was lost when Glastonbury Abbey was stripped of its wealth during the 1539 Dissolution of the Monasteries.

The political motivations behind the fraud are connected to the tradition of Arthur as the once and future king. A powerful culture hero to the Welsh, Cornish, and Bretons, Arthur represented the idea of a unified, post-Roman Britain where a confederacy of kingdoms united under the rule of a high king who successfully fought back the Saxon invaders. Arthur's reign was a time of peace and sovereignty for the Britons—and though it may have only ever been true in legend, it was a legend particularly dear to the medieval Celtic kingdoms actively struggling to maintain their independence against waves of invasions. The belief that Arthur would return to aid them in their darkest hour was a source of hope, especially as Henry II and Edward I sought to conquer the Welsh once and for all. What better way to dash that hope than to find proof of Arthur's demise and discover his remains in solidly English lands?

All of this aside, Glastonbury's connections with Arthur nevertheless took hold in the medieval imagination. If Glastonbury was Avalon, it stood to reason that the landscapes of Arthurian Tradition, particularly those surrounding his final battle, would also be located nearby. In time, for example, Camelot came to be associated with Cadbury Hillfort, and the Pomparles Bridge, spanning the River Brue, is where Sir Bedivere is believed to have returned Excalibur to the Lady of the Lake. Glastonbury as Avalon became cemented in the popular culture and found literary purchase in post-1191 stories of Arthur.

Aside from the discovery of Arthur's tomb, there are other connections between Avalon and Glastonbury that are worth exploring, even though it isn't always clear if these associations have been influenced by the writings of Gerald of Wales or if they represent independent traditions.

Triad 90 of *Trioedd Ynys Prydein* (*The Triads of the Island of Britain*)—a medieval compilation of traditional Welsh lore grouped into triadic verses, or sets of three related motifs, believed to have been used as bardic mnemonic devices—references Ynys Afallach as the location of one of the Three Perpetual Harmonies (*Tri Dyfal Gyfangan*) of the Island of Britain. The perpetual harmonies are referring to *cyfangan*—an uninterrupted choir. According to the explanatory notes that accompany the triad, in each of these three places there were 2400 holy men, a hundred of whom sang every hour so that every hour of every day would be filled with continuous prayer songs, forever. In her gloss of this triad, translator Rachel Bromwich indicates that Glastonbury is what is intended, along with two other important monastic sites. She notes that some versions of this triad substitute *Ynys Widrin*, an alternative Welsh name for Glastonbury deriving from the English, meaning "Island of Glass" (discussed further on page 38).[22]

In the early twelfth century, the English historian William of Malmsebury penned *De Antiquitate Glastoniensis Ecclesiæ* (*On the Early History of the Church of Glastonbury*). In it, he writes that Glastonbury was founded by a man named Glasteing, who—along with his twelve brothers—came to the area from the north of Britain. As Glasteing was passing through the Midlands, he followed his sow from the town of Wells as she made her way along a watery track that came to be called "Sugewege" or Sow's Way. He eventually caught up with her suckling her piglets under an apple tree growing near the Old Church. He took this to be a sign and decided to settle there with his family; the town would eventually come to be named after him.[23] The presence of apples and pigs—both strongly associated with the Otherworld—in this founding tale cannot be coincidental, and it hints at an independent tradition that links Glastonbury with the pre-Christian Otherworld.

While William may have been inspired, as scholars suggest, by a similar anecdote in Virgil's *Aeneid*—where the titular hero founds a city at the site where he discovered a white sow suckling her piglets under a tree on a riverbank, there is an episode in the Fourth Branch of *Y Mabinogi* that also conforms to this motif.[24] In it, Gwydion followed a sow along the banks of a river until she stopped beneath an oak tree where she feasted on the rotting flesh of a wounded eagle—the transformed hero, Lleu.

---

22 Rachel Bromwich, *Trioedd Ynys Prydein: The Triads of the Island of Britain* (Cardiff, UK: University of Wales Press, 2006), 233.

23 William of Malmesbury and John Scott, *The Early History of Glastonbury: An Edition, Translation, and Study of William of Malmesbury's De Antiquitate Glastonie Ecclesie* (Woodbridge, UK: Boydell Press, 1981), 53.

24 John J. Savage, "Insula Avallonia," *Transactions and Proceedings of the American Philological Association* 73 (1942): 405–415, https://doi.org/10.2307/283559, 401.

On Apples and Avallach

Concerning the name of Avalon itself, medieval writers make mention of two competing etymologies. Both Gerald of Wales and William of Malmesbury, for example, suggested the name of the Island of Avalon either had to do with the apples that grew there or was an eponymous reference to a legendary ruler. In his *Liber de Principis Instructione*, Gerald of Wales writes:

> What is now called Glastonbury was, in antiquity, called the Isle of Avalon; it is like an island because it is entirely hemmed in by swamps. In British it is called Inis Avallon, that is, insula pomifera [Latin: "The Island of Apples"]. This is because the apple, which is called aval in the British tongue, was once abundant in that place.[25]

Further, in *Speculum Ecclesiae*, he states:

> Truly it is called Avalon, either from the British word ava, which means pomum [Latin: "apple"], because apples and apple trees abound in that place; or, from the name Vallo, once the ruler of of [sic] that territory.[26]

William of Malmesbury makes similar etymological arguments in *De Antiquitate Glastoniensis Ecclesia*. He mentions another name for Glastonbury, Insula Avallonia, and adds that it could either mean "Island of Apples"—arising from *avalla*, which he called the British word for "apples" in reference to the apples that grew there—or "Island of

---

25 "The Discovery of the Tomb of King Arthur from *Liber de Principis Instructione*," trans. John William Sutton, *The Tomb of King Arthur* | Robbins Library Digital Projects, The Camelot Project 2001, https://d.lib.rochester.edu/camelot/text/gerald-of-wales-arthurs-tomb.

26 "The Discovery of the Tomb of King Arthur from *Speculum Ecclesiae*," trans. John William Sutton, *The Tomb of King Arthur* | Robbins Library Digital Projects, The Camelot Project 2001, https://d.lib.rochester.edu/camelot/text/gerald-of-wales-arthurs-tomb.

Avalloc," so named after a mysterious figure who once dwelt there with his daughters due to its isolation.[27]

Avallach (Afallach, Aballac) is a name that turns up in the mythic genealogies of the Northern Welsh kingdom of Gwynedd. The Old Welsh Genealogies found in the British Libraries MS 3859 names a figure called Aballac, who is either the son or grandson of Beli Mawr—a Brythonic solar divinity. It was not unusual for medieval genealogies to trace noble lineages to biblical, classical, or native folkloric figures who may have once been divine; the practice served to give these families an enhanced degree of authority in their right to rule. One such ruler was King Coel Hen, who traced his linage in the northern genealogies back to Aballach map Beli et Anna—Avallach, son of Beli and Anna; it is possible that Anna is derived from the goddess Dôn, who is married to Beli Mawr.[28]

Afallach appears in several entries in *Trioedd Ynys Prydein*. In Triad 70, he is named as the father of Modron, while in other lore, she is described as the daughter of the King of Annwn; this connection between Afallach and Annwn through Modron is a significant one. Modron has children with Urien, a semi-historical king of Rheged—a Brythonic kingdom of the Old North—thereafter permitting his royal line, which includes the Welsh hero Owain, to trace their lineage back to Afallach. While we will discuss her in greater detail in chapter 6, it is notable that Modron—the daughter of the King of Annwn who is a Brythonic ancestral figure who may also have given his name to Avalon, an island strongly associated with the Otherworld—is herself an ancestress of sorts to Morgan le Fay, who is sometimes called the Queen of Avalon. Their tales become conflated in later lore, as we shall see.

Lastly, it is possible that the figure of Avallach endures into later Arthurian Tradition, appearing in the Vulgate Cycle as Evalach, a

---

27 William of Malmesbury and Scott, *Early History*, 53.

28 Bromwich, *Trioedd*, 274.

pagan king in *L'Estoire del Saint Graal.*[29] Character transferences of pre-Christian figures into the Arthurian legendarium is not uncommon, and we will be discussing several instances of this phenomenon throughout this book.

Apples and the Otherworld

The other etymology for Avalon connects the paradisiacal island with the paradisiacal fruit, the apple. The word derives from the Proto-Indo-European *ab(e)l*—"apple." The Proto-Celtic word was *aballā*; Gaulish, *avallo*; Old Irish, *uball, ubull*; Modern Irish, *ubhal, úll*; Scots Gaelic *ubhall*; Manx, *ooyl*; Welsh, *afal*; Cornish, *aval*; Breton, *aval*.[30]

Apples feature very prominently in Irish tradition as being connected to the Otherworld. Apple branches are often carried by Otherworldly figures who function as Threshold Guardians, such as Manannán mac Lir and the fairy woman who called Bran MacFebal to undertake a journey to the Otherworldly Island of Women (see chapter 2). These silver branches are either hung with golden apples or crystal blossoms and are able to produce beautifully soothing music. Gifts of apples also serve as invitations to the Otherworld from would-be fairy lovers. These magical fruits often have the property of being able to sustain humans for a month or more, even if it is the only thing they eat. This seems to be an extension of a property of Otherworldly Islands of Apples in both Irish and Welsh tradition—that they are self-sustaining places of eternal youth, and restored health.

In the Welsh poem "Yr Afallennau" (discussed earlier in this chapter), Myrddin has gone mad with grief after a terrible battle and hidden himself in the woods, becoming Myrddin Wyllt—Myrddin the Wild. His madness and his living in a place of liminality has granted

---

29 Rhys, *Studies*, 337.

30 James MacKillop, "Apple," in *Dictionary of Celtic Mythology* (Oxford University Press, 2017), 21.

him the power of prophecy; throughout the poem, he makes several prophecies while addressing an apple tree. In addition, this tree seems to have magical properties, among them apparently rendering Myrddin invisible to his pursuers—or perhaps it has opened a pocket into the Otherworld, allowing him to hide.

In lore and legend, then, the presence of apple—fruit or flower, tree or branch—likewise indicates the presence of the Otherworld and mirrors many of its qualities, especially its gifts of self-sustaining bounty, healing and immortality, prophecy and wisdom. Likewise, these qualities mirror the properties of the magical cauldrons of Welsh tradition, as we shall see.

The Isle of Glass

The other Welsh name for Glastonbury given by Gerald of Wales is *Ynys Gwydrin,* "the Glass Island," which he believed to have been the origin of the Anglo-Saxon name "Glastonbury." However, modern scholars think Gerald had it backward and that Ynys Gwydrin, Ynys Widrin, or Ynys Wintrin were the Welsh versions of the Anglo-Saxon name that predated it.

A possible etymology for the name Glastonbury derives from *glaston,* the Celtic word for "woad," a plant that produced a colorfast blue dye used in Celtic cultures as far back as the fifth century BCE. In Welsh, *glas* means "blue," and our English "woad" is derived from the Saxon *waad.* The soil and climate of Somerset is historically conducive to growing woad, and the towns of Glastonbury, Bath, and Wells were centers for its cultivation and production. Woad grew to be an important industry in the sixteenth century, before indigo became more readily available from India. Therefore, a convincing meaning for the name Glastonbury could be "the place where woad grows."[31]

---

31 Frank D. Reno, *The Historic King Arthur: Authenticating the Celtic Hero of Post-Roman Britain* (Jefferson, NC: McFarland & Co., 2007), 222.

Although "Ynys Wintrin" is usually translated to mean "Island of Glass," this appears to be a folk etymology based on the assumption that the *glaston* in Glastonbury literally meant "glass" rather than "woad." A further complication is that the Latin word for woad, *vitrum*, is also one of their words for "glass"; this is potentially a reference to the blue hue of glass resulting from the chemicals used in its production in Roman times. It may be, therefore, that the Welsh *Wintrin* derives from *vitrum*—although it is possible that it too, refers to woad rather than glass.[32]

But perhaps most evocative of all is the association of glass fortresses or towers with Otherworldly islands in Welsh tradition. One of the places visited by Arthur and his men when they raided Annwn is called Caer Wydr ("Glass Fortress") while Tŷ Gwydr ("Glass House") is Merlin's home on Bardsey Island, which has strong associations with the Welsh Otherworld and Ynys Afallon itself. We will discuss these in detail in later chapters.

Glastonbury and the Grail

Aside from the link between Glastonbury and Avalon forged by the alleged discovery of Arthur's grave at the Abbey, there are other traditions associated with Glastonbury that hold resonance with what we know about the Holy Isle. In his 1340 work, *The Chronicle of Glastonbury Abbey*, John of Glastonbury writes that in the time of Arthur, there was a monastery of holy virgins on the island of Avalon on or near Wearyall Hill. While he was certainly referring to a community of nuns, this is the first known reference to a women's religious community at Glastonbury.

---

32 W. J. Keith, *John Cowper Powys's A Glastonbury Romance: A Reader's Companion*—Updated and Expanded Edition (Toronto, 2010), http://www.powys-lannion.net/Powys/Keith/Gcompanion.pdf, 24.

In *De Antiquitate Glastoniensis*, William of Malmesbury wrote that Joseph of Arimathea came to Glastonbury in 63 CE along with twelve companions. They built a church dedicated to the Virgin Mary out of wattle and daub, and what would become Glastonbury Abbey arose around it. Called the *Vetusta ecclesia* ("the old church"), it was likely built in the seventh century CE but was destroyed in a fire in 1184. After the fire, the Lady's Chapel (sometimes called St. Joseph's Chapel) was built over the site of the old church.[33]

Robert de Boron's *Joseph d'Arimathie*, written in the late twelfth century, marks the beginning of Joseph's connection with the Grail materials. In it, Joseph and the Grail company journeyed from Jerusalem to the western lands with the aim of bringing the Grail to *vaus d'Avaron* in Britain, likely a corruption of the Vale of Avalon.[34] This tradition was built upon in other romances, as the Grail was slowly transformed into a Christian relic, culminating in the *Estoire del Saint Graal*, the first book of the Vulgate Cycle, dated to the early thirteenth century, that established Joseph as a Grail guardian and the founder, through his son Josephes, of a lineage of Grail keepers extending to the time of Arthur's rule.[35]

In the late fourteenth century, John of Glastonbury's *Chronicle* served to bring together the various traditions around Joseph to create a definitive version of his life and lore in Britain. Lagorio calls the *Chronicle* "an ingenious blend of elements from the apocrypha, Celtic lore, early Grail history, and extant abbey legends, related a prestigious, yet religiously orthodox version of Glastonbury's founding by Joseph and his eleven

---

33 Benjamin A. Saltzman, "Glastonbury Abbey," in *The Encyclopedia of Medieval Literature in Britain* (Hoboken, NJ: Wiley Blackwell, 2017).

34 Jean Rogers and Robert De Boron, *Joseph of Arimathea: A Romance of the Grail* (United Kingdom: Steiner, 1990), 55.

35 Valerie M. Lagorio, "The Evolving Legend of St. Joseph of Glastonbury," *Speculum* 46, no. 2 (1971): 209–231, https://doi.org/10.2307/2854852.

followers in 63 A.D."[36] Joseph was said to have been buried near the Old Church along with two cruets of Christ's blood and sweat—a reflection of the Church's growing disapproval of the increasingly popular Grail legend as unorthodox. In this account, Arthur is said to be a descendant of Joseph of Arimathea, further connecting both the legendary king and the Grail (or its stand-in relics) with Glastonbury—and, by extension, with Avalon.

Other Potential Locations

Generally speaking, there are three main traditions concerning the location of Avalon in medieval literature: Glastonbury; somewhere in the Mediterranean, most prominently Mt. Etna in Sicily; or locations so far away from Britain—such as the Antipodes—that it is possible they were meant as hyperbole, representing someplace so beyond the imagination of the audience that they came to possess an almost mythical essence.[37] Aside from these explicitly stated traditions, there are also locations in folklore and literature concerning Arthur's last resting place that don't specifically name Avalon but nonetheless reflect the Holy Island's Otherworldly functions and description.

Avalon, Arthur, and Wales

There's at least one medieval account that locates Avalon in Wales, and there are many Welsh sites with folkloric traditions that connect them to Arthur's final resting place; most of the latter are examples of the "king asleep in the mountain" folkloric motif. In these tales, Arthur and his knights are suspended in a magical sleep within a hidden cave where they await the call to come to Britain's aid.

---

36 Lagorio, "Evolving Legend," 218.
37 C. J. Rushton, "Avalon," in *The Encyclopedia of Medieval Literature in Britain*, ed. R. Rouse and S. Echard (Oxford, 2017), 10.1002/9781118396957.wbemlb507.

In the *Vera Historia de Morte Arthuri* (*True History of the Death of Arthur*, c. 1200), Avalon is said to be located in Gwynedd, a county in northwestern Wales that was an independent kingdom from the end of the Roman period up until the Welsh conquest by Edward I in the late thirteenth century. According to the story, after being wounded in the battle of Camlan, Arthur is further wounded by a strange youth who strikes him with a shaft of elm with a poisoned tip. Arthur hurls his spear and kills the unknown enemy, but his own fate is sealed. He is brought to "the delightful Isle of Avalon" where physicians tried and failed to heal him. After his death, he was taken to be buried in a small chapel dedicated to the Virgin Mary but his corpse was too big to fit. During the funeral ceremony, the earth quaked and a strange storm of bright lightning, loud thunder, and powerful winds brought in a mist that obscured Arthur from their sight. When mists lifted hours later, the king was gone and the chapel sealed although no one could say what had become of him.[38]

There are many Welsh folktales that feature the Arthurian "king asleep in the mountain" motif; these are not specifically about Avalon proper, although it is clear from the story's details that the hollow hill or cave beneath the mountain where Arthur and his men are sleeping is part of the Otherworld. These kinds of tales are reflections of the messianic beliefs around Arthur's prophesied return to reestablish Brythonic independence from the rule of the invaders; this is sometimes referred to as the "Breton/Briton hope."

Yet of all the places in Wales that could lay claim to having been the real-world location of Avalon, one far outpaces all the rest: Ynys Enlli.

---

38 Richard Barber, "The 'Vera Historia De Morte Arthuri' and Its Place in Arthurian Tradition," in *Arthurian Literature, Volume I* (Woodbridge, Suffolk: D. S. Brewer, 1999), 88–93.

Ynys Enlli—Bardsey Island

Part of the ancient kingdom of Gwynedd, the Llŷn Peninsula extends southwestward from the coast of northern Wales into the Irish Sea, pointing to a small island with a big legacy: Bardsey Island. Its English name is believed to have derived from Viking raiders who either called it "the Bard's Island," or alternatively named it after one of their chieftains. In Welsh, however, it is called Ynys Enlli—the "Island of the Current," named for the infamously dangerous waters that surround it. It is very difficult to make the crossing to the island from the mainland through Swnt Enlli, (Bardsey Sound); its tides are strongly influenced by the way weather conditions cause the water to flow over the treacherous shoals and reefs below the surface.

There are several traditions concerning these waters. It is said that there are seven tides in Bardsey Sound, and those who would navigate them would need to understand them to make the journey safely. A poem written in the sixteenth century about the journey to Ynys Enlli by the bard Rhys Llywd ap Rhys ap Rhicert describes the waves as being "A flock of the sheep of Gwenhidwy, And nine rams along with them."[39] In Welsh lore, Gwenhidwy or Gwenhidw is a mermaid who tends to the waves of the sea, the latter described as a flock of eight ewes with the ninth—a breaker wave—as a ram.[40] This eight plus one configuration is characteristic of many Ninefold groupings, and there are several associations with waves and the number nine as we shall see in chapter 3.

Over the centuries, many did risk the perilous voyage to this small island lying less than two miles from the end of the Llŷn Peninsula. Against all odds, Bardsey has a long history of occupation. Archaeological evidence shows that the island was first inhabited more than

---

39 T. Gwyn Jones, *Welsh Folklore and Folk-Custom* (UK: Folcroft Library Editions, 1977), 75.

40 P. C. Bartrum, "G," in *A Welsh Classical Dictionary: People in History and Legend up to about A.D. 1000* (Aberystwyth: National Library of Wales, 1993), 359.

four thousand years ago. The stone foundations of Iron Age hut circles were found in the protective western edge of Mynydd Enlli, the mountain in the center of the island that also gives Bardsey its characteristic silhouette, which has been compared to that of a mouse or a whale. With such a long history of habitation, there's no surprise that there is a lot of lore concerning this mysterious island.[41]

According to tradition, a monastery was founded on the island by St. Cadfan in the sixth century; after his death, St. Lleuddad succeeded him as abbot. Tradition says that when Lleuddad was on his deathbed, he was visited by an angel who granted him three wishes. Famously, the dying saint asked that anyone who was buried on Bardsey not be sent to hell. His prayer was said to be granted and as a result, ailing pilgrims traveled to the island to die there while those of means sought burial on the island to obtain its promise of eternity in heaven. Because of this, it became known as the Island of 20,000 Saints and is a real-world Island of the Dead. Even today, stories describing bones emerging from the ground from unmarked burials on Bardsey make the news.

Sometimes called the Welsh Iona, Bardsey was a Holy Island and a popular pilgrimage destination in medieval times; making three pilgrimages to Bardsey was the equivalent of one pilgrimage to Rome. The difficulty of making the journey was an appealing aspect for the penitential functions of pilgrimage. In 1191, Gerald of Wales wrote that Bardsey was inhabited by an order of monks called Caelibes or Colidei, and that the island "has this wonderful peculiarity that the oldest people die first, because diseases are uncommon, and scarcely any die except from extreme old age."[42]

Aside from its Christian connections, Bardsey has strong associations with the Otherworld. According to the sixteenth-century Peni-

---

41 "Ymddiriedolaeth Ynys Enlli / Bardsey Island Trust." Accessed June 27, 2022, https://www.bardsey.org/.

42 Geraldus Cambrensis and Llewelyn Williams, *The Itinerary through Wales and the Description of Wales* (London: J. M. Dent & Company, 1908), 116.

arth Manuscript (No. 147), it is the home of Myrddin Wyllt (Merlin the Wild). There, along with a company of nine bards, he is said to have the Thirteen Treasures of Britain in his keeping, securing them in Tŷ Gwydr (the House of Glass). Bardsey is said to be Merlin's final resting place, with Tŷ Gwydr a variation for his traditional enclosure by Nimue, his student and future Lady of the Lake, at the end of his life. The recurring motif of Otherworldly glass fortresses, towers, and enclosures in Welsh, Irish, and Arthurian Traditions will be explored throughout this book.

Finally, in 1998, a unique species of apple tree was discovered on Bardsey behind a house where it was sheltering from the intense winds that make it impossible for trees to grow on the island. It is believed to be a descendant of the apple orchards cultivated by the monks more than a thousand years ago. This ancient variety is not known to grow anywhere else and is notable as being particularly disease resistant. The variety itself has been named for the island—Ynys Enlli apples or Bardsey Island apples—although they have also been called Merlin's apples because of his mythic association with the island.[43]

And so in Ynys Enlli, we have a Holy Island off the coast of Wales boasting many of the same characteristics associated with Ynys Afallon. It is an Island of the Dead as well as a paradisiacal western island, since anyone buried there will be guaranteed entry to heaven. Everyone who dwells on the island enjoys excellent health and only dies of old age. It is a religious center and a place of pilgrimage that requires a treacherous journey over water. It has a folkloric association with the Nine Waves (and therefore the Otherworld)—a point further reinforced by the Glass House associated with Merlin, who keeps watch over Britain's magical treasures, with nine bards accompanying him. The island has a strong association with apples—apples that are resistant to disease,

---

43 "Ynys Enlli," Pomiferous website, accessed May 16, 2022, https://pomiferous.com /applebyname/ynys-enlli-id-496.

just as those who dwelt on Bardsey were said to live in good health into their old age. Finally, it is significant that some of the early Arthurian stories located Avalon in Gwynedd—the area of Wales to which Bardsey belongs. If we were to seek Avalon in Wales, then, Bardsey Island fits the bill in almost every way.

Avalon, Brittany, and France

Many of the earliest Arthurian tales—and some of the most influential additions to the Matter of Britain—come from Brittany and spread to other areas of France by way of traveling minstrel and the popularity of Breton *lais*—short, rhymed tales of romance and chivalry filled with Celtic magic and fairy lore. It is believed that Chrétien de Troyes was strongly influenced by early Breton lais during the writing of his Arthurian works.

There are a few places in France that have connections to Avalon; these include Avallon in the Burgundy region, and Île d'Aval or Enez Aval, a small island off the coast of Brittany.

Avallon

The works of famed Arthurian scholar Geoffrey Ashe espouse a theory that an historical fifth-century Romano-British king named Riothamus was the basis for the stories of King Arthur. Both figures were known as the King of the Britons, both died due to the betrayal of an ally, and both engaged in campaigns of war in Gaul; these comparisons are based on historical accounts of Riothamus and those of Arthur in Geoffrey of Monmouth's *Historia Regum Britanniae*. Riothamus was said to have died in 470 while fighting the Visigoths in Gaul, and Ashe contends that he would have been buried in the town of Avallon, near to where he fell.[44]

---

44 Geoffrey Ashe, *The Discovery of King Arthur* (Stroud, Glouchestershire, UK: The History Press, 2017).

While there is no direct evidence of a connection between Riothamus and Avallon, the town itself was located on a major Roman road and was very famous as the site of a healing complex on the banks of the River Cure. By the first century CE, there was a Roman temple and spa at the site, and archaeological evidence suggests that it was a place of reverence as far back as the Neolithic period. At the center of all this devotion was Les Fontaines Salées ("the salt springs"), famous for their healing properties. It would make sense that a wounded Riothamus would have been brought to such a place for healing if he were anywhere in the region. And it is very fitting for a center of healing to bear the name "Avallon."[45]

Île d'Aval

There is a small island off the coast of Brittany that is rich in history and has strong Arthurian associations. It is the only potential location for a physical-world Avalon that is an island literally named "the Apple Island": *Île d'Aval* in French and *Enez Aval* in Breton. Archaeological evidence shows that the island was inhabited since the Mesolithic era and that a monastery and chapel dedicated to Saint Marc was built around the sixth century. A large granite menhir is believed to mark the resting place of King Arthur, and late nineteenth-century excavations revealed horse and human burials in association with it. It is currently in private hands.[46]

---

45 Marilyn Floyde, *King Arthur's French Odyssey: Avallon in Burgundy* (Cambridge, UK: Vanguard Press, 2009), 68–69.

46 Kristin Enez, "L'île D'Aval Conte L'histoire," L'île d'Aval Conte l'histoire (Ile-Grande Passion …, January 17, 2016), http://www.ile-grande.bzh/aval-pommes-arthur/.

Finding Avalon

As this brief overview has shown us, the fundamental characteristics that have come to define our understanding of Avalon have a lineage long predating her first appearance in the written record. As a concept, she is broad enough to encompass a variety of interrelated functions while also being flexible enough to inhabit a multitude of locations, from the sun-drenched slopes of Mt. Etna to centers of pilgrimage off the coast of Wales to the westernmost edges of the earth—almost beyond the imagination's ability to see.

There is no question in my mind that Glastonbury is a holy place; indeed, my first book, *Avalon Within,* includes an approach to working with the sites in its sacred landscape as a way to connect with the transformational energies of the Holy Island—but was it once truly Avalon? Modern archaeological excavations of Glastonbury have yet to reveal anything that would support the idea of an ancient Pagan enclave of priestesses, and modern scholars have mostly rejected the veracity of traditions dating back to the twelfth century identifying Glastonbury as the burial place of King Arthur and therefore the real-world location of Avalon. It is believed instead that this connection was fabricated in the Middle Ages for political and economic reasons.

Yet despite the lack of objective evidence, between the power inherent in the landscape of Glastonbury itself as well as the energetic egregore that has been built up through its centuries-long association with Avalon, it is clear that the land itself has come to wear the mantle of myth. This, along with the liminal qualities inherent in mist-ringed islands and orchards of apple trees, has undoubtedly imbued Glastonbury with the power of being a bridge to Avalon, even as there are other places and spaces that have been similarly empowered by legend and local lore, such as Bardsey Island.

There is something inherent in human nature to want to anchor the sacred in what is familiar, what is accessible, and what is around us. There is no question that legends can come to dwell in physical places and become anchored to sites of power, or—alternatively—sites that have come to accrue power by virtue of their association with myth. It represents the same energy and shares the same psycho-spiritual function. This is, in part, the reason why there are so many places in the landscapes of Britain and Brittany that bear the name of Arthur—his seat, his grave, his mountain. When the epic tales of the past are made visible in the landscapes all around us, they remain in consciousness—dynamic and alive.

It is possible to create these strong associations through the power of intention carried by the vehicle of tradition, held and maintained over centuries. These energetic associations are then able to serve as bridges between this world and the myth—this world and the Otherworld. This in turn facilitates a connection between the local landscape and the sacred landscape—like the connection between Glastonbury and Avalon. This kind of connection, especially when built up over time, makes it much easier for people to connect with, for example, the Otherworldly Avalon through the Glastonbury landscape. That is one mechanism at play.

Another mechanism is related to the nature of the Otherworld itself. The traditions of Wales and other Celtic cultures provide us with insights into the characteristics of the Otherworld—where it is located, how it can be reached, and the powers it holds. Places in the physical world that have liminal characteristics are not necessarily part of the Otherworld, but can serve as bridges between the worlds that allow us to connect with it—and it to connect with us. This is the stream we will be exploring in the next chapter.

2

ENTERING THE OTHERWORLD

Broadly speaking, the Otherworld in Celtic traditions encompasses anything and everything not of this world. It is the origin or dwelling place of beings generally classified as being "supernatural," such as the gods, fairies or the Otherfolk, spirits of place, and heroic ancestors. While some scholars find the term "Otherworld" insufficient for expressing the full meaning of "that which is not of this world," it is nevertheless useful for describing supernatural beings and places in Celtic traditions that do not derive from Christian belief systems.

The Otherworld of the Celts is not the same as Underworld realms like Hades; it is not a place for the spirits of the dead to dwell for all eternity, enjoying rewards or suffering punishment for their deeds during life. While it has its darker side—Welsh tradition, for example, speaks of prisoners held in the Otherworld as well as places of gloom or impediment—overall, the Otherworld is characterized as containing great abundance, and those who dwell there are immortal beings blessed with eternal youth. While there are some accounts of Islands of the Dead in Irish and Gaulish traditions, these appear to be temporary sojourns where souls can rest before reincarnating.

In some lore, the Otherworld is a very remote place, sometimes characterized as a far-off land to the west or on the other side of the world. It is often depicted as an island or series of islands that can only be reached by a perilous journey over water. The Otherworld has also been described as a world beneath our own, either found at the bottom of a lake or the sea or literally existing as a subterranean realm below the ground. Still other tales describe characters stumbling into the Otherworld accidentally—implying that there are other places where the two worlds lie side by side—or else accessing it through known entrances, such as hollow hills.

While there are sometimes specific places in the physical landscape that have supernatural associations and are thought to be connected to the Otherworld, extant lore from Celtic lands is unclear on whether there were multiple Otherworldly realms, if it was one vast domain with many points of entry, or if both were true as perceptions of the Otherworld may have varied by culture and time period. Either way, the lore suggests that a close relationship exists between this world and the Otherworld, even as the two realms exhibit marked and important differences.

Characteristics of the Otherworld

Over and over again, tradition emphasizes that the Otherworld functions very differently from our own world. Not only do the laws of physics appear to not apply when it comes to matters such as time, speed, and distance, the Otherworld also operates according to its own set of rules and requirements. Mortals who seek to enter the Otherworld or to engage in some way with those who dwell there are cautioned to understand those rules before they attempt to do so. Unwary human visitors could easily and unwittingly offend their hosts or naively enter into agreements with them containing loopholes that the Other Folk will not hesitate to exploit, to the human's detriment. Stories about the

Otherworld consistently stress that its values and sense of morality are very different from those of humans, and all who come in contact with the Otherworld or its inhabitants would do well to keep these differences in mind.

Time passes differently in the Otherworld, although the amount of time passed in each realm differs greatly from one tale to the next. In some stories, spending one night in the Otherworld is the equivalent of a hundred years in the mortal world, while in other stories a visitor can enter the Otherworld in the spring, and return home the next day to find that winter had come. Measures of distance and perceptions of speed also seem to follow their own rules when it comes to the Otherworld and its inhabitants. Rhiannon's birds, for example, are able to sing from across a far ocean and be heard as clearly as if they were in the same room as the listener. Similarly, when Rhiannon crosses into this world upon a white mare walking at a slow and steady pace, even the quickest of mortal riders are unable to catch up with her. Instead, the faster she is pursued, the further away from her pursuers she becomes even though her mare's pace remains unchanged.

One of the characteristics of the Otherworld is that it has a very contradictory nature; sometimes it is across a vast ocean, and sometimes it is very local, existing alongside our own world or overlaying it in some way. Due to this proximity, it is hidden from mortals through magical concealments, sometimes envisioned as a veil between the worlds. This veil affects time, space, and consciousness, and it is thinnest at instances of transition. These concealments are therefore easiest to bypass in situations of liminality—that is, at thresholds that are neither of one world nor the other. Because of this, the three main ways to access the Otherworld are through boundary places, boundary times, and boundary states.

Boundary Places

Boundary places are the areas of transition that separate one region from another. These can be natural places such as riverbanks and shorelines, or artificial constructs like hedges, fences, or political borders. Boundary places are also present where opposing things come together. This union of opposites can manifest in nature as mist (confluence of air and water), as springs and wells (emergence of water from earth), and as fords (passage through water by earth). Constructed places where opposites unite include burial mounds (hollow hills, where the dead can be met by the living), crossroads (the intersection of two or more roads), and bridges (structures crossing over water or through the sky constructed out of materials sourced from the earth—wood, metal, stone).

Boundary Times

Boundary times are temporal transitions that mark a change from one period to another. Some of these transitions are human-made, arising as a consequence of our efforts to measure time through the use of calendar systems and technology. An example is the threshold between years that occurs when the clock strikes midnight on December 31—artificial but still potent. However, most calendar systems historically are based on natural rhythms that can be used to measure time, such as the revolution of the earth around the sun, the rotation of the earth around its axis, and the relative relationships between the earth, moon, and sun that cause the phases of the moon. Examples of natural boundary times include dusk and dawn, equinoxes and solstices, and the points of transition between seasons.

The great festivals of Calan Gaeaf (Welsh, "First of Winter") and Calan Haf (Welsh, "First of Summer") are powerful examples of boundary times. In Wales, Ireland, and other Celtic lands, traditional observances and rites associated with these days are reflections of a cultural understanding of how the separation between this world and the Otherworld is affected during these transitional periods. These ideas persist today, even as the origins of these beliefs likely stem from pre-Christian times.

In Wales, there are three occasions that hold the designation Ysbrydnos or "Spirit Night": Nos Calan Gaeaf (Eve of the First of Winter), Nos Calan Haf (Eve of the First of Summer), and Noswyl Ganol Haf (Midsummer's Eve). It is believed that on these nights, ghosts and spirits of the dead walk freely among the living and the thinning of the veils makes them good nights for divination. However, these periods could also be dangerous, and so apotropaic folk practices and leaving offerings for the spirits were common on these nights. In Ireland, it is believed that the *síd* mounds—the hollow hills that lead to the Otherworld—are thrown open on Samhain ("Summer's End," the equivalent of Calan Gaeaf); the veils are removed and no concealment is possible during this threshold time that straddles the light and dark halves of the year.

Boundary States

Boundary states are transitions connected to shifts of status and consciousness; they are primarily centered on concepts of personal identity in relation to the outer world, as well as the filters through which the individual is able to perceive the worlds within, around, and beyond them. Some changes of status manifest in relation to the natural cycle of life, and include the thresholds of birth, puberty, adulthood, old age, illness, injury, and death. Periods of liminality connected to shifts in social status vary by culture; within a given culture, the way these transitions are marked can differ based on collectively held concepts around gender, religion, ethnicity, and sexuality.

These changes in status are usually marked by rites of passage, functioning both to assist the individual with the impact these transitions can have on their sense of identity as well as to serve as a signal to the outside world that an individual's status within the social structure has changed. Modern day examples of these rites of passage include baby blessings, first blood ceremonies, bat and bar mitzvahs, quinceañeras, graduation parties, weddings, swearing-in ceremonies, initiation rituals, and the administration of last rites.

Boundary states that accompany shifts of consciousness can be achieved in many ways. They can happen as a result of physical trauma or illness, such as when people become comatose, go into shock, or have a dissociative episode. Near death experiences and sleep paralysis are other examples of shifts in consciousness that are involuntary results of physiological processes.

Shifts of consciousness can be achieved by entering boundary states intentionally through mental, physical, and spiritual disciplines such as martial arts, yoga, and meditation. Other religious and spiritual practices used to enter into trance states include ecstatic dance, repetitive chant, ritual incubation, mediumship, mantra, mandala creation, aspecting deity, and sacred sexuality practices. Of course, altered states of consciousness are also reached through the use of alcohol, hallucinogens, and other intoxicants; however, their use is generally discourage due to the inability to control or direct these experiences coupled with the physical and mental risks these substances can present.

There are techniques specific to some Celtic traditions used to cross into these boundary states and suspend consciousness between worlds. These include the Three Illuminations of the Filli in Ireland and the prophetic trances of the Awenyddion in Wales—both of which are methods used to seek the divine inspiration and poetic prophecy of Imbas and Awen.

Otherworldly Islands

Concepts of the Otherworld are not uniformly held by all Celtic cultures, although there are many commonalities. In Welsh tradition, the

Otherworld is called *Annwfn* (Middle Welsh) or *Annwn* (Modern Welsh), which means either "the Very Deep place" (from *an-*, used as an intensifying prefix and *dwfn*, meaning "deep") or "the Not-World" (from *an-* used as a negating prefix and *dwfn*, meaning "world").[47]

In the Four Branches of *Y Mabinogi*, the passage between Annwn and our world is shown to occur in various ways. We see characters unknowingly wander into the Otherworld by crossing territorial boundaries, illustrating that aspects of Annwn resemble our own world and that there are places where the two worlds exist side by side. Other characters are shown intentionally inviting the presence of the Otherworld by sitting on mounds known to have supernatural properties. We also see examples of Annwn imposing itself on our world by way of a mist that can transport physical objects and living beings between the two worlds; this mist is often heralded by a deafening thunder. Lastly, we observe characters spending time on islands that present with several Otherworldly qualities, including a difference in the passage of time, and an altered sense of distance between things.

The traditions of Otherworldly islands such as these feature in the mythos of many Celtic lands, and they represent a vital component to our understanding of the nature and mythic heritage of Avalon.

Islands in Irish Tradition

Irish tradition is filled with Otherworldly islands, typically envisioned as paradisiacal lands to the west. A famed example of this is *Tír na nÓg* ("Land of the Young"), home of the Tuatha Dé Danann, a race of divine beings. There are several ways to reach Tír na nÓg: through barrows, being transported by mists, or by undertaking a sea voyage.

---

47 Sarah Higley, "Preiddeu Annwn: The Spoils of Annwn," Robbins Library Digital Projects (The Camelot Project, 2007), https://d.lib.rochester.edu/camelot/text/preiddeu-annwn.

There are two categories of Irish tales that are defined by their themes of sea journeys to the islands of the Otherworld. These are called *echtrae* ("adventure" usually older and are more Pagan in context), and *immram* ("voyage," which include Pagan elements but typically exhibit Christian influence). However, the distinctions between the two tale types are not always clear-cut, and there are a few tales classed as immrama that more correctly should be considered echtrai.

Two such tales are "Immram Brain maic Febail" ("The Voyage of Bran Mac Febal") and "Immram Máel Dúin" ("The Voyage of Máel Dúin"). In both stories, the titular heroes and their respective crews journey to the islands of the Otherworld. Among the many strange and wondrous places they visit, two islands are of particular interest to our present discussion. These are *Emain Ablach* (the Place of Apple Trees) and *Tír na mBan* (the Land of Women).

Emain Ablach and Tír na mBan

Emain Ablach is a paradisiacal land in the Otherworld ruled by Manannán mac Lir, one of the Tuatha Dé Danann. Manannán is a sea deity who is also the Guardian of the Otherworld. He possesses a magical silver branch hung with three golden apples; this branch has the power to play music that soothes those who are ill and injured into the comfort of sleep.

In the eighth-century Irish tale "The Voyage of Bran Mac Febal," the eponymous hero is called to undertake a quest to the Otherworldly island Tír na mBan. One day, while walking alone around his stronghold, Bran hears beautiful music behind him, yet no matter how much he turned around to find its source, the music was always behind him. The song was so sweet, it eventually lulled him into a peaceful sleep. Upon waking, he discovers beside him a silver branch bearing apple blossoms—the source of the music. Taking it up, he makes his way into the royal hall where a strangely attired woman appears. Standing before the assembly, she invites him to embark upon a journey to the Otherworld by singing fifty quatrains of a poem to him; her song begins:

> 'A branch of the apple-tree from Emain
> I bring, like those one knows;
> Twigs of white silver are on it,
> Crystal brows with blossoms.
>
> 'There is a distant isle,
> Around which sea-horses glisten:
> A fair course against the white-swelling surge,—
> Four feet uphold it.[48]

During the course of her song, the Otherworldly woman reveals details about Emain Ablach that resemble descriptions of Avalon: it is a place of perpetual spring, abundant with food and drink, and its inhabitants know nothing of illness or sorrow. Another name given to Emain Ablach in her poem is Aircthech ("Bountiful Land"), again recalling Avalon as the Fortunate Isle. When her song is complete, the silver branch—which comes from Emain Ablach—jumps from Bran's hand to hers as she departs.

Bran decides to take up the quest, and when he does so, he embarks upon the journey with three companies of nine men. After many encounters along the way, Bran and his men finally reach Tír na mBan and are warmly welcomed by its inhabitants. They are presented with lavish feasts, and each man found a mate among the women—there were three times nine beds to accommodate them all. The adventurers thought they had spent a year in Tír na mBan, but as it is with the Otherworld, when they returned to Ireland they discovered that hundreds of years had passed in this world.

---

48 Kuno Meyer, trans., "The Voyage of Bran Mac Febal," Celtic Literature Collective (London: David Nutt, 1895), accessed June 16, 2022, https://www.maryjones.us /ctexts/branvoyage.html.

Similarly in "Immram Máel Dúin," also believed to have been written in the eighth century, Máel Dúin and his crew of seventeen undertake a long sea journey in large curraghs (wood-framed vessels covered in animal hides, similar to Welsh coracles) during which they encounter thirty-one strange and wonderful islands. Several times during the course of their travels, when the crew had exhausted their provisions and were suffering from hunger, they encountered islands where magical apples grew; as few as three such apples proved able to sustain the entire crew for forty days.

After visiting many islands, they came upon one that featured a great fortress in the middle of a plain. It was the richly appointed home of a queen and her seventeen daughters; there were eighteen women in all—a multiple of nine—and their number exactly matched that of the Irish journeyers. The women extended their hospitality to Máel Dúin and his men, laying a wondrous feast before them. The next morning, as the men started to take their leave, the queen invited them to remain, saying, "Stay here and old age shall not fall on you, but you shall keep the age you now have; lasting life shall be yours always, and every joy and delight. Why then go wandering longer from island to island over the wide and barren ocean?"[49]

Initially enticed by her offer, the men decide to stay, but after three months—which felt to them like three years—they try to take their leave once more. As the boat begins to leave, the queen rides to the shore on her horse and prevents their departure by throwing a magical ball of thread that Máel Dúin catches; it clings to his hand, and she uses it to pull the boat back to the harbor. In this way, she was able to prevent their leaving three times for a period of three months each. On the crew's fourth attempt to depart, one of the crew catches the clew of thread instead; another of the crew severs his hand, and it falls into the sea along with the magical thread, allowing them to finally escape.

---

49 Joseph Jacobs, ed., *The Book of Wonder Voyages* (NY: The Knickerbocker Press, 1919), https://en.wikisource.org/wiki/The_Book_of_Wonder_Voyages/The _Voyage_of_Maelduin. 116.

Mag Mell

In the Irish tale "Echtra Condla" ("The Adventures of Connla the Fair"), the eponymous hero is the son of Conn, king of Ireland. Standing with his father and his father's Druid on the hill of Uisnech, the sacred center of Ireland, a strangely garbed woman appears that only Connla can see, although the others are able to hear her. She identifies herself as a noble woman who dwells in a *sid* (fairy mound) where the immortal inhabitants spend their days in peace and eternal feasting. Declaring her love for Connla, she invites him to live with her in Mag Mell, the "Plain of Delight." Before she is dismissed by the magic of Corann, the Druid, she throws an apple to the prince. Connla is overcome with love for the mysterious woman, and although the only thing that he eats for a month is the apple she gave him, the fruit itself is never diminished. At the end of the month, she appears to him once more, again extending an invitation for him to join her. When Connla says that he is torn between his love for her and that of his people, she says:

> Thou strivest-most difficult of wishes to fulfill—
> Against the wave of longing which drives thee hence.
> That land we may reach in my crystal boat,
> The fairy-mound of Boadach.
> There is yet another land
> That is no worse to reach;
> I see it, now the sun sinks.
> Although it is far, we may reach it before night.
> That is the land which rejoices
> The heart of everyone who wanders therein;
> No other sex lives there
> Save women and maidens.[50]

With that, he jumped into her crystal boat and sailed away with her into the west, never to be seen again.

---

50 Tom Peete Cross and Clark Harris Slover, *Ancient Irish Tales* (New York: Henry Holt and Co., 1936), 490.

Islands in Welsh Tradition

Likewise, Otherworldly islands are present in Welsh tradition, and share many similarities with those known to us from Irish tales. In the Second Branch of *Y Mabinogi*, the Island of Gwales is the setting of an eighty-year-long Otherworldly feast with Bran and the Assembly of the Wondrous Head. In the Fourth Branch we encounter Caer Arianrhod. Although it is not overtly identified as Otherworldly, it is clearly defined as "other" based on its most unusual characteristic: it is ruled over by a woman, whose name it bears. While it is not explicitly an island of women, a sole woman ruler is definitely out of the ordinary. Most relevant to this discussion are the island fortresses of Annwn.

Islands of Annwn

The ninth-century Welsh poem "Preiddeu Annwn" ("The Spoils of Annwn") tells the story of King Arthur's raid of the Otherworld in search of a magical cauldron. Although the earliest known versions of "Preiddeu Annwn" appear in manuscripts dating to the thirteenth or fourteenth century CE in the compilation of poetry that has come to be known as *Llyfr Taliesin* (*The Book of Taliesin*), linguistic analysis suggests the poem is much older; some scholars date it to somewhere between the sixth and ninth centuries CE.[51]

After a voyage over the sea, Arthur and his band of warriors move through Annwn, encountering seven wondrous and enigmatic fortresses—or alternatively, a single fortress given multiple epithets. It is unclear what the author intended, but at the very least, the poem is similar to Irish immrama tales in that heroes undertake a sea voyage and visit a multitude of Otherworldly areas with different attributes. The names and descriptions of the fortresses in "Preiddeu Annwn" are deeply evocative; many hold resonance with depictions of Oth-

---

51 Norris J. Lacy, "The Spoils of Annwfn (Preiddeu Annwfn)," in *The New Arthurian Encyclopedia* (New York: Garland, 1991), 428.

erworldly magic found in both Welsh and Irish traditions, indicating some cross-cultural influences. These fortresses are:

1. *Caer Sidi*: Fortress of the Old Ones or Fortress of the Mound

2. *Caer Pedryfran*: Four-Cornered or Four-Peaked Fortress

3. *Caer Feddwid*: Fortress of Mead-Drunkenness or Fortress of Carousal

4. *Caer Wydr*: Fortress of Glass

5. *Caer Goludd*: Fortress of Guts or Fortress of Hindrance

6. *Caer Fandwy*: Fortress of Heights or Fortress of the Divine Peak

7. *Caer Ochren*: Fortress of Enclosure or Fortress of the Shelving Tides[52]

A few of these fortress names and attributes are especially relevant to our present discussion, and provide further support for the idea of Avalon as an island of the Otherworld. The name *Caer Sidi* is likely a borrowing from Irish tradition, where sacred mounds called *sid* were considered entrances to the Otherworld and had associations with the gods of the Tuatha Dé Danann as well as the Other Folk. Mounds with connections to the Otherworld also appear in Welsh tradition, such as the Gorsedd Arberth in *Y Mabinogi*. Interestingly, two physical world places that are most strongly associated with Avalon both feature large mound-like areas in their landscapes: the large, terraced hill that is Glastonbury Tor, and Mynydd Enlli, the singular mountain that gives Bardsey Island (discussed in chapter 1) its iconic silhouette.

Caer Pedryfran is the location of the Cauldron of the Chief of Annwn that is kindled by the breath of Nine Maidens. Described in the

---

52 Sarah Higley, "Preiddeu Annwn: The Spoils of Annwn," Robbins Library Digital Projects (The Camelot Project, 2007), https://d.lib.rochester.edu/camelot/text/preiddeu-annwn.

poem as four times revolving, it bears a resemblance to the fortress of Cú Roí in "Fled Bricrend" ("The Feast of Bricriu"), a story from the Ulster Cycle. Cú Roí was an Irish warrior king possessing magical powers, and every night he would chant an incantation that caused his fortress to revolve like a millstone, making it impossible to find the entrance until sunrise.[53]

The carousal and mead drunkenness associated with Caer Feddwid appears to be an Annuvian iteration of Otherworldly feasts that feature prominently in story traditions from many Celtic lands. Mead is a powerful shifter of consciousness, and it brings on an intoxication resembling the trance states that bring on prophecy or the battle frenzies that incite warriors into battle. It is also suggestive of the kingship rites involving mead found in many Celtic cultures. Perhaps the shift in consciousness it brings about acts as a proxy for the shift in status that comes with the granting of sovereignty to a worthy king.

Lastly, in addition to Caer Wydr, there are several mentions of glass buildings associated with the Otherworld in Welsh lore, including Tŷ Gwydr, a glass house on Ynys Enili/Bardsey Island, belonging either to Merlin or to Morgan le Fay, depending on the source. Ynys Witrin, the Island of Glass, is a Welsh name for Glastonbury, although as discussed on page 38, there are several theories regarding the etymology of the name.

King of the Otherworld

The purpose for Arthur's journey was to obtain the Cauldron of the Chief of Annwn, located in Caer Pedryfran in the care of Nine Maidens. This was a perilous journey from which only seven of the entire company of warriors and bards returned. We will discuss the Nine Maidens and other aspects of this poem throughout this book.

---

53 George Henderson, *Fled Bricrend: The Feast of Bricriu* (London: Irish Texts Society, 1899).

Several figures have been identified as the leader of the Otherworld in Welsh mythos. Rather than a contradiction, it is likely that Annwn is composed of several kingdoms; this appears to be what is suggested in the First Branch of *Y Mabinogi*. These named kings include: Arawn, Hafgan, Pwyll, Gwyn, and Avallach. The final two are of particular interest to our explorations as they have strong associations with Avalon—something that further reinforces the location of the Holy Isle as part of Annwn. We discussed Avallach ap Beli in chapter 1. Depending on the source, he has been called either the King of Annwn or the King of Avalon; in the case of the latter, it is also said that the island was named after him.

Gwyn ap Nudd ("White, son of Mist,)" features in Welsh folklore as the leader of the Wild Hunt. There are a variety of traditions about the Wild Hunt. In one version, very year at Calan Gaeaf, Gwyn rides out from the Otherworld with the Cwn Annwn ("Hounds of Annwn") to gather the souls of all who had died in the newly-ending year and bring them back with him to the Otherworld. Gwyn appears in "Buchedd Collen," ("The Life of Saint Collen," sixteenth century) where he is called the King of Annwn and of the Fairies and is said to dwell on or beneath Glastonbury Tor—ostensibly because of Glastonbury's connection to Avalon. In "Culhwch ac Olwen," Gwyn is a warrior in Arthur's retinue, though his story contains hints of his chthonic attributes. The narrative states that the spirits of the demons of Annwn were put in him by God, lest the world be destroyed—which seems to imply Gwyn is able to control them.

Islands of the Dead

Although we have only touched upon a few examples in this brief overview, a rich literary heritage featuring Otherworldy islands can be found in the lore of many Celtic lands. Generally speaking, those who dwell on these islands in Irish and Welsh tradition are the "Ever-living Ones" who, according to Loomis, are the immortal remnants of Pagan deities.[54] There are some exceptions. For example, in Irish tradition, Tech nDuinn ("House of Donn" or "House of the Dark One") is an island where spirits gather after death, though whether as their permanent abode or as a resting place before journeying to other destinations is unclear. This island is associated with Donn, a male ancestral figure in Irish tradition. Tech nDuinn has been identified with several real-world islands near the coast of Ireland, and Irish scholar Kuno Meyer compares it to the Greek realm of Hades. In contrast, the paradisal Otherworldly islands that are located far across the ocean to the west and can only be visited by mortals while still living, have been compared to ancient Greek ideas of the Islands of the Blessed or Elysium.

However, these beliefs do not appear to be limited to the realm of story; there are real-world analogs to these Otherworldly islands as well—some of them sites of Christian monastic settlements and places of pilgrimage, and others manifesting as literal Islands of the Dead. These serve as an excellent illustration of the ways in which lore and literature are important vehicles for the transmission of cultural beliefs. Elements of myths and folk narratives do not arise in a vacuum; they reflect aspects of the cultures from which they arise—whether structures of society, collectively held moralities, historical events, culturally transformative circumstances, or beliefs originating in religion or expressed in folk practices.

There are several examples of islands used in various Celtic cultures primarily for the purpose of burials, usually of people considered holy or high status. Two in particular are relevant to our discussion here; both can be found off the western coast of Britain and both are associated with the Brythonic Celtic cultures found in Cornwall and Wales.

---

54 Roger Sherman Loomis, *Wales and the Arthurian Legend* (Cardiff, UK: University of Wales Press, 1956), 143.

These are Ynys Enlli/Bardsey Island (covered in chapter 1) and the Isles of Scilly—an archipelago off the western tip of Cornwall.

The Isles of Scilly are rich with ancient sites; what is particularly striking is that they feature an unusual number of cairnfields. Cairnfields are clusters of cairns—stones that have been heaped together to create a memorial or marker of some sort; these are often interpreted as burial places, although they generally tend to be shallow, suggesting that bodies may have been exposed to the elements before burial. There are various types of cairns found on these islands, including chambered cairns and entrance graves that may have served ritual purposes as well.

The relative density of cairns and burial chambers compared to the rest of the isle of Britain, in addition to the amount of burials comparative to contemporary population size, is a strong indicator that the Isles of Scilly may have been treated as real world Islands of the Dead. Similar to Bardsey Island, they are islands to the west reached by a journey over water to where people were brought from elsewhere to be laid to rest in holy ground.

Avalon and the Otherworld

Taken as a whole and based on the descriptions of Avalon from extant lore, we can see that the Holy Isle exhibits many characteristics that identify her as an island of the Otherworld. She is located in the west, is surrounded by mists that reinforce her liminality, and can only be reached by a journey over water that requires a knowledgeable navigator. The island is one of healing, joy, and self-propagating abundance. She is known and named for her apple trees, that most Otherworldly of fruit, and she abides by her own set of rules.

While this mythic Avalon holds strong resonance with the Islands of Women and Otherworldly paradises found in the traditions of other Celtic cultures, it does not mean they are all the same island. Ynys Afallon and Emain Ablach may resemble each other, but they exist independently of each other within different cultural contexts. Perhaps it is clarifying to say that they are two examples of the same mytheme—in this case, an Otherworldly island abundant with paradisiacal fruit—held in common by cultures that are related to or in contact with each other. In mythological studies, a mytheme is a unit of story that tends to exist in a similar relationship with other story units in tales across cultures, suggesting a similar origin. For example, the mytheme of the Otherworldly island of magical women often appears alongside the mytheme of the questing hero; we see it with Arthur, Bran Mac Febal, and Odysseus.

Avalon Within, Around, and Beyond

In her most actualized form, I believe that Ynys Afallon exists quite firmly in the Celtic British Otherworld and is one of the islands of Annwn. As such, she may never have had a physical location in this world at all. That said, there is no question that there are places resembling the descriptions of Avalon found in legend, like Bardsey Island, or that have come to wear her mythic mantle over time due to local tradition or long-standing belief, like Glastonbury. This is a long-recognized phenomenon where a particular landscape becomes associated with a legendary locale such that one becomes an energetic proxy for the other. I have come to call this process "spatial euhemerization," and in many ways, it functions to create a liminality—a threshold into the Otherworld.

It is clear from the lore that there is more than one way to reach the Otherworld, and that it touches this world through a variety of liminalities—including boundary places, threshold times, and spaces of transition. While literature from Celtic lands is filled with symbols and folkloric motifs that signal to the audience that the Otherworld—and its influence—is present, I believe these to be more than literary devices. No matter where or what they are, if threshold places, times, and spaces are ways of entry to the Otherworld, then a physical place that expresses liminality is likewise connected to the Otherworld in a very real way.

Perhaps it is then true to say that Avalon is in the Otherworld and that there are physical places and passages in this world through which we can connect with her. For those who know the way, the part of the Otherworld that is Avalon can be accessed in places that are of like energy. Working in liminal spaces that approximate or emulate the characteristics of the Holy Isle—the details of which have come down to us through the Avalonian Stream of Tradition—would allow or encourage the energetic current of Avalon to come through those spaces.

What is true in the outer world also holds true in our inner world. We can find Avalon within us through the pursuit of Sovereignty and the development of mastery that permits us to recognize the presence of liminalities, empowers us to cross thresholds of many kinds, and inspires us to seek the blessings of Awen—in service to self, to others, and to Source.

3

THE NINEFOLD
SISTERHOODS

From the earliest written accounts of Avalon, she is described as a place of extraordinary women who enjoyed powers and privileges beyond those of their contemporaries dwelling within the confines of ordinary society. Nine sisters ruled the island by a fair set of laws of their own devising, and were not beholden to the rules and moralities of the medieval court. They were well educated in the arts and sciences; possessed the powers of healing, augury, and shapeshifting; practiced bard craft; served as allies and advisors to kings; and judged the worth of champions and would-be rulers through tests and challenges.

Groups of nine holy women living in enclaves set apart from the rest of society is a motif found across Celtic, Germanic, and Mediterranean myth and folklore traditions. Although we cannot say with any certainty how these groups are related to each other, if at all, there are several potential explanations for why these Ninefold Sisterhoods appear in so many iterations in so many lands.

On Potential Origins

In ancient prehistory, the Celtic, Germanic, and Mediterranean cultural groups are among those believed to have developed out of a common mother culture that spoke the Proto-Indo-European (PIE) language—a reconstructed root tongue that gave rise to the majority of languages in Europe and on the Indian subcontinent. This root tongue is believed to have been spoken by the Kurgan people who originated in steppes of Eastern Europe sometime between 4500 to 2500 BCE before migrating across Europe and India—carrying their language and its attendant culture with them.

It is theorized that as segments of this Indo-European mother culture migrated to different areas and lost contact with other speakers of their language, separate branches of PIE began to develop over time. These new branches were likely influenced by the languages of the indigenous peoples the Indo-European migrants came in contact with, as well as the different physical environments of the lands they came to inhabit. While there is no direct evidence of PIE, linguists have been able to reverse engineer this theorized mother tongue by retracing common elements in the languages that arose in areas related to the Indo-European migrations.

Language is a powerful carrier of culture; it includes words for things and concepts that its speakers directly experience and want to convey to others. Cultural shifts, such as those accompanying migration, influence changes in language as well. New words arise to reflect new environments, experiences, and beliefs, while words for things that no longer hold relevance gradually fall away.

Using the same techniques as linguists, mythologists and those who study ancient religions have been able to reconstruct elements of a hypothetical core PIE mythos, as well as extrapolate some attendant religious practices. It is therefore possible that some manner of religious expression involving nine sacred women may have originated in the core PIE culture, which would account for reflections of this motif being present in several later belief systems and mythic traditions, each exhibiting some cultural variation.

This core expression could have manifested in several ways. There may have been a PIE religious practice that involved cloistered groups of nine priestesses, and/or there may have been a ninefold divinity group, in the mode of well-attested traditions of triple divinities, who may have had functions associated with water, knowledge, healing, and inspiration.

Alternatively, the motif may be a reflection of a PIE cultural association with the number nine. Likely due to the nine month human gestational period, many societies connect the number nine with women and fertility (and, by extension, with the moon and magic), and therefore nines may have come to be an organizing principle used to measure completion or wholeness—a full set of something. We can see this latter idea, for example, manifest in medieval Welsh culture where warriors are grouped by nine, and contemporary law codes make repeated use of periods of nine days. (The significance of nine is discussed further, beginning on page 79.)

If the Ninefold motif isn't one that originated in the PIE mother culture, it may instead have come to feature in Celtic, Germanic, and Mediterranean cultures as a result of a later transmission of ideas between these cultures. We know, for example, that Gallo-Roman and Germanic tribes venerated triune groups of Mother Goddesses called the *Matres* or *Matronae*. The earliest attested writing of the word *Matres* is believed to be in Gaulish, although dedicatory stelae to various Triple Mother groupings don't appear until the Roman conquests of Celtic and Germanic lands. Before syncretic Roman influence, the Celts either rarely created images of their gods or did so out of materials that did not survive into the present. Was worship of the Matres a Celtic belief that spread to their Roman and Germanic neighbors, who then manifested their devotion to these goddesses in new, culturally relevant ways? Or was this a belief the three cultural groups already had in common, but the Roman manifestation of devotional cult objects to the Matres is what spread during the first century CE? We don't know for sure, but the cross-cultural veneration of divinity groupings of this type is clear. The Matres are discussed further in chapter 5.

Similarly, the concept of a Ninefold Sisterhood may have had its origins in one of the Celtic, Germanic, or Mediterranean cultures that then spread to other areas and into other cultures. Due to the nature of transmission, however, it is possible that what may have begun as the worship of a Ninefold divinity group or as a cultus featuring cloistered priestesses in groups of nine may have made its way into other lands (horizontal transmission) or into the traditions of other times (vertical transmission) in altered forms.

For example, Roman accounts of priestess isles off the coast of Gaul (discussed in detail later in this chapter) are presented as history, but they are not firsthand accounts. There is therefore a possibility that these were instead Gaulish myths or legends preserved in local oral tradition that eventually found their way to the various historians and geographers who recorded them as fact. Furthermore, the stories of Ninefold Sisterhoods may have been transmitted between cultures in the post-Christian era, thereby owing local variations to shared folklore and, later, the literary record.

It is also possible that the Ninefold motif may not have had anything to do with the PIE origins of the cultures where we most strongly identify its presence. Instead, it may have been a religious form that belonged to one of the indigenous cultural groups of Europe that predated the Indo-European migrations of the late Stone Age and early Bronze Age. While there is little that directly attests to this, remnants of cultural histories sometimes show up in the myths, legends, and folklore of a people.

One example is the theory that the stories of Zeus's sexual conquests in Greek mythology are actually may be mythic memories of the cultural shifts that occurred when the Indo-Europeans settled the Greek islands, bringing their gods with them.[55] Broadly speaking, Zeus could be seen to represent the conquering culture, overwriting or integrating that which already existed. Some of the women he slept with—often depicted in the myths as human royalty or semi-divine creatures like nymphs—may have originally been indigenous goddesses of place. The union between the two—as with the rites of the sacred marriage (hieros gamos) and conference of Sovereignty (covered in chapter 5)—could represent the incorporation of preexisting belief systems and cults of worship into the religion of the newcomers. This is a vast oversimplification for the purpose of our current discussion, but it is easy to find support of this theory in Greek mythological studies.

We must also consider the possibility that the Ninefold Sisterhood motif is one that arose in many places independently of each other. It may have served to meet a cultural need common to people living in a particular landscape—whether environmental or social—and so the answering form took a similar manifestation in disparate places and times. Further, it is always possible that instances of Ninefold Sisterhoods arising separately may have nothing in common with each other, and the connections that we see are the result of looking at history and lore through the lens of our present cultural context, causing us to find meaningful patterns having nothing to do with original intention.

Indigenous Beliefs

Like the cultural histories preserved as mythic resonances in ancient Greek myth discussed above, there are related theories on the origins of at least some stories and beliefs concerning the Other Folk in Celtic

---

55 Joseph Campbell, *Goddesses: Mysteries of the Feminine Divine*, ed. Safron Rossi (Novato, CA: New World Library, 2013), xxii

lands. Some scholars posit that tales of Otherworldly figures and their strange customs are based in residual memories of differences between the Celtic peoples whose culture spread from the continent (whether through migration of peoples or transmission of ideas) and those of the indigenous peoples of Britain who predated them.

As cultural shifts tend to be gradual, especially in preindustrial times, it's easy to see how Britons living in remote areas would hold on to their pre-Celtic way of life and belief systems longer. This might account for the fay exhibiting behaviors, rules, and taboos that seemed strange to the now-predominant overculture telling stories about them. In the tale of the Lake Maiden of Llyn y Fan Fach, for example, she is described as laughing at a funeral, crying at a wedding, and stalling so as not to have to attend a christening. This cultural difference may also account for the idea of iron being a ward against the fay; the indigenous Bronze Age peoples wouldn't have been using iron until it arrived along with the Celts and their technologies. Iron therefore could have represented an imbalance of power in terms of weaponry, or else simply marked the difference between the cultures.

This substrata of pre-Celtic cultural forms may be related to the Ninefold Sisterhood groups known to us in Celtic lands. If it is true that women could become Druids in Celtic society—a matter that may not be as settled as we may think, as we shall discuss in chapter 4—why then do there appear to be separate orders of religious women, existing side by side with them? In addition to the classical accounts of Gaulish priestesses living on secluded islands, Tacitus's description of the Roman siege of Mona (Ynys Môn/Anglesey) seems to make a clear delineation between the Druids (famously described by Roman writers as wearing white) and the black-garbed women weaving in and out of the Druidic ranks during the encounter. Described as bearing torches and acting like Furies—fearsome goddesses of vengeance—these women both incited the battle fury of the Britons for the coming battle and stupefied the invading Roman legions, who were immobilized with terror … at least for a time.

As this account is the only information we have about these women of Môn, who they were and what roles they may have played in Celtic British society is unknown; we don't know if they were Druids, a separate order of priestesses, or if they were just women of the island joining in the defense of their land. If they were a separate order of priestesses, it is possible that they were part of Celtic religious culture and their religious service to their people took a more "monastic" form—akin to the Gaulish priestesses on their sacred islands, whom we will be discussing below—than the Druids, who appear to have traveled widely.

Alternatively, these priestess groups may have had their origins in the beliefs of the indigenous inhabitants of Gaul and Britain. As the migration of Celtic culture through Europe seems to be the result of the transmission of ideas, as well as some movement of people—rather than the abrupt changes that tend to accompany military conquests—there may have been a gradual shift of culture that permitted an assimilation of indigenous beliefs with Celtic ideas. If so, this older religious order may have remained, perhaps serving as representatives of the deities and spirits of the land itself. As such, they may have acted as representatives of the genus loci and tutelary divinities—some of whom came to be remembered as Lake Maidens and Fairy Brides—who held the Sovereignty of the land.

With the coming of Celtic tribes that seemed to embrace the idea that one can only be a leader if they have the permission of the spirits of the land in their care to do so, it is possible that the transmission of kingship and the granting of the right to rule may have been among the responsibilities of these priestesses, on behalf of the indigenous deities they served. This dynamic, in turn, could be what the Sovereignty motif in early literature was originally founded upon.

To be clear, this is conjecture—but it derives from a method of mythic analysis that seeks insight from potential subtextual meanings embedded in story narratives. For example, in the Fourth Branch of *Y Mabinogi*, the ongoing tensions between Arianrhod and Gwydion are believed to be a proxy for issues arising from cultural shifts around women's rights and powers in medieval Wales. This is most clearly expressed around the change from matriliny to patriliny. With matrilineal inheritance, estates and titles were passed down through the motherline; it is a man's sister's son who inherits the estate or the throne. Because this form of inheritance fell out of practice, it may explain why later Arthurian writers justified Mordred's claim to Arthur's throne as being the king's son through an incestuous relationship with his half-sister Morgause, rather than because Mordred is his nephew (the manner in which he is originally depicted); that would not make sense to them.

Some characters in *Y Mabinogi* have matrinyms—meaning they are named for their mothers rather than their fathers—including Gwydion ap Dôn and Mabon ap Modron. This kind of naming convention is typical in cultures that practice matrilineal inheritance. Gwydion himself is his uncle Math's heir because he is the son of Dôn, Math's sister. Likewise, Lleu eventually inherits the throne of Gwynedd—ostensibly because he is the son of Arianrhod, Gwydion's sister. However, this was not the type of inheritance practiced in Wales at the time of the writing of *Y Mabinogi*, nor is it present in any extant Welsh law codes. While we are not completely sure how the different British Celtic tribes handled matters of inheritance, there appears to be some proof of matriliny in the earliest portion of the Pictish King List.

The presence of cultural forms in myths and legends that seem out of sync with their contemporary audiences or authors, therefore, can be suggestive of older social structures and conventions—the memories of which have been carried along the stream of tradition. Although they may be reinterpreted by subsequent authors or retellers of tales, doing a close reading of these stories and looking between the lines for meaning can often yield surprising insights that may be supported by other sources.

The Significance of Nine

Before we start to look at the different iterations of the Ninefold Sisterhood motif as it appears over time and across cultures, there is one last thing to consider. The virality of the motif may not be due to the spread of the institution of holy women themselves but is based instead on the significance of the number nine. The Proto-Indo-European root word for nine is *newn*, from which arose the Greek *ennea*, Latin *novem*, Old Irish *noin*, Welsh *naw*, Gaulish *navan*, Old Norse *niu*, Middle English *nīn*, (from Old English *nigen*, from Proto-Germanic *newun*), to name a few related to the relevant mythos.[56]

This connection is worthy of note since language is a primary transmitter of culture; it therefore stands to reason that along with the word for "nine," cultural ideas about what nine represents (aside from its numerical function) could also have been passed along. There is an allusion to perfection that seems to accompany the number nine: "[T]he Book of St. Albans, in the sections on blazonry, lays great stress on the nines in which all perfect things (orders of angels, virtues, articles of chivalry, differences of coat armour, etc.) occur."[57]

In the early fourteenth century, the allegory of the Nine Worthies began to appear in writing. A reflection of chivalric culture, it named three groups of three men (three Pagans: Hector, Alexander the Great, and Julius Caesar; three Jews: Joshua, David, and Judas Maccabeus; and three Christians: King Arthur, Charlemagne, and Godfrey of Bouillon)

---

56 Harper Douglas, "Etymology of Nines," Online Etymology Dictionary, accessed September 3, 2022, https://www.etymonline.com/word/nines.

57 Ernest Weekley, *An Etymological Dictionary of Modern English* (London: John Murray, 1921), 986.

as representing the highest attainment of chivalric virtue within their respective cultures. Although the Nine Lady Worthies began to appear in literature and art by the late fourteenth century, these nine started off as anonymous allegories. They eventually began to be named, but there was never a standard roster; these Worthies included Amazons, queens (both ancient and contemporary), biblical figures, and Christian saints. Included in one version is the Iceni Queen Boudica (see page 121).[58]

Even into the modern era, phrases such as "to the ninth degree" and being "dressed to the nines" persist, with the sense that the point at hand is exhibiting its highest or most perfect level of expression.[59]

Traditions concerning the number nine appear in several Celtic cultures over time, and overall suggest a general sense that it represented a unit of measurement associated with a full set of something, or a wholeness. The body, for example was believed to be composed of nine principle parts, while in medieval society, the recognition of kin relationships extended up to the ninth generation. The herbal formulary of the Physicians of Myddfai (further discussed on pages 357–358) often incorporated nines in their remedies—typically making their medicines from three ingredients that are then taken three times a day for nine days.[60]

According to the Welsh Laws, a serf's house was to consist of a hall with nine penthouses, while the serfs as a class were expected to build nine houses for their king. Similarly, the laws often refer to a holding consisting of a homestead and eight acres; the idea of nine component parts of a home is a common motif. In Wales and Scotland, the Beltane need-fire was built by nine men who each gathered nine sticks of nine

58 François Velde, "The Nine Worthies," Heraldica, December 6, 2006, https://www.heraldica.org/topics/worthies.htm.

59 Weekley, *Etymological Dictionary*, 986.

60 Charles Wagner, Jillian De Gezelle, and Slavko Komarnytsky, "Celtic Provenance in Traditional Herbal Medicine of Medieval Wales and Classical Antiquity," *Frontiers in Pharmacology* 11 (2020), https://doi.org/10.3389/fphar.2020.00105.

different trees. In Irish tradition, companies of warriors were groups of nine made up of a leader and eight others.[61]

The importance of nine is underscored by its repeated appearance in the Welsh Laws. There is a section called "The Nines of Law" where differing units of measurement and components of judgment are presented in groupings of nine. These include the nine types of marriage, the nine accessories of theft, the nine words of pleading, the nine handbreadths, and so on.[62] Elsewhere in the laws, the ninth day of the month is used to mark the end or beginning of a period of time, and units of nine days are common in the literature of the time. Ireland likewise used units of nine days or half days, called *nômad* and *noínden*. There is a sense, then, that some Celtic cultures may have once considered a week to consist of nine nights, and therefore a month would have been composed of three weeks or twenty-seven days.[63]

Perhaps there was always a magico-religious component underscoring the cultural significance of nine in Celtic lands, but if there wasn't, it seems that nines increasingly became associated with the realms of magic and the Otherworld over time. We see this in the naming traditions of stone circles in Cornwall, for example, as discussed below.

Ninefold Sisterhoods

While we may never know the ultimate origins of these Ninefold groups nor be able to make definitive statements concerning how they may be connected, it is clear that the many iterations found in history, lore, and literature bear some similarities to each other. Often dwelling apart from society on remote islands or in hidden groves, they tend to

---

61 Alwyn D. Rees and B. R. Rees, *Celtic Heritage: Ancient Tradition in Ireland and Wales* (New York: Thames and Hudson, 1974), 193.

62 Aneurin Owen, *Ancient Laws and Institutes of Wales* (London: Printed by G.E. Eyre and A. Spottiswoode, Printers to the Queen's most Excellent Majesty, 1841), 563.

63 Rees and Rees, *Celtic Heritage*, 194.

have strong associations with wells, springs, lakes, or other bodies of water. They are variously depicted as either mortal women possessing magical power such as priestesses, enchantresses, witches, and even nuns or saints able to perform miracles—or supernatural beings, such as water spirits, fairy women, or goddesses. Let's take a look at some of these Ninefold groups as they appear in the history and lore of various Celtic, Germanic, and Mediterranean cultures before we reflect on how they relate to, and what they can teach us about, the Nine Sisters of Avalon.

The Ninefold in Classical Accounts of Gaul

Although the pre-Christian Celts didn't write down their own histories, they were certainly written about; the majority of the historical information we have about them derives from Greek and Roman sources. These materials are fundamentally imperfect in several ways. It is important to keep in mind that classical historians did not adhere to the same standards of proof required of modern historians; because of this, their sources are not always well vetted and include second-hand accounts as well as the sometimes-unattributed writings of earlier historians. They often uncritically relayed fantastical accounts of the foreign peoples they wrote about, nor did they generally strive to maintain a sense of detached neutrality when it came to cultures whose traditions seemed barbarous or strange to their "civilized" mindsets.

Even when it comes to firsthand accounts such as those of Julius Caesar, many of these classical historians and geographers have demonstrated personal and political biases in their work, causing modern readers to question the truth of what was described and wonder which details may have been exaggerated or even made up whole-cloth in support of an agenda. However flawed these accounts of the Celts may be, reading them with the proper context can still yield useful information. This is particularly true when details of these writings appear to verify what we see in the archaeological record and when we are able to see echoes of these accounts show up in later literary traditions.

The final concern is not a problem with the sources specifically but with our own interpretations and assumptions about them. It is important to keep in mind that there are a variety of peoples who fall under the "Celtic" umbrella term; there was never a singular, homogenous Celtic culture. Instead, the pre-Christian Celts comprised a multitude of tribal groups living across Europe and in the British Isles and Ireland over the course of about a thousand years. Even though they shared related languages and cultural forms, we cannot assume that the information we have about the Romanized Celts of Gaul also held true for the Celtic tribes of Britain and Ireland, or that first-century BCE accounts of Gaulish religious beliefs are still applicable to the Gauls of the fourth century CE. We cannot even assume that the cultus (system of worship) of one Gaulish tribe would be the same as those of a contemporary but separate Gaulish tribe living a hundred miles away.

With all of this said, it is nevertheless important to recognize that the accounts of Greek and Roman geographers and historians provide us with some of the most detailed information about Celtic cultures that remain to us from the pre-Christian period. This is especially true of the precious few examples of Ninefold Sisterhoods and Celtic holy women appearing in the historical record. With both the context and limitations of our sources in mind, let's take a look at the information available to us.

The Gallizenae

In his book, *De situ orbis*, Roman geographer Pomponius Mela (first century CE) gives an account of the Gallizenae (sometimes written as Gallicenae, "the Gauls of Cena"). They were a group of nine priestesses who dwelt on the Island of Sena (*Enez-Sun* in Breton, *Île de Sein* in French) off the coast of Brittany. Famed for their oracular gifts, healing powers, and possessing the ability to shapeshift and control the weather, these women were said to live in perpetual virginity and perform ecstatic rites in service to the Divine.

> In the Britannic Sea, opposite the coast of the Ossismi, the isle of Sena [Sein] belongs to a Gallic divinity and is famous for its oracle, whose priestesses, sanctified by their perpetual virginity, are reportedly nine in number. They call the priestesses Gallizenae... they have been endowed with unique powers, they stir up the seas and the winds by their magic charms,... turn into whatever animals they want,... cure what is incurable among other peoples,... know and predict the future, but that it is not revealed except to sea-voyagers and then only to those traveling to consult them.[64]

In addition to this description bearing many similarities Geoffrey of Monmouth's account of the Nine Sisters of Avalon, the Île de Sein itself has many things in common with the Otherworldly islands described in chapter 2. The waters surrounding the island are infamously treacherous due to dangerous currents and an enormous area of reefs, requiring ships that pass to rely upon a network of buoys and beacons to help them navigate the area safely. There are the remains of many megalithic monuments on the island, including two large standing stones believed to have been part of a stone circle, evidence of its long history of habitation and association with ritual practices.

Breton folklore about the Île de Sein include tales of boatmen awakened in the middle of the night to ferry loads of invisible yet audible passengers to the island, who then pay with coins as they disem-

---

64 Pomponius Mela, *Pomponius Mela's Description of the World* ed. Frank E. Romer (Ann Arbor, MI: The University of Michigan Press, 1998), 115.

bark…a mythic memory, perhaps, of Sena having once been an Island of the Dead.[65]

The Samnitae/Namnitae

Another island of priestesses is mentioned by the Greek historian Strabo (63 BCE–c. 24 CE), based upon the earlier writings of Posidonius (c. 135–c. 51 BCE).

> In the ocean, he [Posidonius] says, there is a small island, not very far out to sea, situated off the outlet of the Liger River [Loire River]; and the island is inhabited by women of the Samnitae*, and they are possessed by Dionysus and make this god propitious by appeasing him with mystic initiations as well as other sacred performances; and no man sets foot on the island, although the women themselves, sailing from it, have intercourse with the men and then return again. And, he says, it is a custom of theirs once a year to unroof the temple and roof it again on the same day before sunset, each woman bringing her load to add to the roof; but the woman whose load falls out of her arms is rent to pieces by the rest, and they carry the pieces round the temple with the cry of "Ev-ah," and do not cease until their frenzy ceases; and it is always the case, he says, that some one jostles the woman who is to suffer this fate.[66]

(*Historians believe "Samnitae" is a corruption of "Namnitae," a Gaulish tribe who lived in the region of what is today Nantes, in France.)

Archaeologist Jean-Louis Brunaux believes the details included in this account make a case for its historical authenticity. First, he believes the wet climate of western France would necessitate the annual replacement of the thatched reed roofs of Gallic houses. Second, he cites

---

65 Sabine Baring-Gould, *Brittany* (London, UK: Methuen & Co. Ltd., 1902), https://www.gutenberg.org/files/51022/51022-h/51022-h.htm.

66 H. L. Jones, "The Geography of Strabo Book IV chapter 4," in *The Loeb Classical Library, Vol. II* (Cambridge, MA: Harvard University Press, 1923), 249–251.

Pliny the Elder's claim that it was a common religious belief for the Celts to consider it taboo to drop new thatch during the reroofing process. And finally, Posidonius made mention of circumambulation as a Celtic religious practice in his other writings as well.[67]

These priestesses differ from the Gallizenae in several ways: they are not celibate and seem to be especially known for their ecstatic rites in devotion to a divinity whom the Greek Posidonius identified with Dionysus. Some translations of this passage call the women "Bacchantes," undoubtedly in reference to rites in which the priestesses of Dionysus tore apart animals (and sometimes humans) with their bare hands. while overcome with divinely inspired madness In the annotations for this passage, the editor explains that, "*Ev-ah* is a joyful hallelujah in honour of Dionysus, one of whose numerous cult-names is *Evas*."[68] It is uncertain which divinity is meant in a Celtic context.

The Nine Sorceresses of Larzac

A lead tablet interred with a woman in a Gallo-Roman cemetery in Larzac, France, is the longest extant example of Gaulish text yet discovered. Written in a Roman script and dating to the first century CE, some scholars believe it to be a curse tablet or else otherwise associated with the magical workings of a group of nine sorceresses who practice "underworld magic." Although the paucity of written Gaulish texts makes definitive translations difficult, Celticist John Koch has proposed the following translation for a portion of the tablet:

---

67 Jean-Louis Brunaux, *Les Druides: Des Philosophes Chez Les Barbares* (Paris: Points, 2015), 241.

68 Jones, "Geography," 249.

Herein -:
- a magical incantation of women,
- their special infernal names,
- the magical incantation of a seeress who fashions this prophecy.
The goddess Adsagsona maintains Severa daughter of Tertiu in two cult offices, (as) their scribe (?) and offering maker.[69]
[The tablet then goes on to list the names of those in the group involved in this incantation; there are nine in all.]

The Ninefold in Breton Tradition

The Korrigan

In his collection of Breton folklore published in 1917, Lewis Spence recounts traditional tales and beliefs about the Korrigan. In some stories, she is an individual fay creature with nine maiden attendants; she is associated with water and bears resemblance, according to Spence, with "Keridwen."[70] In other stories, the Korrigan (or simply Korrigan, with no "the" before her name) is used as a collective term for a type of fairy woman, typically associated with water. Dwelling deep in the forest of Broceliande in Brittany, they are traditionally found near wells or fountains and are said to have once been Druidesses or pagan princesses who were eternally exiled for eternity for having rejected Christianity. They can be seen engaging in circle dances under the light of the moon, and favor ancient stone monuments like dolmens and standing stones.

In her singular form, the Korrigan is described as having bright golden hair and red glowing eyes; she possessed the power to cause men to fall so deeply in love with her, that her victims die of their longing. Using her magic to give her forest home the appearance of a richly appointed castle, she would lure unwary travelers into her lair. Her

---

69 John T. Koch, *The Celtic Heroic Age: Literary Sources for Ancient Celtic Europe & Early Ireland & Wales* (Oakville, CT: Celtic Studies Publications, 2003), 4.

70 Lewis Spence, *Legends & Romances of Brittany* (Project Gutenberg, 1917), 60.

victims would be so overcome that they would forget everything and everyone in their lives and completely lose themselves to her seductive beauty. However, upon the rising of the sun, all of her enchantments would fall away and the Korrigan would take on the appearance of a hideous hag. It was believed that the Korrigan's infamously insatiable lust was motivated by a desire attain to immortality through sexual union with humans. She is occasionally known to steal human children and replace them with changelings.

A more benign version of the Korrigan is featured in a Breton poem called "Ar Rannoù" ("The Series") that was included in a work called *Barzaz Breiz*, a compilation of folksongs in the Breton language. These songs were gathered from oral tradition and published in 1839 by Théodore Claude Henri, vicomte Hersart de la Villemarqué. Although Villemarqué claimed it to be one of the oldest Breton poems, its true age is uncertain. "Ar Rannoù" seems to be a teaching song, containing what appear to be mnemonic references to a body of Breton lore presented as a dialogue between a Druid and a child. Question and answer formats such as this are a common convention in the early vernacular poetry of Celtic lands.

In Villemarqué's translation of "Ar Rannoù," the child questions the Druid about the meaning of numbers, and the Druid provides a series of correspondences and associations for each. For the number nine, the Druid replies:

> Nine small white hands on the table of the threshing floor, near the tower of Lezarmeur, and nine mothers who utter loud cries. Nine Korrigans dancing, with flowers in their hair, and robes of white wool round the fountain, by the light of the full moon. The sow with her nine young, at the gate of the castle in her sty, grunting and rooting, rooting and grunting, "little one, little one,

little one, run to the apple tree: the boar is going to give you a lesson."[71]

It is notable that the associations for nine have strong connections with women and the Otherworld: the fairy Korrigans dancing around a fountain; the full moon; moaning mothers; sows, piglets, and boars; and the iconic Otherworldly apple tree. Villemarqué provides extensive annotations for "Ar Rannoù," using Breton folklore to give some context to the evocative symbols incorporated in the song's verses. In doing so, he connects the Korrigans with the nine Gallizenae of the Île de Sein, and relays a custom recorded in the middle of the seventeenth century, where those who lived on the Île de Sein honored the new moon by kneeling before it and reciting the Lord's Prayer. Villemarqué believed that the circle dance of the Korrigans linked the cult of the moon to the veneration of fountains, and remarked on another tradition from the Île de Sein: on the first day of the new year, everyone made an offering of bread and butter to the fountains in their village.[72]

Villemarqué expands upon this vision of the Korrigan in the introduction to *Barzaz Breiz*, describing them in a way that aligns with similar fairy creatures in other Celtic lands. They are shapeshifters who can take on the aspect of any animal, possess the powers of prophecy, are able to transport themselves wherever they wish anywhere in the world, and are incredibly skilled warriors. They love singing and music, and tend to be short in stature even though they are fully mature adults. In addition to linking them with the Gallizenae, he also connects them with the Cauldron of Ceridwen (whose name he gives as

---

71 This translation of Villemarqué's French version of "The Series" was published along with some of Villemarqué's notes in "Sayings and Doings of the Cymry" in *Dublin University Magazine* 64: 464–840. Dublin, Ireland: William Curry, Jun., and Company, 1864, 473–474.

72 Villemarqué, "Sayings and Doings," 473.

"Koridgwen") and both of them to a pearl-rimmed cauldron that brews poetic genius. Keep these in mind as we proceed.[73]

Theomacha and Her Sisters

In the seventh century Breton lai called "Vita Prima Samsonis" ("The First Life of St. Samson of Dol"), the eponymous Saint Samson of Dol encounters a woman named Theomacha ("Enemy of God") on the island of Loire. Said to live deep in the forest with her mother and eight sisters, she is described as an old and wild-looking woman flying through the air and carrying a bloody trident that she used to attack one of Samson's young deacons. Confronting her, the saint said, "'Can you not return the monk whom you struck to life again, or at least stir yourself for the good of your soul?' But in reply, she said 'I neither will nor can restore anything to goodness, for I can do no good thing. From my childhood to this day, I have always given myself to wickedness.'" As she attempted to depart, St. Samson began to pray for her evil to be destroyed, and when he was done, she fell down dead.[74]

The Ninefold in Cornish Tradition

Although as a political entity it has been subsumed into England, Cornwall (Kernow) is counted as one of the Six Celtic Nations, along with Wales, Brittany, Scotland, Ireland, and the Isle of Man (some also recognize Galicia and Asturias in Spain as two additional Celtic Nations). Cornwall is located on the peninsula extending into the Atlantic Ocean from the southwestern portion of Great Britain. It was home to

---

73 Theodore Hersart de La Villemarqué, *Barzaz-Breiz. Chants Populaires De La Bretagne, Recueillis Et publieˊs Avec Une Traduction franc¸aise, Des Arguments, Des Notes Et Les meˊlodies Originales*, vol. 1 (Paris: A. Franck, 1846), https://fr.wikisource.org /wiki/Barzaz_Breiz/1846/Introduction, xlvi–xlviii.

74 Richard Sowerby, "A Family and Its Saint in the Vita Prima Samsonis," in *St Samson of Dol and the Earliest History of Brittany, Cornwall and Wales*, ed. Lynette Olson (Suffolk: Boydell & Brewer, 2017), 29.

the Celtic Dumnonii tribe, and in the post-Roman period was part of the kingdom of Dumnonia along with the Isles of Scilly, Devon, and parts of Somerset. It developed a distinctive Brythonic language and culture related to those of Wales and Brittany. Cornwall has many Arthurian associations—including Tintagel, where, according to Geoffrey's *Historia Regum Britannae*, he was born—and is included as part of the collective cultural origin of what has come to be known as "The Matter of Britain."

There is a persistence of folk tradition concerning Nine Maidens in Cornwall that does not appear in written legend; rather, it is attached to the names of megalithic monuments. In Cornish, *Naw Men* means "nine stones" and at least six stone circles in Cornwall are known to have borne this name. In some places, the *men* element is believed to have devolved into "maiden," one potential reason these monuments are also known as Nine Maidens.[75]

There is a stone row composed of nine upright megaliths near the Cornish town of St. Columb Major that is called the Nine Maidens, although it is more traditionally called the Nine Sisters, the direct translation of *Naw Voz*, its name in Cornish. Aside from this stone row, of all the stone circles in Cornwall with the number nine in its name, only the Nine Stones Circle in Altarnun is actually made up of nine stones.[76]

It may be that these circles called the Nine Maidens, the Nine Sisters, and even just the Nine Stones are not named for the number of stones but for the magical traditions connected with nine.[77] The folklore accompanying several of these circles are variations on the same theme: that a group of women were dancing on the Sabbath instead of attending church and were punished by being turned into stone.

---

75   B. C. Spooner, "The Stone Circles of Cornwall," *Folklore* 64, no. 4 (1953): pp. 484–487, https://doi.org/ http://www.jstor.org/stable/1257874, pg. 485.

76   Spooner, "Stone Circles," 484.

77   Ibid., 486.

A similar tale is associated with The Merry Maidens stone circle in Boleigh—another consisting of nineteen stones.

Sometimes these circles and stone rows have a separate upright stone or two in close proximity to them; these are often called Fiddlers—the musicians accompanying the dancers who were turned to stone along with them.[78] The Nine Ladies Stone Circle in Stanton Moor, for example, has a large megalith called the King Stone associated with it which—despite its royal name—is locally considered to have been a fiddler. Similarly, the Merry Maidens are accompanied by a pair of standing stones called the Pipers.

The Ninefold in Scottish Tradition

The Nine Maidens

Nine Maidens traditions are plentiful in Scotland, appearing to straddle Pagan and Christian worlds. The most complete legend of the Nine Maidens speaks of the daughters of St. Donevald (Donald), who—like their father—lived a life of religious piety, eventually becoming saints in their own right after their deaths. Originally from Glen Ogilvy, the sisters came to be under the protection of the Pictish king Garnard after their father's death. Garnard built them an oratory or church under a great oak tree in Abernathy.

Tradition has it that St. Patrick asked St. Brigid to pay a visit to Scotland with her nine holy virgins in order to bless this newly built church. A nearby practice in Dumfriesshire that seems to commemorate this visit was for maidens to visit St. Bride's well on May Day, bringing with them nine white stones as an offering to the saint in memory of her vir-

---

78 Ruth St. Leger-Gordon, *The Witchcraft and Folklore of Dartmoor* (Newton Abbot, UK: Peninsula Press, 1994), 69.

gin attendants.[79] There are many wells and springs in the region that have been named for the Nine Maidens, although local folklore seems to vary as to who they may have been; often they are connected to stories of Nine Sisters being killed by a dragon or other monstrous beast.

Only three of their names are known to us: Mazota (Mayota), Fyncana, and Fyndoca. St. Mazota is known for her miracle of preventing geese from destroying a field of crops, while St. Fyndoca is known for establishing a sanctuary on the island of Innishale in Loch Awe that was used as a burial place for local clans—an Island of the Dead. Another island with a Nine Maidens connection is a crannog in Loch Tay, once called *Eilean nam Bann Naohm* (The Island of the Holy Women); nuns are said to have lived there, and would come to the mainland to celebrate the "Holy Women's Fair" held annually on Nine Virgins' Day, in July.[80]

Edinburgh Castle was once called the Castle of Maidens (*Castellum Puellarum*), and legends say it was built on the site of a shrine to the Nine Maidens. The castle is mentioned in the early Welsh poem "Y Gododdin" and has Arthurian associations. The Castle of Maidens appears in several Arthurian tales, although it is uncertain if they are all meant to be the same castle. Perhaps one of its most noteworthy appearances relevant to this discussion occurs in the Second Continuation of Chrétien's *Perceval*. In the tale, a noble lady accompanied by a hundred maidens dwell in the Castle of Maidens; their task is to test the worth of the knights who pass through their country.[81] This testing function associated with a queen who rules over a land or enclave of

---

79   J. Mackinlay, "Traces of Cultus of the Nine Maidens in Scotland," *Proceedings of the Society of Antiquaries of Scotland* 40, November, 1906: pp. 255–265, https://doi.org/http://journals.socantscot.org/index.php/psas/article/view/7059, 259.

80   Stuart McHardy, *The Quest for the Nine Maidens* (Edinburgh, UK: Luath Press, 2003).

81   Nigel Bryant, *The Complete Story of the Grail. Chretien De Troyes' 'Perceval' and Its Continuations* (Cambridge, UK: D. S. Brewer, 2015), 330.

magical women is a recurring theme in Arthurian Tradition that may have its origins in the Sovereignty motif, as we shall see.

The Ninefold in Irish Tradition

Ruad and the Nine Sisters

In an Irish tale found in "Inber n-Ailbine," poem 4 of *The Metrical Dindshenchas*, Ruad, son of Rigdonn, embarks upon a sea voyage with three ships, each filled with thirty men. While they were en route to Norway from Ireland, the three ships became trapped in the waters, unable to move. Ruad jumped overboard to see what was hindering the ships, and:

> *When he hastened to cut loose the ship in truth*
> *through the salt depths of the sea's treacherous waters,*
> *he found, in the secret spot he swam to,*
> *nine female forms, fair and firm.*
>
> *They said to him in pure clear strains*
> *it was they who had arrested him*
> *…*
> *nine women of them, excellent and strong;*
> *hard it was to approach them.*
>
> *He slept nine nights with the women*
> *without gloom, without tearful lament,*
> *under the sea free from waves*
> *on nine beds of bronze.*[82]

One of the sisters becomes pregnant, and although they allow him to leave and release his ships from their spell, they extract a promise

---

82 Whitley Stokes, "The Prose Tales in the Rennes Dindshenchas," The Prose Tales in the Rennes Dindshenchas (I)–Translation [text], accessed August 27, 2022, https://www.ucd.ie/tlh/trans/ws.rc.15.001.t.text.html.

from Ruad that he return to them on his voyage home. After seven years in Norway, Ruad and his men set sail for Ireland, intentionally avoiding the place where they encountered the nine women. However, as soon as their ships touched the Irish shore, they heard a "martial strain." Angry at the violation of his oath, the sisters pursued Ruad; in the heat of the battle, the one who was the mother of Ruad's child killed her own son, and cast his body onto the ship of his father.

Cill Dara

There are several accounts of the number of women associated with Brigid and her shrine at Kildare (from Cill Dara, the "Church of the Oak"); in some traditions, like in Scotland, she is the leader of nine virgins, while in others there are nineteen. Regardless, the religious center founded by Brigid shares some similarities with the patterns of communities of holy women we've seen thus far—and potentially contains elements of a devotional practice predating the one we know from the Christian period.

The Irish goddess Brigid ("Exalted One" or "High One") is mentioned in the ninth-century *Cormac's Glossary* names her as one of three divine sisters with the same name—a Triple Goddess. Brigid is connected with water through the holy wells bearing her name, as well as with fire—quite appropriate for a goddess of smithcraft, inspiration, and healing. Fire and water are important components of healing in some Celtic traditions and is particularly well attested at the thermal springs of the goddess Sulis in Bath, England.

Brigid is a beloved goddess who is believed to either have been syncretized with a saint of the same name during the medieval period, or was Christianized whole cloth—transformed from a goddess to a saint. Either way, the attributes of the goddess, including her feast day of February 1, became connected with St. Brigid; details of her hagiography and folk practices associated with the saint contain elements that hint at her potentially Pagan past.

St. Brigid is said to have founded a monastery at Kildare in 480 CE—on the site of a cult center dedicated to the goddess Brigid. There, beneath an enormous oak tree, was a shrine featuring a perpetual flame tended by holy women; this is very suggestive of a pre-Christian practice, not unlike the priestesses of Vesta who tended the national hearth in Rome. In fact, Brigid's flame was extinguished in 1220 CE by the Archbishop of Dublin, who objected to its Pagan origin. The sacred fire was revived after his death, only to pass into darkness once more during the Reformation. In 1993, the Brigidine Sisters kindled the perpetual flame anew at the site of the original shrine in Kildare, Ireland. It remains today, along with the Solas Bhríde Centre and Hermitage, as a place of pilgrimage and devotion to those dedicated to Brigid in all of her guises.

In his *Topographia Hiberniae* (*The History and Topography of Ireland*), Gerald of Wales writes that the fire of Brigid was tended by nuns and holy women, who have kept it perpetually alight "since the time of the Virgin"—and even though this flame had been continuously fed for many years, ashes had never accumulated at the site.[83]

Nineteen women were in service to the perpetual flame, and each took a night in turn to ensure that it continued to burn. On the twentieth night, the fire was left in Brigid's keeping; without fail, it was found still burning in the morning.[84] Around this sacred fire was a circular hedge made of stakes and brushwood; this was a boundary no man was allowed to cross. Further, only women were permitted to blow di-

---

83 Giraldus Cambrensis, "The Topography of Ireland" in *The Historical Works of Giraldus Cambrensis*, edited by Thomas Wright, translated by Thomas Forester. (London, UK: George Bell and Sons, 1849), 53–54.

84 Cambrensis and Wright, "Topography of Ireland," 96–97.

rectly upon the fire, but not with their breath; they could only use a bellows or a fan.[85]

Gerald gives several accounts of men who dared to violate these prohibitions. The first was an archer who not only leapt across the hedge but blew upon the fire; once he jumped back over to the other side, he descended into madness. He blew into the mouths of everyone he met and ran from house to house blowing into every fire he could find, each time crying out, "See how I blew St. Brigid's fire!" The townspeople restrained him, and he begged to be taken to the water as he was suddenly overtaken by thirst. Once there, he drank so much water that he burst and died immediately. Another man tried to cross the hedge and was able to get one leg over the boundary before he was dragged away by his friends. The moment his foot touched the sacred ground, his entire leg became withered, rendering him lame and addled in the mind for the rest of his life.[86]

The Ninefold in Norse Tradition

Turning our attention now to cultures outside of the Celtic world, we find that the number nine is very significant in Norse traditions. It is central to their cosmology, manifesting as the Níu Heimar (Nine Worlds) that surround the world tree, Yggdrasil. Norse lore tells us that Odin hung upside-down from an ash tree for nine nights in order to receive the runes, and that he owned a gold ring called Draupnir that possessed a magic whereby every ninth night, eight rings identical in size and weight would drop from it. Nine also seems to have been important in their magical and healing traditions, as evidenced by the famous "Nine Herbs Charm" found in the *Lacnunga*, a compilation of Anglo-Saxon herbal formulae and charms written in the tenth century CE. Containing both Germanic Pagan and Christian elements, the

---

85 Ibid., 97.
86 Ibid., 106.

charm contains several references to the number nine as it describes the preparation of these herbs to make a potent medicine. Unsurprisingly, there are a few Ninefold Sister groups found in Norse tradition as well.

The Nine Daughters of Rán

Some writers have linked the nine women in the story of Ruad (recounted in the earlier Irish section) with one of several iterations of the Ninefold found in Norse tradition, believing them to be an Irish account of the Nine Daughters of the goddess Rán. Often referenced in the poetry of *skalds* (Scandinavian poet-performers, similar to bards), this grouping of nine is also mentioned in both the *Prose Edda* (a thirteenth-century compilation of lore collected from oral tradition) and the *Poetic Edda* (written in 1220 by Icelandic scholar Snorri Sturluson, who based it on a variety of traditional sources, including the *Prose Edda*).

Both the goddess Rán and her husband, the jötunn Aegir, were divine embodiments of the sea. (A jötunn is a primordial entity from a race of beings that preceded the gods in Norse mythos). Their Nine daughters were personifications of the waves of the sea, and each of their names reflect a different manifestation of wave. In his 1916 translation of the *Prose Edda*, Arthur Gilchrist Brodeur lists the names of these Nine Wave Sisters along with their meanings:

Himinglæva: That through which one can see the heaven

Dúfa: The Pitching One

Blódughadda: Bloody-Hair

Hefring: Riser

Udr: Frothing Wave

Hrönn: Welling Wave

Bylgja: Billow

Dröfn: Foam-Fleck

Kólga: Poetical term for "wave"; "the Cool One"[87]

The Nine Wave Sisters may be related to the Nine Maidens of the Mill—giantesses who turn a great mill in the sea at the far edge of the earth, manifesting as a whirlpool that creates the waves and grinds down islands. This mill is a resonance of the Cosmic Mill from Norse tradition that causes the turning of the stars as well as the tides of the ocean.

Nine Mothers of Heimdallr

Another grouping of Nine Sisters in the Norse tradition is the Nine Mothers of Heimdallr. In the *Prose Edda*, Heimdallr is said to be a great and holy deity, and "nine maids, all sisters, bore him for a son."[88] A few lines later, Heindallr himself is quoted as saying:

> *I am of nine | mothers the offspring,*
> *Of sisters nine | am I the son.*[89]

While some scholars have theorized that the Nine Mothers of Heimdallr are identical to the Nine Daughters of Rán, the names provided for these figures in lore are not the same. They are named in the Old Norse poem "Völuspá hin skamma," which contains several stanzas believed to be an accounting of the birth of Heimdallr:

> *One was born in olden days,*
> *endowed with power from the gods.*
> *Nine Jotun maids carried him,*

---

87 Snorri Sturluson, *The Prose Edda: By Snorri Sturluson. Translated from the Icelandic, with an Introd. by Arthur Gilchrist Brodeur*, trans. Arthur Gilchrist Brodeur (New York: American-Scandinavian Foundation, 1916), https://www.sacred-texts.com/neu/pre/pre00.htm, 219.

88 Sturluson and Brouder, *Prose Edda*, 40.

89 Ibid., 40.

a spear-splendid man, along the Earth's edge.

...

Gjalp bore him, Greip bore him,
Eistla bore him and Eyrgjafa,
Ulfrun and Angeyja, Imd,
Atla and Jarnsaxa.

He was endowed with the Earth's power,
with the cold sea, with boar's blood[90]

Here we see that Heimdallr's mothers are described as "jötunn maids." Aegir, the father of the Nine Wave Daughters, is also a jötunn, so perhaps it is possible that two separate traditions arose around the birth of Heimdallr that may account for the Nine Sisters' different names.

Valkyries

There are several instances in Norse myth where Valkyries appear in groups of nine, including in the *Poetic Edda*.[91] Famously serving as psychopomps who gather the souls of dead warriors to escort them to the afterlife, Valkyries bring half of the slain to Fólkvangr, the hall of Freya, while the other half go to Valhalla, to be in service to Odin. In these halls, the dead feast and drink mead brought to them by the Valkyries; these warriors will fight alongside the gods during the events of Ragnarök. Aside from their psychopomp role, Valkyries share several associations with other Ninefold groups and Sovereignty figures—they are shapeshifters, often depicted as swan maidens; they often appear in the company of ravens and horses; they are cup bearers offering mead to dead heroes; and they are famous for their weaving—able to cause

---

90   Jeramy Dodds, trans., *The Poetic Edda* (Toronto: Coach House Books, 2014), 260.

91   Carolyne Larrington, trans., *The Poetic Edda* (Oxford, UK: Oxford University Press, 1999), 128.

or block victories in battle. They are often counted among the *dísir* and *Nornir* as goddesses associated with Fate.

Völva

As we will discuss further in chapter 4, Roman accounts of Germanic tribes detail their belief in the inherently magical nature of women, particularly when it comes to seership. These woman prophetesses were called *völva*, so named for the staff they carried as a mark of status; more properly, it was a distaff—the rod upon which raw wool was held during the spinning process—signifying their connection to the spinning and weaving of fate. They engaged in ecstatic rites, performed rituals of prophecy, and used poetic forms to chant desired outcomes into being. In *The Saga of Erik the Red* is a völva named Thorbjorg, who was chief among nine sisters who were also völva.[92]

The Ninefold in Welsh Tradition

There are several iterations of the Ninefold found in vernacular Welsh tradition, all of which appear in early Arthurian contexts. While on the one hand, the appearance of Ninefold Sisterhoods in some of the first Arthurian tales establishes a long-standing connection between Arthur and the Nine, there is another important piece to keep in mind. The earliest prose sources for Arthur are the *Historia Brittonum* (c. 829–30) and the *Annales Cambriae* (c. 954)—both Latin texts from Welsh sources that present him in a pseudohistorical light as a soldier and winner of victories against the Saxons. We begin to see the heroic traditions of Arthur mixed with early legends and folklore in several early Welsh poems, including "Pa Gur?" ("What Man Is the Porter?")

---

92 Keneva Kunz, "Eirik the Red's Saga," in *The Sagas of Icelanders: A Selection* (New York: Viking, 2010), 653–674, 658.

(ca. eleventh century) and "Preiddeu Annwn," believed to date somewhere between the ninth and early twelfth centuries.

By the tenth or eleventh century, the story of Arthur begins to take on a life of its own, growing in popularity and evolving to the point that many disparate legends and folktales had become attached to him. This makes it difficult to discern whether certain elements of Arthurian tales were native to his story cycle or if Arthur had simply usurped the role of the tale's original central character. It is therefore possible, if not probable, that the Ninefold Sisterhoods that appear in early Welsh literature represent an independent tradition that was preserved because it became associated with Arthur, rather than having only existed as part of the Arthurian legendarium.

Ninefold groups appear in the two aforementioned early Welsh poems ("Pa Gur?"and "Preiddeu Annwn") as well as in a slightly later prose tale titled "Peredur son of Efrawg," dating somewhere between the twelfth and fourteenth centuries. It is worth noting that of these three groups of nine magical women, two of the groups are designated as witches that are ultimately killed by Arthur's companions, while the third is subject to a raid where the magical cauldron in their keeping is stolen by Arthur and his men. Further, "Culhwch and Olwen," a somewhat contemporaneous tale (ca. eleventh–twelfth centuries CE), includes an episode where King Arthur and a few of his men travel north to seek and kill the witch Orddu in order to obtain her blood.

Some scholars have posited that this repeating motif may in fact be a narrative echo—what I call a mythic memory—of the religious and cultural shifts occurring in the fifth and sixth centuries. These changes would at first have been preserved through oral tradition, before eventually entering the written record centuries later. It's not hard to see how groups of nine witches or sorceresses living apart from society, along with the image of the lone cave-dwelling hag—both of which have precedent in earlier lore—could have become representative of the evils of Paganism in medieval writings. Hagiographies from this period—like that of St. Samson, mentioned above—are full of stories of saints using their faith and prayer to overcome demons, fairies, and witches. Similarly, epic tales depicting heroes defeating these so-called evil remnants of the past allow these figures to become paragons of goodness, while also permitting them to illustrate the full power of their might against unsympathetic foes.

On the one hand, there is a fairly extreme position held by Flint F. Johnson, a Medievalist who believes that these motifs are reflections of the Christians' literal purging of Pagan Celtic cult centers.[93] According to him, these surviving remnant "proofs" involve a specific handful of characters—Arthur, Cai/Kay, Peredur/Percival, Gwalchmai/Gawain, and Samson—whose stories are meant to take place during the fifth and sixth centuries, and whom he specifically calls out as being "destroyers of paganism." They display this characteristic in multiple works written by different authors in a variety of languages, including: "Pa Gur?," "Prieddeu Annwn", "Le Conte du Grail," "Perlesvaus," "Didot Perceval," "Diu Crône," "Vitae Samsoni," and "Peredur."[94] While some of these works are believed to have influenced each other or are thought to have drawn upon common sources, Johnson believes that these traditions are so entrenched that the evidence of these purges was able to survive despite the lack of written works from this period of British history.[95]

Arthurian scholar Glenys Goetinck takes a more moderate view contending that the witches may represent elements of an older order trying to reassert itself in a system that has usurped its power. She is not talking specifically about religion here (although it certainly plays a role) but of the cultural shifts in Britain as it moved away from matriliny (inheritance through the mother) into patriliny (inheritance through the

---

93 Flint Johnson, *Origins of Arthurian Romances Early Sources for the Legends of Tristan, the Grail and the Abduction of the Queen* (Jefferson, NC: McFarland, 2012), 121.

94 Johnson, *Origins*, 133.

95 Ibid., 122.

father). Tensions arising from this shift underscore some of the conflicts in *Y Mabinogi*, particularly those between Bran and Efnisien and between Gwydion and Arianrhod (as discussed above).[96] In "Peredur," the Nine Witches of Caer Lloyw caused Peredur's uncle to become lame, and they beheaded his cousin, thereby preventing these men from ruling. In accordance with matrilineal inheritance, kingship should instead have been invested in the son of the king's sister, Peredur. Since the causes for the enmity between the heroes and the witches are often not made clear in these narratives, Goetinck posits that it is meant to represent the overwhelming of an earlier, woman-centered order with that of a male-centered warrior society, such as with the coming of the Celtic tribes to Britain.[97]

Either way, whether the slaying of the witches is a mythic memory of the routing out of Paganism in Britain or representative of the triumph of patriliny over an older matrilineal order, this motif is yet another piece of evidence that supports the idea of the Ninefold Sisterhood as it appears in Celtic lands as being of a much more ancient origin than the medieval writings in which they first appear. Let us now take a more detailed look at some of these Ninefold groups.

Nine Witches of Ystafngwn

Primarily a compilation of early Welsh poetry from the ninth through twelfth centuries, the *Black Book of Carmarthen* (NLW Peniarth MS 1) is the oldest extant manuscript written entirely in Welsh, believed to date to the thirteenth century. Poem 31 of the manuscript—written in Old Welsh and known by its first line, "Pa Gur/Gwr yv Y Porthaur?" ("What Man?/What Man Is the Porter?" as mentioned previously)—has been dated to the eleventh century (although some scholars have

---

96   Glenys Witchard Goetinck, "The Quest for Origins," in *The Grail: A Casebook*, ed. Dhira B. Mahoney (London, UK: Routledge, 2015), 117–148, 136.

97   Goetinck, "Quest for Origins," 137.

argued for an eighth century origin), and is the oldest known Arthurian poem, albeit fragmentary.

The poem describes Arthur and his men being challenged by a porter who will not let them through the gate until Arthur names and vouches for his company. A common literary device of the time, Arthur uses the porter's challenge to describe his men as the best in the world and gives an accounting of their greatest victories and exploits. This company includes figures from Welsh mythology, such as Manawydan and Mabon, as well as those who would later be counted among the knights of the Round Table, including Bedwyr (Sir Bedivere) and Cai (Sir Kay).

When speaking of Cai, Arthur says:

> *Y guarthaw ystaw in gun*
> *Kei a guant nav guiton*

> *At the peak of Ystafngwn*
> *Cai pierced nine witches.*[98]

This very brief verse doesn't give modern readers much information, although its brevity may indicate an assumption by the unknown author that the audience would understand the reference. Since the context of the poem is extolling the virtuous deeds of Arthur and his men, Cai's killing of the Nine Witches of Ystafngwn is framed as a noble deed. Perhaps it also suggests the powers the witches wielded, since it took one of Arthur's best men to defeat them.

The Nine Witches or Sorceresses of Caer Lloyw

"Peredur son of Efrawg," (c. twelfth–fourteenth centuries) is a Welsh tale included in both *Llyfr Coch Hergest* (*The Red Book of Hergest*) and *Llyfr Gwyn Rhydderch* (*The White Book of Rhydderch*). It is one of the

---

98 Jon B. Coe and Simon Young, *The Celtic Sources for Arthurian Legend* (Felinfach, UK: Llanerch Publishers, 1995), 132–133.

Three Welsh Romances which—along with the Four Branches of *Y Mabinogi*, and the Five Native Tales—comprise the eleven tales from the Red and White Books that are often translated and collected under the modern title *The Mabinogion*. The Three Welsh Romances are Welsh versions of Arthurian tales that were either directly inspired by the poems of French writer Chrétien de Troyes, or else drew upon the same Celtic source as Chrétien.[99] While there is a great deal of overlap between the two bodies of work, the Welsh tales include materials not found in their French counterparts.

"Peredur son of Efrawg" is often described as the story of the grail without the grail; it is the analogue of Chrétien's *Perceval ou le Conte du Graal* (*Perceval, or the Story of the Grail*), a twelfth-century epic poem in Old French that serves as the first written account of the grail. *Peredur* broadly follows the storyline of "le Conte du Graal," although there are some marked differences between the two narratives, including clear overlays of native Welsh traditional materials.

For example, the Grail Procession from "le Conte du Graal" has an equivalent in "Peredur," but instead of parading the *graal*—a shining object set with precious stones—along with a bleeding lance and other mysterious elements, the venerated objects in the Welsh tale replace the grail with a severed head, borne by two maidens upon a salver. Anyone exploring the connections between the Celtic Sovereignty motif and the evolution of the Grail Quest would do well delving into both of these works, but for our purposes here, we will focus on one aspect of "Peredur": The Nine Witches of Caer Lloyw–*Y Naw Gwiddonod Caerloyw*.

During the course of his adventures, Peredur finds himself in the hall of a great lady attended by many handmaidens. She offers him the hospitality of her table but suggests that he find somewhere else

---

99   Roger Sherman Loomis, *The Grail: From Celtic Myth to Christian Symbol* (London: Princeton, 1991), 8.

to sleep, as her home is unsafe. Prompted by his questioning, the lady reveals that nine witches who live at their own court with their mother and father have conquered the whole of the land. The lady's household is the only one left that has not yet fallen to them, and they expected to be attacked before morning. Swearing to aid in her defense, Peredur sleeps there that night, and is awakened at dawn by a terrible cry. Clad only in his shirt and trousers, he takes up his sword and rushes out, just in time to see a witch defeating one of the watchmen. Attacking the witch with his sword, Peredur strikes her head with a blow so hard the battle helmet she was wearing becomes flattened like a dish.

The witch cries out to him by name, asking for his protection. Peredur asks how she knew who he was, and the witch replies that through her visions she knows him to be destined to cause suffering to her and her sisters and that he is also fated to receive a weapon and a horse from them. She invites him to depart with her so that she can complete his training in the ways of knighthood and give him further instruction in the use of arms. Peredur agrees, under the condition that she swears no further harm would come to the lady or her holdings. The witch gives him assurances that they would be safe. Satisfied, Peredur departs with her and spends three weeks training at *Llys Gwiddonod*, the Witches' Court. At the conclusion of his time there, he chooses a horse and a weapon and sets out on his journeys once more.

At the end of the tale, Peredur learns the identity of the person whose severed head was borne by two maidens in the strange procession he witnessed in the Castle of Wonders—the hall of his lame uncle: it was his cousin who had been killed by the Nine Witches. Likewise, these witches were to blame for maiming his uncle. He is told that it is his destiny to avenge these wrongs, so he sends word to Arthur asking for his assistance against the witches. Together with Gwalchmai, Arthur, and a number of the king's men, Peredur makes for the witches' court. There, Peredur thrice asks them to hold back, but the witches slay three of Arthur's men in front of his face. Finally,

Peredur draws his sword and attacks one of the witches, cleaving her helmet (and one assumes, her head) in two. As she dies, she cries out to the rest of her sisters that Peredur was among the warriors and that they should flee—he was the one to whom they had taught the arts of war, and he was the one who was destined to destroy them. It is all for naught, however; Arthur and his warriors attack them once more, and every last witch is slain.

These nine witches or sorceresses live in Caerloyw or Caer Loyw. Meaning "Bright or Shining Fortress," it is the Welsh name for Gloucester, a city in the southwest of England on the River Severn. Gloucester features in another medieval Welsh story, "Culhwch ac Olwen," where it is identified as a location of the prison of Mabon ap Modron, who was famously taken from his mother's side three days after his birth, with no one knowing if he was alive or dead. As part of a series of difficult tasks or *anoethau*—which Arthur's cousin Culhwch needed to accomplish in order to marry Olwen, the daughter of the giant Ysbaddaden—two of Arthur's warriors, Cei and Bedwyr, track down the location of Mabon and free him from his prison. That both Mabon and Peredur have a connection with Gloucester is notable in that some scholars believe the Welsh hero Pryderi may have been a precursor to the character of Peredur—while Pryderi himself is considered a reflex of Mabon. (In mythological studies, deities in related cultures who are similarly named or have similar characteristics or stories are called "reflexes" of each other. It acknowledges that there may be a relationship between these deities, even if the nature of that relationship is not completely clear.)

Of potentially greater significance to this discussion, however, is how these details from "Culhwch ac Olwen" and "Peredur" serve to make connections between Gloucester and Annwn, the Welsh Otherworld. A detailed description of Annwn can be found in "Preiddeu Annwn" that appears to draw upon various strands of lore to paint a picture of an Otherworld with a variety of disparate regions or named fortresses.

One area, called *Caer Sidi* or "the Fortress of the Mound," is described as the prison of a figure named Gweir—who, along with Mabon, is mentioned in Triad 52 as one of the Three Exalted Prisoners of the Island of Britain.

Another area mentioned in the poem is Caer Pedryfan, "the Four-Peaked Fortress" that stands on Ynys Pybyrdor, "the Island of the Strong (or Radiant) Door"; the latter harkens back to Gloucester as the Shining Fortress. Generally speaking, things that are described as shining/white/holy have strong associations with the Otherworld in Welsh mythos. What's more, Caer Pedryfan is the home of another group of nine magical women: the Nine Maidens of Annwn, whom we will discuss below.

It is possible that the Nine Maidens and the Nine Witches both refer to the same group of Otherworldly women, and the differences in how they are presented in each story are reflections of varying cultural perspective on magic and Otherworldly beings at different points in time. However, they each appear to embody different magical functions. The Nine Maidens seem to serve primarily as inspirers, performing a creative function as Muses of the Awen, although an argument can be made that they hold a protective role as well, since a priceless cauldron that tests the worth of heroes is in their keeping. The Nine Witches, on the other hand, seem to have a more destructive function as we are told that they have used their powers to subjugate the land. However, they also appear to serve an initiatory function; their training of Peredur and gifting him with weapons and a horse is strongly reminiscent of the Fairy Queen motif that commonly recurs in Arthurian Tradition.

Warrior women who train heroes in weaponry and the art of combat are found in the literary traditions of other Celtic lands as well. One such example is Scáthach ("the Shadowy One"), who trained many Irish warriors, most famously the legendary hero Cú Chulainn. She dwelt on the Island of Skye, where her daughter Uathach ("Specter") stood guard at the gate of her home, Dún Scáith ("Fortress of

Shadows"). Although many warriors sought to train with her, she would only accept those who had proven themselves worthy, either by overcoming a dangerous challenge or defeating her in a test of arms. Cú Chulainn proved himself worthy and trained with her for a year; some sources say he was granted "the friendship of her thighs," possibly a remnant of sexual rites associated with the initiation of warriors.[100]

Naw Morwyn of Annwn

> I am honored in praise. Song was heard
> in the Four-Peaked Fortress, four its revolutions.
> My poetry, from the cauldron it was uttered.
> From the breath of nine maidens it was kindled.
> The cauldron of the chief of Annwfyn: what is its fashion?
> A dark ridge around its border and pearls.
> It does not boil the food of coward; it has not been destined.[101]

The Naw Morwyn or Nine Maidens of Annwn are featured in "Preiddeu Annwn", a poem from *The Book of Taliesin* that potentially dates back to the ninth century, making it one of the older sources of extant lore from Welsh tradition. We've previously discussed its various fortresses in chapter 2. "The Spoils of Annwn" describes a raid on the Otherworld by King Arthur and three ships full of men. One of the journeyers is the great bard Taliesin himself, and the poem is told from his perspective. It is a perilous voyage that results in the loss of many lives; the poem repeatedly intones that only seven survivors are said to have "risen up" from Annwn, seemingly placing the Otherworld both across the water and below our own world.

---

100 MacKillop, "Scáthach," in *A Dictionary of Celtic Mythology*, 378.

101 Sarah Higley, "Preiddeu Annwn: The Spoils of Annwn," Robbins Library Digital Projects (The Camelot Project, 2007), https://d.lib.rochester.edu/camelot/text/preiddeu-annwn, lines 13–17.

The purpose of this raid is to obtain the Cauldron of the Chief of Annwn, which is in the keeping of the Nine Maidens. This is a wondrous vessel with many magical attributes. Recalling the discussion that opens this section, the presence of the Nine Maidens seems to signal that this poem contains an older narrative strata, one with potential roots in pre-Christian beliefs. As with the Nine Witches of Caer Lowy and the Nine Witches of Ystafngwn, Arthur and his men bring violence with them. While the poem isn't completely clear, the following verses seem to suggest that the cauldron is stolen from the maidens at sword point:

> Lleog's flashing sword was thrust into it,
> and it was left behind in Lleminog's hand.[102]

There is some confusion over the names given in these verses, and it is likely that they have been garbled over time by scribal error. However, many scholars agree that Lleawch is intended to be a warrior from Arthur's retinue named Llenleawc Wyddel, who features in yet another cauldron quest, found in "Culhwch and Olwen."[103] In that tale, Arthur and his men travel to Ireland in order to obtain a cauldron from Diwrnach the Giant, so that it could be used to boil the meat for Culhwch's wedding feast. Diwrnach refuses, and is struck down by Llenlleawg Wyddel using Arthur's sword Caledvwlch (Excalibur); the cauldron is then filled with treasure and brought back to Britain. This appears to echo the events in "The Spoils of Annwn," although the poem says nothing of the fate of the Nine Maidens as a result of the raid.

There is a resonant quest in the Second Branch of Y Mabinogi, where Bran and his warband travel to Ireland in order to free Branwen from mistreatment by her husband, the Irish king Matholwch.

---

102 Marged Haycock, *Legendary Poems from The Book of Taliesin* (Aberystwyth, Wales: CMCS Publications, 2007), 443–444.

103 Sarah Higley, "Preiddeu Annwn: The Spoils of Annwn," Robbins Library Digital Projects (The Camelot Project, 2007), https://d.lib.rochester.edu/camelot/text/preiddeu-annwn, note for line 18.

This tale involves a magical cauldron that has the power to bring dead warriors back to life. The cauldron was given by Bran, himself a giant, as a gift to Matholwch to make up for the maiming of the Irish king's horses on the night of his wedding to Branwen; this insult was made by Bran's half brother Efnisien, because he was unhappy that their sister had married a foreign king. As in "The Spoils of Annwn," of the entire war band, there are only seven survivors who return from the journey across the water; Taliesin, once again, is among them.

When we understand that Ireland is sometimes used as a stand-in for the Otherworld in medieval Welsh literature, it suggests the possibility of a core mythos that underscores these tales. In the annotations for her translation of "Preiddeu Annwn," Sarah Higley suggests that the commonalties between "Preiddeu Annwn" and the Irish poem "Dun Scáith" from *Lebor na hUidre*, (*The Book of the Dun Cow*)—all of which include a journey over sea, a raid on an island fortress with iron doors, a treasure-filled cauldron, and a harrowing escape—makes a strong case that "there was a source legend known in both Irish and Welsh lore that may have furnished the materials for all these stories, and which involved a raid upon a god's fortress for a divine cauldron."[104]

We don't know anything about the Nine Maidens aside from the few verses provided above; except for the apparent theft of their cauldron, there is no interaction between the raiders or the maidens. However, their presence looms large in this tale—perhaps due in part to the ancient tradition from which they appear to descend, but also due to their role and relationship with the cauldron in their keeping.

The cauldron is a vessel of poetry and prophecy; that it will not boil the food of a coward is a testing attribute seen in other lore that can also be seen to serve an oracular purpose. The testing attribute is often connected to the granting of Sovereignty, suggesting that Arthur's purpose in obtaining the Cauldron of the Chief of Annwn—*Pair Pen*

---

104 Higley, "Preiddeu Annwn," note for line 13.

Annwn—is also connected to the conference of Sovereignty from the Otherworld. Indeed, the Welsh word *pair* can be translated to mean both "cauldron" and "sovereignty"; given the bardic belief in the magical power of language (and penchant for worldplay), this is likely not a coincidence.

That the cauldron is kindled by the breath of the Nine Maidens suggests that they have a role in the vessel's activation. Perhaps they are Muses, goddesses of inspiration; perhaps Taliesin's statement that his poetry was kindled by their breath is a metaphor for the reception of that inspiration—a divine force in Welsh tradition called the Awen. This is discussed further in chapter 8. Perhaps the nine are oracular priestesses, breathing in the potent vapors of the boiling cauldron to speak mantic verses like the Pythia of Delphi. Certainly, seership is a power commonly found in the women of the various Ninefolds we have discussed, as well as in individual holy women known to us from history and legend.

It seems likely, however, that both possibilities are true: that these Otherworldy maidens are both Muses and oracles, for the two are strongly linked in Celtic cultures. The ability to create prophetic poetry is a hallmark of the most accomplished of Welsh bards, while the greatest of Irish poets are similarly granted foresight through the receipt of *Imbas forosnai*, "the inspiration that illuminates."

In the final line of the verse concerning the Nine Maidens and their cauldron, we are given another name for their dwelling place. Earlier, it is identified as Caer Pedryvan, the "Four Peaked" or "Four Times Revolving Fortress." At the end, as the poem intones that only seven rose up from the fortress, it is now called Caer Vedwit, "the Fortress of Mead-Drunkenness." This is significant because mead's powers of intoxication are related to the crossing of thresholds—such as those that permit passage into the Otherworld—and play an important role in kingship rites in several Celtic lands. Perhaps the name of the fortress is meant to mirror the like functions of the cauldron.

This overview of Ninefold Sisterhoods in Celtic, Norse, and Arthurian Traditions is intended to provide us with a broad cross-cultural context for the Ninefold Sisterhood that is central to the work of this book: the Nine Sisters of Avalon, who are the inspiration for the path of the priestess we are seeking to emulate. Before we do so, let us take a look at the information available to us about priestesses and holy women in ancient Celtic cultures, so that we may obtain a deeper understanding of the roles they played in service to their people and their gods.

4

CELTIC PRIESTESSES
AND HOLY WOMEN

Many modern Pagans, polytheists, and practitioners of magic who are drawn to the legends of Avalon are inspired by the idea of being a priestess of the Holy Isle. While there are hints that enclaves of holy women once existed in various parts of the Celtic world, we know very little about who they were, what they did, and to whom they were devoted. Nonetheless, in order to undertake a service of priestessing inspired by Celtic lore and in service to Celtic divinities, it is important to ground ourselves in what information is available about these holy women.

The insulated communities of Otherworldly or magical women of the Ninefold Sisterhood type is one way in which holy women appear in the historical accounts, legends, and folklore of Celtic lands. They also appear as a solitary woman in service to her gods and her people; although she is not cloistered communally, she is still often set apart and working alone.

As with most things concerning early Celtic cultures, we do not have a great deal of information about their holy women; the Celts famously didn't write down their histories, lore, and religious beliefs, preferring instead to pass this information along through an oral tradition preserved by professionally trained bards and poets. The two main sources we will be looking at are classical written accounts, and the later literary record. Neither of these sources are without their issues, but perhaps we can come to a general sense of things by examining what each is able to tell us, while also acknowledging their limitations.

Classical Accounts

Classical accounts of Celtic cultures can be problematic for many reasons. For one, they were prone to exaggeration for political reasons; they sometimes conflated continental Celtic tribes with Germanic tribes; they overlaid their accounts with *Interpretatio Romana*, where (for example) they substituted the names of their divinities for those of the Celts; and they didn't differentiate between received history or recounted legend in their records. As modern readers, we must also keep in mind that the majority of their writings concerned only some tribes of the Celts of Gaul and similarly limited information about the pre-conquest Celts of Britain. This is an important thing to note, as there is a tendency for modern practitioners to take these accounts and apply it all to pre-Christian Celts, no matter when or where they existed in the Celtic world.

With all of this in mind, let's take a look at some of these descriptions of Celtic women whose vocations and actions are those we would associate with priestesses, wise women, or those engaged with the magical arts. It is notable that the powers they possess and the services they provide to their people and their gods greatly overlap those associated with the women of the Ninefold groups.

Women of the Cimbri

The Cimbri are a tribe from Jutland whose identification as Celtic or Germanic has varied from one classical writer to another, perhaps due to their known migrations into Gaul. The famed Gundestrup cauldron was found in a bog in Himmerland, Denmark, which was part of their territory. Modern scholars note that while Cimbric place names in Jutland appear to be Germanic in origin, those Cimbric chieftains who are known to us bear names of Celtic derivation. In light of this uncertainty, most scholars take the middle road and consider them primarily Germanic with very strong Celtic influences.

In his *Geography*, Greek historian Strabo gives an account of Cimbric priestesses and their practices of seership:[105]

> Writers report a custom of the Cimbri to this effect: Their wives, who would accompany them on their expeditions, were attended by priestesses who were seers; these were grey-haired, clad in white, with flaxen cloaks fastened on with clasps, girt with girdles of bronze, and bare-footed; now sword in hand these priestesses would meet with the prisoners of war throughout the camp, and having first crowned them with wreaths would lead them to a brazen vessel of about twenty amphorae; and they had a raised platform which the priestess would mount, and then, bending over the kettle, would cut the throat of each prisoner after he had been lifted up; and from the blood that poured forth into the vessel some of the priestesses would draw a prophecy, while still others would split open the body and from an inspection of the entrails would utter a prophecy of victory for their own people; and during the battles they would beat on the hides that were stretched over the wickerbodies of the wagons and in this way produce an unearthly noise.[105]

---

105 Strabo, *The Geography of Strabo*, ed. Horace Leonard Jones (Cambridge, MA: Harvard University Press, 1917), https://www.perseus.tufts.edu/hopper/text?doc=Perseus:abo:tlg,0099,001:7:2:3.

CELTIC PRIESTESSES AND HOLY WOMEN   117

Veledā

In his *Histories*, the Roman historian Tacitus (c. 56–c. 120 CE) records an account of a powerful holy woman named Veledā who lived in the first century CE. A member of the Bructeri tribe, living east of the Rhine, her people were considered Germanic by the Romans. Modern scholars, however, believe it more likely that the Bructeri—or, at the very least, their leaders—were Celts. Indeed, Veledā's very name comes from the Proto-Celtic word *welet*, meaning "seer," related to the Irish ogham *velitas*, meaning "poet," and is the feminine form of Old Irish *file*—the title given to the highest rank of professional poets. Likewise, Veledā may have been a title rather than a personal name.[106]

Tacitus tells us that the Germanic tribes believed that many women naturally possessed a degree of prophetic insight, and those whose abilities were particularly powerful were deeply revered, to the point of being considered a divinity.

> They even believe that the sex has a certain sanctity and prescience, and they do not despise their counsels, or make light of their answers. In Vespasian's days we saw Veledā, long regarded by many as a divinity. In former times, too, they venerated Aurinia, and many other women, but not with servile flatteries, or with sham deification.[107]

Veledā's prestige as a seer derived from the correct prediction that her tribe and their Germanic allies would be victorious in the Batvian revolt against Rome. She was held in such high esteem that she was chosen—along with General Civilis, the leader of the revolt—to arbitrate a peace treaty between the Romans and the rebelling tribes.

---

106 Koch, "Veleda" *Celtic Culture: A Historical Encyclopedia*, 1728.

107 Cornelius Tacitus, *The Complete Works of Tacitus*, ed. Alfred John Church, William Jackson Brodribb, and Lisa Cerrato (New York, NY: Random House, Inc, 1942), http://www.perseus.tufts.edu/hopper/text?doc=Perseus%3Atext %3A1999.02.0083%3Achapter%3D8.

Tacitus informs us that Veledā was a holy virgin, and that in the course of the arbitration, that the ambassadors could not speak with her directly.

> They were not, however, allowed to approach or address Veledā herself. In order to inspire them with more respect they were prevented from seeing her. She dwelt in a lofty tower, and one of her relatives, chosen for the purpose, conveyed, like the messenger of a divinity, the questions and answers.[108]

Ganna

In his *Roman History*, Cassius Dio (155–c. 235 CE) makes a brief reference to Emperor Domitian (ruled 81–96 CE) having an audience with Veledā's successor, a virgin priestess from Germany named Ganna. She was honored by him, before returning home. Ganna was accompanied by Masyus, king of the Semnones tribe, and like Veledā before her, she likely served a diplomatic role in negotiations with the Emperor. Her name is believed to have roots in the Old Norse word *gandr*, "magic wand," or is related to the Proto-Celtic word *geneta*, "girl."[109] I've seen references in recent works that call Ganna a Druidess, but that is not directly supported by the source material.

Camma

During the Iron Age, three Celtic tribes settled in an area of Asia Minor, part of modern-day Turkey. This area was called Galatia, reflecting their connection to the Celtic peoples of Gaul; these settlers were the survivors of a failed campaign by an enormous Gaulish war band that sought to conquer Greece in 281 BCE. The famed Gaulish chieftain

---

108 Tacitus, Church, Brodribb, and Cerrato, *Complete Works*.

109 Matasović Ranko, *Etymological Dictionary of Proto-Celtic* (Leiden, NL: Brill, 2009), 157.

Brennus was part of this force, which was routed by the Greeks just short of raiding the temple of Apollo at Delphi. Galician warriors were known for their skill and often hired to fight as mercenaries in Greek and Roman wars.

The story of a powerful Galatian woman named Camma is relayed in the works of Greek historians Plutarch (c. 46–120 CE) and Polyaenus (second century CE); she is lauded as an exemplar of bravery and fidelity. Camma is said to have been a princess of the Tolistoboii tribe and is described as virtuous, beautiful, and kind; she was said to possess a great wit and a sharp mind. Her high status in Galatian society is connected to her service as a priestess of the goddess Artemis; this is likely referring to the syncretized Artemis-Cybele, who took on the attributes of the Anatolian goddess and had a famous cult center in Pessinus, one of the Galatian capitals. Although they were Celts, the Galatians gradually incorporated local beliefs with their own.

Of Camma, Plutarch writes:

> A thing that brought her into greater prominence was the fact that she was the priestess of Artemis, whom the Galatians especially reverence, and was seen magnificently attired always in connexion with the processions and sacrifices.[110]

Polyaenus adds:

> … she was priestess of Artemis, which is an office of the highest rank that a woman can hold in Galatia.[111]

Camma was married to the Galatian tetrarch Sinatus, but another tetrarch named Sinorix had fallen in love with her; although he pur-

---

110 Plutarch, "Bravery of Women," in *Moralia*, trans. Frank Cole Babbitt (Cambridge, MA: Harvard University Press, 1927), http://data.perseus.org/citations /urn:cts:greekLit:tlg0007.tlg083.perseus-eng1:20.

111 Polyaenus, *Stratagems of War; Translated from the Original Greek by R. Shepherd*, trans. Richard Shepherd (London, UK: Printed for G. Nicol, 1793), § 8.39.1.

sued her aggressively, Camma was loyal to her husband. Unable to accept Camma's refusal of him, Sinorix arranged the murder of his rival and renewed his campaign to take her as his wife. Camma continued to deny him and took refuge in the temple to evade his advances. But as time passed, her friends and family began to encourage her to accept his proposition of marriage.

Instead of giving in, Camma invited Sinorix to meet her in the temple so that she could give consent to the marriage in the presence of the goddess. They shared a bowl of milk and honey as a libation, but she had poisoned it. Plutarch tells us that:

> … she lifted up a shrill loud voice, and fell down and worshipped her goddess, saying: I call thee to witness, O most reverend Divinity! that for this very day's work's sake I have over-lived the murder of Sinatus, no otherwise taking any comfort in this part of my life but in the hope of revenge that I have had. And now I go down to my husband. And for thee, the lewdest person among men, let thy relations prepare a sepulchre, instead of a bride-chamber and nuptials.[112]

Sinorix died later that evening, but Camma lived through the morning. Having heard of his fate, she died happy.

Boudica

While she many not have been a priestess per se, the Roman account of the famous warrior-queen Boudica includes details of religious practices facilitated by her that are relevant to our discussion. During the time of the Roman conquest of Britain in the first century CE, Boudica's husband, Prasutagus, was one of eleven Celtic British chieftains who chose to ally themselves with Rome as client kings; doing so

---

112 Plutarch, *Plutarch's Morals: Translated from the Greek by Several Hands*, trans. William Watson Goodwin (New York: Athenaeum Society, 1905).

allowed them to maintain some independence in their rule and secure safety for their people. Prasutagus ruled over the Iceni, the Celtic tribe that once inhabited the region of Britain that is known today as East Anglia. In his will, Prasutagus left half of his kingdom to Emperor Nero and the other half to his two teenaged daughters, with Boudica serving as regent until they came of age. However, upon his death in 60 or 61 CE, the Romans ignored Prasutagus's will. They seized his wealth, annexed his lands, and ousted the Iceni nobility.

When Boudica protested, the Romans flogged her publicly, raped her two daughters repeatedly, and called all outstanding Iceni debts due, decimating the tribe economically. The Iceni were outraged at this treatment, and Boudica staged a ferocious revolt against the Romans, allying with the neighboring Trinovantes tribe. Together they raised an enormous war band and attacked the Roman city of Camulodunum (Colchester). With the majority of Roman forces fighting to capture the island of Mona—the Roman name for Ynys Môn/Anglesey, the Holy Island of the Druids—in the northwest under the direction of general Suetonius Paulinus, there were very few Roman troops available to defend Camulodunum. Boudica's army was able to raze the city to the ground, taking as plunder the colossal head of the bronze statue of the deified Claudius that had been erected in front of his newly built temple. Emboldened, her armies marched on the Roman cities of Londinium (London) and Verulamium (St. Albans), where they were again able to overwhelm the Roman forces and destroy the settlements.

Roman historians Tacitus and Cassius Dio recorded accounts of Boudica's rebellion; neither men were eyewitnesses to the events, although Tacitus's father-in-law served at a military tribunal in Britain during the time of Suetonius's term as governor, so he may have had direct knowledge of these events. Having completed his conquest of Mona, Suetonius gathered his troops and rushed down south after learning of Boudica's revolt. While unable to defend Londinium or

Verulamium, it is believed that he was able to defeat the much larger Celtic army by engaging them in a narrow pass along the Roman road today known as Watling Street. Of their victory against Boudica's warriors, Tacitus writes that the Romans were as ruthless as the Britons had been and did not spare anyone—even killing women and animals, which was not their usual practice.

How Boudica ultimately met her end is unclear. In one account, Tacitus states that she poisoned herself rather than fall into Roman hands. Cassius Dio, however, writes that some of the Britons escaped the Romans with plans to regroup and mount another offensive, and it seems that Boudica was among them. Before that could come to pass, Boudica became ill and died; she was greatly mourned and given a costly burial. With Boudica gone, the Britons lost heart and opted to return to their homes in defeat rather than try to muster a force against the Romans once more.

Boudica's story is remarkable in that it provides historical evidence that British Celtic women—of the Iceni tribe, anyway—were able to train and fight as warriors, could inherit land and titles, were empowered to rule as independent queens, and could command an army while making alliances with neighboring tribes. Since her story was recorded by Roman historians, we must take their biases into account, especially when it comes to the words that have been put into the mouths of the figures involved. Cassius Dio, for example, relays speeches given by Boudica and Suetonius to their respective armies. Since he was writing more than a hundred years after these events, he almost certainly crafted these speeches himself.

According to Dio, after giving a speech railing against the injustices of the Romans, and inciting her people for battle, Boudica does the following:

> … she employed a species of divination, letting a hare escape from the fold of her dress; and since it ran on what they considered the

auspicious side, the whole multitude shouted with pleasure, and Buduica, raising her hand toward heaven, said: "I thank thee, Andraste, and call upon thee as woman speaking to woman ... those over whom I rule are Britons, men that know not how to till the soil or ply a trade, but are thoroughly versed in the art of war and hold all things in common, even children and wives, so that the latter possess the same valour as the men. As the queen, then, of such men and of such women, I supplicate and pray thee for victory, preservation of life, and liberty against men insolent, unjust, insatiable, impious ... But for us, Mistress, be thou alone ever our leader."[113]

Here we see Boudica using a method of augury to determine whether the coming battle would end in victory for her people. The direction of the hare released by the queen in a ritual context brought a message from the Gods, and upon receiving a sign that they would prevail, Boudica then calls upon the goddess Andraste to ask for her blessings on their endeavor.

We learn a bit more about Andraste in the next segment of Dio's writings, where he recounts the brutality of Boudica's forces as well as some of their religious behaviors. While we know from the archaeological record that the Britons burned the Roman cities to the ground, it is quite possible that what he writes here is an example of anti-Celtic propaganda as it bears a lot of resemblance to earlier Roman accounts of the Druids whose sacred groves were covered in the gore of their human sacrifices. It may be that the cult activity in these sacred precincts included augury using entrails—a practice well known to the haruspices, or "gut seers" of Rome.

They hung up naked the noblest and most distinguished women and then cut off their breasts and sewed them to their mouths,

---

113 Cassisus Dio, *Roman History*, trans. Earnest Cary (Cambridge, MA: Harvard University Press, 1925), 93.

in order to make the victims appear to be eating them; afterwards they impaled the women on sharp skewers run lengthwise through the entire body. All this they did to the accompaniment of sacrifices, banquets, and wanton behaviour, not only in all their other sacred places, but particularly in the grove of Andate. This was their name for Victory, and they regarded her with most exceptional reverence.[114]

Note that here that the goddess of the grove is called Andate; this is likely a misspelling or an alternative form of Andraste, although some have posited that she is related to the Gaulish goddess Andarta, "the Great Bear" who herself may be connected to Artio, another Gaulish bear goddess. Either way, Dio describes this deity as the Celtic counterpart of the Roman goddess of victory—a statement further supported by the proposed meaning of Andraste as "unconquerable."[115] This carries extra significance because—according to Celticist Kenneth Jackson—Boudica's name arises from the Proto-Celtic feminine word *boudīkā*, which means "victorious."[116]

One wonders at the connection between the goddess and the queen; perhaps the correspondence of meaning between their names indicates a devotional relationship between Boudica and Andraste. While the names of legendary figures can often presage a person's accomplishments or character or else be given to them retrospectively in honor of their accomplishments, it is also possible that the queen may have taken on the name for atavistic purposes at the beginning of her campaign against the Romans.

---

114 Dio and Cary, *Roman History*, 96.

115 Miranda J. Green, *Celtic Goddesses: Warriors, Virgins and Mothers* (London: British Museum Press, 1995), 32.

116 Paul T. Bidwell, R. Bridgwater, and R. J. Silvester, "The Roman Fort at Okehampton, Devon," *Britannia* 10 (1979): 255–258, https://doi.org/10.2307/526061, Boudica etymology note, Kenneth Jackson, 255.

In a discussion of the cult activities of Boudica and her forces during their rebellion, archaeologist Miranda Aldhouse-Green notes the absence of Druids in Dio's account. This is significant because rituals of sacrifice are said to have been performed after the battles, and this was something only a Druid was empowered to do. Coupled with the strong narrative suggestion that Boudica herself performed these rituals, Aldhouse-Green considers the possibility that—like the Gaulish chieftain Aeduan, who was an ally to Caesar and a friend of the Roman statesman Cicero—the queen may have herself been a Druid.[117] But what does that mean? Let us explore this further.

Druidesses

Ancient Celtic societies are often praised for their progressive treatment of women in both secular and sacred realms, especially when compared to their contemporaries in other cultures. We know from early sources that Celtic women could inherit property, fight as warriors, rule as queens, and lead their people into battle. It would make sense that women would also have the ability to train and serve their people as Druids. Unfortunately, there is no direct evidence for female Druids in antiquity; while there are references to female Druids in the accounts of classical historians as well as in early medieval literature of Ireland, both are problematic in their own ways, as we shall see.

Let us first start by defining what it means to be a Druid. Etymologically speaking, the word itself derives from the Proto-Celtic *druwid*, *druiwides* (pl), meaning "oak knower." It first appears in writing as *Druides*, a Latin word believed to have been borrowed from Gaulish.[118] As we know, ancient Celtic cultures practiced oral tradition, and so the earliest written evidence of the Druids come to us from clas-

---

117   Miranda Aldhouse-Green, *Boudica Britannia: Rebel, War-Leader, and Queen* (Harlow, UK: Pearson Longman, 2006), 154.

118   Koch, "Druid," in *Celtic Culture*, 615.

sical accounts. While these writings certainly have their inherent biases, they represent the only sources we have about the Druids that are contemporary to the period when Celtic Pagan religion was still in practice. Even with this, we know precious little about what the Druids believed.

There is an important distinction to be made here: while ancient Druidism had a religious function, it was not itself a religion. Instead, according to Greek and Roman writers, the Druids were an elite learned class among the Iron Age Celts, and there is mention of them both in Continental and Insular Celtic societies. They were priests and augurs, teachers and judges, transmitters of history, and holders of sacred memory. According to Caesar, it took twenty years to become a Druid, and all teachings were transmitted orally and committed to memory. They enjoyed many privileges—such as exemptions from paying taxes and serving during war—and were accorded a great amount of respect and social power.

Caesar wrote that Druidism originated in Britain and that those who sought the finest training in the discipline would travel there to study. The Druids held annual gatherings in Gaul at the sacred grove in the territory of the Carnutes tribe, the near the site where the famed Chartres Cathedral was built. Druids would gather here from all over the Celtic world, and from this center would mediate conflicts and set policies. There was one Druid who held leadership over the entire order, and succession was determined by merit, not inheritance, showing that they valued achievement over bloodline—although sometimes succession had to be determined by force of arms.

In many ways, the Druids were the primary unifying factor in the otherwise fiercely territorial Celtic tribal landscape. They appear to have wielded great influence over the agricultural Celts, overseeing the festivals and propitiating the gods with ritual and sacrifices. The Druids performed many of the tasks a centralized government would perform. They composed a learned elite upon which the mass populace was dependent for matters both spiritual and mundane; yet no matter how profane, an element of the religious was always present.

Archaeologist Barry Cunliffe describes Druidism as developing out of the changes to agriculture and the shift from the guiding neolithic axis of solstices and summer/winter encampments to seasonal, lunar-based agricultural practice that came with permanent year-round settlements. The Druids, therefore, may have integrated pre-Celtic native beliefs and traditions with the newer practices defined by people's needs as settled agriculturalists, thus giving them a great deal of power over the socioeconomic lives of the Celts.[119]

Strabo describes a tripartite division of this priestly caste.

> ...there are three sets of men who are held in exceptional honour; the Bards, the Vates and the Druids. The Bards are singers and poets; the Vates, diviners and natural philosophers; while the Druids, in addition to natural philosophy, study also moral philosophy.[120]

This, combined with other contemporary accounts, paints a picture of the Druids as philosophers and judges, who oversaw ritual and arbitrated disputes. The Vates performed auguries both through interpreting natural occurrences such as the movements of birds and by examining the entrails and death spasms of sacrifices, both animal and human. The Bards were the keepers of knowledge, recorders of genealogies, and seekers of divine inspiration; they were required to memorize vast amounts of lore, sang poetic verses that praised great deeds, memorialized the dead, and satirized the unrighteous. Over time, the divisions of duties appear to become less discrete, and later classical ac-

---

119   Barry W. Cunliffe, *Druids: A Very Short Introduction* (Oxford, UK: Oxford University Press, 2010), 134.

120   Strabo, *The Geography of Strabo. Literally Translated, with Notes, in Three Volumes*, trans. W. Falconer and HC Hamilton (London, UK: George Bell & Sons, 1903), http://data.perseus.org/citations/urn:cts:greekLit:tlg0099.tlg001 .perseus-eng2:4.4.4.

counts seem to refer to any person of Celtic derivation that practiced magic or some sort of seership as a "Druid," regardless of whether they were actually a part of the ancient order.

With this understanding of the Druids in mind, let us take a look at what evidence is available to show that women were a part of this order.

The Archaeological Record

Generally speaking, the archaeological record has not provided us with very much direct proof of ancient Druidism at all, irrespective of gender. While there is archaeological evidence of religious activity in Celtic areas, we cannot know for sure who was responsible for it. For example, we know the Celtic Britons propitiated the gods with votive offerings, often by ritually breaking and depositing high status items in bodies of water—but we cannot say for certain that Druids were involved. And while we have discovered rich Celtic burials containing high status grave goods and objects that could be interpreted as having ritual use or religious provenance, there really is no definitive proof that the person they were buried with had been a Druid.

An example of this is the mound burial of the "Woman of Vix," dating to about 500 BCE, discovered in 1953 near the town of Vix in Burgundy. The untouched burial chamber was filled with rich grave goods, including a trove of jewelry and a large gold torc; the latter is an especially important item as it marks the woman as someone of very high status. Because of this, she is often titled the Lady, Queen, or Priestess of Vix, and some have argued that she was a Druid. However, while the richness of her grave makes it clear that she was a woman of great importance, it does not prove she was a Druid.

The Metz Inscription

There is an intriguing piece of epigraphic evidence discovered in France often cited as proof of the existence of female Druids. Dating to the second or third century CE, it is a votive inscription in Latin that reads:

> *Silvano sacr(um) et Nymphis loci Arete Druis antistita somnio monita d(edit)*[121]

While researching this, I discovered several proposed translations, the differences between them all hinging upon the meaning of the word *Druis*. Most sources consider it a proper name, while others translate it to mean "Druid." To get a fresh opinion, I consulted with Kitos Digiovanni, a friend of mine who has a PhD in Classical Philology. I sent him the Latin inscription, and he translated it to read as follows:

> *Being advised in a dream, Druis Arete the high priestess has dedicated this offering [meaning the votive tablet] to Silvanus and the Nymphs of the place.*

I asked if the word *Druis* could mean "Druid," and he replied that translating Roman inscriptions can be tricky, as the syntax is not always straightforward. In this case, it is possible for Druis to be a patronymic (that is, a personal name deriving from the name of one's father or another male relative), but it could also be translated as "Druid"; according to Digiovanni, there is no sure way to tell. If it does mean "Druid," the inscription would read:

> *Being advised in a dream, Arete the Druid high priestess has dedicated this offering to Silvanus and the Nymphs of the place.*

---

121 "Votive Inscription from Divodurum–Metz (Belgica)," EDH: Inscription Database–Heidelberg University, accessed August 26, 2022, https://edh.ub.uni -heidelberg.de/edh/inschrift/HD000334.

If the syntax alone is not sufficient in helping us determine the meaning of this inscription, perhaps looking at the dedication in its cultural context will prove useful. This inscription was discovered near Metz, a French city whose name derives from the Gaulish tribe Mediomatrici (from the Gaulish *Medio-māteres*, meaning "middle-mothers"); the tribe may have been so named because their territory was between the two mother-rivers of Matrona (Marne) and Matra. They worshipped the goddess Nantosuelta ("winding stream"), whose consort is Sucellos ("good striker"). She is often represented as a raven or as a woman with a birdhouse mounted on a staff, while Sucellos is often depicted holding a large hammer.[122]

The dating, use of Latin, and dedication to Roman divinities places this offering tablet squarely in the provenance of Gallo-Roman culture. However, while Druidism in Gaul was repressed under Emperors Augustus and Tiberius, it is said to have been completely eradicated under the rule of Emperor Claudius, who was in power in the middle of the first century CE. As this dedicatory inscription was created at least fifty to a hundred and fifty years after the socioreligious institution of Druidism had been dismantled in Gaul, it is far more likely that *Druis* is a name rather than a title.

Whether or not the dedicator in question is a Druid, it is clear that she is in any case an *antistita*—a high priestess. It is uncertain what sort of high priestess Arete was; did she serve in a Roman temple, or did she honor Gallo-Roman gods? Was she in service to Sylvanus, the Roman god of the woodlands, or did she make an offering independent of her vocational dedication? It is notable that Sylvanus was often syncretized with the Gaulish deity Sucellos, given her tribal veneration of

122 P. L. Kessler and Edward Dawson, "Mediomatrici / Mednomatrici (Belgae)," The History Files: European Kingdoms–Celtic Tribes, May 5, 2011, https://www .historyfiles.co.uk/KingListsEurope/BarbarianMediomatrici.htm.

Nantosuelta.[123] Even the provenance of her name is unclear, as *arete* is a Greek word meaning "excellence" or "virtue," so we cannot tell if she is a Romanized Gaul or if she hailed from elsewhere. Ultimately, the most we can say about this with any certainty is that Arete was a priestess of high status.

Classical Accounts

When we speak of classical accounts of the Celts—observations written by ancient Greek and Roman historians, geographers, and generals— we need to keep in mind that they are talking primarily about the Celts of Gaul and Britain. Even here, their experiences are limited to certain tribes encountered in specific geographic areas in particular time periods. Because of the longevity of Celtic cultures, their widespread distribution across continental Europe and into the British Isles and Ireland, and their tribal nature that resisted any sort of centralized government or national identity, we cannot assume that the points of Celtic culture described in these classical accounts were universal to all Celtic peoples.

Earlier Classical Accounts

None of the earliest classical writings discussing the Druids mention anything about women. In fact, in his first-century-BCE work *De Bello Gallico* (*The Gallic War*), Julius Caesar explicitly states that those who seek training as Druids are young men, writing:

> The Druids usually hold aloof from war, and do not pay war-taxes with the rest; they are excused from military service and exempt from all liabilities. Tempted by these great rewards, many young

---

123 Miranda J. Aldhouse-Green, *The Gods of the Celts* (New York: The History Press, 2011), 94.

men assemble of their own motion to receive their training; many are sent by parents and relatives.[124]

There are several things that might explain the absence of women Druids in the earliest classical accounts:

1. The writers may not have encountered or been told about women Druids.

2. The writers may not have recognized a woman Druid for what she was when they encountered one.

3. The writers may have encountered or heard about women Druids, but did not consider them worthy of specific mention.

4. There weren't any women Druids.

Many classical writers took great pains to point out differences between Celtic cultures and their own, especially when it came to gender roles. Of course, women served as priestesses in Greco-Roman cultures, so the presence of priestesses would not be particularly notable in a Celtic context. However, the service of priestesses of Greece and Rome was directly connected to aspects of the cultus to which they were dedicated. Since the Greeks and Romans wrote about the Druids as a high-status professional class that included judges, natural philosophers, astronomers, and mathematicians, they would likely have made note of women performing these roles had they observed them. Without proof, the writers may have defaulted to the assumption that women would not be part of this learned class and so only spoke of it in terms of men.

There is, however, one account that shows women serving in what would be considered a Druidic role, although they are not specifically named as such. This comes to us from Plutarch, a Greek historian,

---

124   H. J. Edwards, *Caesar: The Gallic War* (New York, NY: G.P. Putnam's Sons, 1917), 339.

biographer, and philosopher who also served as a priest of Apollo at Delphi. One of his works, *Mulierum Virtutes* (*The Virtues of Women*), is a collection of stories about women—both collectively and as individuals—from different cultures that speak to his opinion that women and men are equals when it comes to their moral character. In a section entitled "Of the Celtic Women," he writes:

> There arose a very grievous and irreconcilable contention among the Celts, before they passed over the Alps to inhabit that tract of Italy which now they inhabit, which proceeded to a civil war. The women placing themselves between the armies, took up the controversies, argued them so accurately, and determined them so impartially, that an admirable friendly correspondence and general amity ensued, both civil and domestic. Hence the Celts made it their practice to take women into consultation about peace or war, and to use them as mediators in any controversies that arose between them and their allies. In the league therefore made with Hannibal, the writing runs thus: If the Celts take occasion of quarrelling with the Carthaginians, the governors and generals of the Carthaginians in Spain shall decide the controversy; but if the Carthaginians accuse the Celts, the Celtic women shall be judges.[125]

Here, we see women in the roles of judges and arbitrators, something supported in other contemporary writings, as we saw in the cases of Veledā and Ganna above. What is particularly interesting about this account is that it echoes something Greek historian Diodorus Siculus (first century BCE)—based upon works of Posidonius (c. 135– c. 51BCE)—wrote about the Druids of Gaul in his *Bibliotheca Historia* (*The Library of History*):

---

125 Plutarch, *Plutarch's Morals: Translated from the Greek by Several Hands*, trans. William Watson Goodwin (Cambridge, MA : Little, Brown, and Company, 1874), http://data.perseus.org/citations/urn:cts:greekLit:tlg0007.tlg083.perseus-eng2:6.

Nor is it only in the exigencies of peace, but in their wars as well, that they obey, before all others, these men [Druids] and their chanting poets, and such obedience is observed not only by their friends but also by their enemies; many times, for instance, when two armies approach each other in battle with swords drawn and spears thrust forward, these men step forth between them and cause them to cease, as though having cast a spell over certain kinds of wild beasts.[126]

While Plutarch does not identify the women in his account as Druids, they seem identical in function to the Druids described by Diodorus, who wrote a century earlier than he. While this is an indirect identification, it does make a good case for women being a part of the early Druidic institutions of Gaul.

That said, absence of evidence is not evidence of absence. The fact that women in at least some Celtic lands enjoyed rights and privileges unknown to their contemporary counterparts in other cultures makes the existence of women Druids more likely than not. The fact that there are references to Druidesses in later classical writings may also support the idea of their inclusion in the powerful Iron Age Druid order described by Caesar and earlier writers.

However, we must also take into account the social changes that accompanied the Roman occupation of Gaul and Britain; there are huge sociocultural differences between the unconquered Celtic tribes of the first century BCE and the Gallo-Roman and Romano-British peoples of the fourth century CE. The power of the Druids was broken, both due to the Roman repression of their order and by Roman bureaucracy that took over many of the legal and socioeconomic roles the Druids previously held. With this in mind, let's take a look at these direct mentions of Druidesses from later classical accounts.

---

126 Diodorus Siculus, *The Library of History*, trans. C. H. Oldfather (Cambridge, MA: Harvard University Press, 1939), https://penelope.uchicago.edu/Thayer/E /Roman/Texts/Diodorus_Siculus/5B*.html.

Later Classical Accounts

Several references to Druidesses can be found in the *Historia Augusta* (*August* or *Augustan History*), a fourth-century-CE compilation of writings on the lives of several Roman emperors and other personages associated with the imperium, spanning the years 117 to 284 CE. Modern scholars find this collection somewhat problematic. First, there are questions about its authorship. It purports to have been written by six different authors, but scholars today believe it to be the work of a single writer.

More critically, its historical validity has been questioned; the many fictional and satirical elements woven into these biographies suggest they represent authorial commentary on the social and political realities of their contemporary society, rather than striving to be a straightforward record of history. However, since it is one of the few extant Latin commentaries for this period of late Roman history, it continues to be studied and evaluated by academics and researchers. As with most Roman sources concerning the Celts, therefore, it is important to keep this context in mind as we proceed.

The first mention of Druidesses comes from an account of the life of Emperor Severus Alexander who ruled from 222 to 235 CE; he was assassinated by his own men while at war against an invasion of Germanic tribes. The author makes a list of the omens that predicted the emperor's demise, which included the following:

> Furthermore, as he went to war a Druid prophetess (*mulier Druias*) cried out in the Gallic tongue, "Go, but do not hope for victory, and put no trust in your soldiers."[127]

---

127 Lampridius, "The Life of Severus Alexander, Part 3," in *Historia Augusta* (Cambridge, MA: Harvard University Press, 1921), https://penelope.uchicago.edu /Thayer/E/Roman/Texts/Historia_Augusta/Severus_Alexander/3*.html#60.6.

The next account concerns an incident from the youth of Diocletian, who would become Emperor in 284 CE, and rule until 305 CE:

> When Diocletian … while still serving in a minor post, was stopping at a certain tavern in the land of the Tungri in Gaul, and was making up his daily reckoning with a woman, who was a Druidess (*Druias*), she said to him, "Diocletian, you are far too greedy and far too stingy," to which Diocletian replied, it is said, not in earnest, but only in jest, "I shall be generous enough when I become emperor." At this the Druidess (*Druiade*) said, so he related, "Do not jest, Diocletian, for you will become emperor when you have slain a Boar (*Aper*)."[128]

Ever mindful of this prophecy, Diocletian (according to the author) would always be sure to slay boars while out hunting. He rose through the ranks of the Roman military, eventually becoming a cavalry commander and serving in a military campaign in Persia years later. It was during this campaign that Emperor Numerian was assassinated by a prefect of the imperial guard named Aper who hoped to gain the throne for himself. When Aper, whose name means "boar," was found guilty of the crime by tribunal, it was Diocletian who insisted on executing him personally—solely because of the words of the Druidess. The troops in the field then proclaimed Diocletian emperor.

Finally, there is an account concerning the Emperor Aurelian, who ruled from 270 to 275 CE:

> … on a certain occasion Aurelian consulted the Druid priestesses (*Druiadas*) in Gaul and inquired of them whether the imperial power would remain with his descendants, but they replied, he related, that none would have a name more illustrious in the

---

128 Vopiscus, "The Lives of Carus, Carinus and Numerian," in *Historia Augusta*, trans. David Magie, vol. III (Cambridge, MA: Harvard University Press, 1921), https://penelope.uchicago.edu/Thayer/E/Roman/Texts/Historia_Augusta/Carus_et_al.html#14.3.

commonwealth than the descendants of Claudius. And, in fact, Constantius is now our emperor, a man of Claudius' blood, whose descendants, I ween, will attain to that glory which the Druids foretold.[129]

Of the three mentions, it is this final account that feels the most authentic in that it describes a formal consultation of these Gaulish Druid priestesses for oracular purposes, rather than the unsolicited prophecies depicted in the other two accounts. Regardless of the overall intentions of their authors, all these episodes speak to a belief in the possession of prophetic powers by the Druids—particularly, of women Druids. This aligns with Roman accounts of Celtic and Germanic seeresses mentioned earlier in this chapter.

As an aside, I noted the Latin words used to refer to the Druidesses in each of these accounts, as some versions of *Historia Augusta* describe these women by using the term *Dryades*, leading some modern works to claim it as an official name for female Druids. However, religious scholar Adam Anczyk explains that these Gallic "dryads" are "identified as Druids *per analogiam*, since other authors of antiquity have sometimes modified or misspelled the term *Druides* into *dryades* or similar."[130] This term has also led to some confusion with the Greek tree nymph of the same name, although the similarity between the words "Druid" and "dryad" is based upon their common etymology stemming from the from PIE root *deru*—meaning "tree," particularly the oak.

We must also take note that the preceding accounts specifically concern Gaulish women; the Gauls were groups of continental Celtic peoples whose Iron Age culture and language arose around 500 BCE

129 Vopiscus, "The Life of Aurelian, Part 3," in *Historia Augusta*, trans. David Magie, vol. III (Cambridge, MA: Harvard University Press, 1921), https://penelope.uchicago .edu/Thayer/E/Roman/Texts/Historia_Augusta/Aurelian/3*.html. 43.4

130 Adam Anczyk, "Druids and Druidesses: Gender Issues in Druidry." *Pantheon. Journal for the Study of Religions* 10, no. 2 (2015): 21–33. https://www.academia .edu/22186011/Druids_and_Druidesses_Gender_Issues_in_Druidry.

from the earlier La Tène culture and spread across Europe. Over the centuries, they fought many wars against the Romans until they were finally conquered by Julius Caesar in 50 BCE. After becoming annexed into the Roman Empire, a gradual assimilation gave rise to Gallo-Roman culture, marked by religious expressions that syncretized Gaulish deities with those of Rome. In the Roman period, therefore, we start to see Gallo-Roman temples, dedicatory steles, and statuary—the first direct archaeological and epigraphic record of Celtic divinities—as the Romanized Gauls worshipped alongside their Roman counterparts.

However, the Druids of Gaul did not fare quite as well. While Julius Caesar's accounts of the Druids in his *De Bello Gallico* is one of the richest sources of eyewitness information we have about this priestly caste, his exaggeration of some of their religious practices—particularly their human sacrifices—was intended to be propaganda in service of gaining financial support from Rome that would allow him to continue his campaign against the Gauls. The images of gore-filled groves were taken up by subsequent Roman writers and certainly did not endear Druids to the public mind.

However, it is likely for political rather than religious reasons that the empire came to see the Druids as enemies of the state. Augustus Caesar forbade Roman citizens from practicing Druidism, while the imperial senate under Tiberius set forth a decree against Druids, *vates* (diviners), and related healers.[131] And according to Suetonius, it was under the reign Claudius that:

131 Jane Webster, "At the End of the World: Druidic and Other Revitalization Movements in Post-Conquest Gaul and Britain," *Britannia* 30 (1999): 1–20, https://doi .org/10.2307/526671, 11.

The religious rites of the Druids, solemnized with such horrid cruelties, which had only been forbidden the citizens of *Rome* during the reign of Augustus, he utterly abolished among the Gauls.[132]

Beneath the surface of this Roman distaste, there was a real fear of the unrest being fueled by Druidic prophecies concerning the downfall of Rome. Historical archaeologist Jane Webster writes:

> ...prophecy appears to have been a key medium through which dissent was voiced. Tacitus...explicitly refers to Druids using prophecy as incitement to unrest in post-conquest Gaul. He states that during the Civilis revolt (A.D. 70–71) the Druids prophesied the downfall of the Empire, and incited rebellion in Gaul.[133]

She also notes that "Augustus, in particular, was extremely distrustful of the subversive potential of divination and prophecy: in 12 B.C. over 2,000 books on prophecy were confiscated and burnt on his orders."[134]

It is especially interesting, therefore, that the three accounts of Druidesses included in *Historia Augusta* concern their powers of prophecy. Are these accounts true, apocryphal, or purposefully fictional? Are they examples of the satire or social commentary modern scholars perceive in *Historia Augusta*? Do they reflect a reality where Gaulish female Druids are known for their skills in seership, at least during the late Roman period?

Given the prohibitions against Druids in Gaul—and their outright slaughter in Britain during the first-century campaign against the Druidic enclave of Môn—are these women Druids at all, or has the term come to be used in that period to mean anyone with prophetic powers? Historian Ronald Hutton posits: "It is possible that terms related to

---

132 Suetonius, *The Lives of the Twelve Caesars*, ed. J. Eugene Reed (Philadelphia: Gebbie and Co., 1889), http://www.perseus.tufts.edu/hopper/text?doc=urn:cts:latinLit:phi1348.abo015.perseus-eng1:25.

133 Webster, "At the End of the World," 14.

134 Ibid., 13.

Druid were being applied by Roman authors who knew little of Gaul and Gallic language, to kinds of magical practitioner very different from the original Druids."[135]

While I understand that questioning the veracity of these sources is much less satisfying for the modern day practitioner who would prefer to take them at face value in order to use these accounts as direct proof of women Druids, I nevertheless think it is important to be clear-eyed with the nature and context of these materials. While we cannot be sure of the veracity of these accounts as describing actual events, at the very least they tell us something about the Roman perception of Druids in this period—and that is not without value.

Irish Sources

As we have already discussed with Wales, it is likely that the stories that compose the Irish mythological tradition existed in orality for centuries before being written down; the earliest Irish vernacular literature, however, benefits from having been redacted sooner than the comparable materials in Wales. Additionally, since Rome never conquered Ireland, its native Celtic culture was able to continue to exist uninterrupted for centuries longer than in Britain and Gaul. Lack of Roman rule also resulted in the Irish conversion to Christianity to be more gradual than in other Celtic lands, permitting Ireland to maintain its Pagan social institutions—including the continued influence and power of Druidism—into later periods as well.

Because of these factors, the earliest Irish mythological works include more overtly Pagan elements (e.g., figures directly identified as divinities) and generally tend to present a more tribal cultural essence centered on the war band. In contrast, due to its very different cultural history and having written down its vernacular tales in a later period, the ostensibly

---

135 Ronald Hutton, *Blood and Mistletoe: The History of the Druids in Britain* (New Haven, CT: Yale University Press, 2009), 21.

Pagan elements in the mythic tales of Wales are subtextual, and the cultural settings overall tend to reflect early medieval courtly society.

Early Irish myth and legend contain references to women bearing the titles of Druidess (*bandruí*), poetess (*banfhili*), and seeress (*banfháith*) The very fact that there are words in Old Irish for these female figures is itself a fairly persuasive proof of their existence. Some scholars, however, have argued that their presence in mythic literature does not necessarily prove their existence in ancient Irish culture. It is important to remember that the cultural context within which Irish stories were written down (the early medieval period) is not the same as the context that first birthed these tales (for some, at least, the pre-Christian period). Further, many of the stories consciously reflect earlier times in Irish history; as such, they are writing about a remembered history through the filter of their contemporary mindset, which does not always result in an accurate depiction of the past.

Language is a powerful carrier of culture, and shifts in language are hallmarks of social change. While the impact of collective experiences (like foreign conquest) and new technologies (like the internet) often result in the addition of words to a given lexicon, more gradual changes can cause language and meaning to shift over time. These changes in meaning are particularly important to keep in mind when comparing information obtained from different cultural contexts. As we discussed with the classical accounts of Gaulish women (predating the Irish materials by centuries), it is unclear whether the women—or even the men—identified as Druids in Irish myth were actually connected to the institutions we recognize belonging to the Iron Age Druidic social class.

According to Anczyk, the Old Irish word *druídecht* simply means "magic" or "sorcery." He goes on to say:

> It is also noteworthy, that in the opinion of scholars, Druidesses are not often mentioned in the medieval texts (with the usage of the name). The figures of witches, women-warriors, prophetesses and other magical or holy women, are often connected with Dru-

idry or they are called Druidesses by the means of association, as they dealt with similar issues to those which the Druids probably did. Therefore it is only one of the many possible interpretations of the provenience of these characters.[136]

It appears that by the early medieval period, any literary figures who used magic or had oracular powers could be called a Druid, including nonhumans otherwise identified as fairy women or divinities. Further, Hiberno-Latin texts (Irish texts written in Latin) use the word *magus* to refer to Druids, while translations of texts from Latin into Irish will render the word *magus* as "Druid." That said, the type of magic most frequently associated with Druids in medieval Irish texts is that of divination or prophecy.[137]

Some researchers have made the case that in the Irish sagas, the literary depictions of Druids—and the idea of Druidry in general—serve as personifications of native Paganism rather than reflecting any organized cultus or order. When Druids appear in Irish hagiographies during the Conversion period, for example, their purpose in the narrative is to symbolize the antithesis of Christianity rather than any actual form of Paganism.[138]

There is a famous Irish lorica, or prayer of protection, known as "The Cry of the Deer" or "The Breastplate of St. Patrick"; its writing is attributed to the fifth-century saint, although the prayer itself has been dated to the eighth century based on linguistic analysis. Combining Christian and Pagan elements both in subject and form, this lorica is a fascinating reflection of a time of cultural transition. The prayer goes

---

136 Anczyk, "Druids and Druidesses," 7.

137 Radu Razvan Stanciu, "Attitudes towards Paganism in Medieval Irish and Old Norse Texts of the Trojan War," *Apollo* (dissertation, Cambridge University, 2016), https://www.repository.cam.ac.uk/handle/1810/290141. 129–130.

138 Ibid., 129.

into great detail listing the various evils from which it petitions God's protection, including those mentioned in the following lines:

> *fri dubrechtu gentliuchtae,*
> *fri saíbrechtu heretecdae,*
> *fri imchellacht n-ídlachtae,*
> *fri brichtu ban ocus gobann ocus druad*

> *Against the black laws of paganism,*
> *Against the crooked laws of heretics,*
> *Against the encirclement of idolatry,*
> *Against the spells of women and smiths and Druids*[139]

First, it is interesting to note that women and Druids are mentioned separately; while this does not necessarily rule out women as Druids, it does seem to suggest that women had their own form of magic. (Many cultures have historically considered smiths to be magical practitioners of sorts, likely due to their ability to transform raw materials, engage in the "alchemy" of smelting, and to create alloys.) Modern Catholic translations of this prayer gives the line about spells as "Against spells of witches and smiths and wizards."

The differences in these translations underscores the ways in which words shift meaning over time, typically in response to changes in culture. It also illustrates how the translator's perspective makes all the difference as to whether we are talking about women and Druids or witches and wizards, and it informs our understanding of how these words can be used interchangeably.

There is a tendency in modern Neopaganism to conflate the Druidism we see described in first-century-BCE Gaul with the practices and

---

139 Jacqueline Borsje, "Druids, Deer and 'Words of Power': Coming to Terms with Evil in Medieval Ireland," in *Approaches to Religion and Mythology in Celtic Studies*, ed. Katja Ritari and Alexandra Bergholm (Newcastle-upon-Tyne, UK: Cambridge Scholars Publishing, 2009), pp. 264–291, 137–8.

beliefs of the figures identified as Druids in early medieval Irish texts. As mentioned earlier, we cannot even confidently connect the Druidesses in the Roman accounts of fourth-century-CE Gaul with the Druidic order mentioned in accounts of Gaul three centuries earlier.

One of the biggest differences between these groups is that before the Roman annexation of Gaul and Britain and in addition to being a learned caste of professionals and elites, Druids also served a priestly role. In contrast, the accounts of Druidesses from the Gallo-Roman period show them functioning as prophetesses, but only one of the three episodes suggests a religious context for their powers. Though we cannot prove any direct connection between these women and the Druidic order from the first century BCE, it does still demonstrate that there were holy women serving as seers in Gallo-Roman culture.

Similarly, the women who are called Druidesses in early Irish literature and lore were usually in service as poets or seers, functions possessing a great deal of overlap. Other magic-wielding women were called witches or enchantresses, and if they were supernatural in origin, could be given an epithet identifying them as fairy women. However, those women who are given the title of Druidess appear to be disconnected from any form of religious service; their titles instead seem based on the fact that they could wield magic. While this may be a result of the biases of the Christian scribes who wrote these stories down, it appears to reflect what we know of the shifted status of Druids in Ireland after the coming of Christianity and its gradual suppression of the order.[140]

Where once Druids were part of Ireland's highest social class, their function as royal advisors was taken over by Christian clerics, and their prophetic powers merged with those of the *filidh* (poet-seers) until, by the seventh century, the Druids were no longer a distinct order. They are mentioned in Old Irish law codes and status tracts like the *Uraicecht*

---

140 Cunliffe, *Druids)*, 94.

Becc, but they are no longer part of the privileged class; instead, they are looked upon as magicians and makers of charms, equivalent in class to freemen farmers. The filidh, however, saw their prestige increase and their powers expand, and they served as poets, seers, advisors, lawyers, and teachers well into the seventeenth century, when English rule effectively ended their order.[141]

This is not intended to take anything away from these accounts of female Druids in Irish literary traditions, but it is important that we move forward with the understanding that the cultural significance of the word "Druid" appears to have evolved over time. While this means we cannot necessarily draw a direct connection between the figures in Irish myth who are called Druids and those who performed sacerdotal functions within a Pagan context—whether in pre-Christian Ireland or elsewhere in the Celtic world—it doesn't discount the existence of women serving as Otherworldly intermediaries. And while we cannot rely upon these stories as proof positive that women had been part of the formal religious orders, studying to be Druids alongside men, the abundant presence of bandruí and banfhili in Irish vernacular tales strongly suggests this was likely the case.

Welsh Sources

Caesar wrote that Druidism originated in Britain, but aside from their potential presence in the following Roman account, there does not appear to be any direct mention of female Druids in any surviving Welsh texts. Tacitus describes the siege of Anglesey, stronghold of the Druids, in 61 CE by General Suetonius Paulinus, thus:

> On the beach stood the adverse array, a serried mass of arms and men, with women flitting between the ranks. In the style of Furies, in robes of deathly black and with dishevelled hair, they

---

141 Ibid., 97–98.

brandished their torches; while a circle of Druids, lifting their hands to heaven and showering imprecations, struck the troops with such an awe...their limbs were paralysed, they exposed their bodies to wounds...Then, reassured by their general, and inciting each other never to flinch before a band of females and fanatics, they charged...cut down all who met them....[142]

In this harrowing account, the black cloaked women described as Furies appear to be engaging in battle incitement of their fellow Britons, while striking fear in the hearts of the enemy. It is notable that these women are dressed in black, rather than the white garb other classical writers have ascribed to the Druids, although that's not necessarily proof that they were not Druids; neither is the fact that Tacitus lists the women separately from the Druids, calling the enemy "females and fanatics." While many modern practitioners have their opinions on who they were, the truth is we will likely never know for sure if these black-robed figures were Druids, a separate order of allied priestesses, or simply women living on Môn taking a stand against the invading Romans alongside their menfolk.

Finally, there is an interesting piece of Welsh folk belief that some of Y Tylwyth Teg ("the Fair Folk") were the souls of righteous Druids who had died before the coming of Christianity. Unable to go to heaven, they were nevertheless too good to be sent to hell, and so instead they were allowed to dwell freely on Earth as immortal spirits, with particular connections to the natural world.[143] As Y Tylwyth Teg is an umbrella term for the many different types of fairy folk in Welsh tradition (including those appearing solely in female form such as the Gwragedd Annwn), a belief that they were the souls of righteous Druids can be

---

142 Tacitus, "The Annals," in *Tacitus–The Annals*, ed. John Jackson, vol. V (Cambridge, MA: Harvard University Press, 1937), https://penelope.uchicago.edu/Thayer/e/roman/texts/tacitus/annals/14b*.html.

143 Evans-Wentz, *Fairy Faith*, 147.

seen to indirectly imply the existence of woman Druids—or, at least, a belief in their existence.

In our examination of the sources thus far, it is fair to say that even where we have located their presence, very few names of these holy women remain in history, lore, and legend. Perhaps this serves to underscore the idea that the wisdoms they have for us today are not so much centered on who they were, but what they did. Their functions, powers, and modes of service are what remain to us today, forming a call to action of our own. Let us begin to look at the powers ascribed to these priestesses and holy women, these nature spirits and goddesses—especially as they appear in subtextual contexts in legends and lore—so that we may come to a deeper understanding of the powers they had and the nature of their service.

5

VESSELS OF
SOVEREIGNTY

There are two main Goddess types attested in Celtic traditions, both found on the continent as well as the British Isles and Ireland. While they appear to sometimes be at cross-purpose—with Sovereignty Goddesses often having martial characteristics and acting as a psychopomp for dead warriors on the battleground, while the Divine Mothers are nurturing goddesses invested in birthing and maintaining life—the supposed dichotomy between the Divine Mother and the Sovereignty Goddess is not as clear-cut as some may think. Indeed, Celtic divinities tend to possess multiple attributes, some of which overlap with those of other gods.

Both types of deities often present as tutelary goddesses—divine embodiments of their lands. As such, their primary concern is the well-being of their territories and all who dwell there. Divine mothers are often ancestral figures and progenitors of divine lineages, some of which bear their names. In continental Europe, there is an enormous amount of archaeological evidence that supports the existence of a widespread cultus centered on the veneration of mother goddesses. Found primarily in Gaul, Britain, and the Rhineland and later spreading throughout out the Roman Empire, inscriptions called these goddesses variously

Matres, *Matronae*, and *Deae Matronae*—simply, "the Mothers" or "the Divine Mothers." Most have bynames or epithets describing the nature, place of origin, or function of the divinity. Some are clearly tutelary divinities, while others hint at local ancestral worship.

Sovereignty Goddesses act to protect their lands by testing candidates to determine their worthiness to become king. If they pass her test or meet her challenge, she confers Sovereignty upon them through the medium of her body, which acts as a physical bridge between the king and the land. The act of sexual union links the well-being of the land to the well-being of the king; they have a shared fate, making it important that he rules justly and remains healthy. Should he prove to be unrighteous or come to suffer any kind of blemish, malady, or injury, his kingdom will suffer as well. Sovereignty will withdraw her blessings and seek to replace the king.

In many stories where the representative of Sovereignty appears, she is often found near wells or bodies of water; in addition to offering her body to kingly candidates, she also proffers them a drink. Bodies of water, as we have seen, are boundary places marking the overlap of this world and the Otherworld, and when they appear in stories, it signals that supernatural influences are present. As in Irish immrama tales, the Otherworld is accessible by crossing bodies of water, and many Welsh tales feature magical or fairy women who live beneath the surface of a lake, as in the tale of Llyn Y Fan Fach, or on islands at the center of a lake, like Ceridwen in the tale of Gwion Bach.

While these divine women are seen as the literal Vessel of Sovereignty (in Irish myth especially), tales that feature quests for magical vessels—such as the chieftain's cauldron sought in *Preiddeu Annwn* and the Cauldron of Regeneration in the Second Branch of *Y Mabinogi*—may well be symbolic proxies for the Sovereignty of the land. Nowhere is this clearer than in Arthurian legend, where the quest for the holy grail is undertaken to heal the wounded king and bring restoration to the Wasteland.

There is an evolution of symbolism here, where goddess becomes woman becomes cauldron becomes grail, but the underlying meaning remains the same. In simplest terms, the sacred marriage between the king and the goddess of the land confers fertility to the realm through the vitalistic power of their sexual union. Similarly, the cauldron is a transformer that both creates and sustains life.

The Cauldron

The cauldron is a potent symbol in many Celtic cultures. In the reed-thatched roundhouses of Iron Age Britain, cauldrons were suspended from roof beams to hang over the hearth—the provenance of women—where they played a central role in daily life. Within these vessels, food was cooked, medicines were brewed, and bathwater was heated. Gathered around it and the hearth fire's warmth and light, feasts were given, hospitality shared, stories were told, songs were sung, and life was celebrated.

Crafted from either bronze or iron for everyday use, and ranging from utilitarian to incredibly ornate, cauldrons were highly valued objects. They have often been found in votive deposits in sacred lakes and at river sources, ostensibly in hopes of propitiating the gods or spirits of the land. They also appear in burials, particularly of high status persons, alongside other objects thought to have been used for feasting; perhaps they were a part of a funerary feast or else included so that the deceased could offer hospitality to their ancestors in the Otherworld.

Given the cauldron's cultural significance, we find that its mythological counterparts are vessels of transformation, rebirth, wisdom, abundance, and poetic inspiration—and as in life, these are most often in the keeping of women.

The Nature of the Cauldron

We can identify several types of magical cauldrons in the Welsh tradition, some that may be different iterations of related types or that may exhibit more than one magical attribute.

The Cauldron of Wisdom

Also called (or related to) the Cauldron of Knowledge and the Cauldron of Inspiration. The best known example is the Cauldron of Ceridwen from "The Tale of Gwion Bach" from *Ystoria Taliesin (The History of Taliesin)*. Ceridwen uses her cauldron to brew an elixir for her son; it required the work of a year and a day—an Otherworldly period of time—and, when finished, would bestow wisdom and the powers of poetic prophecy upon whomever took the three drops that would emerge from the vessel. The rest of the potion was a poison that cracked the cauldron and befouled everything it touched.

When Gwion, her servant, stole the drops meant for her son, it triggered a shapeshifting pursuit between Ceridwen and Gwion that ultimately saw him devoured by her in the shape of a hen after he transformed into a grain of wheat. He was later reborn of her, becoming the great bard Taliesin—he who possessed the Shining Brow. Most scholars believe this story is an encoded initiatory ritual for Welsh bards, who considered Ceridwen their mother and Muse.

The Cauldron of the Chief of Annwn is another iteration of the Cauldron of Inspiration; it is described as having the ability to utter prophetic poetry and praise song. This vessel is kindled by the breath of Nine Maidens, who also appear to function as Muses. This is not the only magical property attributed to this cauldron, as we shall see.

The Cauldron of Abundance

"Preiddeu Annwfn" tells the story of Arthur's raid on the Welsh Otherworld to claim the Cauldron of the Chief of Annwn. In addition to being a source of divine inspiration, the vessel has a testing component: it will not boil the food of a coward. It is this property of the cauldron to only be activated on behalf of a virtuous person that most strongly resonates with Sovereignty Goddesses; in both cases, abundance is granted when the candidate is found worthy.

A cauldron with similar attributes is Pair Dyrnwch Gawr—the cauldron of Dyrnwch the Giant—one of the Thirteen Treasures of the Island of Britain (in Welsh, *Tri Thlws ar Ddeg Ynys Prydain*). "If meat for a coward were put in it to boil, it would never boil; but if meat for a brave man were put in it, it would boil quickly (and thus the brave could be distinguished from the cowardly)."[144]

The Thirteen Treasures is a listing of magical objects found in various late medieval Welsh manuscripts; although there is some variation in the listed objects from manuscript to manuscript, the list is always composed of thirteen items. In addition to the Cauldron of Dyrnwch the Giant are two vessels of abundance among them: the Hamper of Gwyddno Garanhir (*Mwys Gwyddno Garanir*), which would multiply a meal sufficient for one person into enough to feed a hundred; and the Horn of Brân Galed from the North (*Corn Brân Galed o'r Gogledd*), which would provide any type of drink one could wish for. The Cauldron of Abundance has a clear influence on the later Grail Traditions, where that sacred vessel is often described as being able to provide each person it serves with bountiful food and drink, in accordance with their desires.

The Cauldron of Regeneration

Also called the Cauldron of Rebirth or Cauldron of Transformation. This vessel, called *Pair Dadeni* in Welsh, is featured in the Second Branch of *Y Mabinogi*; it possesses the ability to bring dead warriors

---

144 Rachel Bromwich, *Trioedd Ynys Prydein: The Triads of the Island of Britain* (Cardiff: University of Wales Press, 2006), 240.

back to life, albeit without speech. The keepers of this cauldron were two giants from Ireland who lived beneath the waters of the Lake of the Cauldron. The male giant carried the cauldron on his back, and the female giant had the ability to conceive every six weeks; every six weeks after that, the child would become a fully grown warrior.

This cauldron eventually found its way into the keeping of Bendigfran, king of the Island of the Mighty—a poetic name for Britain. In order to cement lasting alliances between Britain and Ireland, Bran's sister Branwen married Matholwch, the king of Ireland. During the wedding feast, their half brother Efnysien mutilated the horses of the Irish, and as partial compensation for this violation of the laws of hospitality, Bran gave the Cauldron of Regeneration to Matholwch. When Britain and Ireland later go to war due to Matholwch's mistreatment of Branwen, the Irish use the cauldron to revive their dead warriors. Efnysien, whose actions catalyzed the unrest between the two kingdoms to begin with, hides among the dead so that he can enter the cauldron and destroy it.

The Cauldron of Regeneration may also be the vessel depicted on one of the inner plates of the famous Gundestrup Cauldron, found in a Danish bog but believed to be of Celtic origin; the image shows a large figure, possibly a deity, thrusting the body of a warrior headfirst into a large vat or cauldron.

Sovereignty as Relationship

One of the reasons the Sovereignty motif is so well attested in the lore of various Celtic traditions is because it seems to represent a foundational cultural concept of how to be in right relationship with their lands and the gods of their people. At its core, the fundamental function of the Sovereignty figure is to serve as a mediator between two opposing states of existence. As a Threshold Guardian, she straddles the border between what is known and what is unknown. And humanity, when faced with an unknown—with all its attendant fear and uncertainty—seeks to find a way to influence an outcome, so that whatever they find when they reach the other side of the transition is as good a place as possible. Thus, cultivating positive relationships with those who hold mastery over the in-between spaces is a good survival strategy.

Sovereignty as a Bridge

One of the primary roles of the Sovereignty figure is to serve as a catalyst—a vessel for change able to pour forth the energies of creation from the Otherworld into this world. She is a bridge for the regenerative energies that flow through her as a result of her union with a worthy king. It is this catalyzing spark that transforms the hag into the maiden, births summer from winter, brings abundance to the Wasteland, and heals the wounded king.

When the king and Sovereignty are in a balanced relationship, her mediating presence will ensure that the land is fertile and abundant, its boundaries secure. Likewise, Sovereignty will respond to an imbalance. She will withdraw her blessings from the unworthy king, and like the drawbridge of the Grail Castle, the passageway between this world and the Otherworld closes—the creative force she channeled is cut off, and the realm becomes a Wasteland. As the goddess of the land, Sovereignty's choice of king is an extension of her powers to protect her territory and all who dwell within it. If need be, she will incite war to safeguard her people and defend her boundaries.

She will seek to restore the relationship between the king and the land by investing a new king—one who is whole, and one who has proven their worth by meeting the challenges of her testing. The energies that sustain life, fertility, and abundance return when balance is restored and Sovereignty's bridge connects the worlds once more. The hag becomes a maiden, the wells begin to flow, the land becomes abundant once more, and life can thrive in peace. The spark of creation returns, bringing with it the powers of regeneration and rebirth.

When we consider what we know about the gifts and powers that have been attributed to the women of the Ninefold Sisterhoods, we can see that, fundamentally, their roles are also to serve as bridges— to cross and help others cross thresholds of various kinds. As seers, shapeshifters, and vessels of prophecy, they cross between this world and the Otherworld to bring back guidance in service to others. As healers, midwives, and receivers of the dead, they harness liminalities of sickness and health, death and rebirth. As inciters to battle, intoxicators of kings, and granters of abundance, they bridge the spaces that shift one sociopolitical reality into another. As Muses and initiators and granters of Awen, they open the doors between the worlds to allow the creative essence of the Universe to flow forth and catalyze change.

Sovereignty as Threshold Guardian

Let us take a look now at the various ways in which the Sovereignty figure—or, more precisely—the function of the Sovereignty figure to serve as a Threshold Guardian, reveals itself in the legends of Celtic lands and in the Arthurian Tradition. Understanding these dynamics can help us better understand the role of the Avalonian priestess as a bridge between the worlds.

The Lake Maidens

Tales of Lake Maidens are a uniquely Welsh iteration of the Fairy Bride folk motif. Counted among Y Tylwyth Teg, these Lake Maidens are also known as *Gwragedd Annwn* ("Wives/Women of Annwn") a benevolent class of Welsh fairies who present as beautiful women who live beneath lakes and rivers. In many of these Lake Maiden stories, these Otherworldly women leave their watery homes to marry human men, bringing with them rich dowries of fairy cattle. These unions are described as marked by abundance and good fortune—but the continuance of these marriages are dependent upon a contract, the provisions of which must be upheld by the husband. These are behavioral prohibitions, which include the promise to never touch the Lake Maiden with iron, or to never strike her with three unworthy blows, lest the marriage be ended.

When we consider that literary fairies and Otherworldly women often originated as deities or genii locorum who were reduced in stature over time, we can see how Lake Maiden tales appear to feature devolved Sovereignty figures, functioning on a smaller, more localized scale. As with other Sovereignty stories, there is an element of testing in order to prove the suitor's worth. Just as the hieros gamos between goddess and king renews the fertility of the land, so does the marriage between the human man and the Otherworldly woman bring with it great abundance and good fortune. And just as with an unrighteous or physically blemished king, all of the bounty granted by the Otherworld is rescinded once the relationship becomes one of imbalance through the violation of the contract between them.

In the story of "The Lady of the Lake" (also called "The Lady of Llyn y Fan Fach"), after the third unworthy blow, the Lake Maiden returned to her home beneath the lake—taking all of her dowery animals with her, leaving her husband poor once again. No matter his tears and pleading—in truth, all his strikes were small taps of frustration that nevertheless broke the fairy contract—her former husband would never see her again. Yet she continued to appear to her sons and gifted them with the knowledge of an herbal formulary that brought them great renown as the Physicians of Myddfai. In this tale, the Otherworld reveals itself as a source of wisdom, abundance, and healing whether gifted through the vessel of the woman as Mother or agent of Sovereignty or through the mysteries of the Cauldron.

The Cup Bearer

In some tales that feature the Sovereignty motif, the goddess or her proxy demonstrates favor by gifting a cup of mead to the man she has deemed worthy of rule. There are hints of mead rituals associated with kingship rites in early Irish literature, and the idea persists that the mead itself was considered divine and was sometimes personified by a goddess, such as Queen Medb from the Irish Ulster Cycle. Not only is she believed to have been a Sovereignty Goddess, her very name means "Intoxicating one" or "Mead-woman."[145]

Likewise in Gaul is a grouping of the triple Divine Mothers called the *Matronae Comedovae*, whose name either meant "the Ones Who Intoxicate with Mead" or the "Ones Who Rule." According to Dr. Noémie Beck, "two etymologies are acceptable, since *med-* and *medu-* are derived from two homonymic roots, respectively referring to intoxication and sovereignty; notions that were interrelated."[146]

The altered states of consciousness achieved through inebriation, especially arising from the ritual drinking of mead, was considered a method of entering into the Otherworld. Achieving this ecstatic trance state during king-making rites may have played a role in the conference of Sovereignty onto the new king. Here, the intoxicating properties of mead may represent, or seek to replicate, the shift of consciousness that accompanies the sexual union with Sovereignty—a threshold crossing

145   Britta Irslinger, "Medb 'the Intoxicating One'? (Re-)Constructing the Past through Etymology," in *Ulidia 4: Proceedings of the Fourth International Conference on the Ulster Cycle of Tales*, Queen's University, Belfast, 27–9 June 2013, ed. Ó Mainnín Mícheál B. and Gregory Toner (Dublin, Ireland: Four Courts Press, 2017), 39.

146   Noémie Beck, "Goddesses in Celtic Religion: Goddesses of Intoxication," Brewminate (blog), February 10, 2018, https://brewminate.com/goddesses-in-celtic -religion-goddesses-of-intoxication/.

that both connects the king to the Otherworld, and marks his shift of status as the new sovereign.[147]

In the Irish tale "Baile in Scáil" ("The Phantom's Frenzy"), the warrior Conn journeys to the Otherworld where he meets the enthroned deity Lugh, who is accompanied by a woman wearing a crown of gold. Identified as the Sovereignty of Ireland, she holds a golden cup she filled from a silver vat using a golden dipper. When she asks Lugh to whom the cup should be given, he names Conn and then lists all the kings of Ireland who will come after him.

Lugh of Ireland—as well as the Welsh Lleu—are reflexes of the Gaulish divinity Lugus, who appears to have held a triple function as magician, warrior, and craftsman. Lugus is commonly syncretized with Mercury in Gallo-Roman iconography and inscriptions; he is often paired with the Celtic goddess Rosmerta, whose name potentially means "Great Provider." Her attributes are the cornucopia, a Roman libation cup called a patera, and a large vessel (sometimes interpreted as a bucket or casket of mead).[148] Her association with the abundance of the land, as well as her potential connection to mead may indicate her status as a goddess of Sovereignty. Certainly her symbolic attributes are quite similar to those of the Sovereignty of Ireland in "Baile in Scáil," and there may be some significance to their respective relationships with Lugus and Lugh.

The trance of mead intoxication may have also been used to bring poetry and prophecy back from the Otherworld, thus serving as a means to obtain divine inspiration. Further, the relationship between war goddesses and goddesses of inebriation speak to the battle frenzy of Celtic warriors; the Morrígan, for example, is famous for her powers of incitement.

---

147 Charles Bowen, "Great-Bladdered Medb: Mythology and Invention in the Táin Bó Cuailnge," *Éire-Ireland: A(n Interdisciplinary) Journal of Irish Studies* 10, no. 4 (1975): 21.

148 Koch, "Rosmetra," *in Celtic Culture*, 1542.

References to mead also feature in Welsh tradition, in several poems from *The Book of Taliesin*, including "Kanu y Med" ("A Song to Mead") and "Kadeir Taliesin" ("The Chair of Taliesin"); the latter ends with the following lines:

> Let the brewer give a heat,
> Over a cauldron of five trees,
> And the river of Gwiawn,
> And the influence of fine weather,
> And honey and trefoil,
> And mead-horns intoxicating
> Pleasing to a sovereign,
> The gift of the Druids.[149]

In our earlier discussion of "Preiddeu Annwn," another poem from *The Book of Taliesin*, we encounter an area of the Otherworld called Caer Vedwit—the Fortress of Mead-Drunkenness. The presence of this caer in Annwn may be testimony to the sacred nature of mead as well as its ability to open a door between the worlds. The Well Maidens and the Grail Maidens, described below, are related to the Cup Bearer, and seem to be literary descendants of this Threshold Guardian type.

The Well Maidens

The story of the Well Maidens comes to us from "The Elucidation," a prologue to Chrétien de Troyes's thirteenth-century *Perceval ou Le Conte du Graal* written by an anonymous author sometime between the thirteenth and fifteenth centuries. Because Chrétien died before completing his great work, he left behind many questions about the grail's nature and origin. The prologue appears to be an attempt to

---

149 "The Chair of Taliesin, Book of Taliesin XIII," The Celtic Literature Collective website, accessed February 28, 2023, https://www.ancienttexts.org/library/celtic/ctexts/t13.html.

weave together the various strains of story that had arisen around Perceval with the aim of providing a context for the origins of Wasteland, the significance of the Fisher King, and the purpose of the knightly quests to recover the Grail. One of these narrative strains is the tale of the Well Maidens. It holds a very strong resonance with the Sovereignty motif we have been discussing, such that it is possible there may have been a conscious effort on the part of the author to connect Chrétien's work with related but independently evolved story traditions. Here is that story, in brief.

Once, the many sacred wells that graced the portion of Britain called Logres were tended by Otherworldly women known as Well Maidens. These magical oases, called Courts of Joy by some, were places of sanctuary and hospitality for travelers in need of rest and replenishment. Any time of day or night, a weary journeyer could arrive at one of these wells and ask—with all due courtesy—for whatever food or drink they most desired. Immediately, a beautiful Maiden would emerge from the well bearing a golden bowl of the finest drink, followed by another Maiden carrying a silver platter laden with the richest food, all in accordance with the traveler's desires.

One day, an evil king named Amangon visited one of these Courts of Joy and desecrated its holy precinct by taking hold of the Maiden who emerged from the well and raping her. He stole her golden bowl and carried her off to his holdings where he forced her to remain in his service. From that day forward, the well was still and silent; no Maiden ever again arose from its waters to offer hospitality. Emboldened by the actions of their king, the vassals of Amangon likewise set aside their honor and raped the other Well Maidens and stole their vessels of gold … until one day, all the wells had gone silent and no Maidens ever again came forth from them.

These evil deeds did not go unpunished, we are told, and the king and his men came to horrible ends—but the damage done ran deeper. The springs and rivers all dried up, the plants withered, the trees bore no fruit, and the court of the Fisher King and all its riches became hidden from the world. The once-bountiful earth became blighted and was transformed in to a Wasteland.

It was during the time of King Arthur that a band of his noble knights discovered the descendants of the Well Maidens hidden deep in the forest. When they learned of the violations that caused the blighting of Logres, the knights vowed to avenge the crimes of Amangon and his men, restore the golden bowls to the wells, and find the court of the Rich Fisher who possessed the key to restoring the Wasteland: the Grail.

The narrator of "The Elucidation" goes on to reference many adventures and the seven knights who would go on to find the Fisher King's court. But it is only through the powers of the Grail that the waters of Logres began to flow once more. The land became thick with forests, great courts rose up, and the abundance of the land was restored. Of the descendants of the Well Maidens, we are told that the famed Castle of Maidens was built for their home and protection, and each was the beloved of one of the great knights of the land.

As Threshold Guardians, the Well Maidens present very clearly as analogs of the goddesses or genii locorum responsible for the conference—or removal—of Sovereignty. The abundance of the land is tied to the behavior of its king, and and the horrific violence of sexual assault and kidnapping, compounded by violations of the social contracts governing the rules of hospitality result in an imbalanced relationship with the agent of Sovereignty, causing the blessings of the Otherworld to be withdrawn.

The Well Maidens' Otherworldly origin is underscored by their connection to water, particularly to holy wells. Some scholars have argued that the Old French of "The Elucidation" is ambiguous in its use of the word *puis*, which is typically translated as "well" but could also be a corruption of the word for "hill."[150] For me, this ambiguity only serves to reinforce the Maidens' Otherworldly identity, especially since hollow hills are also known gateways to the Otherworld.

The story of the Well Maidens very clearly depicts the consequences of violating the sacred trust of hospitality, a core tenet in many Celtic societies and indeed many European cultures from Germanic tribes to the city-states of Greece. This violation causes imbalance between society and the Otherworld, and the resulting withdrawal of the life-giving energies that come through these Threshold Guardians leads to ruin and the Waste.

This tale serves as a powerful allegory for the disempowerment and oppression of women and may be a mythic memory of the cultural shifts of late antiquity and the early Middle Ages as that accompanied the spread of Christianity. It is also a warning against humanity's ongoing rapine treatment of the earth that sees capitalism engaging in an unsustainable exploitation of resources without thought of consequence, only short term pleasure and gain. By demonstrating all that we stand to lose, the Well Maidens teach us the importance of being in a balanced relationship with our world. When our actions dishonor our planet and violate the sovereignty of all who dwell upon it, we bring the Wasteland upon ourselves.

The Grail Maiden

In Chrétien de Troyes's *Le Conte du Graal*, a young and freshly knighted Percival rides out from Arthur's court to return to his secluded home in Wales to comfort his grieving mother who did not want him to leave home. On his journey, Percival encounters a river that is too wild and wide to cross, but he must somehow do so in order to reach his destination. While seeking another way across, Percival encounters two

---

150   Albert Wilder Thompson, *The Elucidation: A Prologue to the Conte Del Graal* (Genève, Swizterland: Slatkine, 1982), 37.

men fishing in a boat on the river who direct him to a nearby keep to lodge overnight. Percival follows their advice, and after struggling to locate the elusive keep, discovers that the water-ringed and seemingly run-down castle was a much grander court than appeared from the outside. What's more, the holder of the keep was one of the men in the boat from earlier in the day—the Fisher King, who suffers from a terrible wound to the thigh that renders him lame.

While feasting with his host in the strange court, Percival is gifted with an almost unbreakable sword and then witnesses an odd procession wherein a young man holds a bleeding lance, two youths carry lit candelabras, a beautiful maiden bears the shining vessel called the graal, and a second maid carries a silver tray; all of the wondrous items are carried from room to room throughout the meal. The jewel-encrusted golden platter of the graal is so incredibly beautiful and shines so brightly that it renders the flames of the candles themselves dim in comparison. No explanation is given for this procession, and Percival chooses to leave his questions unasked, fearing they would be perceived as unknightly and rude.

The next morning, Percival awakens to find that the keep is completely empty; he calls out in search of anyone from the night before, but finds no one except a waiting and well-equipped horse for his journey. Still confused about the events of the previous night, Percival departs. As he leaves, the drawbridges to the castle are lifted against him so that he cannot return. As he resumes his journey to see his mother, he encounters a young woman who asks Percival if during the procession, he had asked that which we have come to know as the grail question—"Whom does the grail serve?" Percival admits he had not done so, and the maiden scolds and shames him, telling him that asking this question would have healed the king and restored the land. Instead, his failure will result in a great deal of grief and suffering.

While the strange scene at the feast and Percival's failure by inaction may seem to be impenetrable mysteries, one of the roles of the Sovereignty figure is to test her potential champion or kingly candidate to determine his worth. The beautiful maiden in the procession bears the wondrous vessel from room to room, waiting in vain for the Grail question to be asked. Later on in the story, an incredibly ugly woman riding a mule reminds Percival that the Grail could have been used to heal the wounded king and restore the bounty of the land had he asked the question; it is likely that this woman is the transformed Grail Maiden.

In many Sovereignty tales, the Sovereignty figure presents as a hideous hag when the land is without a whole and righteous king; when a righteous candidate joins with the hag sexually, she is transformed into a beautiful woman. Her ugliness is both a test of the man's character and a metaphor for the state of the land without its rightful king—barren, harsh, and challenging. In the "Echtra mac nEchach," Sovereignty compares her form to the realities of kingship saying, "and as you have seen me loathsome, hound-like, fearsome first and beautiful afterwards, the sovereignty is like that."[151]

The presence of a Loathly Lady (a motif discussed in more detail in the next section) in this tale reinforces the relationship between the Grail and the Cauldron of Regeneration that preceded it. The Grail Maiden is the bearer of the regenerative principle—no longer embodying it in her person but nevertheless reflecting the testing aspect of the Vessel of Sovereignty in her appearance. She is in service to that which grants Sovereignty, and the vessel she carries has the ability to bridge states of being. Because the champion failed his test, the Wasteland persists, the king remains unhealed, her beauty turns to ugliness, and the rejuvenating bounty of the Otherworld is denied.

There are some uncomfortable things about this dualism, to be sure. Medieval legends abound with praise of women for their beauty and purity—smooth white skin; slim arms; buxom breasts; red lips;

---

151 Mary Jones, "Echtra mac nEchach", Leabhar Buidhe Lecain, Celtic Literature Collective (website) accessed June 10, 2014, http://www.maryjones.us/ctexts/eochaid .html.

golden, ruddy, or night-black hair—and there was an intentional symbolic connection between beauty and goodness. But in the context of the Sovereignty mytheme, it is mostly centered around the polarity of abundance and lack—fertility and the Wasteland—rather than commentary on age or the honor accorded to older women in Celtic cultures. Indeed, in the legends and lore of Celtic peoples, hags and crones were fearsome, powerful forces to be reckoned with.

The hag becoming the maiden when kissed can be considered a reflection of the patriarchal preference for youth and beauty, but perhaps this is also a modern perspective. We must keep in mind that the Hag and Maiden are two sides of the same woman, two aspects of the same whole. We too possess a dual nature—parts that are wounded and parts that are healed. If we seek the blessings of a sovereign life, then we must reclaim the power of both aspects of ourselves.

Loathly Lady

The figure of the Loathly Lady appears in several Arthurian legends. She is an evolution of the Sovereignty motif that sees the focus shifted from concern with the collective health of the land to the individual agency of women; indeed, rather than being granters of Sovereignty, women are seeking to obtain their personal sovereignty from men. This variation is found in early English literature, including *The Weddynge of Sir Gawen and Dame Ragnall*, as well as Chaucer's *The Wife of Bath's Tale*. Here, the threshold moment takes the form of a question, "What is it women most desire? Answer: Sovereignty." When the correct answer is given, the transformation of the Loathly Lady occurs, and she becomes a beautiful young maiden.

In *The Weddynge of Sir Gawen and Dame Ragnelle*, Arthur and his retinue are engaged in a stag hunt, a motif that often presages an encounter with Sovereignty. Upon felling the beast, Arthur is confronted by Sir Gromer Somerjour, the "man of the summer day," who tells Arthur he has wronged him by giving some of his lands to Sir Gawain. Arthur asks what he must do to make amends, and Gromer tells him that he must return to this wood a year hence, dressed in the same garments, with the answer to the question of "whate wemen love best in feld and town." (line 91) Should Arthur not be able to supply the correct answer, Gromer will cut off his head.

Arthur agrees to the challenge and returns to his court, where Gawen suggests they two ride out over the countryside, pose the question to everyone they meet, and write each answer down in a book. After collecting responses over a year's time, the night before the fated meeting an uneasy Arthur encounters a Loathly Lady in the forest; she is Sir Gromer's sister, Dame Ragnelle. Described in the tale as an incredibly ugly woman, Ragnelle tells Arthur she will give him the correct answer in exchange for Gawen's promise to marry her. Gawen agrees, and she reveals that what women want most is sovereignty. Arthur's life is saved, and once the danger to the realm has been averted, the two wed. On their wedding night, Gawen is less than amorous toward his new wife. Ragnelle scolds Gawen and reveals that she has been cursed: she can either be beautiful by day and ugly by night, or beautiful by night and ugly by day. She tells him to choose which option he prefers. Gawen considers his reply and then remembers the answer Dame Ragnelle gave that solved the riddle.

Gawen tells Ragnelle that the choice is hers, not his, and immediately she transforms into a radiantly beautiful woman. She tells him he has broken her curse—she will be beautiful now, both day and night. Here, the champion has passed the test, is thus found worthy, and joins with Ragnelle in their wedding bed. However, in this inversion of the Sovereignty motif, he is already in possession of the lands she represents; in fact, it was Arthur's gifting of that land to Gawan that initiated this whole scenario. Now that Ragnelle is wed to Gawan, her brother no longer has cause to reclaim the unlawfully transferred land.

The Washer at the Ford

This iteration of the Threshold Guardian is connected with both prophecy and fate. It is best known in Irish tradition as a death omen associated with Badb, one of the aspects of the Morrígan. In Scotland there is a rich trove of lore concerning fairy women called *bean-nighe* or washer-women who inhabit remote liminal spaces connected with water. Should someone come across a woman washing bloody clothing or the trappings of war at the ford of a river, it is a sign that they will soon die or not survive the coming battle. Both Badb and these other fay women were known to utter prophecies as well.

This motif takes a bit of a different form in Welsh tradition, where it is primarily associated with Modron (discussed in detail in chapter 6). She is fated to wash (whether herself or clothing is unclear) at the ford of a river until she delivers a son to a Christian man. The place was called "the Ford of the Barking" because all the dogs in the area would gather there to bark and howl at something unseen, their sound terrifying to all who head it. Uriens of Rheged, a semi-historical figure, was the only man brave enough to approach the ford—when he arrived, he found only silence and a woman in the river.

Uriens is said to have "taken hold of her," and she became pregnant with twins, the maiden Morfudd and the Arthurian hero Owain, who, like his father, also has an historical counterpart. After their sexual encounter, the woman in the river (whose name is not given in the tale but we know based on other lore) blesses Uriens for fulfilling the requirements that will release her from her fate. She then reveals her Otherworldly origins by telling him that her father is the King of Annwn.

In contrast to Irish tradition where it is an omen of death, this encounter is more aligned with the powers of Sovereignty to test a potential king; Uriens proved himself through his bravery. The implied rape in this story (which some question, as Modron blesses him afterward) highlights the probability that this may be a corrupted version of the hieros gamos, or sacred marriage component of the conference of Sovereignty to the worthy candidate. Indeed, Uriens is a famed king of the Old North kingdom of Rheged in both historical accounts and literary tradition. Modron is clearly of divine origin; her name means "Divine Mother" and is cognate with the Gaulish river goddess Matrona, who will be discussed further in the next chapter. River goddesses are often major tutelary divinities, and as such, are prime candidates for facilitating the conference of Sovereignty.

As with the Loathly Lady, this medieval Welsh variant of the Washer at the Ford may also be a devolved Sovereignty figure. Mirroring the cultural changes of their times, these two subtextual representations of Sovereignty both rely upon the actions of the man with whom they partner to free them from their curse or fate rather than themselves serving as changers of destiny and speakers of prophecy.

The Lady of the Lake

Arthurian Tradition contains several characteristic examples of the ways in which the conference of Sovereignty shifted to become something symbolic. Perhaps the most renowned—and subtextual—example of this is the Lady of the Lake giving the sword Excalibur to Arthur.

Geoffrey of Monmouth mentions Arthur's sword in *Historia Regum Britanniae*, and although he doesn't describe the circumstances of how Arthur obtained it, he does write that this most excellent sword was forged on Avalon. This detail has powerful ramifications about the Holy Isle's involvement in the conference of Sovereignty, especially if it derives from native tradition. Geoffrey called it Caliburnus (or Caliburn)—a Latinization of its Welsh name, Caledfwlch, which first appears in "Culhwch ac Olwen" as one of Arthur's most prized possessions. Its name evolved over time to become the more familiar Excalibur.

There are two swords associated with Arthur: the one he famously drew from the stone, and the one he received from the Lady of the Lake; it is the latter sword that is most often named Excalibur, strengthening the connection between the sword-granting Lady and Avalon. It may be that these are parallel (rather than competing) traditions, since both include subtle sexual symbolism, settings of liminality, and the testing element associated with the conference of Sovereignty.

When Arthur breaks the sword he drew from the stone, Merlin takes him to see the Lady of the Lake in order to be given Excalibur, ostensibly so that his covenant with the land can be renewed. She is described as a fairy woman who possesses strange magics and dwells with her sisters on an enchanted island or in a wondrous realm below the water. Merlin rows Arthur out to the middle of her lake to speak with the Lady, who seems to be standing on the surface of the water itself. Another woman's arm holds a sword aloft from beneath the water, and Arthur asks the Lady if he can have the sword. She gives it to him—along with a scabbard that magically prevents the wearer from bleeding—in return for a promise that he will grant her a future request of her choosing.

In Thomas Malory's *Le Morte d'Arthur*, after his fatal wounding at the Battle of Camlann, Arthur bids his knight Sir Bedivere to cast Excalibur into a nearby lake. At first, Bedivere is reluctant to part with the sword and lies to his king about having thrown it into the lake, but Arthur sees through the knight's deception and demands his order be carried out. Bedivere returns to the lake and throws the sword. To his surprise, the richly garbed arm of the Lady of the Lake catches the sword, brandishes it thrice, and disappears back into the lake with Excalibur.

Scholars believe that these mythic episodes involving Excalibur could be reflections or resonant memories of ancient British Celtic traditions of making votive offerings of swords, shields, and precious objects to holy lakes and sacred rivers. As water was considered a gateway to the Otherworld, placing offerings into these bodies of water—either to gain the favor of the gods or thank them for an answered prayer—would ensure that the gods received them in the Otherworld.

Famous votive deposits were found in Llyn Cerrig Bach on Ynys Môn, and the River Thames at Battersea, England. Even Julius Caesar commented on this practice in Gaul, stating that gifts of precious metals would be deposited in lakes and no one would dare touch them upon a punishment of painful death. To be gifted with one of these swords would indeed confer honor upon the bearer and represent the blessing of the Otherworld—gods and ancestors both.

Depictions of the Lady of the Lake in the French Vulgate cycle are strongly informed by the Fairy Queen motif. In this motif, an Otherworldly woman who rules over an island paradise becomes either the foster mother of an orphaned baby or takes a knight she has deemed worthy as her lover. In either case, she arms the hero and bestows upon him a horse. Here, we see the Sovereignty figure choose her defender, who takes on the role of the Otherworldly champion—like the Nine Witches of Caer Lowy who train and arm the hero Peredur. There are many variations on the motif of magical women playing the role of initiator—whether into adulthood, manhood, or the Sovereignty of kingship.

It is not difficult to see the symbolism present in the piercing hardness of the unsheathed sword; the virility of the empowered male rising from, and with the blessings of, the waters of the sacred feminine. We have already seen this type of shift in symbolism with images of the feminine as well, as with the mediating powers of the Grail that evolve to become so central to Arthurian Tradition.

The Barge Queens

One of the most enduring episodes in Arthurian Tradition is the journey of the mortally wounded Arthur to Avalon for healing. In all accounts of this journey (save for the first one), Arthur is brought to the Holy Isle by a barge or ship filled with Otherworldly women or black-veiled queens. These women are often described as shrieking or weeping as Arthur is remitted to their care.

The passengers in the barge differ from account to account. Typically, although there may be others present, there are three queens who ferry Arthur to Avalon. In Malory's *Le Morte D'Arthur*, these are the Queen of Northgalis (North Wales—who may be the enchantress Sebile), the Queen of the Wasteland (who may be Perceval's aunt), and Morgan le Fay (whom we will discuss in detail in chapter 6). At this point in the development of Arthurian lore, Morgan is the wife of Uriens and therefore the Queen of Gore (a legendary land believed to exist in the area of North Rheged, part of the kingdom ruled by the Urien of history).

It is notable that Morgan le Fay is always present in the barge to Avalon, even in those later Arthurian tales where her character has evolved from Arthur's benevolent helper and ally to his staunchest enemy. Still, in Malory—after chapter upon chapter of challenging the king in an effort to end his reign—she tenderly lays his head upon her lap and asks, "Ah, dear brother, why have ye tarried so long from me?"[152]

Nimue, the chief Lady of the Lake, is often among the women in the barge as well. This is another point of note, since in *Le Morte d'Arthur* and subsequent works influenced by Malory, Arthur's journey to Avalon begins directly after Bedivere famously returns Excalibur to the Lady of the Lake's waiting hand. It seems almost as if the return of the sword is what triggers the events that follow.

The Barge Queens who ferry Arthur to Avalon are guardians of the threshold between life and death. They are serving in a capacity that is sometimes associated with Sovereignty Goddesses: the psychopomp—one who guides the souls of the dead to the Otherworld. This duty is a reflection of her dual role as life giver and life taker, initiator and usurper, one who enlivens the land and she who withdraws her bounty, leaving a Wasteland behind.

---

152 Thomas Malory, *Le Morte D'Arthur*, vol. 2 (London: J.M. Dent and Sons, Ltd., 1915), 389.

Other examples of Sovereignty Goddesses as psychopomps include the Morrígan, whose crows gather the souls of dead warriors on the battlefield; this is mirrored by the collection of severed heads after battles (it was a widely-held belief in Celtic cultures that the soul of a person resides in the head) known as "Macha's Nut Harvest." This, in turn, has a resonance in Norse myth, where Valkyries gather the souls of heroes slain on the battlefield, and bring them to Valhalla or Fólkvangr.

The first written account of Arthur's journey to Avalon is in the *Vita Merlini*, where Geoffrey of Monmouth writes that Arthur's men enlist the services of Barinthus—one "to whom the waters and the stars of the sky were known"—to navigate their ship to Avalon.[153] Barinthus is believed to be an Otherworldly figure, and some have connected him to St. Brendan the Navigator, an Irish saint famous for his sea voyage in search of the Isle of the Blessed. Barinthus may have a mythic predecessor in Manannán mac Lir—the Irish god of the sea and himself a Threshold Guardian of the Otherworld. This is especially worthy of note, as Ynys Afallon bears a strong resemblance to Emain Ablach, the Otherworldly island ruled by Manannán.

Manannán is said to possess a magical silver branch hung with three golden apples that plays music with the power to soothe a soul to sleep. Another figure with a similar branch is the Otherworldly woman who appears to Bran mac Febal and calls on him to undertake a quest to the Land of Women. Her branch is silver with crystal blossoms on it and is taken from an apple tree on Emain Ablach. These branches clearly have strong connections with the Otherworld. They are reminiscent of the distaffs carried by the Norse völva as well as the famed winged caduceus of Hermes. It seems that in many cultures of Indo-European derivation, those who fulfill the roles of psychopomps or messengers of the gods often carry these symbolic "keys" that open the ways between

---

153 Geoffrey of Monmouth, "The Life of Merlin," trans. John Jay Parry, *Vita Merlini: The Life of Merlin* (Sacred Texts), accessed August 26, 2022, https://www.sacred-texts.com/neu/eng/vm/index.htm.

the worlds. (Human envoys likewise wore or carried something indicating their status that protected them as they journeyed, especially during times of war.)

The act of casting Excalibur into the lake signifies the return of the land's Sovereignty to its source; the mediating element of the sacred lake serves as a doorway to the Otherworld. Likewise, it is over the medium of water that Arthur is taken to Avalon, that Otherworldly island where the broken and battered sovereign of a nation is held and healed until he is ready to return and reclaim his full power.

But the promise of the once and future king is not solely a covenant of the past—a light of hope for the Britons during a dark time of war and occupation. It is also a promise to us here and now—that we, like Arthur, can return to the truth of who we are, that Avalon is a place where our sovereign selves await us … a place where we can be healed, a pathway where we can learn to be whole.

The Sovereignty of Avalon

In many ways, Avalon is a mirror of attributes and functions of Sovereignty. She is associated with water and functions as an Otherworldly threshold. She is a tester of worth; it is not easy to reach the Holy Isle. In some tales, she is well concealed by magical mists, and those who seek her must undertake an often-difficult journey over water. She is a land of endless abundance, youth, and health—all of which are given freely to those who abide by her fair laws. She has the power to heal the wounded king and is depicted in the lore as the origin and keeper of the symbol of Sovereignty. Excalibur was forged on Avalon and is received back into her care until another worth ruler emerges.

Likewise, the characteristics attributed to Avalon in the lore are quite similar to those of magical cauldrons in Celtic tradition:

- Like the Cauldron of Wisdom, it is a place tended by Nine Sisters of great learning and talent in the arts who—like Ceridwen and Taliesin—possess the knowledge of shape changing.

- Like the Cauldron of Plenty, it is a place of abundance where food grows without toil, arising from the island itself.

- Like the Cauldron of Regeneration, it is a place of healing and rest for the souls of the dead until they are ready to return to the world once more.

Now that we have explored the three main currents that inform the Avalonian Stream of Tradition—Otherworldly Islands, Ninefold Sisterhoods, and Vessels of Sovereignty—let us now turn our attention to the women of the Holy Isle itself: the Nine Sisters of Avalon.

6

THE NINE SISTERS
OF AVALON

Thus far, as part of our immersion in the waters of the Avalonian Stream of Tradition, we have explored the ways in which Avalon's identity as an Otherworldly Island has precedent in earlier writings from other Celtic cultures as well as from classical lore. We have examined the role of the Otherworld and its agents in the granting and rescinding of Sovereignty. We have sought out the information available to us from history and lore concerning the roles and powers of priestesses and holy women in Celtic lands. And we have engaged with the traditions of Ninefold Sisterhoods from around the Celtic world and beyond. With all of this as our foundation, we now turn to the women most directly associated with the Holy Island of Avalon from Arthurian lore, in order to get an understanding of who they were, what they represented, and what lessons they hold for those of us who seek to walk the paths of Avalon today.

Generally speaking, the earliest written accounts of Avalon are the most instructive when it comes to identifying the fundamental elements of her core nature. Avalon's first appearance in the written record is a brief mention made by Geoffrey of Monmouth in his influential *Historia Regum Brittaniae*. In it, he says only that Arthur's great sword Caliburn was forged on Avalon, and that it is to this isle that Arthur is taken to be healed of his mortal wounds. He expands upon his account of Avalon in the *Vita Merlini*, a lesser-known work written about a decade after the *Historia*. There, he describes Avalon as a self-sustaining island paradise, ruled over by nine learned sisters who have established a code of laws that visitors to their land have deemed pleasing and fair. He details the powers and expertise of these sisters and very deliberately names each of them.

> There nine sisters rule by a pleasing set of laws those who come to them from our country. She who is first of them is more skilled in the healing art, and excels her sisters in the beauty of her person. Morgen is her name, and she has learned what useful properties all the herbs contain, so that she can cure sick bodies. She also knows an art by which to change her shape, and to cleave the air on new wings like Daedalus; when she wishes she is at Brest, Chartres, or Pavia, and when she will she slips down from the air onto your shores. And men say that she has taught mathematics to her sisters, Moronoe, Mazoe, Gliten, Glitonea, Gliton, Tyronoe, Thitis; Thitis best known for her cither.[154]

Like the other Ninefold groups of holy women, the Nine Sisters of Avalon possess special powers and live apart from the rest of society. Named for the apples of immortality and eternal youth that grow in abundance on its shores, their island home is a place of healing and blessed with bounty. Accessible only by a journey over water requiring the assistance of a knowledgeable guide, the liminal nature of Avalon places her firmly in the Otherworld alongside many similar islands found in early Irish and Welsh legends.

---

154 Geoffrey of Monmouth, "The Life of Merlin," trans. John Jay Parry, *Vita Merlini: The Life of Merlin* (Sacred Texts), accessed August 26, 2022, https://www.sacred-texts.com/neu/eng/vm/index.htm, lines 927–928.

Note: The original Latin gives *cithara*, a lyre-like instrument; the cither is another stringed instrument but was not invented until the sixteenth century.

In addition to the Nine Sisters of Avalon, early Welsh literature features three other examples of Ninefold Sisterhoods: the Nine Maidens of Annwn, the Nine Witches of Ystafngwn, and the Nine Witches or Sorceresses of Caer Lowy. These are discussed in detail in chapter 3. While these Ninefold groups share some commonalities, it is unclear if these are different stories about the same group of nine, if they are different iterations of the same mytheme with a common mythic origin, if they are a mythic residue that has preserved memories of a divinity group or a priestess order with a Ninefold organization, or if—as I suspect—they are a little bit of all three.

If they are resonances of a core Brythonic myth that has been lost to us, it makes sense that there would be various interpretations of the mytheme arising at different points in time along the flow of its Stream of Tradition. What this means is that—depending on the time and place these stories were written down—the cultural and authorial perspective on women's power and on magic is what dictates whether the Nine were characterized as benevolent allies, Otherworldly enigmas, or magic-wielding antagonists needing to be defeated.

We definitely see this process at work when it comes to Morgen, specifically. While her nature as the benevolent healer and goddess-like figure we first meet in the *Vita Merlini* changes to become something altogether more sinister as the Arthurian Tradition develops over the centuries, as Morgan le Fay she nevertheless remains a core character in the Matter of Britain and beyond. However, although they are presented alongside Morgen as corulers of Avalon in the *Vita Merlini*, her sisters never appear in any subsequent works, nor do they appear to have any precedent other than, perhaps, Geoffrey's imagination.

Because of their obscurity and the almost impossible task of tracing their etymologies in any academic or linguistically satisfying way, it is possible that the names of Morgen's sisters arose from a mélange of references rather than any genuinely existing tradition. Simply put, Geoffrey seems to have created the names himself, styling them with a Greco-Roman essence in order to invoke a sense of antiquity—and authenticity. As we have already discussed, Geoffrey appears to draw upon native British tradition as well as Classical sources as inspiration for his writings. In the case of the Nine Sisters of Avalon, this inspiration—fittingly enough, considering the nature of the Nine Maidens of Annwn—may have included the Nine Muses: the divine source of art and poetry in Greco-Roman tradition.

Not only is the learned nature of the Nine Sisters suggestive of the Nine Muses, it may also allude to the seven liberal arts that formed the foundation of medieval education. These seven arts were the *trivium*—grammar, rhetoric, and logic—and the *quadrivium*, made up of geometry, arithmetic, music, and astronomy. Like the Nine Muses, the seven arts were often personified as women in writing and art.[155]

Whether or not he intended a direct comparison with the seven liberal arts, Geoffrey mentions that the Sisters of Avalon are experts in the healing arts, particularly when it comes to knowing the medicinal properties of herbs—in medieval times, these were a physician's stock and trade. Morgen is said to be able to change her shape in order to fly where she wills, and the places named by Geoffrey are famous centers for learning. In a medieval context, mathematics is just as likely to refer to the science of numbers as it is to the study of astrology, and so may also serve as a reference to the divinatory arts.

Finally, music is mentioned in connection with "Thitis best known for her cithera"—a lyre-like instrument famously associated with Apollo, divine leader of the Nine Muses in some Greek myths. While this may be another ingress of classical influence, perhaps in a Welsh context the cithera may have been intended to represent the harp, given its strong bardic associations.

---

155 Iain Tidbury, "Philosophy and the Liberal Arts," Liberal Arts website, July 28, 2022, https://liberalarts.org.uk/philosophy-and-the-liberal-arts/.

Regardless of Geoffrey's intentions, there seems to be an enduring tradition of Avalon as a place of women's learning. In a fragmentary fourteenth-century Welsh account of the birth of Arthur called "Arthur and Kaledvwlch" (Llanstephan MS 201), Uther is said to have sent one of Eigyr's (Igraine) daughters with Gwrleis (Gorlois) to "the Isle of Avallach, and of all in her age she was most skilled in the seven arts."[156] The daughter's name is given as Diotima, but it's clear that she is a substitute for Morgan, who, by that time, had become Arthur's half sister and daughter of Igraine and Gorlois. In *Le Morte D'Arthur*, Malory writes that Morgan was sent to a nunnery as a child, where she "became a great clerk of necromancy." As seen in chapter 1, there was a women's ecclesiastical center in Glastonbury that, by the time of Malory's writing, had been associated with Avalon for at least three hundred years—could this be the nunnery he intended?

Who Are the Nine Sisters?

Aside from Morgen, the names of the Nine Sisters of Avalon do not appear in any other account of Avalon nor elsewhere in Arthurian Tradition. Some scholars have nevertheless attempted to identify these magical women, or else sought to understand where Geoffrey drew his inspiration from in naming them. As we otherwise have very little information about these sisters, it is worth exploring these findings.

The 1973 translation of the *Vita Merlini* by Basil Clarke includes an in-depth name notes index where he seeks to connect the Sisters to similarly named figures from classical and Irish traditions. In his book *Quest for the Nine Maidens*, Stuart McHardy references these annotations, adding his observations that some of the names bear similarities

---

156 J. H. Davies, "Arthur a Kaledvwlch: a Welsh Version of the Birth of Arthur (From a Fifteenth Century M.S., with Translation)," *Y Cymmrodor: Transactions of the Honourable Society of Cymmrodorion* 24 (1913), http://www.maryjones.us/ctexts /kaledvwlch.html.

with figures associated with Ninefold groups from Germanic and other Celtic sources, especially the Nine Maidens traditions of Scotland.[157] What follows is a brief compilation of their theories for each of the Sisters, with a bit of lore to fill in some of the details.

Moronoe

In P-Celtic or Brythonic languages, *mor* means "sea," while in Q-Celtic or Goidelic languages, *mor* means "great" or "big."[158] Clarke had no suggestions for any connections save noting a similarity with Moronoc, the name of a seventh-century Irish bishop.[159]

Mazoe

Of all Morgen's sisters, Mazoe has the strongest association with another Ninefold Sisterhood—the Scottish Nine Maidens of Glen Ogilvy, discussed in chapter 3. The name *Mazoe* bears a strong similarity to Mazota, the eldest of St. Donevald's nine daughters. In a surviving story about Mazota, she is said to have performed a miracle by convincing a flock of geese to stop destroying crop fields. The best known of her sisters, who were collectively honored as a group of saints—the Nine Maidens or Nine Holy Virgins, whose grave beneath an oak tree in Abernathy became a place of pilgrimage—Mazota was a saint in her own right. Her feast day was December 22—the Winter Solstice. Her ability to speak to animals and association with Midwinter may suggest a potential connection to pre-Christian beliefs, perhaps as a deity or a priestess.[160]

---

157   Stuart McHardy, *The Quest for the Nine Maidens* (Edinburgh, UK: Luath Press, 2003), 81.

158   Ibid., 82.

159   Geoffrey of Monmouth, *Life of Merlin. Vita Merlini*, ed. Basil Clarke (Cardiff, UK: University of Wales Press, 1973), 207.

160   McHardy, *Quest*, 83.

Gliten, Glitonea, Gliton

McHardy links these three together as resonances of forms of the name Cliodhna: Clindna, Cliodhna, Cliodna. In Irish lore, Cliodhna is a powerful banshee associated with County Cork, who is also known as the Queen of the Munster Fairies. She features in several stories. In one of them, she is one of the three daughters of Manannán mac Lir's chief Druid and is said to dwell in *Tir Tairngire*, the Land of Promise. In another, she is described as being the most beautiful and most noble woman in the world. She possesses three birds that eat the fruit of an Otherworldly apple tree; their song has the power to heal the sick by lulling them into a restorative sleep.[161]

Cliodhna has many associations with water, several of which involve her drowning. When she follows her lover Ciabhán to Ireland, she is overtaken by a wave that drowns her while she is sleeping.[162] According to the early Irish text *Acallamh na Senovah*, every ninth wave is named Cliodhna's Wave and is said to be the strongest.[163] In Irish and Welsh traditions, it is necessary to pass over the ninth wave in order to enter the Otherworld; everything beyond this wave is unknown territory, and therefore is considered to be Other. A connection with waves can be found in a few other Ninefold Sisterhood groups: the Nine Daughters of Ran and the Nine Maidens of the Mill, both from Norse tradition, as well as the Irish story of Ruad and the Nine Sea Maidens (chapter 3). Cliodhna's Wave holds resonance with the Nine Waves of the Welsh mermaid Gwenhidwy; as with Cliodhna, Gwenhidwy's ninth wave is the strongest but is considered the ram among the eight ewes of the mermaid's sheep-like waves (chapter 1).

---

161 MacKillop, "Cliodhna," in *Dictionary of Celtic Mythology*, 80–81.

162 Ibid., 80.

163 McHardy, *Quest*, 83.

Tyronoe

Watery connections continue as Tyronoe may derive from the Greek mythological figure Tyro, princess of Thessaly.[164] In *The Odyssey*, Homer relays how Tyro fell in love with the river god, Enipeus. However, Poseidon desired her and took the form of Enipeus to lay with her. "And the dark wave stood about them like a mountain, vaulted-over, and hid the god and the mortal woman. And he loosed her maiden girdle, and shed sleep upon her."[165] Tyro bore twin sons to Poseidon, Pelias and Neleus. Interestingly, Pelias was the father of Nine Daughters, known collectively as the Peliades. He died at their hands when Medea convinced them that cutting him up and placing him in her pot to boil would cause him to be rejuvenated and emerge young and strong. Tyrone is also an Irish place name, but any connection between it and Tyronoe, Sister of Avalon, is unclear.

Thitis, Thiten, and Thiton

There's a bit of confusion concerning the names of Thiten and Thiton. Depending on the source, there are two sisters named Thiten, two sisters named Thitis, or one named Thiten and the other Thiton. It is unclear if Geoffrey intended for their names to be doublets or a scribal error was introduced somewhere along the way that has been preserved into the present. Whatever the case may be, the last sister is distinguished from her namesake by her musical gifts.

In Greek mythology, Thetis is a primordial goddess of the ocean who, in later tales, is said to be a nereid—a sea nymph—who becomes mother of the hero, Achilles. Another Greek water deity with a similar

---

164 McHardy, *Quest*, 84.

165 Homer, *The Odyssey, with an English Translation by A.T. Murray, PH.D. in Two Volumes*, trans. A. T. Murray (Cambridge, MA: Harvard University Press, 1919), http://data.perseus.org/citations/urn:cts:greekLit:tlg0012.tlg002.perseus-eng1:11.

name is Tethys, a titan.[166] The daughter of Uranus and Gaia, Tethys was the wife of Oceanus and mother of three thousand Potamoi (river gods) and three thousand Oceanids—nymphs who are usually (but not always) associated with water.

Potential Divinities?

So where does this leave us? Aside from Morgen, whom we will consider in detail shortly, we have very little information about the nature and identities of the Nine Sisters of Avalon. As we have seen, the etymological origins of their names are unclear, a fact that may simply reinforce the theory that their names originated in Geoffrey of Monmouth's imagination. However, if we soften our gaze somewhat as we look at their names, we can detect some tenuous connections to water deities from Greek myths, as well as a few potential resonances with a Scottish holy woman and a few Irish goddesses or Fairy Queens—again, having some watery associations.

Over the years, scholars have had various theories concerning the origins of the sisters' names. Medievalist Lucy Allen Paton embraces the notion that they were completely made up.

> The necessity of naming her eight sisters is apparently embarrassing to the poet; he economizes by ringing three changes on one name—and his ingenuity deserts him completely before he reaches the eighth. Where he found these names has never been determined.[167]

Folklore researcher Sarah Allison has posited that the internal similarities of their names may suggest they were once a set of three Triple

---

166 McHardy, *Quest*, 84.

167 Lucy Allen Paton, *Studies in the Fairy Mythology of Arthurian Romance* (Boston: The Athenaeum Press, 1903), 44.

Goddesses, composed of Morgen/Moronoe/Mazoe, Gliten/Glitonea/Gliton, and Tyronoe/Thitis/Thitis.[168] While there's nothing that directly supports this theory, there are instances where all three aspects of triune divinities in Celtic lands have the same name. In Gaul, for example, there are inscriptions to the deity Lugus in his triple form, and his name is simply made plural: Lugoves. This may have been intended to illustrate the potency of the divinity through the power of the sacred three. While the three goddesses collectively called the Morrigàn in Irish tradition all have different names (and show up in different stories as being composed of different sets of three deities), the three aspects of the goddess Brigid are all called Brigid, albeit with different epithets.

There are no direct examples of Triple Goddesses that have survived in extant Welsh lore, but there are a few hints that suggest this may not have always been the case. For example, Triad 56 speaks of Arthur's three wives:

ARTHUR'S THREE GREAT QUEENS:
  + Gwenhwyfar, daughter of (Cywryd) Gwent;
  + Gwenhwyfar, daughter of (Gwythyr) son of Greidiawl; and
  + Gwenhwyfar, daughter of (G)ogfran the Giant.[169]

One gloss of Gwenhwyfar's name renders its meaning as "White Phantom"; Welsh name elements meaning "white/shining/holy" (like the suffix -wen, and the prefix gwen-) are often associated with characters who had once been divine. It is also possible that Gwenhwyfar's involvement in various love triangles and abduction stories suggests that she may once have been a seasonal Sovereignty Goddess—and, perhaps, as

---

168 Sarah Allison, "Morgan Le Fay and Her Sisters," Writing in Margins website, January 18, 2021, https://writinginmargins.weebly.com/home/morgan-le-fay-and-her-sisters.

169 Bromwich, Trioedd Ynys Prydein, 161.

Triad 56 may allude—a Triple Goddess as well. Another "hidden" Triple Goddess can be discerned in the figure of Modron, discussed here.

Another theory proposed by author August Hunt posits that Geoffrey of Monmouth drew upon Irish tradition for the names of the Nine Sisters, and that they appear in the *Vita Merlini* as corrupted versions of the names of Irish divinities. Hunt makes the following identifications:

+ *Morgen* is the Morrígan, triple Sovereignty Goddess.

+ *Morone* is Muirne or Muireann, mother of Fionn mac Cumhail.

+ *Mazoe* is Macha, one of the Goddesses that comprise the Morrígan.

+ *Gliten*, *Glitonea*, and *Gliton* are Clidna in triple form, as McHardy also theorized (see above).

+ *Tyronoe* is Tuireann/Uirne, who is the sister of Muirne, and aunt of Fionn mac Cumhail.

+ *Thiten* and *Thiten* of the lyre are Etain Echrade (Etain the Horse Rider), doubled.[170]

In my opinion, there is no clear reason why Geoffrey would have drawn inspiration for these figures from disparate Irish myths rather than from his native Welsh tradition, although Clarke does concede that there is some possibility that Geoffrey could have been exposed to Irish materials given the old connections between Ireland and Llandaff in south Wales, where Geoffrey may have been based for some of his life.[171] Be that as it may, if the names as they appear in the *Vita Merlini* do represent genuine oral tradition, I was unable to find any sources that illustrate clear linguistic bridges between Middle Irish and Latin

---

170   August Hunt, *The Mysteries of Avalon: A Primer on Arthurian Druidism* (CreateSpace Independent Publishing Platform, 2012), 32.

171   Clarke, *Vita Merlini*, 208.

(the language in which Geoffrey was writing) that would account for the forms of these names as he recorded them.

All of this said, I find the idea that the names of the Nine Sisters of Avalon suggestive of an underlying theme that connects them to water is worthy of note, especially as we turn now to consider Morgen herself.

Morgan le Fay

It cannot be a coincidence that the Sister of Avalon connected to the most lore is also the one whom Geoffrey took pains to designate as being first among her sisters. Of course we are speaking about Morgen—who will eventually become known as Morgan le Fay. She is the most gifted in herbs and healing, the one who instructed her sisters in mathematics, the most beautiful, and the most learned. This is not unusual; often when companies of nine appear in early legends from Celtic lands, they tend to comprise a leader and their eight attendants, with only the central figure named. It is therefore possible that Geoffrey took Morgen directly from preexisting lore, which, by convention, may have named her but not her eight sisters. This could potentially explain the lack of clear derivation for the names of Morgen's sisters: because native Welsh sources didn't provide for them, Geoffrey was in a position where he needed to make them up. While this theory doesn't clarify the difficulties with name etymology, it does lend support to the possibility that Avalon, and the Nine Sisters who rule there, derive from older tradition.

Morgen's first literary appearance is in the *Vita Merlini*. There, Geoffrey uses the Old Welsh spelling of her name, Morgen, derived from the Common Brittonic name *Mori-genā*, meaning "sea born." In modern Welsh, the name Morgan is masculine and thought to derive from the Old Welsh name *Morcant* ("sea circle"), rather than from *Mori-genos* (the masculine form of *Mori-genā*) that instead gave rise to the Middle Welsh names Morien and Moryen.

Since the etymology of her name is so well attested, it allows us to see that Morgen's strong association with water is very long-standing, giving additional support to the idea that her sisters' names are purposefully suggestive of water deities or spirits. This watery affiliation is further emphasized by the fact that she shares a name with a class of water spirits from Welsh, Cornish, and Breton lore called Morgens or Mari-Morgens. Add to this the description of her powers of healing, shapeshifting, and flight, and it is plain to see that Morgen is no ordinary mortal woman.

Tracing Tradition

Perhaps there is no clearer example of the way in which legends evolve as a reflection of shifts in cultural mores than Morgan le Fay, whose characterization changes greatly over the span of close to a thousand years' worth of tales in which she features. A brief examination of her evolution is useful not only for gathering information that suggests her true nature and identity but also helps us gain an understanding of the ways in which sociocultural perspectives on women's status, power, and sexuality—as well as those concerning the belief in and practice of magic—shifted over time.

When taken as a whole, Morgan's characterization over the centuries-long span of Arthurian Tradition is at odds with itself. Although she starts her literary journey as a learned healer and powerful Otherworldly woman—sometimes called a goddess, a nymph, a fairy, or a Fate—over time, she gradually becomes more human. Her magic shifts from something originating from her personal nature to something that can be learned, often reportedly deriving its power from connections with dark forces. Over time, her magic starts to be depicted like that of an enchantress or an increasingly dark sorceress. She is said to have become a great clerk of necromancy during her education in a nunnery, a detail eventually added to her backstory that may serve as a narrative echo of her original cloistered home with her sisters on the Holy Isle.

Similarly, Morgan shifts from being a benevolent ally to Arthur and his knights, to one of Camelot's greatest enemies. She is increasingly motivated by jealousy, invested in vengeance, and fueled by her hatred for Queen Guinevere. She will stop at nothing to bring down Arthur and his court, and uses her dark magics to set traps, seduce questing knights, take captives, and attempt to murder her enemies. She is said to dwell in a variety of strongholds, sometimes living with other sorceresses who share her desire for power and match her legendarily robust libido. Eventually, she seems to lose all sense of her former self—at best, becoming a scapegoat for the evils of women's sexual freedom and the use of demonic magic, and at worst devolving into a two-dimensional literary trope and convenient villain.

For the most part, Morgan remained in this degraded form into modern times, until—with Malory's *Le Morte D'Arthur* serving as a primary influence—a resurgence of interest in the Matter of Britain during the Victorian period influenced a new era of Arthurian writing, art, and theater extending into the present day. Morgan was the subject of paintings by Pre-Raphaelite artists and included in poetic works by Alfred, Lord Tennyson, and novels by authors such as Marion Zimmer Bradley (*The Mists of Avalon*) and Fay Sampson (*Daughter of Tintagel/ Morgan le Fay* series). She also featured prominently in films such as John Boorman's *Excalibur* (1981), as well as in television series, such as the BBC's *Merlin* (2008) and Starz's *Camelot* (2011).

Her characterization varies in these retellings and revisionings. She sometimes remains an antagonist, but some of the most engaging stories reclaim her earliest literary attributes; in these, she is often depicted as a priestess, a powerful healer, and a supernatural being. Even when she is still the foe of Camelot, modern stories tend to delve more deeply into her perspectives and motivations, making her a more sympathetic character, rather than a stock villain.

But perhaps the most powerful reclamation of Morgan le Fay is to be found in today's Neopagan movement. Although varying from practitioner to practitioner, and from tradition to tradition, Morgan is viewed by many as a deity or a powerful Fairy Queen. She is appealed to as a patron of Witches, a paragon priestess of the Old Religion, and an iconic mistress of the magical arts. Some honor her as the Goddess of Avalon, the Divine Queen of the Summerland where the souls of the dead rest, and a chthonic divinity of death and the Otherworld.

While there is no question of her current divine status, thanks in no small part to the power of apotheosis, was Morgan le Fay a goddess in pre-Christian Celtic tradition? To answer this question, we must return to the place where we first found her—with her Sisters on Avalon—to trace her Stream of Tradition back to its source. And because this Stream of Tradition is both long and wide, we will focus on one particular current for the sake of this discussion: Morgan's relationship with Avalon and the realms of water.

Goddesses, Fairies, and Saints

It is the nature of tales transmitted through oral tradition to mirror the cultural changes of the people who remember and share them. Because of this, it is not unusual to see figures who had once been divinities gradually shift to become reduced in status—often becoming fairy women or saints with the coming of Christianity. While we do not have any direct evidence that attests to Morgan's divinity in the pre-Christian period, there are some historical texts written in the medieval period that identify her in this way.

In *Speculum Ecclesiae*, II.9, (c. 1216) Gerald of Wales claimed that the bards considered Morganis, who bore Arthur to Avalon, a fairy goddess (*dea quaedam phantastica*). A Welsh manuscript from c. 1400 (Llanstephan MS.4, fo.507r) gives a similar account:

"The bards of Ynys Prydein and its storytellers used to imagine that it was Margan dwywes o Annwfyn ['Margan a goddess of Annwn'] that had hidden him [Arthur] in Ynys Afallach to heal him of his wounds."[172]

Morgan is also called a goddess in the late fourteenth-century Middle English poem "Sir Gawain and the Green Knight." At the end of the tale, it is revealed that in the guise of an old woman, she used her powerful magics to set up the challenges encountered by Gawain as a way to test his worth—a role she often plays in later Arthurian tales and an echo of the functions of the Sovereignty Goddess. Morgan's famed epithet, le Fay—from Old French meaning "the fairy," or Latin, meaning "the Fate"—is likely a reflection of the process known by mythologists and folklorists as reverse euhemerization. While we first see her name given as Morgan le Fay in the French Arthurian Romances known as the Vulgate Cycle (from c. 1215), she received similar appellations in other literary traditions as well.

Morgan and the Morrígan

There is a common misconception, primarily due to the perceived similarities between their names, that Morgan le Fay is the British iteration of the Morrígan, the Irish goddess of battle and Sovereignty. However, this is not possible linguistically as the etymologies of their names are quite different. As we have already seen, the name Morgen derives from the Common Brittonic word *Mori-genā—"sea born." In contrast, one gloss for the Morrígan derives her name from *Rīgantona, a reconstructed Gallo-Brittonic deity name that means "Divine" or "Great Queen." The Welsh reflex for *Rīgantona is Rhiannon, who is— like the Morrígan—a goddess of Sovereignty. An alternative meaning

---

172 Timothy Lewis and J. Douglas Bruce, trans., "The Pretended Exhumation of Arthur and Guinevere: An Unpublished Welsh Account Based on Giraldus Cambrensis" *Review Celtique* 33 (1912): 423–451, https://archive.org/details /revueceltique33pari/page/432/mode/2up.

of the Morrígan's name is "Phantom Queen," deriving from the reconstructed Proto-Celtic name *Moro-rīganī-s, where the *mor* derives from the Indo-European root word for "terror," or "monstrousness."[173]

On the other hand, the Old Irish cognate of *Mori-genā is the name Muirgein. There is an Irish tale—a version of which appears in *Lebor na hUidri* or *The Book of the Dun Cow*—that tells how the overflow of a sacred well caused an inundation that created a lake called Loch Eathach. A woman named Liban survived the flood that killed her family, and lived in a palace under the lake for a year before becoming a mermaid who was half salmon and half woman. She was caught in a net three hundred years later, and when she converted to Christianity, she was given the name Muirgein. She later became a Christian saint, whose feast day is January 27.[174]

Morgan and Modron

There is, however, another Goddess with whom Morgan becomes associated. The sixteenth-century manuscript Peniarth Ms. 147 recounts a story about Urien, the historical sixth-century ruler of the Brythonic Kingdom of Rheged in *Yr Hen Ogledd* ("The Old North"). In Llanferres, in the northeast of Wales, is a place called the Ford of the Barking where all of the dogs in countryside would gather on the side of the river ford to howl and bark. They sound they made was so terrifying that no one was brave enough to investigate—except Urien Rheged.

He followed the sound to the ford where he saw a woman washing in the water. Immediately, the dogs fell silent and Urien took hold of the

---

173 "English–Proto-Celtic Wordlist" (University of Wales), accessed March 4, 2022, https://www.wales.ac.uk/Resources/Documents/Research/CelticLanguages /EnglishProtoCelticWordList.pdf.

174 Standish H. O'Grady, ed., *Silva Gadelica: (I–XXXI.) A Collection of Tales in Irish with Extracts Illustrating Persons and Places. Edited from MSS. and Translated by Standish II. O'Grady. Irish Text, (Translation and Notes.)* (London: Williams, 1892), 266–269.

woman and "had his will of her." Asking for God's blessing upon him, she revealed to Urien that she was the daughter of the King of Annwn and had been fated to wash at the ford until she conceived a son by a Christian man. She directed him to return to the ford in a year to receive his son. When he did, he found that she had born him a daughter as well: the twins Owein and Morfudd.[175]

As the daughter of the King of Annwn, the woman identifies herself as an Otherworldly figure, but does not give her name nor that of her father. However, more information is to be had from Triad 70 of *Trioedd Ynys Prydein*—a much earlier source—listing the Three Fair Womb-Burdens of the Island of Britain; the second of which is: "Owain, son of Urien and Morfudd his sister who were carried together in the womb of Modron, daughter of Afallach."[176]

Taken together, it is clear that the woman in the river is Modron and that she is the daughter of Afallach, the King of Annwn. As we have already discussed in chapter 1, there is longstanding medieval tradition that makes an etymological connection between Avalon and Ynys Afallach (the Island of Afallach), named for an Otherworldly figure who was its king. In some lore Afallach lives on the island with daughters, while in other traditions he is named as the son or grandson of Beli Mawr, a Welsh solar divinity, and Dôn, an ancestral goddess. Dôn is the matriarch of a lineage of important Brythonic divinities known collectively as *Plant Dôn*, the Children of Dôn. Among her children are Arianrhod, Gwydion, Gilfaethwy, Govannon, and Amaethon.

Modron therefore has a respectable divine lineage within the context of Welsh tradition proper; it was not uncommon for noble families to trace their bloodline back to important figures from local folk tradition, classical mythos, and the Bible. As mother of the hero Owain, Modron provides the royal house of Rheged with a respectable lineage. But the

---

175 Bromwich, *Trioedd Ynys Prydein*, 449.
176 Ibid, 449.

story of the encounter between Urien and Modron suggests that even more is going on than this.

The motif of the Washer at the Ford is found in Irish and Scottish tradition where it is a death omen for whomever has the misfortune to encounter an Otherworldly woman washing bloodied clothing in a river. Babd, one of the aspects of the Mórrigan, is especially connected to this motif. In the story of Modron, however, the encounter at the ford leads to the lifting of a destiny rather than the foretelling of one, and it has a great deal in common with stories of Sovereignty Goddesses, themselves often associated with rivers or other bodies of water.

That her union with Urien is likely a mythic memory of a Sovereignty rite is underscored by Modron's connection to the Gaulish goddess Matrona; the two divinities are said to be cognate, because their names have the same meaning: "Divine Mother." Matrona is the tutelary goddess of the Marne river in Gaul—a river the Romans called "Matrona." Modern scholars believe that Matrona is connected to the widespread worship of the Matronae or Matres, that she is a singular form of the Triple Divine Mother. As such, Modron's connection to Matrona—and therefore the Matronae—may make her a "stealth" Brythonic Triple Goddess, as mentioned in connection with Gwenhwyfar above.

We don't know very much about Matrona; her myths are lost to us. As the personification of the longest river in France, it is very likely that she was a major tutelary figure and therefore a Sovereignty Goddess as well. We do know with some certainty that Matrona is the mother of Maponos, the Gaulish god whose name means "Divine Son." Maponos was widely worshipped in Gaul and into Britain, and was often syncretized with the god Apollo during the Gallo-Roman period. We believe that Roman legionaries from Gaul who were garrisoned along Hadrian's Wall in Britain—the area directly north of the Kingdom of Rheged—brought the worship of Maponos and Matrona with them from the continent. It is along this area of Hadrian's Wall—the northernmost border of the Roman Empire—that we find the highest concentration of artifactual evidence of cult activity dedicated to Maponos and Matrona in Britain.

Just as the Gallo-Roman Matrona became the Welsh Modron, "Divine Mother," so did her son Maponos become the Welsh Mabon, "Divine Son." It is likely that worship of this sacred dyad entered into Brythonic tradition from the region of the Old North, although it is possible that these divinities may have already been worshipped by the Celtic tribes in the area, and we only start to see evidence of this worship during the Roman occupation because the Celts didn't create dedicatory altars or inscriptions in the pre-Roman period.

Triad 70 states that the son of Modron and Urien is Owain. While it is possible that Mabon is Modron's son by a different father, it is interesting to consider that a potential etymological root for the name Owain is the Welsh word *eoghunn*, "youth." Further, the historic Taliesin is believed to have served as a bard in the court of Urien; as such, the bard wrote praise-poems in honor of Urien and Owain, who ruled Rheged after his father's death. Scholar Rachel Bromwich has suggested that the name Mabon is used as a pseudonym for Owain in some of the praise poetry in *Llyfr Taliesin*. In a sense, the historical Owain is functioning as an avatar of the Divine Youth, to whom he can trace his family's lineage.

Given all this context, there is one last piece to put into place when it comes to Modron. We have already shown her to possess a powerful divine heritage, connecting her both to the Gaulish goddess Matrona and to Afallach, a King of Annwn, said to dwell on Ynys Afallach—the Island of Avalon—with his daughters. As mentioned in chapter 1, it is not unusual for figures from Brythonic mythos to make their way into the tales of Arthurian Tradition; Modron and her family are no exception. Afallach may have become King Evalach, and Mabon is likely the figure behind such characters as Mabuz and Mabonagrain.

Although they may have had real-world counterparts, Urien and Owain also become absorbed into Arthurian Tradition, placing them in a squarely pseudohistorical context. Owain becomes one of the greatest Arthurian heroes, featuring in two different versions of the same romance: *Owain, or the Lady of the Fountain* from Wales, and *Yvain, the Knight of the Lion* from France. Urien or Uriens enters Arthurian Tradition as father of Owain and king of a fictional northern kingdom called Gore. He is often depicted as being wed to the sister of Arthur, and together they are the parents of twins: Owain and Morfydd. The name of Arthur's sister? Morgan le Fay.

The degree to which Morgan almost completely assumes Modron's identity is uncanny; they have the same husband and the same children. It's unclear exactly why this may have occurred—aside from the phenomenon we've already discussed that sees Welsh deities and figures from early Welsh literature that became absorbed in the Arthurian legends—but there are many similarities between the two. They each have deep associations with water, possess strong Otherworldly connections, and—as is often the case where these two characteristics occur together—both women exhibit functions associated with the Sovereignty Goddess motif. It is this association with Sovereignty that, more than anything else, indirectly connects Morgan (and Modron) with the Mórrigan. They did not evolve out of each other, nor do they appear to have a common origin other than fulfilling related functions in their respective cultures.

Perhaps the strongest link that connects Modron and Morgan is their shared relationship to Avalon. Morgan's connection with Avalon predates that of Modron (given our extant sources) and is rooted to her identity as one of the Nine Sisters who rule the island. In contrast, Modron's connection to Avalon is both through her father's identity as the king of Annwn and the identification of his namesake Ynys Afallach as an Otherworldly island. At its core, the connection of both women to an Island of Apples in the Otherworld may just be mythological short-hand for "Pay attention: these magical women were once goddesses."

As Morgen, first among the Nine Sisters who corule the Other-worldly Island of Avalon, Morgan's divinity appears to be independent of her connection to Modron; the latter's claim to divinity is directly stated in her name ("Divine Mother"). However, the confluence of Morgan's Stream of Tradition with that of Modron may serve to rein-force the truth of her original status. Morgan bears all of the hallmarks of a reverse euhemerized water divinity who is reduced in status first to a fairy woman, and later to an all-too-human enchantress.

Morgan, Morgens, and Mari-Morgens

With the coming of Christianity to Britain, the water deities who sur-vived the shifting belief systems did so by evolving into a new form. Some goddesses were recast as Christian saints, complete with hagi-ographies that sometimes included elements of the former divinities' myths. Their holy wells and sacred springs were reconsecrated in their sainted names, and the sometimes-complex process by which pilgrims made petitions for healing—such as circumambulating the well head in a clockwise fashion on the saint's holy day while reciting a set num-ber of prayers—at the very least reflects a pervasive type of folk magic that may have origins in pre-Christian beliefs. Some of these ritual pe-titions seem to have only marginally been changed, swapping out some words to make Christian prayers out of more earthy invocations. For example, Modron's Stream of Tradition seems to have bifurcated—part of it flowing into sainthood in the forms of St. Materiana and St. Madrun (whose Holy Well in Cornwall has a testing aspect…a con-tinuation, perhaps, of her Sovereignty aspect), and part of it entering into the fairy realms with Morgan.

Some deities did not become saints and instead maintained a por-tion of their Otherworldly powers while also becoming demoted in status over time. They eventually became water spirits or magical creatures such as nymphs and fairies, guises in which they were able to endure alongside Christian beliefs. For example, the goddess Sabrina of the River Severn (*Afon Hafren*)—the longest river in Britain—is remembered in folklore as a beautiful nymph who was known to assist the poor and heal sick animals who grazed along her shores.

Within the context of these traditions also arose entire groupings of water fay that may hold echoes of particular kinds of local tutelary divinities. Examples of these include the Welsh and Breton water spirits called Morgens or *Mari-Morgens* ("Sea-Morgens"), and the *Gwragedd Annwn* ("Women/Wives of the Otherworld"), who became the Lake Maidens of Wales. There are several Welsh folktales about Lake Maidens who emerge from their homes beneath the waters of sacred lakes to become the Fairy Brides of mortal men and raise families with them.

Unlike the Gwragedd Annwn, who were known for their benevolent natures, most folklore depicts the Morgens and the Mari-Morgens as having more in common with their mermaid cousins who lure unsuspecting men to their deaths. In one Breton tradition, there is a Morgen who is said to live beneath the sea in an opulent palace, eternally young and virginal. Possessing unsurpassed beauty, she would rise to the surface of the water accompanied by other fairies who served her as their queen, to comb her long shimmering hair in the moonlight. As she did so, she sang a song so irresistible that any sailor who heard it would be ensnared in her charm and unable to break free, even as his own boat was dashed to pieces on the reefs that surround her. Once he was in the water, she joyfully took him in her arms, but at her touch, he would die. This was the source of her longing and her virginal nature, for her sexual desires could never be satisfied—every potential lover died in her embrace.[177]

---

177 W. Y. Evans-Wentz, *The Fairy-Faith in Celtic Countries* (London: H. Froude, 1911), 200–201.

A different Breton legend attributes the origin of this Morgen to the inundation of Ys, the lost city ruled by the legendary King Gradlon. There are several versions of this story. In some, Gradlon's daughter, the princess Dahut falls in love with an evil man, later revealed to be the devil, who convinces her to steal a key from around the neck of her father as he sleeps. Placed under a spell, she believes she is unlocking the gates of the city to let her lover in, but in actuality she has used it to open the floodgates that kept the city safe from the sea, and the waves crash in to destroy everything.[178] In other versions, Dahut rejects warnings against her nightly revelries and Pagan rituals, causing her city to be destroyed as a punishment.[179]

As the calamity unfolds, King Gradlon is awakened by a saint (different names are given in different versions of the tale) in time for them to mount the king's horse and make their escape. They pass Dahut as they ride, and at her pleading, her father lifts her onto his horse, but as the waters threaten to overtake them, the saint tells Gradlon that he must throw off his betrayer lest they all drown, and the king does so. The king and the saint survive, but Dahut has been transformed into the Mari-Morgen whom fishermen catch a glimpse of as she combs her hair and sings her plaintive song while sitting on the rocks where her father cast her away.[180]

Folklore from the Breton Île d'Ouessant (Ushant Island) presents a gentler version of the Morgen; in fact, there are many Morgens or Morganezed, composing a race of water fairies who live in palaces beneath the sea. Male and female both, they dwelt in harmony with the humans of the isle and were even known to fall in love with them; they could marry and have children together, and the humans were able to join with them to live beneath the waves.[181]

---

178 Evans-Wentz, *Fairy-Faith*, 201.

179 MacKillop, "Dahut," in *A Dictionary of Celtic Mythology*, 112.

180 Evans-Wentz, *Fairy-Faith*, 202.

181 Ibid., 200.

Magical Women

Sometimes these figures continued to evolve. After shifting from the deities of myth to the fairies of folklore, they often entered the realm of legend as mortal queens and courtly ladies. Sometimes these women possessed magical items, like Rhiannon's bag that could never be filled, or the Cauldron of Regeneration that accompanied Branwen to Ireland when she wed its king. In other tales, noblewomen who are the literary descendants of these more ancient lineages were themselves learned in the arts of magic. This is Morgan as clerk of necromancy, the mystical seductress, the fearsome enchantress whose powers derived not from her own divine essence or from her connection to nature, but from contracts with demons.

In a shift that moved these figures further away from their original (perhaps divine) natures, the tales in which they are featured began to reflect the later medieval belief that magic was something that could be taught or obtained through study; one did not need to possess any inherent power to be able to wield it. In some tales, Morgan learned her magic from Merlin, Arthur's famous advisor. In others, Merlin's female protégé is called Nimue, who becomes the chief Lady of the Lake—another reference, perhaps, to a former fay or divine form.

The Lady of the Lake

The Arthurian figure of the Lady of the Lake—in French, *La Dame du Lac*; in Welsh, *Arglwyddes y Llyn*—is the result of the confluence of several interrelated streams of tradition. Both as a title and several individuals bearing that title, she may have originated as a water deity—a divine embodiment of a sacred lake in the same way that Matrona and Modron were river goddesses. Other, similarly titled figures in Arthurian lore—such as the Lady of the Fountain from *Yvain*, and the Fairy Queen who fostered Lancelot also called the Lady of the Sea—may likewise have divine origins.

There are several women who are called the Lady of the Lake in Arthurian Tradition, and it appears to be a title passed from one woman to another upon her death. Nimue takes over as chief Lady of the Lake (a designation that seems to imply there are multiple Ladies of the Lake, ruled by one who is first among them—not unlike Geoffery's account of Morgen and her sisters) when her unnamed predecessor is killed in an act of vengeance by the knight Balin—who believed her to be responsible for the death of his mother—in Arthur's court. The murdered Lady is the one who gifted Arthur with Excalibur, when Merlin rowed him out to meet her in the middle of her lake.

Nimue is probably the best known of the Arthurian Ladies of the Lake; she enters Arthurian Legend through the French romances, drawing upon both Breton and Norman traditions. Nimue's connection to divinity is stated outright rather than hidden (as became the case with Morgan); some scholars have theorized that the name "Nimue" and its various iterations may have originally derived from that of the goddess Diana, with whom she shares many associations. Nimue appears alongside animals connected with the virgin goddess of the Hunt (such as harts and hounds), and she is literally stated to be a descendant of Diana in the Vulgate Cycle (an early thirteenth-century group of Arthurian prose stories written in French that is also known as the Lancelot-Grail Cycle), and she is shown dressed as a huntress in the *Suite du Merlin*.

Nimue is believed to be the Dame du Lac who fostered Lancelot as a child, bringing the orphaned son of King Ban to live with her in her home on the banks of *Lac Diane* ("Lake of Diana") in Brittany's enchanted Brocéliande Forest. In the Vulgate Cycle, Brocéliande is where Morgan le Fay used her magic to create the *Val sans Retour* ("the Vale of No Return"). But the forest is probably most famous as the place where Viviane was said to entrap Merlin beneath a stone.

In the early twelfth-century German verse-story *Lanzelet*, written by Ulrich von Zatzikhoven, it is the Lady of the Sea who fosters Lanzelet and brings him to live with her in the Land of Maidens. In addition to fostering Lanzelet, the Lady has a son named Mabuz, cognate to Mabon; this naming suggests that the Lady of the Sea is somehow connected with Morgen and Modron—and the Land of Maidens, to Avalon.

In *Le Morte D'Arthur*, Thomas Malory alludes to a hierarchal governance of the mystic Land of Women ruled over by the Chief Lady of the Lake—a place of women's magic. Known to visit Arthur's court as an ally and advisor to the king, many of the Lady of the Lake's exchanges with Arthur are challenges to uphold the balance between the ruler and the ruled. She is also a prime force in gently guiding Arthur and his court to remember their chivalric obligations to women.

Similarly, many of the quests the knights of Arthur's court embarked upon were catalyzed by mysterious women, and often included opportunities for these knights to demonstrate their commitment to the protection of women's lives as well as to their sovereignty of will. The knights did not always succeed.

While many modern retellings of the Matter of Britain often conflate Morgan le Fay with the Lady of the Lake, they are clearly separate characters in the medieval tales. At this point in the development of Arthurian legend, Morgan le Fay is no longer the semidivine benefactor of the king but instead his fully human, magic-wielding half sister. In this guise, Morgan also challenges the imbalances between men and women under the code of chivalry but does so from outside the system. Morgan blatantly refuses to tolerate chivalric standards for women and dedicates a great deal of her time and magic to actively working to bring the whole system down. In contrast, Nimue, as chief Lady of the Lake, uses her position as a trusted royal advisor to try to shift the system from within.

Indeed, in many tales, Morgan and Nimue are often at odds with each other, appearing to represent two sides of the same magic. One a benevolent and nurturing ally who uses her powers to support her chosen king, the other a malevolent and destructive enemy who uses her powers in a bid to overthrow the king she (for various reasons) finds lacking. There is a strong resonance of the Sovereignty motif at play here but instead of there being one figure with two attributes, both aspects of Sovereignty are embodied by different magical women.

When we consider the evolution of Avalon over the centuries, we see that while the fundamental purpose of Avalon remains constant, the Sisterhood who ruled the Holy Isle at its beginning have faded to mere shadows until the modern era. Of the Nine, only Morgan continues forward in the narrative tradition, although the idea of Avalon as a community of magical women persists in the background.

Eventually, even Morgan herself becomes uprooted entirely from her rule and home on Avalon, instead living in various castles in the wilderness or the aforementioned Valley of No Return—fully outside of the regular order of things. And yet, in the end, she is always one of the Barge Queens conducting the mortally wounded Arthur to the Apple Isle.

It is only in the last few decades that interest in the Nine Sisters of Avalon has caused them to re-emerge from the mists in a variety of forms. For me, they are the Sea Born, holy ancestresses arising from the waters of the collective unconscious, where they have been awaiting our need. And so, we come full circle as we once again seek the healing of Avalon through the wholeness of the Nine.

TO BE IN SERVICE

Thus far, we have spent a lot of time examining the roles of holy and Otherworldly women in the history and lore of Celtic lands: goddesses, priestesses, fairies, and literary iterations of the Sovereignty motif with roots in pre-Christian notions of being in right relationship with the goddess of the land. So what does all of this tell us? While we know very little about any formal Celtic priestesshoods, we can obtain some insight into what their roles many have been from the glimpses preserved in history and lore. These come to us both from accounts of cloistered groups of holy women, as well as those about individual women serving as seers, priestess-queens, and Druidesses.

Gathering the Threads

Pieced together from history, lore, and legend, here are some of the general characteristics commonly exhibited by many of these holy or Otherworldly women:

1. They often dwelt apart from society—living on islands, in towers, in remote parts of forests, on the other side of forbidden

hedges, and in sacred enclosures with well-defined boundaries. These separations have multiple purposes:

- They indicate that the holy women live in sacred spaces, beyond the authority or influence of the mundane world; they are wholly dedicated to their service to the Divine.

- They signal that the holy women dwell in neutral spaces outside of regional or tribal boundaries, placing them beyond personal allegiances so that they can be in service to everyone equally.

- When used as a literary device, the separation signals to the audience that these women are "other," which explains why their powers and privileges did not directly reflect the reality of women contemporary to the writing of the tale. This also permits their stories to be used as morality plays without encouraging regular women to make the same choices. These figures in stories could dare to use magic, for example, or be sexually liberated because they were already outside of the natural order of things.

2. They have clear connections to the Otherworld and are often depicted as dwelling in liminal spaces, near or under bodies of water, and on islands associated with eternal youth, endless joy, and inexhaustible abundance. These islands often feature apple trees, which have strong Otherworldly associations in Irish, Welsh, and Breton traditions; magical apple branches have been used to call adventurers to undertake a journey to the Otherworld.

3. They are depicted as being outside of the regular order of things; in addition to dwelling apart from the rest of society, they often do so on islands or in courts that are ruled over—and primarily, if not solely, inhabited—by women.

4. They are typically unmarried. In later accounts, their chastity reinforced their holiness and "purity"; however, some early accounts show them taking lovers at will, or traveling to the mainland to be with their "husbands" before returning to seclusion. The virginity of these women—when meant in the old way of being beholden to no one but themselves—underscores their independence from the limitations imposed upon women in their contemporary societies, and signifies the maintenance of their personal Sovereignty.

5. They often appear in groups or multiples of nine—a number associated with wholeness, a full set, and completion in Britain and in other Celtic lands.

6. They were highly skilled and possessed powers that were out of the ordinary. They were often depicted as learned women who were well educated in both the liberal and magical arts, and who served as teachers to the women in their closed communities. These abilities included the following:

  - They established fair laws over their own lands. They are shown as sisters who ruled collectively, or else as having a Lady of the Lake or a singular queen who presided over a kingdom of women.

  - They were famous for their healing powers, for the making of medicines, and as tenders of the dying.

  - They possessed the powers of prophecy or the Sight, and therefore served as oracles, seers, diviners, and performers of augury.

  - They were testers who assessed the worth of those they would reward, arbiters who ensured that oaths were kept and contracts fulfilled, and initiators who granted and rescinded Sovereignty.

- They sometimes performed political roles—acting as advisors to kings and chieftains, taking on the role of diplomats who negotiated treaties and mediated disputes in situations of conflict, and serving as Peace Weavers who bridged kingdoms and nations with their literal body through political marriages.

- They were said to be shapeshifters, possessing the power to change their appearance (as with a glamour), turn themselves into animals (especially birds, permitting them to fly wherever they willed), or transform into objects such as standing stones. This shape changing may also have been associated with ecstatic religious practices that induced trance states and allowed them to journey between the worlds.

- They were poets and musicians, banfhili and bards, and perhaps priestess-muses in service to the Cauldron of Annwn. In legends, their verses inspired heroes to undertake quests into the Otherworld, and they used their skills to obtain the prophetic poetry of divine inspiration.

- They are sometimes shown in service to a divinity—ensuring the maintenance of their temples or tending their sacred flames.

- They participated in battle—sometimes as warriors, sometimes as trainers of warriors or inciters of the warband, and sometimes acting to terrify the warriors of their enemies. They were challengers of injustice and protectors of women, especially within the courtly system.

- They had the power to calm the ocean and command the weather. They studied mathematics—which, in medieval context, likely refers to the study of astronomy and astrology.

✦ They are described as engaging in ecstatic rites, facilitating the offerings of pilgrims at shrines, and performing necessary sacrifices—even of one of their own, if required.

Reclaiming and Reweaving

With all of this in mind, how can what we know about the traits, abilities, and modes of service attributed to historical Celtic priestesses—as well as their analogs from legend and lore—be used to inform our practice and guide us on our own path of priestessing? While some of the powers detailed in these works are reflections of cultural perceptions of magic during the time they were written down, and some of the practices are difficult to adapt to the realities of the present day, there are still seeds of wisdom to be found within them. Let's take a look at some of the main characteristics ascribed to these holy women to explore their possible psycho-spiritual underpinnings while also considering practical applications for the practice of modern seekers.

Dwelling Apart

Living in a place or state of separation from the rest of the world is a common thread present in many examples of holy women that have come to us down the Stream of Tradition. While some of these women lived collectively on islands, others dwelt in communities deep in the forest or under a lake, protected by concealments. Still others formed community within enclosures defined by hedges and sacred precincts, or else dwelt in towers—inviolate and alone.

Certainly while many of us may find a deep and longing resonance with the idea of living in a cloistered spiritual community centered on the sacred in every aspect of our daily lives, it is a reality that is out of reach for most of us in this day and age. Aside from a few exceptions in some mainstream religions, there isn't the kind of social support for these types of communities that once existed, at least in the Western world. For example, today most Christian nuns are supported directly by their churches, while Buddhist nuns, like monks, continue to rely upon the support of their communities; Paganism is too small and too young of a movement to be able to do the same. However, this way of life doesn't necessarily have to be practiced literally.

There is beauty and power to be found when spending time in sacred community with those who share a spiritual tradition or practice with us. These gatherings can be temporary, like an evening ritual, an overnight celebration, or a weeklong devotional retreat. Or they can be long-term living arrangements like intentional communities, cohousing arrangements, or even communal living on sacred land. That said, not everyone has spiritual community close to them, and even fewer people have the means or desire to live in intentional communities.

Perhaps we can take a different approach to the idea of being cloistered. We can work to extract ourselves from the influence of the social and cultural currents that serve to sweep us up into collective conformity, and strive instead to consciously build and live a life reflective of our authentic selves. Perhaps we can build a life that is defined and shaped by what is sacred to us, while bringing an attitude of sacred service to everything we do. We can and should work to create and maintain good boundaries in our relationships, both with ourselves and others. And if we choose or must, we can keep our sacred service hidden from view so that our safe and holy haven—both within and around us—remains intact.

We can also consider those times in our lives when we find ourselves living alone or unpartnered, either by circumstance or choice, as opportunities for us to more deeply commit to our sacred work, more clearly reveal our sacred purpose, or more consciously engage in building a sacred and sovereign relationship with ourselves. Instead of empty spaces, we can see ourselves surrounded by opportunities for expansion. Instead of isolation, we can see ourselves learning to recognize the ways in which we are connected with the All.

It may be that part of the reason these priestesses lived separate from the people they served was to foster and maintain a sense of neutrality in their vocation. Celtic tribes were often at odds with each other; dwelling outside of these social and political dynamics and owing allegiance only to their gods meant these priestesses may have been considered more trustworthy in their work as oracles, advisors, and judges in service to everyone, regardless of tribal affiliation.

Similarly, we can strive to infuse our priestessing with a sense of selfless service. For example, we can commit to keeping ourselves and our personal biases out of situations we are asked to mediate, we can work diligently to remain clear and unattached to outcome when serving as an oracle or counselor, and we should continuously strive to achieve mastery of the self—clearing away our fears and illusions, recognizing when our ego becomes engaged, and working to be able to overcome the triggers that stimulate the compensatory reactions of our Shadow. This is the work of a lifetime, to be sure, but the more whole we become, the better we are able to serve others from the Vessel of the Self.

Purity and Virginity

Cloistered women's communities often include proscriptions about sexuality, with notions of virginity being connected to spiritual purity appearing to come to the fore in Celtic lands during the Christian period. This may not always have been the case, as we can see from Strabo's account of the Samnitae priestesses: no men were permitted on their island, but these holy women were known to sail to the mainland in order to have sex with men and then return alone. It is worth noting that in the same way no men were permitted on their island, none were allowed to cross the hedge defining Brigid's sacred precinct, so the ideas of seclusion and celibacy are not necessarily related.

It is unknown if the Samnitae priestesses are of a like order to the Gallizenae, who likewise lived on a secluded island off the coast of Brittany. According to Mela's account of them, the Gallizenae were said to dwell in perpetual virginity, but they could be visited on the island by those seeking their wisdom and healing. Mela does not report any prohibition against men specifically, but that doesn't necessarily rule one out. To round out the variations, later Roman accounts of the prophetess Veledā state both that she was a holy virgin and that she dwelt in a secluded high tower, with trusted male relatives serving as messengers between her and those seeking her counsel.

Finally, keeping in mind the caveats concerning Druidesses discussed in chapter 4, it is worth noting that many of the Druids and Druidesses in Irish tradition are described as being married and having children. Given the many permutations of sexual status present in the lore, it is difficult to say whether any can be considered "the norm" when it comes to ancient Celtic holy women.

Perhaps when it comes to our own priestess service, we can orient ourselves to a state of virginity in alignment with its old meaning—being beholden only to one's self rather than as a patriarchal construct that defines purity by a singular sexual metric.

While certainly there are sacred practices related to sexuality—whether connected to devotional choices around abstinence or through conscious explorations of sexuality's liminal mysteries with others—perhaps we can consider other approaches to purity and virginity as well. Instead of living separately from a partner and others, perhaps we can work toward ways of being in relationship that do not distract us from our life's work and priestessing path, or ones that do not see us pouring out our energetic resources to meet the needs of others they are able to meet for themselves.

That said, sometimes we must balance these needs with the demands of other choices we have made in our lives, such as the raising of children, or needing to be a caregiver for our partners or parents.

As long as these usually self-limiting situations are entered into from a place of sovereignty, our "purity" remains intact: it is a purity defined by authenticity of spirit, a sense of emotional independence, and a Sovereignty of self in body, mind, and heart.

Control over Storms and the Sea

Given the strong associations between bodies of water and the Otherworld in Celtic traditions, it is understandable that these holy women would be described as having power over sea and storms. This is especially true of those figures who are believed to have arisen either from tutelary divinities connected with lakes and rivers or fay creatures specifically associated with the sea.

Giving offerings to these spirits in exchange for safe passage or using apotropaic magic in the form of charms, prayers, and chants to avoid bad fortune were common practices for island-dwelling peoples depending upon the sea for travel and sustenance; safe passage and bountiful nets would be common concerns. It makes sense that travelers, traders, and those engaged in fishing would also seek the aid of those who understood how to appease the spirits of the sea and sky with magic, or the knowledge of priestesses who knew how best to seek the intercession of the gods. They would also do what they could to avoid offending or upsetting these spirits lest they whip up a storm in revenge.

The modern Avalonian Tradition includes many water-centered practices. If your area supports it, it is a beautiful thing to enter into relationships with local bodies of water and their attendant spirits. I recommend first researching any local folklore about the body of water in question, and any folk practices concerning water spirits in your area. If you cannot find any, read up on some of the folkloric practices from Wales, Brittany, and other Celtic lands and use them as a guide.

Other practices center on making use of water's function as an Otherworldly threshold. We know that bodies of water such as lakes, rivers (especially at their source), springs, and wells were venerated in Celtic lands. Offerings to the gods were cast into lake waters, as with Llyn Cerrig Bach on Anglesey. Tablets inscribed with requests were placed in sacred springs, like the thermal waters of Sulis in Bath, as were offerings gifted in thanks for prayers answered and healings received. We can use water for the same purpose of transmitting our intentions, requests, and offerings of gratitude between the worlds and to our gods. This can be achieved in a natural setting, if one is accessible to you, or by using a cauldron or other vessel filled with water as a stand in. Water scrying is a key tool in the Avalonian Tradition, and a detailed outline on how to engage it can be found in *Avalon Within*.

Making pilgrimages to wells and springs famous for their healing properties is an ancient practice found all over the British Isles and Ireland. Likewise, many Avalonians today journey to Glastonbury to connect with the energies of Avalon through the sacred landscape. Beneath the shadow of Glastonbury Tor, they will connect with and collect the waters of the Red and White Spring, and spend time in veneration at the Chalice Well. There are healing and immersion pools in the Chalice Well Gardens as well as the White Spring Temple. The newly emerging so-called Black Spring or Black Well is also a powerful place of contemplation. More widely known as St. Joseph's Well, it can be found next to the Lady Chapel in the ruins of Glastonbury Abbey.

Taken from another perspective, having power over sea and storm may be a call for us to develop a mastery of the self and an inner reserve of perseverance in the face of challenge as part of our priestess path. As we continue the inner work that brings us to the self-knowledge necessary for the reclamation of our Sovereignty, we will gain an understanding of our emotional selves—the tender places within us, the vulnerabilities we seek to protect, the triggers that unleash our rage, the Shadow responses that cause us to lash out. Perhaps this is the thunder and the fury we are called to control, the deluge of emotion that threatens to overwhelm us, the wave upon wave of anxiety and fear that crashes upon the shore of our consciousness.

We all know the power of these inner tempests, we all possess a sea-deep reserve of tears. But to be in best service to our gods, the world, and ourselves, we must find a way to smooth these inner waters, calm these buffeting winds, and find a place of solace and center in the face of the howling vortices both around us and within us. A Holy Island, perhaps, where we can retreat and rest ... filled with orchards of plenty, restorative springs, and Otherworldly guides who will help us with our healing.

Shapeshifting

The power to change form is a common attribute of Otherworldly beings; it manifests either as the ability to shift one's own shape or to cause someone else to take on a different form through the use of magic. Most commonly, this power involves humans (or human-presenting beings) changing into animals or taking on animal qualities; the shift in form can go in the other direction as well, with animals (or animal-presenting beings) becoming human. Sometimes the shift only affects one aspect of appearance, such as age or beauty. Other times, it's a type of glamour that allows someone to take on the likeness of another or an illusion that allows someone to hide in plain sight.

Generally speaking, shapeshifting in the lore and literature of Celtic lands is related to a shift in status of some sort. In some tales, Sovereignty figures transform from fearsome hags to beautiful maidens and back again; the appearance is a reflection of the state of the land and the status of the king. In other tales, the transformation is a form of punishment; those judged guilty lose their human status and take on a bestial form. Sometimes the transformations are encoded mysteries, mythic memories of initiatory rites and tests of worth—both of which result in shifts of status within the community.

When it comes to priestessing, shapeshifting is often related to ecstatic spiritual practices. Here, the practitioner uses deep trance techniques to change their form on the inner realms in order to journey between worlds; these journeys can be made for a variety of reasons, particularly for effecting healing and obtaining prophecy.

In addition to the various tools and techniques that facilitate our ability to engage in ecstatic spiritual practices, we can harness the power of shapeshifting in other ways. It can support our ability to adapt ourselves to the shifting situations of our lives—whether triumphs or challenges—so that we may return to a state of balance. It is also present as we engage in the ongoing process of personal transformation resulting from our quest for Sovereignty—changes that shift us mentally, physically, emotionally, and spiritually.

A form of shapeshifting can also be achieved through the cultivation of compassion that allows us to understand and empathize with the journey of others. It is also part of the mechanism that underscores mindfulness practices that allow us to soften the boundaries of our identities and give ourselves over completely to the experiences of the here and now.

Flight

This ability is connected to shapeshifting and commonly appears in many of the Ninefold groups as well as later depictions of enchantresses. In some tales, groups of magical women or Otherworldly sisters appear as flocks of crows or ravens, to fight on behalf of their chosen champions. One example of this can be found in the late twelfth-century French Arthurian tale, "Didot Perceval." In it, a flock of black birds attack Perceval in defense of Urbain—a knight in service to an Otherworldly Lady. When Perceval lands a killing blow on one of the birds, she falls to the ground and is transformed into a beautiful maiden whose body is carried by her sister-birds to their home on Avalon to be healed.

We may not be able to literally turn into birds, but we can learn to rise above adversity, to shift our perspective in order to see the big picture or the long view that may not be visible from our usual vantage point. Flight brings freedom—being unfettered by attachment to what is material; this can be achieved through our inner spiritual journeys, or through the cultivation of a liberated state of mind.

And it is the power of the mind that is especially being called upon here. For in the *Vita Merlini*, Morgen is said to fly through the air on wings like Daedalus, appearing wherever she wishes, such as Brest, Chartres, or Pavia. These places are notable for having been named with such specificity, and it is believed that they were chosen because they were the sites of some of the greatest learning centers of Geoffrey of Monmouth's time. Perhaps connecting Avalon to these sites underscores the high degree of learnedness possessed by the Nine Sisters. A learnedness and a raising of consciousness that we too can seek to achieve.

Oracular Service

A common attribute ascribed to the Ninefold Sisterhoods and individual holy women we find throughout Celtic lands, including the Gallizenae of Brittany and Veledā of Gaul, is that they were respected oracles possessing widely sought-after gifts of seership. It is possible that, in addition to activating the Cauldron of Annwn with their breath, the Nine Maidens of Annwn uttered poetic prophecy after inhaling the vapors emerging from the Otherworldly cauldron.

Classical accounts tell us that Druids and ovates performed auguries through interpreting natural occurrences, such as the flight of birds, and by examining the entrails and death throes of sacrifices both animal and human. We also know that elaborate incubation rituals to obtain prophetic verse were performed by bards and poets in Celtic lands. These include the Irish rite of Imbas Forosnai, a kind of sensory deprivation ritual detailed in the text of *Cormac's Glossary*, as well as the induced ecstatic speech of the Welsh *Awenyddion* ("Inspired Ones"). As described by Gerald of Wales in the twelfth century, when consulted by someone seeking their guidance, the *Awenydd* (singular) would behave as one possessed, entering into a trance state without any control over their senses.

> *Words stream from their mouths, incoherently and apparently meaningless and without any sense at all, but all the same well expressed... When it is all over, they will recover from their trance, as if... waking from a heavy sleep, but you have to give them a good shake before they regain control of themselves.... They seem to receive this gift of divination through visions... in their dreams. Some... have the impression that honey or sugary milk is being smeared on their mouths; others say that a sheet of paper with words written on it is pressed against their lips.*[182]

The ability to produce mantic (prophetic) verses infused with the Awen was the mark of the greatest of bards. When the potent essence of the Awen was present, it may have invested their very words with the power to create that which they spoke. This may, in part, explain why these poems appeared to be prophetic.

The strong association between holy women and seership makes a compelling case for those who wish to walk a priestess path inspired by Celtic traditions to include some form of divination as part of their personal practice—regardless of whether one has a calling to be in oracular service to others.

Developing clarity of sight and trust in one's intuition is foundational to the work of priestessing. This can be achieved in several ways:

---

182 Giraldus Cambrensis, *The Journey through Wales and the Description of Wales*, trans. Lewis Thorpe (Harmondsworth, UK: Penguin Books, 1978), 246–247.

1. Through the development of discernment that is the by-product of the quest for self-knowledge; this allows us to know the difference between Shadow-based illusions and Sovereignty-centered truths. One way of achieving this is undertaking the work of the Avalonian Cycle of Healing and Cycle of Revealing.

2. By engaging in an ongoing and consistent discipline of energetic practices that serve to clear and balance our energy fields; these practices help us to release expectations, become uncoupled from attachments, and move through the world in as present a way as possible. In turn, we gradually become more sensitive to energetic shifts, more open to receiving guidance, and more trusting of our own inner wisdom. Examples of these practices include the Ninefold Breath, the Three Realms Working (*Avalon Within*), and the Awen Trance posture (chapter 12 for both).

3. By committing to learning or developing a symbolic language that opens a two-way channel of communication between the parts of the self, between the self and the world, and between the self and the gods. This can be achieved through the use and eventual mastery of a divinatory tool of your choosing.

Our Sight becomes clear when we turn the inner eye within, and as a result of this quest to know ourselves, our perspectives shift and the world around us changes—a mirror of our own internal changes. When we can see the people, circumstances, and events in our lives for what they are, rather than through the filter of our past hurts, future worries, and self-imposed restrictions, we hone our Sight—the ability to see beyond our limitations and the illusions they bring.

Healing

The power to heal wounds and restore health is probably one of the attributes for which holy and Otherworldly women are most famous. Whether it is through the use of magical ointments crafted by figures such as Morgan le Fay, the restoration of the mortally wounded Arthur by bringing him to Avalon, or the Cauldron of Regeneration's ability to bring dead warriors back to life—healing is a central part of a wise one's identity. Geoffrey of Monmouth specifically details Morgen's mastery of herbal medicines to cure all illnesses—an art she has also taught to her sisters, although she exceeds them all.

Working with plant allies for medicinal and magical purposes is a cornerstone of the modern Avalonian Tradition, and many sisters immerse themselves in this study. In addition to their healing properties, herbs can be used as energetic tools that facilitate personal growth and build bridges of connection with the Divine. There are many healing modalities, however, and whether one chooses a vocation in a field of medicine, through the practice of a wholistic discipline, as a mental health professional, as one who midwives babies into the world, or who supports the dying as they depart the world—healing is a deeply effective way to be in service as a priestess.

Yet, even if this is not where one's call to service lies, healing is nevertheless foundational to the work of the Avalonian Tradition. It is a powerful commitment to do the work required of us to bring the whole self into balance, to use our inner and outer resources wisely, to honor our limitations, to claim and celebrate our accomplishments, and to take time to engage in meaningful self-care. The more whole we are, the more we know the truth of ourselves—both the light and the dark— the more healed we become. With that healing, we are able to be in better service to ourselves, our communities, and the goddesses of Avalon.

Ritual and Sacrifice

One of the more obvious tasks of a priestess is to serve as a facilitator: to build a bridge between the self and the Divine, to create sacred spaces and experiences that facilitate the building of bridges on behalf of others, and to spend time in devotional works intended to honor the deities we serve and to receive their guidance.

We know that in ancient times, priestesses in Celtic cultures performed ceremonies of sacrifice that also served as methods of augury, engaged in ecstatic ritual practices, facilitated rites of kingship, and acted as initiators into mystery traditions. They also served to maintain sacred precincts dedicated to the Divine—whether annually rethatching the temple on their island home, tending the eternal flame at Brigid's shrine, or inciting Druids and the warriors on Ynys Môn in defense of their sacred groves.

While some modern priestesses are called to be caretakers of sacred spaces, facilitators of spiritual communities, and celebrants of rituals and ceremonies, there are other ways to integrate this kind of service in our lives. For many of us, it's important to establish our own ritual space, shrine, or working altar. Another way is to tend to the temple of the self—the vehicle through which all service is rendered.

Emulating the practice of the Samnitae priestesses to rethatch the roof of their island temple every year, we can commit to undertaking an annual self-evaluation—of body, mind, spirit—in order to maintain the sacred space both within and around us. What needs to be sacrificed or released for the whole to prosper? How can we let go of what no longer serves us in a way that brings us joy, even when the choice to do so was a difficult one? How can we replace what has been worn out—whether it means learning new things, making different choices, or finding other ways to replenish our inner resources? How can we better reinforce our life's structure so that we can ensure the integrity of the temple?

Learnedness and Mastery

In the *Vita Merlini*, Geoffrey of Monmouth extolls the learned nature of Morgen and her sisters, and mentions Morgen's visits to famous contemporary centers of learning, flying there upon her magical wings. She is described as sharing her knowledge with her sisters, who themselves are said to display mastery, especially in the healing arts and music. Later Arthurian tales describe Morgan as excelling in the seven liberal arts—the gold standard of medieval classical education, almost exclusively reserved for men—and Morgan is said to have become a great clerk of necromancy while she studied at a nunnery in her youth.

An elite and well-educated priestly class, the descriptions of Gaulish Druids in the accounts of early classical authors emphasizes their dedication to, and appreciation for, education. They were said to gather in secret locations, such as caves or deep forests, where they undertook their studies. According to Caesar, it took twenty years to become a Druid, and while he reports that the Druids used Greek letters to write their language for mundane purposes, they preferred to commit their sacred learnings to memory and impart them through verbal instruction. Caesar believed this was a control tactic on their part that let them retain their power.

There is a strong connection between sacred service, learnedness, and professional mastery. As we see in ancient accounts, the priestesses and holy women of Celtic tribes were sought after for their prophetic guidance and their ability to act as respected mediators during times of conflict. We see these qualities carry over into the medieval literature of Ireland and Wales: female poets and seers were consulted for their Imbas by Irish kings and queens; magic-wielding women trained heroes in the arts of war in both Irish and Arthurian Traditions; and Otherworldly rulers and queens, like the Lady of the Lake, Branwen, and Rhiannon were invaluable advisors at royal courts.

While not every modern priestess is called to service through study or teaching, it is important for us to obtain a foundation in the lore, literature, and culture of the divinities we serve. Not only is attaining this grounding in tradition and primary source materials a powerful devotional act, it may also reveal ways to build bridges of connection to our gods that we may never have recognized through secondhand information.

More than this, both history and lore appear to emphasize being skilled in some field as a component of sacred service. As this overview has shown, while there are many components of practice that contribute to being a well-rounded priestess, there were—and are—many different manifestations of priestessing. A full palette of tools, skills, and fields through which we can express our priestess service is available to us. Using them with sacred intention and a sense of passion centered in the fulfillment of our calling is the pathway the leads us into mastery. And it is this mastery which, in turn, unlocks the door to being in our highest service to the Divine.

8

THE STREAM OF TRADITION

As we work our way through this book, we have identified three primary energetic sources that feed Avalon's Stream of Tradition: Traditions of Otherworldly Islands, Traditions of Ninefold Sisterhoods, and Traditions of Vessels of Sovereignty. Having some sense of the source of these waters, we can now reflect on how its course shifted in response to the different cultural landscapes through which it flowed over many centuries.

It can be difficult to look at these shifting courses from a purely temporal perspective due to the intermingling of different story traditions arising from, and contributing to, both the oral and literary transmission of tale. While the first written accounts were likely influenced by traditions already established in orality, albeit presented through the lens of the author, later on things become more complicated. The Stream of Tradition flowing through literature began to evolve on its own trajectory, while oral tales continued to be shared and spread by professional bards and casual performers alike.

The stories that have come to comprise the whole of Arthurian Tradition expanded and evolved as they passed through the hands of different authors, writing from different cultural perspectives, in different periods of time. Some of these shifts were caused by the addition of regional heroic tales, characters, and story elements arising from different cultural contexts. One such shift can be seen in the works comprising the French Vulgate Cycle, which introduced the character of Lancelot, the Quest for the Holy Grail, and added themes of chivalry and courtly love into the Arthurian mix. In other cases, authors incorporated traditions of Arthur and his court that grew out of the same source tradition as the Matter of Britain but evolved separately from the written materials.

Because some of these strands of tradition separated, evolved on their own accord, and then were folded back into the whole again (alongside other strands woven in from other, perhaps even older sources), it isn't always helpful to look at the Ninefold as it presents in Arthurian Tradition from the perspective of a linear evolution over time. Indeed, from what we know of Brythonic bardic tradition—which was responsible for the preservation and transmission of their cultural knowledge—elements of story drawn from history and legend were presented side by side, sometimes intermingled without distinction.

Instead, I have come to identify three distinct but interrelated currents within the Avalonian Stream of Tradition: the Current of Myth, the Current of History, and the Current of Legend. Each informs and reflects the others in a ways that makes it difficult to pick out the original form that gave rise to the others. It may be, for example, that local traditions about historical priestess enclaves evolved into legends of sister enchantresses ruling over a land of magic. Or it is possible that mythic tales of shape-changing river goddesses who granted sovereignty to their chosen mates—and took it back from those deemed unworthy—gave rise to tales of water spirits who seduced men with their beauty before drowning them in their depths. I believe it is likely that both scenarios are true, and they represent just some of the possibilities.

Because we cannot know for sure, let us group these manifestations of the Ninefold found in Gaulish, Welsh, and Arthurian Traditions according to the type of current that carried it into the Stream of Tradition.

Three Currents from the Stream of Tradition

The Current of Myth

For me, the Current of Myth is associated with the Realm of Sea. It contains wisdoms that have been unconsciously transmitted through the symbols embedded in tales which have their origins in sacred stories. This current therefore carries a religious component and can inform our spiritual beliefs.

One manifestation of the Ninefold associated with this current is the Nine Maidens of Annwn, whose mythic qualities suggest their original divine nature. They present as Ninefold Goddesses of Inspiration, Sister Muses who are tenders of an Otherworldly cauldron. This vessel, the Pair Pen Annwn—exhibits two primary natures. It is a source of poetry and prophecy, making it similar to the Cauldron of Ceridwen. It is also a cauldron of testing that will not boil the food of a coward. This last quality, coupled with the fact that Arthur's primary reason for raiding the Otherworld was to obtain this cauldron, suggests that it is also connected to the conference of Sovereignty.

The Current of History

The Current of History is associated with the Realm of Land. It contains wisdoms reflected in chronicled accounts of communities of religious women that were physically established in several forms over time and in different cultures. This current therefore carries an historic component and can inform our spiritual practices.

The manifestations of the Ninefold associated with this current include those communities of Gaulish priestesses described in the accounts of Roman historians: the Gallizenae and the Samnitae/Namnitae

Women—two different groups of nine priestesses dwelling on separate secluded islands. There are also traditions of cloistered communities of religious women in the early Christian period in Celtic lands that may be related to—or perhaps grew out of—similar communities from Pagan times. These include the traditions of the Nine Maidens of Scotland (the nine chaste daughters of St. Donald), as well as the fourteenth-century account by John of Glastonbury of "a monastery of holy virgins" on Wearyall Hill, the first such mention of a women's community of this type in Glastonbury

The Current of Legend

The Current of Legend is associated with the Realm of Sky. It contains wisdoms transmitted through literary works that have been consciously constructed, albeit based upon folkloric traditions that may have been transmitted in orality for centuries before being written down. Many strands of Arthurian Tradition follow this trajectory, even incorporating traditions from other cultures. Because of the enduring nature of these stories—having been retold over many years and in many lands—it is understandable that some of the folk motifs and symbol sets found in Arthurian stories were reinterpreted over time to reflect their new cultural contexts.

The Current of Legend, then, evolved to take a form that is not directly dependent upon history nor mythology, even though the story motifs they contain may have their origins in both. As such, the Current of Legend can be used to inform our understanding of tradition through the shifting of sociocultural contexts. Manifestations of the Ninefold associated with this current include the Nine Sisters of Avalon, the Ladies of the Lake, as well as the folk motifs of Lake Maidens, Fairy Queens, witches, and enchantresses.

These women are depicted as autonomous, able to hold power in their own right, and often possessed magical abilities or objects. Within the context of these legends, aside from those characters with clear supernatural heritages, sorceresses like Morgan le Fay were said to be regular humans who obtained their magic through study. This is a reflection of the medieval belief that magic—then strongly related to various disciplines of science—was something that anyone could learn; no innate powers were required.

When we do a deep reading of these tales, however, the high social status and magical skills of at least some of these figures from literature and folklore suggest their potential origins as goddesses, water fairies, or tutelary spirits. While the ability to use magic doesn't automatically prove that a character is a devolved deity, it is a good indicator that further exploration into the character is warranted. Alternatively, these characters may have developed out of memories of ancient priestesses, Druidesses, or other types of wise women.

Straddling the Currents

Because of the interlacing of myth, history, and legend in cultures that practice oral tradition, some iterations of the Ninefold straddle currents. Perhaps the most famous example is embodied by the holy women in service to Brigid. Whether priestesses who tended the fire temple of the exalted goddess of craft, healing, and poetry, or the Brigidine sisters charged with maintaining the eternal flame of the beloved Irish saint, these women carry several currents of the same Stream of Tradition—a reflection of the complex nature of the whole.

When it comes to the various manifestations of the Ninefold Sisterhoods over time and across cultures, we must ask if each is an independent entity in and of itself or if they are memories or echoes of each other. Are these groups of nine—the Sisters of Avalon, the Witches of Caer Lowy, the Korrigan, the Priestesses of Sena, and so on—meant to be the same nine individuals, each a reflex of a core myth? Are they nine divinities, like the Muses of Greece or the maidens who kindle the Cauldron of Annwn with their breath—or are they nine priestesses in service to a divinity? If so, which divinity? Is it Ceridwen, the bardic muse? Is it a king of the Otherworld—Arawn or Pwyll, Gwyn or Afallach? Are they in service to the Goddess of Sovereignty? Perhaps Branwen and her Cauldron of Rebirth, or else Morgan, Queen of the Apple Isle?

Perhaps there are many iterations of the Ninefold found all over the Celtic world and beyond because it was a common manifestation of devotion to the gods—threshold women, living in a liminal place, working with the creative force of the Universe. Or is it simply that the number nine was a common grouping in cultures of Indo-European derivation, a natural representation of a wholeness—a complete set of something?

When we seek these answers, it is important to keep in mind that the quest is not necessarily about finding the one true or "correct" version of the Ninefold... some original, superior form that renders all subsequent variants too changed to be authentic, or too watered down to be powerful. Just as there are many ways to enter the Otherworld— many thresholds through which it is accessible, and many places that resonate with Avalon or other aspects of Annwn—so has the Ninefold revealed itself in many ways. Whether through the varied paths of history, legend, or mythology, each presents different facets of what is collectively the same whole.

So whether your vision or experience of one of the Ladies of the Lake is that of a Celtic water divinity, an embodiment of mists, or a medieval Fairy Queen clad in white samite, what matters is that you have arrived in that threshold place where she dwells. Once in her presence, you may be tested. Should she find you worthy, a portion of Sovereignty's blessings may be yours.

In the same way, no matter how the Ninefold reveals itself to you— whether through the medium of myth as the Nine Maidens of Annwn, the medium of history as the nine Gaulish priestesses of Enez-Sun, or the medium of legend as the Nine Sisters of Avalon—the form they take is less important than the Stream of Tradition from which they arise and the wisdoms they can therefore carry. In the end, the absolute truth of the Ninefold and the ultimate origin of Avalon's Stream of Tradition may never be known to us—but that is less important than the truths she can reveal to us.

Experiences of the Avalonian Ninefold

In my work with Avalon over the years, I've experienced several iterations of the Ninefold when I've journeyed to the Holy Isle using the mythic map left behind for us in legends: undertaking the inner journey over the waters of the unconscious, passing through the threshold of mists that hinder the clarity of sight, and entering the Mythic Otherworld.

Once there, I have encountered an iteration of the Ninefold that I have associated with the Realm of Land: a community of priestesses, dwelling apart from the rest of society, on an island of sacred springs and groves of apple trees. There, emerging from the mists of a distant history, these real and mortal women lived in a cluster of roundhouses, nine of them encircling a tenth … interconnected like the spokes of a wheel, with the central space a place for all to gather. This was a place of learning, and each of the women known to me as Morgens was the high priestess of one of the Nine Paths of devotion. Each one a teacher, and a builder of bridges. Each possessing the magics obtained through study and shared in service of community. Each undergoing trials and becoming a Morgen—one who was "Born of the Sea"—that is, an initiate of the deep mysteries.

I have also encountered an iteration of the Ninefold I have come to associate with the Realm of Sea. These are the fairy aspects of Avalon, in this realm revealed as a brume-enshrouded island dwelling in a twilight place of deep mystery. I have met these literal Ladies of the Lake on the shores of the Holy Isle, their swirling, tenuous forms arising from the waters—the Gwargedd Annwn or Women of the Otherworld. I've come to know these mist-wrought beings as spirits of place who serve as intercessors between this world and the Otherworld—the Morgens of Y Tylwyth Teg. These amorphous ancestral energies are Threshold Guardians, straddling the realms of Land and Sea, themselves arising from the liminality existing between the Realms of Sea and Sky, primordial mists ancient beyond memory.

And finally, I have encountered an iteration of the Ninefold I believe to be associated with the Realm of Sky. They can only be reached through the building of bridges and the crossing of thresholds, for they dwell in the remotest of Otherworldly fortresses, in the Fourfold Revolving Caer at the heart of Annwn. Tenders of a most precious treasure, they are the Nine Maidens whose breath kindles the pearl-rimmed Cauldron of the Chief of Annwn. They are the keepers of the energies of creation, divine Muses who catalyze change and apportion the blessings of poetic prophecy—that force, that Awen, which speaks all things into existence—to those who are proven worthy.

As I worked with these three iterations of the Ninefold, I got the sense that while they are each connected to Avalon—and certainly hold resonances with each other—they aren't identical to each other. I have come to understand them as being related to a common origin that has manifested itself in each of the Three Realms, and what makes them different is the medium through which they have become manifest.

It has also been my experience that these threshold beings aren't necessarily exclusive to the Avalonian Otherworld. For example, I have stood on the shore of Llyn y Fan Fach, home of the Lady of the Lake whose sons became the famed Physicians of Myddfai. Connecting with her there, I found her to feel very much like the Ladies of the Lake I've worked with who are associated with Avalon, but this Lady is not specifically connected with Avalon.

Seeking the Awen

If the ninth-century dating of "Preiddeu Annwn" is correct (it is the earliest date accepted by scholars), then the poem predates the *Vita Merlini* by around three hundred years. This means that Geoffrey of Monmouth may have been aware of this poem, and it could have potentially inspired his description of the Nine Sisters of Avalon. Given his education, it is also quite possible that he was aware of classical accounts from the first century CE describing communities of Gaulish priestesses living on islands off the coast of France—another possible influence on his depiction of the Nine Sisters. A third possibility is that the motif of nine Otherworldly women may have been a traditional element in the tales of the bards and minstrels of Geoffrey's day, making it a natural inclusion in the *Vita Merlini*. Finally, although we will likely never know, the Nine Sisters of Avalon may have been an established element in traditions of Avalon transmitted in orality and existing independently of Geoffrey; he may simply have been the first to commit this motif to writing.

There is another mythic resonance held by the Nine Maidens of Annwn and the cauldron in their keeping—a resonance that strongly harmonizes with the Welsh figure of Ceridwen, who also possessed a wondrous cauldron. Divine Muse and mother to the bards of Wales long into the Christian period, Ceridwen was believed to be the source of the Awen—the creative force of divine inspiration. It flowed from her cauldron to illuminate the verses of poets whose mastery made them worthy of her gift. She was the mother of the mythic Taliesin, whose Shining Brow attested to his initiation into the mysteries of Ceridwen's cauldron—a vessel that also possessed the power to bestow wisdom and catalyze transformation.

There is also an historical figure named Taliesin, believed to have lived in the sixth century CE, who was renowned as a court bard in service to Urien of Rheged and his son Owain mab Urien, among other patrons. Works attributed to him and to later bards who composed poetry through the assumption of his persona—perhaps as a way to tie into the bardic lineage of the one called "Taliesin Ben Beirdd" ("Taliesin, Chief of Bards")—were collected in the manuscript known as *Llyfr Taliesin* (*The Book of Taliesin*). In "Preiddeu Annwn," which is part of this collection, Taliesin speaks in the first person as he describes a raid on the Otherworld by Arthur and his men; he counts himself as one of Arthur's companions, and is one of only seven survivors of this dangerous quest through seven Otherworldly fortresses. This Taliesin identifies very strongly with his mythic namesake, and he speaks of being reborn of Ceridwen in several poems in this collection—possibly a reference to bardic initiation.

One interesting theory about "Preiddeu Annwn" suggests that the raid on the Otherworld depicted in the poem is actually intended to be a metaphor for the bardic quest to obtain the divine inspiration of the Awen.[183] This perspective unlocks a new layer of understanding for this enigmatic poem that assists in unifying the whole piece. The first half of the poem describes the various fortresses of Annwn and their mythic attributes, while the second is filled with the complaints of Taliesin; he spends several stanzas railing against the inadequacies of those whose poetic education is lacking compared to his own—even likening their songs to the howling of wolves.

In contrast, Taliesin says, "**My** poetry, from the **cauldron** it was uttered. From the **breath of Nine Maidens** it was kindled." (emphasis mine). He seems to be comparing the traditional training of the bards—with all of its knowledge of natural sciences and the cycles of the world—to what he has deemed the inferior education of monks and "little men." Perhaps this is part of the reason Taliesin compares a bard's inner exertions of mind and spirit in the quest for Awen to the perilous journey of warriors through the fortresses of the literal Otherworld. It may be that in his

---

183 Sarah Lynn Higley, "The Spoils of Annwn: Taliesin and Material Poetry," in *A Celtic Florilegium: Studies in Memory of Brendan O'Hehir*, ed. Brendan O. Hehir et al. (Lawrence, MA: Celtic Studies Publications, 1997), 43.

mind, they are both in search of the same thing—the vessel that gifts inspiration and tests the worthiness of kings.

While Ceridwen is not mentioned in "Preiddeu Annwn," the kindling of the cauldron that brings forth poetry, prophecy, and praise songs—all bardic powers obtained through the gift of the Awen—is accomplished by the Nine Maidens in Caer Pedyvran. As we learn in *Ystoria Taliesin*, while Ceridwen brought together the components necessary to create her brew of wisdom, she herself did not tend the cauldron for the year and a day this magical operation required; she replenished the water and added ingredients at their appropriate times. Instead, it was young Gwion Bach whom she charged with stirring the brew, while a blind man named Morda was tasked with keeping the fire beneath the cauldron alight. Perhaps there is some significance in the fact that Ceridwen is not the tender of the fire beneath the cauldron in either tale, while also being the established source of Awen in Welsh tradition. Alas, the extant lore appears to be silent on this point.

However, it is significant that it is the breath of the Nine Maidens mentioned so specifically in the kindling of the Otherworldly cauldron. Of course, air is necessary to keep fires burning; oxygen is a critical component in the process of combustion, also requiring heat and fuel. Similarly, oxygen is critical to life; without it, our cellular metabolism—which operates in a way that strongly resembles the combustion process—comes to a halt, resulting in death.

Breath is related to speech and, by extension, song. The use of breath to fuel the formation and express the vibration inherent in words is, in addition to being a fundamental component of Welsh bardic poetry, connected to the act of creation in many religious and magical traditions. In the Hebrew creation story, God speaks the universe into being, and the so-called magic word "abracadabra" is believed by some (although there is disagreement among scholars) to derive from Hebrew or Aramaic phrases roughly meaning "I create what I speak."[184]

Taliesin's quest for Awen reveals the true nature of the bardic arts, which—in its most exalted form when infused with the Awen—was not simply the composition of poetry, but the utterance of prophecy; a foretelling. From a magical perspective, therefore, words and verses empowered by the Awen can be seen as intentional acts of creation—whether directly manifested by the speaker, or as catalysts for change in the hearts of those who hear or read those sacred words. And so, fire is related to breath. Breath is related to life … and both fire and breath are connected to the generation and transmission of the Awen—the creative spark arising from the energies of divine inspiration.

On Inspiration

The etymology of the word "inspiration" can be traced back to the Latin word *inspirare*, meaning "blow into, breathe upon," used figuratively to mean "excite, inflame". This gave rise to the Old French word *inspiracion* ("inhaling, breathing in"), which entered the English language as a word used to describe the influence of the Divine, particularly as related to the writing of holy books. In Middle English, the verb *inspire* meant "to breathe or put life or spirit into the human body; impart reason to a human soul." In modern English, "inspire" of course means the literal act of taking in breath, as well as the act of influencing others and/or calling them to action.[185]

In turn, *inspirare* is connected to the Latin *spiritus*, "a breathing, breath; breath of a god," and is the origin of the English *spirit*: the "animating or vital principle in man and animals." Both *inspirare* and *spir-*

---

184 "Abracadabra," Oxford English Dictionary, accessed February 228, 2022, http://www.oed.com/view/Entry/539.

185 "Inspiration (n.)," Etymology, accessed August 28, 2022, https://www.etymonline.com/word/inspiration#etymonline_v_9343.

itus are believed to have arisen from the Proto-Indo-European (PIE) *(s)peis—*, meaning "to blow".[186] The etymology of the word "Awen" itself comes from the Indo-European root word *-uel*, meaning "to blow," which gave rise to the Old Irish *ai* (< *aui*) "poetic art," and the Welsh *awel*, "breeze." Koch writes that Awen comes from the same root as the Irish words *fath* "prophecy" and *faith* "prophet," as well as the Welsh *gwawd*.[187] Interestingly, *gwawd* is a term that used to refer to praise poetry but has come to mean satire or mockery—both of which were tools of the bard.[188]

Tracing the etymologies of these words reveals ancient connections between the concepts of breath, the spirit or soul, and the taking in of divine or vitalistic (that is, life-giving or sustaining) energies. These energies impel humans into action, fill us with a sense of divine purpose, and reveal wisdoms directly from Source. This concept of divine inspiration, therefore, seems to be what is implied by the kindling breath of the Nine Maidens of Annwn. In turn, this suggests that by nature, these nine function as Muses—those who inspire—connecting them both to Ceridwen and to the Nine Muses of classical tradition.

Muses and Maidens

Whether the appearance of a Ninefold Muse in a ninth-century Welsh poem is due to the author being influenced by the classical world or because they were a part of indigenous bardic tradition—which may have shared PIE roots with Greek poetic traditions, thereby accounting for their similarities—is unclear. However, there are several commonalities between the two groups that are worth exploring, especially since we know so much more about the Greek Muses than we do the

---

186   "Spirit (n.)," Etymology, accessed August 28, 2022, https://www.etymonline.com/word/spirit#etymonline_v_24031.

187   Koch, "Awen," in *Celtic Culture*, 148.

188   MacKillop, "gwawd," in *A Dictionary of Celtic Mythology*, 262.

Nine Maidens of Annwn. One similarity that particularly stands out to me is that both groups of nine are associated with liminality.

The Muses are a group of Nine Sisters who live together; while they are not specifically called virgins, their unmarried state sets them apart from the natural order of things for women in ancient Greek culture. Encounters with the Muses typically occurred at places of liminality, such as on mountaintops or out in the rural landscape beyond the confines of cities—in wild places outside of civilization's order. Similarly, the Nine Maidens are found in the Otherworld and can only be reached after a threshold journey over water.

Although each of the Muses eventually came to be associated with specific realms of art and science, it happened at a fairly late stage in their development, usually attributed to the Hellenic period spanning the last three centuries BCE. These attributions are:[189]

Nine Muses of Classical Tradition

Calliope BEAUTIFUL OF SPEECH	Chief Muse, Muse of epic poetry and rhetoric
Clio GLORIOUS ONE	Muse of history
Erato AMOROUS ONE	Muse of erotic poetry and marriage songs
Euterpe WELL-PLEASING	Muse of music and lyric poetry
Melpomene CHANTING ONE	Muse of tragedy
Polyhymnia MANY HYMNS	Muse of sacred song, oratory, and rhetoric

189 Tomasz Mojsik, "Muses and the Gender of Inspiration," *Sakarya University: The Journal of Art and Science*, no. T. 10 (2008), 67.

Terpsichore **DELIGHTS IN DANCE**	Muse of choral song and dance
Thalia **BLOSSOMING ONE**	Muse of comedy and pastoral poetry
Urania **CELESTIAL ONE**	Muse of astronomy

Before this period, the Muses were typically depicted as acting as a group, and this anonymity contributed to their sense of liminality. Since the Muses and their realms of influence were fully established long before the writing of "Preiddeu Annwn," it may suggest that the nameless Nine Maidens of Annwn are derived from an older tradition, rather than as a result of classical influence on its author.

In contrast, the Nine Sisters of Avalon have names and are expressly stated to be learned in the arts and sciences, and several are associated with specific areas of mastery, such as Morgen with healing and Thitis with music. As noted elsewhere, details in the *Vita Merlini* may have been influenced by Geoffrey of Monmouth's classical education. However, this may be another detail that suggests that the Nine Sisters of Avalon (whose home on an Otherworldly island is also an expression of liminality) may be a later iteration of the Nine Maidens of Annwn.

Finally, the liminal qualities of the Muses extends to the idea that they, as with the Nine Maidens, can be reached at threshold times and in threshold places. This leads us to our second point of similarity. Poetic mystery traditions—involving rites of initiation for those who would enter into divine service as a poet or bard—are features of both Welsh and Greek cultures. As previously mentioned, allusions to these rites are scattered throughout the writings of Taliesin, including "Preiddeu Annwn." Further, the story of the mythic Taliesin's death and rebirth as a son of Ceridwen as relayed in *Ystoria Taliesin* has long been considered an allegory for the process of bardic initiation.

Similarly, Greek tradition contains references to those who receive gifts of skill or song after transformational encounters with the Muses. For example, in the opening of his eighth-century-BCE work *Theogony*, the poet Hesiod declares his fitness to create this piece by including an account of what appears to be his own initiation by the Muses. After describing them in a way that underscores their liminal qualities—hailing from their home at top of Mount Helicon, dancing around a spring and bathing in holy waters, traveling by night in a veil of thick mists as they sing—he writes:

> And one day they taught Hesiod glorious song while he was shepherding his lambs under holy Helicon, and this word first the goddesses said to me—the Muses of Olympus, daughters of Zeus who holds the aegis: "Shepherds of the wilderness, wretched things of shame, mere bellies, we know how to speak many false things as though they were true; but we know, when we will, to utter true things."
>
> So said the ready-voiced daughters of great Zeus, and they plucked and gave me a rod, a shoot of sturdy laurel, a marvellous thing, and breathed into me a divine voice to celebrate things that shall be and things there were aforetime; and they bade me sing of the race of the blessed gods that are eternally, but ever to sing of themselves both first and last.[190]

Not only do Muses function to impart the gifts of divine inspiration, it appears they also serve as initiators who facilitate the shifts of status and consciousness that accompany the initiation of poets. We know

---

190 Hesiod, Hugh G. Evelyn-White, and Homer, *Hesiod, the Homeric Hymns, and Homerica. With an English Translation by Hugh G. Evelyn-White* (London: Heinemann, 1914), https://archive.org/details/hesiodhomerichym00hesi_0/page/n9/mode/2up, 78–81.

that Ceridwen was hailed as a Muse by the Welsh bards, and that she is mother/initiator of Taliesin; by extension, this appears to also make her the mother of those who have undergone traditional bardic training culminating in an initiatory rite that confers the rank of bard upon them. Since we know that the "Muse as initiator" concept is not foreign to Welsh tradition, it is therefore not a stretch to assign this same quality to the Nine Maidens of Annwn as well. Not only does the cauldron in their keeping dispense the gifts of poetry and prophecy, it is also a testing vessel—it will only function for those who have been deemed worthy.

Inspiration and Sovereignty

Tests of this sort are often related to the granting of Sovereignty, and the transformations accompanying the investiture of kingship are catalytic in nature. When Sovereignty is granted to a candidate who has been found fit to rule, not only does he experience a shift in status as he becomes king, but the land he now rules is likewise shifted; the fate of the land has now become bound to the fate of the king.

In tales where Sovereignty is a goddess and the divine embodiment of the land, her sexual union with the king is the rite that binds him to her territory. Her physical being acts as the bridge between the king and the spiritual essence of the land, and the energies that flow forth from this union serve to restore vitality and abundance to the region in his keeping. This renewal of the land is reflected in the appearance of the Sovereignty Goddess, who transforms from hag to maiden. In stories where the Sovereignty has become sublimated into a symbolic vessel such as the grail, the attainment of the vessel by those who are worthy triggers the release of a vitalistic energy that, in this example, restores the Wasteland and heals the wounded king.

Legends and lore teach us that the Otherworld is a place of richness and plenty; among its gifts are the life-giving waters of rivers and fresh water springs. Considering the high volume of votive deposits found at the sources of rivers that were also often the location of cult activities such as healing shrines, the threshold places where these waters miraculously emerged out of the earth from the regions below were considered especially sacred. These are the waters of the river mothers, like Matrona of the Marne river, the thermal healing springs of Sulis-Minerva, and the locations of the Courts of Joy, where Otherworldly maidens freely shared platters of food and golden cups of restorative drink with travelers who happened upon their forest springs.

Just as the Otherworld can be reached through water, it also has a subterranean component; it can be reached through fairy mounds and hollow hills. In "Angar Kyfyndawt" ("The Hostile Confederacy"), a poem from *The Book of Taliesin*, Annwn is described as being below the earth.

This subterranean aspect of the Otherworld is also the source of the vitalistic energies that make life possible—the food we grow; the trees we harvest for shelter, warmth, and transportation; and the healing herbs we use to make medicines. It is also a storehouse of great treasure; we mine it for precious metals and other raw materials such as crystals, minerals, salt, and clay—things that bring us joy with their beauty and improve our lives through their use in technology. It is no coincidence that chthonic deities like the Greek Hades are also often gods of wealth. Interestingly, Julius Caesar wrote that the Gauls believed that they were descendants of Dis Pater (another name for Pluto, whose name means "the Giver of Wealth"), although certainly he was applying the *Interpretatio Romana* and actually referring to an equivalent Gaulish underworld divinity.

Fertility, abundance, peace, creativity, and health are among the gifts the Otherworld grants to those who live in right relationship with the land. These gifts are bestowed upon those deemed worthy by the Goddess of Sovereignty—the indwelling spirit of the land; maintaining these blessings requires being in a balanced relationship with her. Likewise, when we collectively live in accordance with the earth's cycles and are respectful of its boundaries through sustainability, we experience prosperity and continued survival as a species. For us individually, right relationship with Sovereignty is achieved when we work toward wholeness and practice being righteous, honorable, generous, compassionate, courageous, dedicated, wise, learned, and skilled.

However, tradition also teaches that leaders who are in an imbalanced relationship with the land cause their people to experience poverty, famine, war, and misfortune. The Wasteland descends, and the blessings of Sovereignty are withdrawn—whether represented in the lore by the dissolution of a marriage relationship, the reclaiming of the sword of kings, the incitement of war against a dishonorable chieftain, or the transformation of the Sovereignty Goddess from maiden to hag. For us individually, the withdrawal of Sovereignty occurs in the face of an imbalanced relationship that arises through lawlessness, dishonor, greed, mercilessness, cowardice, disloyalty, foolishness, laziness, and arrogance.

Just as the Otherworld is a giver of gifts, it is also a receiver of life. Thresholds allow both entry and exit; the door to the Otherworld opens in both directions in order to maintain balance. It seems, therefore, that agents of Sovereignty are like the agents of Inspiration; they are figures of liminality who serve as bridges between the worlds, and the result of that bridging is to bring energies of transformation and renewal from the Otherworld into this world. These bridging figures are initiators and catalysts of change—both for the individuals who receive their gifts and those who are touched by the works of those that they have gifted. In the case of kings, the renewed abundance of the land and the peace and justice that accompanies right rule benefits all the people in his charge. In the case of the bard, the Awen gifts inspired speech and poetry that can change minds, shift hearts, shame the lawless, and—especially in the case of prophecy—alter courses of action and manifest things into being.

The Gifts of Awen

Awen is the divine spark that underscores all acts of creation, change, and creativity. It is a holy sacrament that, when directed with consciousness, can be harnessed as a force to power the mechanisms of change. As we strive for wholeness, we obtain a clearer picture of our work in the world and how we can best be in Sovereign service to ourselves, to others, and to the Divine. With this sense of Sovereignty comes the ability to direct Awen in accordance with our authentic will, a transformational act that allows us to be conscious participants in the ongoing creation of the Universe.

In my experience, there are two ways in which the Awen is received that I have come to call *Awen Fawr* (pronounced "ah-WHEN vow-ER") and *Awen Fach* (pronounced "ah-WHEN va-CH," sounds like the "ch" in the Scottish *loch*). The energy of Awen itself is the same; what differs is the amount of Awen that comes through and its subsequent impact.

Awen Fawr: Greater Awen

The receipt of Awen Fawr is rare but transformational; a sacred gift catalyzed by experiences of emotional extremes and through the use of directed spiritual techniques. Although it can pour fourth in various quantities, it is often accompanied by a sense of universal oneness and connection with the Divine. It is marked by enormous energetic shifts that ignite what has been described as the bardic "fire in the head"—a temporary condition of enlightenment that forever changes those who experience it.

Awen Fawr can be actively sought through the use of tools and techniques that shift consciousness, such as: ritual trance, incubation practices, and mantic states achieved through ecstatic chant, dance, drumming, plant medicine, and other means of crossing inner thresholds to enter the Otherworld. It can also pour through the thresholds of imbalance that accompany our highest joys and deepest sorrows—the latter best summed up in the sentiment "No angst, no Awen."

Awen Fach: Lesser Awen

The receipt of Awen Fach is much more common, often experienced as the "lightbulb moments" in our day-to-day lives. It comes through as a flash of insight or intuition, a dawning of understanding, the feeling of things falling into place, a sudden understanding when mental connections are made, and ideas that seem to pop into our heads.

Experiences of Awen Fach pave the way for the receipt of Awen Fawr. We can intentionally seek to open ourselves to Awen Fach through mindfulness practices, by clearing our inner energy channels to allow our intuition to flow with less hindrance, and by developing a deepening skill set in any priestessing discipline. Some examples of these include engaging the Ninefold Breath daily, performing the Awen posture regularly, and practicing traditional Welsh poetry forms in order to create a word vessel that can be filled with Awen. These tools will be explored in detail later on in this book.

Otherworldly Cauldrons

What else do Sovereignty figures and those we have designated as Muses in Welsh tradition have in common? Both dispense their gifts through the medium of a sacred vessel. As we have seen in our discussion of the Vessels of Sovereignty from chapter 5, these vessels can take several forms, but the most potent iteration—outside of the physical presence of the Sovereignty Goddess herself—is the cauldron.

Although they often possess more than one attribute, there are three main types of Otherworldly cauldrons in Welsh tradition:

1. Cauldrons of Inspiration that gift wisdom, poetry, and prophecy to those who have earned it.

2. Cauldrons of Plenty that gift abundance and fertility to those who are worthy.

3. Cauldrons of Regeneration that gift rebirth, healing, and transformation to those who have paid the price.

It may be, then, that the gifts poured forth from these cauldrons derive from the same Otherworldly source, and that what pours forth from them is the same divine energy of creation. The ways these creative forces manifest—and the changes that they catalyze—are dependent, in my belief, on the vessel from which they pour and the realm in which that vessel is operating. I am unaware of any lore that identifies the Awen gifted from the Cauldron of Wisdom with the creative and revivifying energies that empower the Cauldron of Plenty or the Cauldron of Regeneration. However, I have come to strongly feel that if these energies are not identical to the Awen, they are at least closely related, and this is the understanding that informs the basis of the work that follows.

9

RECLAIMING
THE NINEFOLD

In the course of my quest to connect with the Nine Sisters of Avalon, as well as with their counterparts in the depths of Annwn, I came to the conclusion that I needed to understand and experience the nature of the Ninefold from a purely energetic perspective. In studying the various Ninefold Sisterhoods from history and lore and exploring the variety of skills and gifts ascribed to them, I eventually came to recognize a pattern. These priestesses, Druidesses, oracles, and holy women…these fairy women, enchantresses, and sea-born Morgens…these Sovereignty figures, Well Maidens, Grail Bearers, and Peace Weavers all had something in common: service as a bridge.

As initiators and challengers, they bridged states of being. As intoxicators and inciters, they bridged states of consciousness. As oracles and seers, they bridged the worlds through trance. As healers and psychopomps, they bridged life and death. As shapeshifters and weather workers, they bridged forms of being. As poets and prophets, they bridged ignorance and knowledge, the past and the present, the present and the future. Regardless of how these holy women served as bridges—magically, spiritually, or symbolically—the result of their various forms of mediation was to catalyze change, by releasing a divinely sourced creative energy I associate with the Awen.

Therefore, I needed to obtain an understanding of the Awen as an active and activating creative force, able to manifest in different ways while still maintaining its fundamental essence. I began to explore the Awen in relation to the Three Realms that define our understanding of Celtic cosmology—their concept of how the universe is ordered. It made sense to me to explore the energies of creativity relative to all of creation. It was when I took the symbol for Awen (discussed below) and overlaid its Three Rays on the Three Realms, that the discrete energies of the Ninefold began to reveal themselves to me, particularly as functions of creation.

A Ninefold Cosmology

My explorations of the Avalonian Stream of Tradition taught me that the Ninefold has many iterations. Not only has it manifested in different forms and made itself known in different cultural contexts over time, but through my work with its energies I discovered that it is also fractal in nature—each aspect of the Ninefold holds the Ninefold within it. Its association with both creation and wholeness allows it to hold correspondence with every act of change and manifestation in each of the Three Realms.

To understand the Ninefold, we must therefore understand the energies of the Three Rays as well as the essence of the Three Realms. Once we know them separately, we can come to understand them collectively, thereby gaining a greater understanding of the whole. When we look at them together, we can understand the ways in which each component of the Awen inspires or catalyzes change in each of the Three Realms—revealing the creative wholeness that underscores the holy creation embodied by the Ninefold.

The Three Realms

The number three held great significance in ancient Celtic cultures, particularly concerning matters of the spirit. We know that some of their deities were triple aspected, and they appear to have held a tripartite cosmological viewpoint wherein the world around them was generally in one of Three Realms: Sea, Land, and Sky. Existing in space and over time, the Three Realms comprise all that ever was, all that presently is, and all that shall ever be.

Here are some of the main attributes I have come to associate with the Three Realms. Please note that this system in this form is not of direct ancient provenance; these definitions are informed by modern Celtic Pagan thought and are based on my personal experiences and interpretations of lore.

+ **The Realm of Sea** is the deepest depths of the Otherworld; it is the abode of the ancestors and the resting place of the spirits of the dead as they await rebirth. It is within this red-hued cauldron of the past that all memory resides. From a psycho-spiritual perspective, it can be seen to represent the unconscious self. It is the realm of the personal and is reflected in—and experienced by—our emotional body.

+ **The Realm of Land** is the manifest world existing all around us; it is the abode of all living things, including spirits of place and the energies that comprise the living planet. It is the eternal present, the rich black soil that births and nurtures all creation. From a psycho-spiritual perspective, it can be seen to represent the conscious self. It is the realm of the interpersonal and is reflected in—and experienced by—our physical body.

+ **The Realm of Sky** is the highest height of the Otherworld; it is the abode of the Divine and the source of the great cosmic patterns that reveal themselves throughout all of nature. It is the bright and shining future that encompasses the fullness of potentiality and an infinity of possibilities. From a psycho-spiritual perspective, it can be seen to represent the superconscious self. It is the realm of the transpersonal and is reflected in—and experienced by—our mental body.

When we use this triplicity as the filter through which we see all of creation, we can identify correspondences both as we drill down microcosmically and expand out macrocosmically. No matter what aspect of manifestation we are contemplating, we can identify each of the Three Realms within it because the relationship they have with each other remains constant, as illustrated in the following correspondence chart.

Three Realms Correspondence Chart

SEA	LAND	SKY
–	=	+
depth	width	height
below	around	above
behind	here	ahead
past	present	future
unconscious	conscious	superconscious
personal	interpersonal	transpersonal
the ancestors	the living	the gods
self	world	Source
emotional body	physical body	mental body
intuition	instinct	logic
soul	body	mind
dependent	interdependent	independent
roots	trunk	branches

SEA	LAND	SKY
experience	skill	knowledge
ochre	soil	chalk
red	black	white
blood	body	breath

The Three Rays

The essence of the Awen has come to be represented by a symbol created by the controversial Welsh antiquarian Iolo Morganwg in the late eighteenth or early nineteenth century. While this symbol of the Three Rays (sometimes called the Tribann) is not ancient, I believe it to be a masterfully crafted glyph that, among other things, holds strong resonance with the three drops of wisdom that emerge from the Cauldron of Ceridwen.

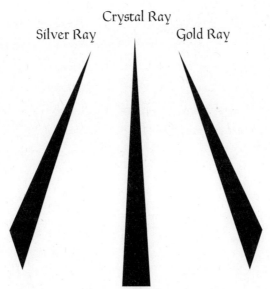

The Three Rays of Awen

Taken as a whole, the symbol describes a triple emanation of the divine energies of creation streaming from source and entering the realms of manifestation. The glyph itself functions as a bridge. When tracing the direction of the rays from the top down, /|\ can be seen as a channel that disseminates the creative force from its source in the Otherworld into this world. When tracing the rays in the reverse direction, it presents a map outlining the process of returning manifest energies to back to Source.

There are many interpretations of the meaning of each of the Three Rays of Awen, and many ways to engage with their energies. In modern Druid traditions, most approaches center on various iterations of the sacred three. I found that a powerful correspondence for the Three Rays is to see connection with the energies of the three pillars on the Qabalistic Tree of Life, another glyph that (among other things) presents a cosmological key to the process of creation and teaches the seeker how to create a pathway back to union with Source.

On the Tree of Life, the three pillars, or downward paths, are called (from left to right) the Pillar of Severity, the Middle Pillar, and the Pillar of Mercy—essentially representing feminine/receptive energy, neutral/balanced energy, and masculine/emissive energy. Similarly, the Three Rays of Awen can be seen as emanations of creative energy from Source, with receptive energy represented by the Silver Ray on the left, balanced energy represented by the Crystal Ray in the center, and emissive energy represented by the Gold Ray on the right.

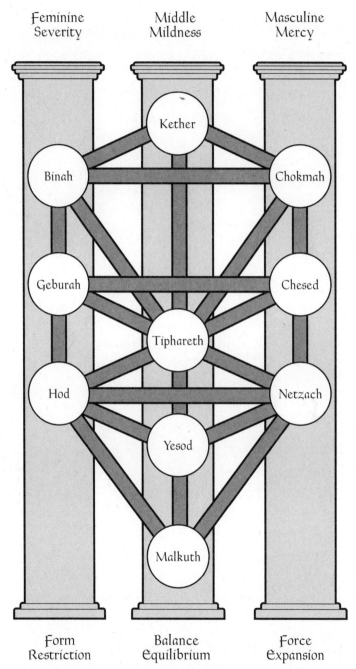

The Three Pillars on the Tree of Life

The following chart is a list of major correspondences for the Three Rays. Each column is a list of resonances of individual rays, while each row shows how the rays relate to each other in the context of the whole.

Three Rays Correspondence Chart

SILVER	CRYSTAL	GOLD
−	=	+
receptive	integrative	expressive
passive	neutral	active
consolidate	coordinate	disperse
regressive	maintaining	progressive
feminine	nonbinary	masculine
magnetic	neutralized	electric
stabilize	order	catalyze
form	transitional	force
antithesis	synthesis	thesis

These energies also hold resonance with a teaching from the ancient Greek tradition in that there were originally only three Muses from whom the nine later arose. These were Mneme (memory), Aoide (song), and Melete (practice).[191] All three parts are necessary for the manifestation of a piece of music. Memory, corresponding to the Silver Ray, is what receives the song, be it an original piece or something traditional that must be learned and remembered. Practice, corresponding to the Gold Ray, is an action that builds skill and mastery in preparation for performance.

---

191 Pausanias, *Description of Greece with an English Translation in 4 Volumes* by W. H. S. Jones, and H. A. Ormerod, (Cambridge, MA: Harvard University Press, 1918), http://data.perseus.org/citations/urn:cts:greekLit:tlg0525.tlg001.perseus-eng1:9.29.2.

The integration of practice and memory infuses the song, the Crystal Ray, with life—creating a dynamic experience for both audience and musician.

The Nine Energies

One way of thinking about the Three Rays is that they represent the activating principle of creation, broken down into three complementary but distinct modes of energy, each presenting a quality of action. Each ray embodies the kind of action being taken or the manner in which something is done.

Three Modes of Action

- **The Silver Ray** builds bridges of reception. It catalyzes inner reflection, stimulates intuitive connections, and functions to create form.

- **The Crystal Ray** builds bridges of integration. Within us, it catalyzes centered presence, stimulates balanced connections, and functions to create order.

- **The Gold Ray** builds bridges of expression. It catalyzes external action, stimulates logical connections, and functions to create change.

Similarly, we can conceive of the Three Realms as representing the receptive principle broken down into three complementary but distinct areas of manifestation—each presenting an aspect of creation. Each realm embodies a domain that is being acted upon, or the medium where change is made or through which something is done.

Three Areas of Change

- **In the Realm of Sky,** energy is expressed through the mind. Guidance can be found in what is possible and from the Divine.

Changes made in this realm manifest in the mind or spirit, affecting our understanding of, and relationship with, the Universe.

+ **In the Realm of Land,** energy is expressed through the body. Guidance can be found in the present and from the living. Changes made in this realm manifest in the physical plane, affecting our understanding of, and relationship with, others and the world around us.

+ **In the Realm of Sea,** energy is expressed through the emotions. Guidance can be found in the past and from the ancestors, and changes made in this realm manifest in the heart or psyche, affecting our understanding of, and relationship with, the self.

When we overlay these two triplicities, it creates a grid that reveals the nine component parts of the Ninefold. We can use the resulting glyph as a key to understanding how the three modes of action—the Three Rays comprising the creative energies of the Awen—present themselves in the three areas of change—the Three Realms of creation.

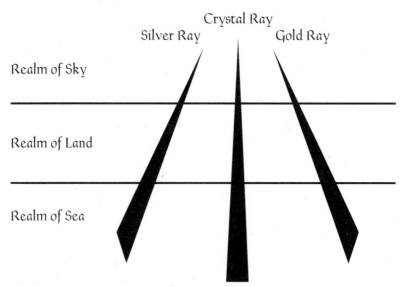

The Three Rays of Awen through the Three Realms

In turn, this glyph allows us to describe the nine specific energies and actions suggested by this overlay. The properties of these energies are summarized in the following chart. For the purpose of clarity, it uses representative correspondences for the rays and the realms but is not limited to them.

Ninefold Energetics Chart

	Silver Ray − Receptive	**Crystal Ray** = Integrative	**Gold Ray** + Expressive
Realm of Sky + Mental	**Silver Sky** −+ Mental reception Receive through mind; reates mental form	**Crystal Sky** = + Mental integration Integrate through mind; creates mental order	**Gold Sky** + + Mental expression Express through mind; creates mental change
Realm of Land = Physical	**Silver Land** −= Physical reception Receive through body; creates physical form	**Crystal Land** = = Physical integration Integrate through body; creates physical order	**Gold Land** + = Physical expression Express through body; creates physical change
Realm of Sea − Emotional	**Silver Sea** −− Emotional reception Receive through psyche; creates emotional form	**Crystal Sea** =− Emotional integration Integrate through psyche; creates emotional order	**Gold Sea** +− Emotional expression Express through psyche; creates emotional change

The energies and actions described in this chart can be further condensed into keywords that broadly describe their nature.

Ninefold Keywords Chart

	Silver	Crystal	Gold
Sky	Learn	Discern	Convey
Land	Make	Sustain	Grow
Sea	Perceive	Restore	Transform

Nine Currents in the Avalonian Stream of Tradition

A Ninefold pattern of function is revealed when the Three Rays of Awen (creative force) overlay the Three Realms of existence (created form). With this energetic map of the Ninefold as a guide, I revisited what history and legend had to say about the roles and powers of priestesses and holy women in the traditions of Celtic lands and sought to find correspondences between them and these nine discrete energies.

Ninefold Roles Keyword Chart

	Silver	Crystal	Gold
Sky	Learn Bard/Poet Knowledge	Discern Judge/Mediator Truth	Convey Counselor/Diplomat Harmony
Land	Make Artist/Crafter Skill	Foundation Host/Benefactor Abundance	Grow Champion/Advocate Honor
Sea	Perceive Oracle/Prophet Wisdom	Restore Healer/Midwife Wholeness	Transform Celebrant/Sacrificer Oneness

I then sought out energetic correspondences from the various components of lore and history that have come to comprise the Avalonian Stream of Tradition—particularly those dealing with traditions of Ninefold Sisterhoods, Vessels of Sovereignty, and the roles of holy and Otherworldly women. I named these nine functions quite broadly, seeking to establish umbrella terms that reflected the fundamental energies of the Ninefold pattern and that could hold a variety of aligned roles within them. For example, to describe the function represented by the Gold Ray in the Realm of Sky, I used the term "emissary"; it is fairly inclusive and can include the roles of mediator, counsellor, advisor, messenger, diplomat, and peace weaver. At other times, this naming convention does directly represent what those in these roles would have been called, such as with the Seer and the Healer.

After sorting through all of this information, I worked to trace each of these nine component currents as far back to their sources as I could—seeking out the being I have come to recognize as the Threshold Guardian or Spiritual Ancestor of that particular path—the essence of whom inhabits all related manifestations of her function along the stream but who takes on different embodiments over time and through cultures. For example, She Who Sustains is related to the Otherworldly hospitality of the Well Maidens, the mead intoxication of kingship rites that ensured the bounty and well-being of the people, the noblewomen whose household hosted feasts and offered hospitality to travelers, and the women who tended the central hearthfires around which families were raised and communities were fed.

The Ninefold Path of the Priestess with Major Correspondences

Path	Lorekeeper	Lawspeaker	Emissary
Spiritual Ancestor	She Who Preserves	She Who Measures	She Who Connects
Role	Bard/Poet	Judge/Mediator	Counsellor/ Diplomat
Domain	History Culture	Justice Oaths and Contracts	Relationships Communication
Key	Learning	Discernment	Understanding
Threshold	Memory	Integrity	Trust
Vessel	Knowledge	Truth	Harmony

Path	Artisan	Hearthtender	Guardian
Spiritual Ancestor	She Who Creates	She Who Sustains	She Who Incites
Role	Artist/ Craftsperson	Host/Benefactor	Champion/ Advocate
Domain	Skill Vocation	Kindred Community	Sovereignty Security
Key	Discipline	Responsibility	Purpose
Threshold	Mastery	Generosity	Valor
Vessel	Art	Abundance	Honor

Path	Seer	Healer	Ritualist
Spiritual Ancestor	She Who Reveals	She Who Restores	She Who Transforms
Role	Oracle/Visionary	Healer/Midwife	Celebrant/Initiator
Domain	Prophecy Guidance	Treatment Caregiving	Sacrifice Ceremony
Key	Clarity	Acceptance	Reverence
Threshold	Awareness	Compassion	Sanctity
Vessel	Wisdom	Wholeness	Oneness

The Ninefold Today

There is no question that we live in a very different cultural context than the ones from which these legends and their underlying myths arose. What personal insights, devotional practices, and guidance in our service as priestess can we obtain from our understanding of the roles, powers, and privileges of Celtic holy women found in lore and history?

As we have seen from the traditions of Wales and Ireland that have remained to us in law codes and through lore, there was a tendency to sort things into groups of nine. The number nine could be therefore understood as a unit of measurement wherein nine of a thing was considered a complete set and, by extension, representative of a whole. When we also consider the traditions of priestesses and Otherworldly women presenting in groups of nine or multiples of nine, a pattern emerges that associates the number with things of a sacred nature. This may be an extension of the significance of the number three to

Celtic peoples; a tripling of the sacred number three can only serve to amplify its sense of holiness. It may also be related to the nine months of pregnancy that results in the birth of a child—a natural teaching of what is required to manifest a wholeness.

This idea that wholeness—something complete—is comprised of nine component parts is one we can adopt for use in our own quest for wholeness. The energetic matrix of the Ninefold we have been exploring can be used as an organizing principle that can be applied to the world within us, the world around us, and the world beyond us. It is a potent lens through which we can reflect upon our inner selves, a clarifying method to assess the nature of our connections with the outer world, and a devotional process that can guide us in growing our relationship with the Divine.

The Ninefold is a system that describes a set of fundamental manifestations of energetic actions, permitting it to be used as an organizing principle with limitless applications. It can be a filter through which to order one's world, a rubric with which to assess one's work, a tool by which to measure one's progress, and a guide through which we can develop sovereign relationships with ourselves, others, the world around us, and with the divinities, Guardians, and guides of the Holy Isle.

Three Levels of Service through the Ninefold

	Self	Others	Source
Lorekeeper	Personal history, reclaiming one's own story, study	Cultural history, archiving, teaching, researching, song, storytelling	Mythic history, chant, poetry, song spells, seeking Awen
Lawspeaker	Personal morality and sense of honor, beliefs, perspectives	Community standards, values, social justice, equity, accountability	Religious tenets, philosophy, spiritual teachings, oaths

	Self	Others	Source
Emissary	Inner relationship, self-expression, clarity of communication	Outer relationships, diplomacy, mediation, counseling, networking	Divine relationships, prayer, meditation, journey work, aspecting
Artisan	Personal mastery, gifts and goals, develop skills, creative practice	Vocation and avocation, innovate, manifest, meet needs, right work	Sacred art, devotional creations, spiritual tools, magical arts
Hearthtender	Self-care and sustainability, inner flame as sacred center	Caring for others, hospitality, generosity, community container	Shrine-tending, maintaining sacred space, religious feasts
Guardian	Personal boundaries, recognition of true will, passions, purpose	Championing causes, honoring and protecting others, activism	Spiritual quests, sacred land protection, ecstatic embodiment practices
Seer	Self-trust, developed intuition, discernment, clear self-assessment	Collective visioning, reflection on group Shadow, guidance	Divinatory and oracular service, mantic trance, ancestor work
Healer	Wholeness, inner and outer balance, tending body, mind, and spirit	Healing through many modalities, midwifery, psychopomp work	Spiritual and vibrational healing, plant ally work, soul retrieval
Ritualist	Alignment, honoring personal cycles, devotional practice	Community ceremony, rites of passage, seasonal workings	Ritual practice, theurgy, sacrifice, offerings, initiation into mysteries

For these reasons and more, seeing ourselves and our world through the filter of the Ninefold while working to develop relationships with each of the nine fosters a better understanding of the corresponding aspects within ourselves and around us in the world. In turn, these understandings empower us to be more conscious in our choices and more directed in our efforts to manifest change. The bridges to the Otherworld represented by the nine can be walked in both directions—they channel the Awen to us through the Vessel of the Self we have prepared to receive it, as well as permit us to cross the thresholds of the Otherworld to seek out energy by using the keys developed through mastery.

The Avalonian Priestess

At its very core, the work of the Avalonian priestess is to know how to navigate these thresholds, recognize times and places of liminality for what they are, and be in service as a bridge. In the Second Branch of *Y Mabinogi*, when Bendigeidfran (Bran the Blessed, King of the Island of the Mighty) leads a war band to Ireland in order to rescue his sister Branwen, he is met by impediment in the form of an impassable river. A literal giant in stature, the king lays his body across the waters so that his men may walk over him to the other side. In doing so, he utters the words of this powerful Welsh axiom: *A fo ben, bid bont*—"Who would a leader be, let him be a bridge."

As an adage, *A fo ben, bid bont* expresses the wisdom of embracing an ideal of leadership founded on two things: the ability to facilitate connections between and on behalf of those in one's charge, as well as the willingness to be a servant leader. A leader should use their position and authority on behalf of others, rather than for their own personal benefit. For me, this philosophy underscores the ethic of the Avalonian priestess as one who is in service to others, who shares empowering guidance, and who is able to act as a bridge at times and in places of transition.

Being the Bridge

Here are examples of bridging that underscore the powers and functions attributed to priestesses and holy women from Celtic traditions:

Shapeshifting creates a bridge between forms

Seership creates a bridge between worlds

Weather-working creates a bridge between conditions

Healing creates a bridge between states of being

Incitement creates a bridge over boundaries

Intoxication creates a bridge between states of consciousness

Initiation creates a bridge between identities

Similarly, each of the Ninefold Paths functions as a bridge:

Lorekeeper creates bridges between ignorance and knowledge, between past and present

Lawspeaker creates bridges between injustice and equity, between chaos and order

Emissary creates bridges between conflict and peace, between misconception and understanding

Artisan creates bridges between essence and form, between practice and skill

Hearthtender creates bridges between need and fulfillment, between isolation and inclusion

Guardian creates bridges between vulnerability and safety, between openness and boundary

Seer creates bridges between darkness and light, between present and future

Healer creates bridges between illness and health, between disconnection and wholeness

Ritualist creates bridges between humanity and the Divine, between the individual and the All

No matter the service we are engaging in, the ability to build bridges requires that we are first able to identify thresholds: their location in time and space, the nature of the worlds they straddle, and the reasons they are present. We must then be able to discern how and when to cross these thresholds, if at all. Finally, we must learn how to direct these crossings so that we arrive on the other side in the state of being or place of our choosing. It is only through the understanding gained from the personal experience of crossing thresholds that we can then seek to facilitate these crossings for others.

Priestess as Verb

IIn the Sisterhood of Avalon, priestessing is something we do rather than something we are. It is an act of service and devotion. We are guided in this service by the energetic paradigm offered to us by the Ninefold.

Bridging into Wholeness

When we engage with the Ninefold in service to the self, it can be used as a tool of personal assessment as well as a pathway that connects us with Otherworldly guidance, both of which assist us in the quest for self-understanding. This, in turn, facilitates the growth, healing, self-acceptance, and wholeness that arises from the inner work required of us in our quest for Sovereignty.

Bridging into Connection

When we engage with the Ninefold in service to others, it can be used as a paradigm for building and maintaining healthy and conscious communities, as a perspective that reframes the nature of sacred service, and a means through which we can make use of our gifts, skills, and passions to facilitate positive change as we participate in active cocreation of the world.

Bridging into Oneness

When we engage with the Ninefold in service to source, it reveals thresholds through which the Divine makes itself known to us and through us. It facilitates the development of authentic devotional relationships with our goddesses, and opens us to an increasingly more transcendent understanding of the Universe and its processes.

While of course we can emulate the skill set specifically included in lore and attributed to the sacred women we've been exploring, we can also consider that any act of conscious creation, and intention to serve as a bridge can be a sacred act of service. If "priestess" is a verb, then "Avalon" is an adverb: an Avalonian priestess is one who is priestessing in the manner of Avalon. Therefore, an Avalonian priestess is one who is priestessing in the manner of Avalon: serving as a bridge between this world and the Otherworld while accessing the transformational power of liminalities.

The Many Paths of the Priestess

The Ninefold Path of the priestess embraces the perspective that there are many paths of service and many ways to build bridges of connection.

This perspective is in alignment with one of the central pillars of the Avalonian Tradition: the pursuit of personal sovereignty, defined as "fully conscious self-determination." This is a state of being that arises from an ongoing practice of inner contemplation and outer manifestation in support of spiritual transformation—work that results in a high degree of self-knowledge, a discernment-based clarity of vision, and an increasing experience of wholeness.

When we know the truth of who we are, we are empowered to make decisions that are informed by authenticity, rather than arising from illusion. This knowing derives from several things: an understanding of where we have come from, an acknowledgment of the experiences that have shaped us, and an acceptance of who we are. We work toward a wholeness that allows us to recognize the things we can see with clarity as well as the places we cannot bear to look; it acknowledges both the power of our dreams and the limitations of our fears.

This personal sovereignty must also inform our sacred service so that we may engage in priestessing in accordance with our gifts, in alignment with the work of our lives, and as a reflection of our true will. I believe our inherent talents and most passionate aspirations come to us from the Divine. The more we work to embrace, develop, and express them, the more we become vessels the gods work through in the world, allowing us to become active cocreators of the Universe. Because of this, I believe that the work of priestessing must reflect the sovereign nature of each individual, so that one's service as a bridge extends from the heart and sings the song of the soul.

As we have seen from our review of the lore, there appear to have been many forms of sacred service in Pagan Celtic cultures. The many powers and types of knowledge attributed to the Ninefold and various holy women in Celtic lands include healing, prophecy, augury, shapeshifting, weather working, water magic, necromancy, music, combat, testing and initiation of kings, fosterage, leadership, teaching, advising, diplomacy, smithcraft, gifting inspiration, incitement in battle, acting as psychopomps, working with animal allies, granting sanctuary, tending holy places, being well educated in science and mathematics, and establishing a just rule of law.

It follows, therefore, that those who feel a call to priestessing today can be in service in similarly diverse ways. We tend to think of priestesses primarily as ritual facilitators, practitioners of divination and the healing arts, teachers and leaders of groups or circles, and as tenders of shrines and sacred spaces. There are also those whose service involves interfaith work, Pagan prison ministries, and acting as celebrants for community rites of passage much like clergy from other religious traditions. These are certainly all forms of priestessing, but there are other ways to be in sacred service, other ways to be a bridge.

The priestess Facilitator, the priestess Oracle, and the priestess Healer are easily recognizable in their roles. Expanding our vision of priestessing allows it to encompass many more paths of service. Among them are the priestess Scholar, the priestess Mediator, the priestess Artisan, the priestess Carer, and the priestess Activist.

Sovereignty and Service

We can discover our best path of service through a continued commitment to our sovereign authenticity. Once we find our inner grail or Cauldron of Sovereignty—the authentic Vessel of the Self—we must then reclaim it by asking ourselves the grail question: "Whom does it serve?" Once the vessel is found and we undertake a journey into understanding the totality of what it is (and what *we* are), we begin the process of reclaiming its potency. Only then will we be able to use it as a vessel in service—to self, to the world, and to the Divine.

What we are able to pour out of the vessel is determined by what we use to fill it. A key part of self-knowledge is the understanding of our gifts, strengths, and goals: Where do our passions lie? What inspires us to action? What do we seek to create for ourselves and in the world—beautiful art, a stable household, a fulfilling vocation, a healthy family, a just society, an exciting adventure, a mastery of skills, a welcoming community, a thriving business, an authentic relationship with the Divine? There are so many choices, and we may turn to one or another at different times in our lives; we may seek several at once, or we may give ourselves wholly to just one or two.

I believe that our gifts, goals, and passions are granted to us by the Divine for a reason. The Matres Fatae—the Gallo-Roman Triple Goddess of fate—is said to attend the birth of every child and gift them with the threads and patterns with which they will weave their lives. Every thread is a different length and thickness, a different material and color. Every pattern is set at the beginning by the circumstances of birth.

Today, we frame those circumstances in terms of socioeconomic class, availability of resources, stability and functioning of the family, physical circumstances of health, as well as the safety and nurturing of the individual. What then comes of the weave depends on the manner in which the child's life unfolds. Each experience, each lesson, each challenge, each victory contributes to the living tapestry of their life's journey.

The more we are able to know our selves and live from a place of authenticity, the more we are able to be conscious weavers of our life's tapestry. Instead of unconsciously repeating patterns that have been set by the people and experiences of our past, the path of wholeness permits us to weave a tapestry that increasingly becomes a reflection of our Sovereignty.

Once we know what moves us, what we strive for, what impels us into action…we know where lies the Awen. And to fill the Vessel of Sovereignty with this creative energy, this divine spark of inspiration, we must then give ourselves permission (time, space, resources, discipline) to go where the Awen flows. This is the path toward authenticity, where we find how we can best be in service as a priestess.

This is the mystery: the Vessel of Sovereignty can only be found deep within us. It is in the keeping of the Guardians of the Holy Island, at the heart of Avalon. The more we are whole, the more we can express what is holy. What we are able to pour out in service through our priestessing is empowered—and inspired—by the Awen. That is the reason we are granted the Awen in the first place: so that we can pour it out—into projects, choices, actions, service. Reclaiming the Vessel of Sovereignty within us empowers us to enter the liminal and bring through the energies needed to catalyze change in ourselves, in our communities, and in the world.

Our approach to priestessing is informed by this model: Self as Vessel, Awen as Service, Sovereignty as Bridge.

The Self as Vessel

Manifesting wholeness through the integration and balancing of the Ninefold within creates a worthy vessel that is ready and able to receive Awen; it does not leak and is of sufficient depth to hold what is required. The further down into the unconscious we go, the deeper our vessel will be. The personal unconscious is what connects us to the collective unconscious, granting us access to the wisdom of the Otherworld.

We can prepare the Vessel of the Self by doing our inner work—obtaining the degree of self-knowledge, personal mastery, and inner Sovereignty necessary to own, acknowledge, and honor all parts of ourself. This is the path that leads to wholeness. Wholeness is not perfection. Wholeness celebrates our gifts and strengths, has compassion for our wounds and fears, and actively seeks to transform the self in order to obtain an ever-greater degree of Sovereignty. Wholeness permits us to be conscious enough to make choices that are in alignment with our Sovereignty—as well as recognizing the truth of the choices not arising from Sovereignty.

Engaging in the work of the Avalonian Cycle of Healing and the Avalonian Cycle of Revealing can assist us on the path of readying the Vessel of the Self for use in our priestess service. The refinement of this vessel is an ongoing process. As we continue to reveal more of our authentic self, as we achieve an increasingly greater degree of wholeness, the Vessel of the Self will shift and evolve as a reflection of our growth. And because this growth continues over the course of our lifetime, we should not wait until we've achieved some sense of completion before we endeavor to seek the Awen.

Awen as Service

The Awen is a gift from the Otherworld, streaming through sacred vessels and granted to those who seek it by means of mastery. It is a sacrament of divine inspiration—a creative energy meant to fill those who seek it so that it may be poured out in service of creation. Wherever it flows, through whatever medium of service, the Awen catalyzes change.

In chapter 8, we discussed the differences between Awen Fach and Awen Fawr, and how the smaller inspirations we receive in our day-to-day lives pave the way for the receipt of the greater energies that come through the vehicle of mastery. Self-mastery comes as a result of our work to refine the Vessel of the Self. The state of that vessel is what determines our ability to receive the Awen, as well as our ability to pour it forth in service. Once we feel that we are able to discern the state of our vessel and its readiness to be used it service, we can begin preparing to receive the energies of Awen by actively seeking it out. The Awen posture presented in chapter 12 is a tool we can use every day to clear the way for the receipt of Awen.

Sovereignty as Bridge

When filled with and empowered by Awen, the Vessel of the Self becomes a Vessel of Sovereignty that, in turn, can be used in service as a bridge—pouring out the energies of Awen in service to self, to the world, and to Source. We are in service to ourselves when we do the work to bridge the nine aspects of the self. With this service, our Vessel pours fourth the gifts of Cauldron of Regeneration and Rebirth. It is service in support of wholeness. We are in service to the world when we act as a bridge between ourselves and the world. With this service, our Vessel pours forth the gifts of the Cauldron of Abundance. It is service in support of our community and our planet, achieved through acts of active or passive priestessing.

We are in service to the Divine when we act as a bridge between ourselves and Source, as well as serving as a bridge to facilitate the connections between Source and others. With this service, our Vessel pours forth the gifts of the Cauldron of Wisdom, Knowledge, and Inspiration. It is a service in support of receiving divine guidance and insight, of forging a personal relationship with divinity through devotional practice, and of engaging in acts of creation that serve as a bridge between others and Source.

FOLLOWING THE
MYTHIC MAP

Whether storming the Otherworld to obtain the chieftain's cauldron or embarking upon the quest for the grail to heal the wounded king, seeking the Vessel of Sovereignty can be an allegory for our soul's yearning for connection to something greater than ourselves, for our desire to obtain a sense of our life's purpose, and for the process of self-awareness that brings us to a place of integration or individuation. The object of the quest, therefore, is wholeness, while the vessel itself is catalytic—the spiritual alembic or Cauldron of Transformation that rarifies, clarifies, and brings about change. Our ability to perceive this inner vessel, and for it to manifest with increasingly greater substance within our consciousness, improves with each step we take along the inner pathways into wholeness. Likewise, the vessel becomes increasingly filled with the energies of creation, abundance, and renewal with each choice we make from a place of Sovereignty.

Although we will be using the mental construct of the Ninefold as a way to organize our approach to wholeness by breaking it down into its composite parts so that we can understand it better, the truth is that a wholeness cannot be separated from itself. All that exists is an aspect of the creative Universe still actively in the process of being made manifest.

Because of this, each of the Nine Paths can enable us to build a bridge of connection to the creative source of the Universe. Further, each path can lead to a revelation of the whole within it—a testimony to their inherently fractal nature.

When these nine aspects of self are working together in balance, we are better able to receive the flow of Awen and for it to fill the Vessel of the Self. This energy can then be poured out into the world through our works of inspired service, thus contributing to the Universe's ongoing process of creation. Our goal, therefore, is to integrate the nine parts of the self to create balance. This activates the Vessel of Sovereignty within us and permits the Awen to flow forth in whatever service we give— our vessels overflow, gifting to others and changing the vessel itself. The more the nine parts of self are in balance, the more we are able to kindle our inner vessel—in support of the knowledge of our service, our authentic self, and our Sovereignty. (See chart facing, on page 277.)

So how can we obtain this inner balance? How do we find the Vessel of Sovereignty within us so that we may activate its powers of transformation, abundance, and wisdom in our lives? One way is by following the mythic map left for us, embedded in the thresholds of symbol found in bardic lore. In this case, we know the location of the Otherworldly cauldron kindled by the breath of the Nine Maidens: Caer Pedyrvan, the Four-Peaked revolving fortress of Annwn.

Because of the longevity of her story and the potential ancient religious underpinnings of her tale, Avalon has come to be expressed in a variety of ways through multiple systems of cognition. Each of these informs the others, and together they not only serve to empower multiple pathways to the Holy Island but also contribute to the energetic essence of Avalon as a whole. In this light, we can conceive of Avalon as a cosmological paradigm, an Otherworldly island, a mythic archetype, an international folk motif, a medieval legend, a romanticized egregore, a psycho-spiritual metaphor, a fragment of reclaimed history, an illusion off the coast of Sicily—and so much more.

Nine Aspects of the Self

Lorekeeper	Lawspeaker	Emissary
What we know and how we learn.	*What we believe and how we think.*	*What we hear and how we respond.*
Knowledge	Values	Communication
Memory	Judgment	Diplomacy
Tradition	Ethics	Relationships
Artisan	**Hearthtender**	**Guardian**
What we create and how we work.	*What we have and how we contribute.*	*What we experience and how we grow.*
Vocation	Resources	Strength
Skill	Generosity	Courage
Mastery	Foundation	Passion
Seer	**Healer**	**Ritualist**
What we perceive and how we trust.	*What we are and how we feel.*	*What we love and how we live.*
Intuition	Restoration	Devotion
Prophecy	Compassion	Alignment
Wisdom	Wholeness	Transformation

So where is the barge that will bring us to Avalon? How can we develop authentic, discernment-based relationships with her guardians? How can we be in service as an Avalonian priestess? How do we cross the threshold to reach the Otherworldly Isle?

To begin, let's consider what we know. There are places that serve as bridges to Avalon, such as historically holy islands and other places where her legends have come to reside. These include specific places—such as Glastonbury and Bardsey Island—as well as places featuring physical characteristics similar to descriptions of Avalon: remote islands, misty lakes, and apple orchards.

Places and times of liminality can also be used as bridges to Avalon, particularly when coupled with some of the characteristics here described. A misty apple orchard at Calan Gaeaf and the shimmering silver pathway formed by the reflection of the setting moon on the surface of a the ocean are examples of entryways to Avalon.

Symbols with strong connections to Avalon can also serve as a bridge to her shores. The most potent of these symbols are those drawn from legend and lore because their connections to Avalon have been well established over centuries; these include apples, a barge with three dark-veiled queens, swans, harps, an island in mist, and the hand of the Lady of the Lake receiving Excalibur.

There are also more recent symbols that have become interwoven with the energies of Avalon; although they don't have the benefit of being empowered over time and through generations, they have been potentiated by the sheer number of people who hold them to be connected in their consciousness—a process facilitated by the technologies of the modern era, from the printing press to the internet. In this way, symbols empowered by consciousness over time (depth) find themselves side by side with symbols empowered by consciousness over space (surface area) because the latter reside in the minds and spirits of millions of people today. These symbols include the *vesica piscis* symbol on the cover of the Chalice Well, the silhouette of Glastonbury Tor, and the blue crescent priestess tattoo from *The Mists of Avalon*.

These latter symbols reinforce the idea that story, art, and music are powerful bridges to Avalon. Legends and lore weave the matrix of the underlying energetic tone encapsulated by the idea of Avalon, but the vessels that hold this idea—the garments it wears, the facets it reveals—change as cultures change and as the needs of society change. However, in the end, if it is something that is consciously connected to the Avalonian Stream of Tradition, it is part of the same whole, because the same waters run through it.

All of these together—the mythic maps found in story, the spiritually activating symbol sets, the catalytic properties of poetic language, the energetic mechanics of working with liminalities—can be used to craft bridges to Avalon through spiritual practices that draw upon all of these things. These practices include ritual, trance journeys, ecstatic rites, and devotional works—all practices that cause a shift in consciousness and reveal an inner threshold.

And where there is a threshold, there is the Otherworld.

Parsing the Otherworld

The Welsh Otherworld is called Annwn (or *Annwfn*, in Middle Welsh), a phrase that means either "the Very Deep" or "the Un-World," depending on the etymology. I think these are related concepts that reflect the Celtic British understanding of both the nature and location of the Otherworld. A cosmological paradigm that consists of "the world" and "not the world" fits into the system of dualities that seems to underscore a great deal of Celtic thought.

What follows is my own take on the Otherworld, informed by my studies as well as the experiences I have had over the years as a practitioner. If Annwn is defined as the Un-World or the Not-World, it stands to reason that anything not of this world is of the Otherworld.

The Realm of Land is analogous to the present; it is the place of manifestation and form and the region where all living things dwell. It is this world and contains all that is.

The Realm of Sea is related to the past; it is the realm of the dead, the place of the ancestors and of deep memory. It is comprised of all that once was and is therefore part of the Otherworld.

The Realm of Sky is connected to the future; it is the realm of perfection, divine patterns, and the gods. It contains the totality of all that may yet be—the sum of all possibilities that have not yet come into manifestation in the Realm of Land. Therefore, it, too, is part of the Otherworld.

In the Welsh tradition, the colors red and white are associated with the Otherworld; when we see these colors, especially together, it is a strong indication that Otherwordly energies are present. For example, the dogs of Arawn, King of Annwn, are white with red ears. The red and white dragons in the story of Lludd and Llefelys are surely Otherworldly entities, and the sacred waters of Glastonbury's Red and White Springs reinforce its connection to Otherworldly Avalon. The colors many modern practitioners have come to associate with the Three Realms are: red for the Realm of Sea, black for the Realm of Land, and white for the Realm of Sky. If the Realm of Land is this world, the two realms associated with the Otherworld are red and white, accordingly—in alignment with traditional correspondences from lore.

When I think about the Three Realms, I see the Realm of Land as the thinnest layer; all that is present at this point in time is much less than the collective sum of all that has once been present—which in turn is infinitely smaller than all possibilities of future presence. The Realm of Sea contains all that once was, and so is steadily increasing in size, representing that which is eternal. The Realm of Sky contains all that may yet be, and so is an infinitely expansive plane of possibilities. If we look at this another way, we see:

Realm of Sky—Future—Potential—the Limitless Expanse

Realm of Land—Present—Manifestation—the Eternal Now

Realm of Sea—Past—Dissolution—the Endless Deep

The Realm of Land is the place where things become manifest—where potentialities from the Realm of Sky take root. Once these things have run their course, they move beyond the present into what once was, becoming part of the eternal Sea that contains all that has passed. The Realm of Land can therefore be visualized as a very thin plane or horizon where energy moves from potential (Realm of Sky) into manifestation and from manifestation into dissolution (Realm of Sea).

One way to look at this cosmogenic mechanism is to envision the Realm of Sky—that which is not yet, the future and all of its possibilities, all that is beyond our ability to experience and comprehend—as full of the limitless energies of creation, emanating from the divine source. This solar, cosmic energy radiates outward, expanding in all directions, seeking to fill the void—just as science teaches us that energy will move from a place of higher concentration to lower concentration until equilibrium is achieved.

When a portion of this energy is received in the Realm of Land—whether by plants awaiting sunlight to grow, bards seeking the Awen in order to compose prophetic poetry, or artisans seeking inspiration to guide them in the creation of something new—that force takes on form and becomes manifest.

If Annwn is the "Not-World" and the "Very Deep", it follows that the manifest world around us—everything that is not considered the Otherworld—is not very deep. The Realm of Land can be envisioned as resting upon the rim of the ever-deepening Cauldron that contains the Realm of Sea. Extending infinitely above it is the Realm of Sky—the expanse of the Universe, and all of its possibilities. And here, between the two, is the coracle of our lives—a little vessel supported by the waters of the past below and open to the future potential of the Universe above. I see this in the symbol of the upright vesica piscis with the cauldron below and the torc of sovereignty above, forming the coracle at the place where they overlap, bridging them both.

As we have learned from the lore, sometimes passage to the Otherworld requires a journey over water—past the Ninth Wave, into the west, along the shining pathway formed when the sun sets over the ocean, toward the threshold of the horizon where the sea meets the sky. Sometimes the journey is underwater—to the bottom of the ocean or below sacred lakes where groups of water spirits or whole civilizations of fairy folk dwell.

Other times, the Otherworld is reached through hollow hills and fairy mounds—often, in reality, Neolithic and Bronze Age burial mounds, and therefore connected to the ancestors and the realm of the dead. This suggests that another way into the Otherworld is through death. Sometimes the Otherworld imposes itself on our own world, its presence heralded by a sudden descent of mist, or a thunderous noise, or a pack of baying hounds described as white with red ears.

However we encounter it, however we connect with or enter it, the Otherworld has its own set of rules—and we would do best to honor them. First, we are warned not to eat or drink the food of the Otherworld; doing so may result in never being able to leave, and those who do manage to leave the Otherworld will eventually pine away and die because nothing in the mortal realm will ever satisfy them again. The warning here is that illusions cannot nourish us; they may be beautiful, but they aren't real and can trap us in a pattern of liminality where we want what we cannot have and have what we do not want.

Likewise, we must remember that the laws of time and space work differently in the Otherworld—far seems near, time runs differently, and speed is relative. We must not linger overlong in the Otherworld or allow it to distract or befuddle us; staying focused on our goals when we find ourselves between the worlds prevents us from getting stuck there. Finally, we must be clear in expressing what we need when we are in a period of liminality, or when the Otherworld is near. Loopholes are also types of thresholds, and the Otherworld loves to exploit them. Direct and unambiguous speech is required, as is ensuring that there can be only one meaning in your spoken intention. If you have any doubt, rephrase or be clear with what you don't want to happen.

The Location of Avalon

So where is the true location of the Holy Isle? Whether we traverse the shining trackways of legend, or follow the faint trails laid by history, it is my belief that Avalon is part of Annwn, the Welsh Otherworld that has its origins in a Brythonic Pagan past.

In legend, she bears all of the hallmarks of the Otherworld—a western island paradise associated with healing, abundance, and eternal youth that is named for the fruit of the Otherworld, and ruled by learned and powerful women. Whether a resonance of ancient Pagan myth, or a fantastical tale conjured in the collective imagination and perpetuated in consciously created literary tradition, Avalon of legend is associated with the Realm of Sky—that part of the Otherworld that contains all possibilities but no certainties—the realm of inspiration that holds and carries the creative energies of the Universe.

On the other hand, if the Roman accounts of islands of Gaulish priestesses are true and the widespread motif of Ninefold groups of holy or magical women found throughout the Celtic world and beyond are the potentially euhemerized recollections of a cultus served by groups of priestesses with oracular and healing powers, then the Avalon of history is associated with the Realm of Sea—that which once was but is no longer and has passed into the watery domain of deep memory.

We may never know the definitive answer to the question of whether Avalon as we have come to know it is a purely literary creation or a resonance of forgotten history—or, as I suspect, a little bit of each. However, as spiritual seekers working to engage with the Holy Isle in this place and at this time, the answer to that question may not matter. Either way, no matter what she may once have been, Avalon exists in the Otherworld—in the cosmological Not-World, and/or the Very Deep within us all.

The Realm of Land is thus a place of bridging where those who seek to be in service as an Avalonian priestess must be able to traverse the various thresholds between the worlds, questing for Avalon both in what is past and what is possible—seeking the guidance of the past and an inspiration for the future. The Realm of Land, the present, is the domain of action—where creation becomes manifest and change is set into motion. We build a bridge from Land to Sky when we seek to create that which isn't yet manifest and build a bridge from land into sea when we seek to change what has manifested.

The manner in which Avalon appears to us depends on the bridge we use to reach her—what mythic map we follow—but I believe the essence of Avalon, the energy she holds, and the functions she fulfills underscore every known iteration of the Holy Isle. The ultimate truth may look like something else entirely.

Whatever falls below the threshold of the Realm of Land and enters the Realm of Sea can be brought up into the land again, welling up out of the Otherworld like a sacred spring. I believe that this is what the modern Neopagan movement has done with the gods and what those whose spiritual path is inspired by Avalon have done with the Holy Isle.

We speak of bringing Avalon out of the mists, but truly, our work is to cross that sacred boundary, the threshold through which we can enter the Otherworld so that we can walk in truth on Avalon's shores. Once we do so, we become able to share her gifts with others through this act of bridging. We can bring back the apple of knowledge and immortality, the mercy of healing ointments, the blessings of Sovereignty, the insights of prophetic poetry, divinely inspired guidance, and the transformational powers of initiation.

Avalon and the Otherworld

There is no question that there are physical locations that resemble the descriptions of Avalon in legend that, over time, have come to wear her mythic mantle. Sometimes it's because long-standing tradition has created a powerful bridge between lore and landscape, while other times the connection is founded on physical similarities of the liminal and symbolic kind—islands that are difficult to reach, islands traditionally associated with the blessed dead, or places known for the rarity and uniqueness of their apples.

However, I believe that in her most actualized form, Ynys Afallon exists quite firmly in the Celtic British Otherworld and is one of the islands of Annwn, the Otherworld of Welsh tradition. This mythic Avalon is akin to paradisiacal islands in the traditions of other Celtic cultures, such as the Irish Emain Ablach, although we may never know if these similarities are a reflection of a core belief common to those peoples arising from the PIE mother culture or one that spread between neighboring peoples long after they evolved into separate cultures.

Either way, even taking into account the complexities that arise when trying to trace the evolution and transmission of myth in cultures that practice orality, we must acknowledge that a relationship exists even when we cannot fully decode the nature and origin of that relationship. This is also true for the ways in which the earliest elements of the Arthurian Tradition have their origins in Brythonic legends and lore, even as centuries of evolution and a variety of narrative influences from across Europe have drowned out some of the foundational aspects of the Matter of Britain.

I reference the poem "Preiddeu Annwn" quite often in this book; it is important to this discussion for many reasons, not least because of its mention of the Naw Morwyn—the Nine Maidens whose breath kindles the Cauldron of the Chief of Annwn. In addition to being one of the earliest Arthurian tales, it is also one of the earliest extant descriptions of the Brythonic Otherworld. Elements of earlier traditions are preserved in Welsh bardic poetry, even as bardism as an important cultural institution endured in Welsh courts into the thirteenth century and well beyond that in nonroyal contexts; indeed, bardism continues to blossom as a cultural movement in Wales today.

Since the Nine Sisters is one of the defining characteristics of Avalon in its earliest written account by Geoffrey of Monmouth—who was likely familiar with "Preiddeu Annwn" or the oral legends that informed it—the area of Annwn that most closely resembles Avalon is Caer Pedyvran, home of the Nine Maidens and the cauldron in their keeping. Some modern Pagan writers have identified Avalon with Annwn as a whole—a one-to-one equivalence—but I disagree; I feel that Avalon is part of Otherworld and does not represent its entirety. This is because Annwn is represented as having many facets and functions in Welsh lore—ranging from joy to restriction—and "Preiddeu Annwn" appears to be describing many of them.

Ynys Afallon—Cosmological Geography

The glyph below is a cosmological map of the Avalonian Tradition as practiced by the Sisterhood of Avalon. It presents a visual organization of the ways in which the various layers of our tradition interconnect and work together, informed by the description of Caer Pedryvan in "Preiddeu Annwn" specifically. The synchronicities between our tradition and the details of Caer Pedryvan (the area of Annwn that most strongly resonates with the energies of Avalon) served as beautiful validation for the mythic map we had been following. I sketched out the foundation of this glyph of integration; it was beautifully re-rendered in the form below by SOA Council of Nine member Kate Brunner.

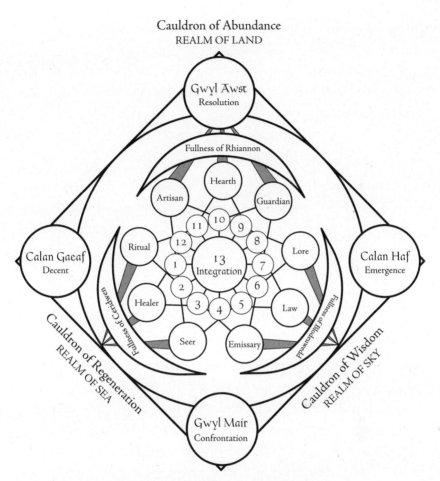

Cosmological Map of the Avalonian Tradition

As with the roundhouses of the Celtic Britons, at the center of the Avalonian Tradition is the cauldron—the Vessel of Sovereignty. Using the cauldron as a bridge into Annwn, we find it in the guise of Peir Pen Annwn, the Cauldron of the Chief of Annwn. It is described as dark and ringed with pearls; it utters poetry, praise, and prophecy, and will not boil the food of a coward. The cauldron is located in Caer Pedryvan, the Four-Peaked Fortress four times revolving, where it is in the keeping of Naw Morwyn, Nine Maidens who kindle the cauldron with their breath. In order to reach Caer Pedryvan, one must undertake a perilous journey over water.

Here is how this description is expressed in the glyph along with an explanation of each element's corresponding aspect within the Avalonian Tradition.

The Sacred Center: The Seeker

In the middle of the glyph is the sacred center, an anchor point in space and time that serves to define one's position relative to the cosmos. There are several overlapping elements that converge at the sacred center, beginning with the essence of the seeker—the self as *axis mundi*. All else proceeds from this point.

The Vessel of Sovereignty: The Avalonian Cycle of Revealing

Occupying the center of the glyph is the Peir Pen Annwn, the Cauldron of the Chief of Annwn. In the Avalonian Tradition, it is called the Vessel of Sovereignty for several reasons. First, it has a testing attribute; it will not boil the food of a coward—which is to say, it will not function for the unworthy. Second, the purpose for Arthur's raid of Annwn is to obtain this cauldron; although we aren't told why he wants it, the testing attribute coupled with it being the property of the Chief of Annwn (the Sovereign of the Otherworld) strongly suggests a Sovereignty motif.

The bottom of the cauldron is represented by the small central circle (the first overlap of the seeker), while its rim is defined by twelve small circles that represent the pearls. Together, these thirteen circles represent the Lunar Keys of the Avalonian Cycle of Revealing. Each Key is comprised of one of the thirteen full moons (each a pearl) in the year, a mythic portion from one of the Welsh goddesses honored in the Avalonian Tradition (Ceridwen, Blodeuwedd, Rhiannon, Arianrhod, and

Branwen), and an herbal ally that energetically corresponds to both the time of the year and the goddess being honored.

The circle at center of the cauldron is the thirteenth moon, the Blue Moon of Reflection; that it overlaps the seeker serves to emphasize how this yearlong and cyclic process changes how we see ourselves and the world around us though the rarifying, clarifying, and transformational powers of the cauldron. At its heart, the work of the Cycle of Revealing is to guide the seeker in reclaiming their Sovereignty, while forging authentic relationships with the goddesses of the Avalonian Tradition. A guide to this process is outlined in my 2019 book, *The Mythic Moons of Avalon*.

The Nine Maidens of Annwn: The Ninefold Path

Surrounding the cauldron are nine larger circles representing the Nine Maidens. Threshold Guardians of the Ninefold Path in Annwn, they are Muses through whose breath the creative energies of the Awen flows, activating the cauldron in their keeping. The cauldron pours forth wisdom and fate, eloquence and art, abundance and incitement, prophecy and healing, and the transformational powers of initiation. Their continued kindling of the cauldron represents both the responsibilities of their guardianship of the Ninefold Path as well as the importance of continuing to work toward the Sovereign wholeness that is facilitated by the Cycle of Revealing.

Just as the Cycle of Revealing is powered by the thirteen lunations of the year and the Cycle of Healing (discussed in the next section) is powered primarily by the seasonal cycle of the sun, so is the Ninefold Path of the Priestess aligned with and empowered by the monthly cycle of the phases of the moon (discussed further in chapter 13).

The Three Fullnesses of Prydwen: The Journey into Wholeness

The three crescent-shaped ships crowning three groups of three Maidens represent the three fullnesses of *Prydwen*, Arthur's ship, whose name means "Fair Face." How can three fullnesses of one ship undertake a single journey at the same time, as suggested in "Preiddeu Annwn"? Perhaps it represents the seeker's need to move through the Three Realms of Sky, Land, and Sea? Or perhaps it is a call for the whole self to participate in the quest to receive the cauldron's bounty—for the seeker to engage the work of the Holy Isle with mind, body, and spirit?

In this cosmological glyph, each of the crescent-shaped ships (which also resemble shields, as "Prydwen" is the name Geoffrey of Monmouth gives to Arthur's magical shield) represents one of the realms—and all its attendant correspondences. The three ships are overlain with the Triple Awen, which emanates from Source before passing through each realm. Each of the nine illuminations or currents that result from the passage of the Three Rays through the Three Realms touches one of the Nine Maidens. These currents and their corresponding maidens represent one of the Nine Paths of the Avalonian priestess. One aspect of the work of the Ninefold Path is to deconstruct the parts of ourselves so that we may better understand the whole.

A repeating refrain in "Preiddeu Annwn" is that of all of Arthur's warriors, only seven returned or "rose up" from the raid on the Otherworld. While any journey into the Otherworld can be fraught with danger, when reflecting this tale within us, perhaps here it can be viewed as referring to the aspects of the self that are sloughed off or left behind. Perhaps it is a statement that those who would obtain the cauldron and its gifts will be rarified by the process, stripped of what no longer serves: illusions, outmoded ways of being, and limiting perspectives. Parts of the old self will fall away; what is not worthy will stay behind and in its place we will have partaken of the Vessel of Sovereignty—and become forever changed.

Caer Pedryvan: The Avalonian Cycle of Healing

The entirety of this energetic map is contained within Caer Pedyvran, the Four-Peaked Fortress symbolized here by the square enclosing the whole. The fortress itself is said to be four times revolving, and while the meaning of this is open to interpretation (and we know of other examples of revolving Otherworldly fortresses from Irish mythos), it is possible that this may refer to the seasonal round.

In each corner is a large circle; these represent the four outer stations of the Avalonian Cycle of Healing: Descent, Confrontation, Emergence, and Resolution. The fifth station, Integration, is located in the center of the glyph, where it is aligned with the Moon of Reflection (the thirteenth moon of the Cycle of Revealing), the cauldron itself, and the wholeness of the Seeker. The Cycle of Healing has many correspondences; among them are the cycle of the seasons, the phases of the moon, the daily positions of the sun, and the four holy days of the Celtic year.

The Cycle also holds resonance with features in the Glastonbury landscape; embodiment practices emulating these portal places connected to Avalon in the Otherworld permit us to grow in understanding of our own inner landscapes. The five stations in the Cycle of Healing hold resonance with the five goddesses honored in the Avalonian Tradition, as well as the five seeds within the sacred apple that, when cut, reveals the star within. Perhaps most of all, the Cycle of Healing is a reflection of the five transformations that result from partaking from Ceridwen's cauldron—the initiatory process through which wisdom is obtained. A guide to this process is outlined in my 2010 book, *Avalon Within*.

This cosmological map of the major elements of praxis within the Avalonian Tradition as practiced by the Sisterhood of Avalon accomplishes several things. It depicts the internally consistent system of engagement wherein the Avalonian Cycle of Healing, the Avalonian Cycle of Revealing, and the Ninefold Path of the Priestess all overlap and work together like a series of interlocking gears that empower our growth with us, encourage our alliance with the wisdoms of the natural world around us, and facilitate our building bridges of connection with the goddesses and guardians of the Holy Isle beyond us.

This map also serves to ground these foundational aspects of the modern Avalonian Tradition in the lore that connects the Holy Isle with the Welsh Otherworld—thereby deliberately building a bridge between these present-day practices and both the Avalonian and the Annuvian Streams of Tradition. Using this cosmological map to guide us in our approach to these Otherworldly realms assists us in our quest to reach the Holy Isle and enter into authentic relationships with her goddesses and guardians. Tying into these two very well-established streams of tradition also serves to further empower our bridges of connection to Avalon, so that we may be in priestess service to the Holy Isle.

THE NINEFOLD PATH OF THE PRIESTESS

While the vision of Avalon that we have inherited from her Stream of Tradition is likely not a reflection of a physical place that existed outside of the realms of legend, it doesn't mean that Avalon isn't real. It is the nature of myth to transcend the limitations of space and time in order to transmit the universal truths contained within it.

The Avalonian Stream of Tradition is a living elixir that holds within it several potent currents of consciousness that are reflections of the beliefs, perspectives, and deep-rooted psychic/psychological needs of the cultures (and individuals) through whose landscapes it has flowed since emerging from the Otherworld at its source. These main currents are:

- **The Islands of the Otherworld,** which represent the nature of our relationship with ourselves—that which is unconscious or hidden in us, that which we fear, that which represents our personal limitations, and the specter of facing our own mortality.

- **The Vessel of Sovereignty,** which represents the nature of our relationship with the world—the ways in which we are in balance with the land, the ways in which we connect with others in safety and authenticity, and the ways in which we can obtain mastery in the things we are passionate about while also being in service to the greater good.

+ **The Ninefold Sisterhood,** which represents the nature of our relationship with the Divine—the paths we walk in search of deeper meaning, the paths that connect us to our higher truths, the paths that reveal the Universal mysteries of wholeness, and oneness, and the transformational bliss of Awen's fire in our heads.

All three are resonances of the same unconscious needs held by all who have participated in this Stream of Tradition over the course of time and through the landscapes of many cultures: the need for connections beyond the bounds of solitude, the need for a hand to guide us over the uncertain thresholds of change, and the need for a bridge to facilitate our journey into the unknown.

What follows is an exploration of this system broken down into its nine component parts in order to reveal the Ninefold Paths of service of an Avalonian priestess. An immersion in any one of these pathways has the ability to bring us to a place of inner healing, outer connection, and relationship with the Divine. This is because, as a system, the Ninefold represents a wholeness, while each path represents a call to mastery—to excellence, to achievement, to fulfillment. Because of the fractal nature of the Ninefold, each of the paths holds a wholeness within it, even in the context of its directed focus. This directed focus is what gives rise to mastery—and it is the mastery of any path that reveals the thresholds that are the foundation of Avalonian magic and that underscore the service of an Avalonian priestess.

Mastery of the self and mastery of an art are both creative forms of self-expression that permit us to cross the divide between what is and what could be. Mastery of the self allows us to build bridges between consciousness and unconsciousness, allowing us to lay down new pathways of cognition that move us away from the limitations of our fears and into the potentials unlocked by our wholeness. The process of building these bridges is similar to how we engage with obtaining and refining a new skill—be it painting, writing, music, dance, martial arts, an academic discipline, homemaking, organization, healing, counseling, craft, teaching, cycling, gardening, midwifery, chess, and so on. The more we practice this skill—forming habits and laying down neural pathways—the more we are able to get out of our own way and allow the art to come through.

This occurs when we are not required to engage the skill consciously. When we have obtained a degree of mastery that does not require us to have to think about what it is we are doing—e.g., the next note to play, the next step in a recipe, the correct form of a yoga pose, and so on—we can allow our innate expression of the skill we have mastered to emerge. When we do not need to concentrate on process, we are able to direct our conscious resources to be present with what we are doing in a new way. This permits us to make new connections, to see previously unobserved patterns, and to process information from a different perspective. When we are "in the zone," we are immersed in the flow of Awen, unimpeded—a state of being that leads to innovation, integration, and the creation of something in the moment. This manifests in ways that include musical improvisation, automatic writing, or pulling together disparate threads of data in a way that leads to a cognitive breakthrough.

To do this, we must find our vocation, our path of dedication, our passion, our true work in the world. We can begin by asking ourselves: What part of the world do I wish to cocreate, to birth into being? Then, whatever it may be—passionately advocating for needed social change, manifesting a life of security and joy, writing an orchestral score that is a journey through the seven fortresses of Annwn, creating a retreat space where our spiritual family can gather and celebrate with us—we must choose it and work toward it. Finding our soul's vocation—that is, following the call of our spirit—is the path that will lead us into mastery.

When we find the flow and identify the thresholds that birth the Awen into the world—that bursts our old vessels apart and leaps joyfully through the cracks—we will then be able to share forth our gifts in a way that will inspire souls, integrate wholeness, and incite change.

The Nine Paths and Their Correspondences

In the following section, we will look at each of the Nine Paths individually and examine certain aspects and applications of their energies. At the beginning of the section for each path, I have shared some of its main correspondences including symbols, animals, stones, herbs, and trees. These are provided to facilitate connections with the energetic essence of each path through a vehicle of correspondence that resonates with the seeker.

Certainly, one could incorporate all of these items (or images of them) on the working altar we will build when immersing in each of the Nine Paths (beginning in chapter 12); since like energies attract, the more your altar reflects the energy of the Path you are currently working with, the easier it will be to connect with that energy. However, don't think you need to obtain all of these items or use all of these tools.

Remember that one of the ways in which the Ninefold Path is empowering is that it seeks to honor the uniqueness of the person walking in service as an Avalonian priestess. Use things that help you connect in a meaningful way. If you are most comfortable with stones, you can focus on the stone correspondences. If you receive strong messages through animal guides, you can focus on their energies. If working with herbs is your passion, using them as a doorway into the energies of the Ninefold is a good place to concentrate.

Please also keep in mind that these correspondences are not the only ones you can use. As you proceed along your path of connections with the Ninefold, other symbols—other vessels that hold the energies of the paths—may present themselves to you. I suggest that once you have worked with a pathway long enough to identify (with clarity and discernment) the energies it represents, you should absolutely honor your inner wisdoms around other correspondences. This should happen after you have completed the first two phases of the Ninefold Immersion presented in the last part of this book.

Trioedd Ynys Afallon

Many years ago, I was gifted by the Awen with a set of triads that are reflections on each of the Nine Paths. I have come to collectively call them the *Trioedd Ynys Afallon*, "the Triads of the Island of Avalon," as they emulate the pattern of the triads preserved for us in *Trioedd Ynys Prydein*. These are all modern creations, and Sisters have found them to be helpful to meditate on when engaging with the Ninefold. These triads are included for each path in the section to come.

Dedicatory Project

Each of the Nine Path sections also includes a dedicatory project designed to immerse the seeker in the creative energies of the path while connecting with the Nine Currents inherent within it. Not only does this Ninefold within the Ninefold open us to a greater understanding of its fractal nature, it also demonstrates that the Ninefold Path of the priestess is actually comprised of a full spectrum of ways to be in priestess service—9 x 9 ways, a wholeness of wholenesses!—such that any woman who feels a call to Avalon will find a reflection of herself that is empowered, whole, and sovereign.

THE PATH OF THE
LOREKEEPER

The harp—what is its nature?
Does it not echo in halls of deep memory?
Does it not burn with the satirist's brand—
Singing praise, Stirring hearts,
Chanting song?

The Triad of the Lorekeeper

Three Honored Teachers of She who Seeks Knowledge: The Natural World, that the mysteries be revealed; the Ancestors, that their wisdoms be remembered; the Elders, that their services be respected, and to these be added Experience—the greatest of all teachers.

Correspondences

Role: Bard/Poet

Threshold Guardian: She Who Preserves

Archetype: The Muse

Energy: Silver Ray in the Realm of Sky

Moon phase: Waning gibbous

Stone: Bluestone (spotted dolerite), hazelnut

Herb: Rosemary

Animals: Swan, blackbird

On the Path of the Lorekeeper, learning is the key that permits access to the threshold of memory through which the Vessel of Knowledge can be accessed. The Vessel of Knowledge pours forth the aspect of Awen connected to culture, tradition, history, and genealogy. It empowers the magic of words, both for memory and for manifestation.

The gifts of this vessel are poured out in priestess service to others when we take on the work and responsibility of engaging in the study of ancient wisdoms, cultural histories, traditional tales, and folk beliefs and then share them with others through words spoken, written, and sung. Practicing these ancient arts is part of this service, such as studying Welsh poetry forms and seeking the blessings of the Awen through various tools and techniques. Archiving today's wisdoms is also part of this service, as we breathe life back into the old ways and enter into relationship with these tales and the figures within them once more.

The Path of the Lorekeeper
Informed by Tradition

Reflecting on those from ancient times whose names we do not know, those whose sacred work aligned with the energies of the Lorekeeper served their people in bardic roles. They were the guardians of the collective memory, historians who received the knowledge of the past while preserving the events of their day for the future. Recorders of noble lineages, and the arbiters of reputation—writing praise songs for princes or biting political satire with equal passion. They were responsible for the oral transmission of wisdom teachings, sacred stories, and cultural knowledge. They encoded these memories in teaching songs and inspired verses. They sought the Awen so that their poetry was infused with prophecy. They understood how to harness the power of words and used the resonance of music to evoke emotion, change minds, and soothe souls.

In the mythic realm, they were learned women who accompanied themselves on instruments, such as Thitis, Morgen's sister and coruler of Avalon who was known for her cither or harp. They spoke verses of prophecy like Merlin's sister, Ganieda. And they were revered as both *banfhili* (poetesses) and *banfháith* (prophetesses), like Fedelm in the Irish epic *Táin Bó Cuailnge*, who was skilled in obtaining the *imbas forosnai*—the inspiration that illuminates.

Inner Reflections on the Path of the Lorekeeper

Reflecting the Path of the Lorekeeper within prompts us to remember our personal history and embrace the story of our life: from the ancestral streams that inform our family dynamics, to all that we have experienced on our journey to the present, and the ways in which both have resulted in the person we have become in the here and now. Doing so grants us the ability to write the story we wish to live: from teasing out the lessons we bring with us from our past, to releasing what no longer serves us as best we can, and reframing our story in mythic terms that empower us to move our life's narrative forward from a place of Sovereignty.

We must be resolute in our commitment to obtain the self-knowledge necessary to become the person we are meant to be: from recognizing that the songs of the past need not be the soundtrack of our future, to harnessing the magic of the present to sing our best destiny into being, and building a bridge of poetic inspiration that guides our journey forward into a life of ever-increasing Sovereignty. Just as we look to the past to seek the source of the Avalonian Stream of Tradition with all the various currents that have contributed to the whole as we have come to know it today, so must we seek out our own Stream of Tradition as part of our path to self-knowledge.

Dedicatory Project for the Path of the Lorekeeper: The Ninefold Englynion

Englynion are traditional Welsh short poetry forms that make use of strict rules on stress, rhyme, and meter called *cynghanedd*—the "confined song" that brings together skill and inspiration in harmony. Arising out of Welsh Bardic tradition, multiple englynion forms have developed over the centuries, varying in pattern and complexity. Creating englynion is a beautiful devotional undertaking that is also a path to developing poetic ability; understanding and being able to use *cynghanedd* is what transforms craft into art, and it marked the difference between a poet and a bard.[192]

This is a very intensive study and more-in depth of a process than can be presented here, so I have suggested a few resources below to help start you along this path. If you want to jump right in, I will share one form I have worked with called the *englyn penfyr* ("short-ended englyn"), which happens to be one of the oldest forms known.

It is made of three-line rhyming stanzas or verses called tercets; a poem using this form can be one or more stanzas—there are no set numbers of verses. The first line has ten syllables and the last two have seven syllables each. It has a set rhyming pattern that looks like the following chart: each *x* represents a syllable, *A* represents the main rhyme (or half rhyme), and *b* represents a secondary rhyme that appears in the *caesura* (pause) added to the end of line one and echoed at the beginning of line two.

> *x x x x x x x A x b*
> *x x b x x x A*
> *x x x x x x A*[193]

---

192   Mererid Hopwood, *Singing in Chains: Listening to Welsh Verse* (Llandysul, Ceredigion: Gomer Press, 2016), xii.

193   Lawrence Eberhart, "Englyn Penfyr," Poetry Forms, June 7, 2020, https://poets collective.org/poetryforms/englyn-penfyr/.

I've tried my hand at writing poems using the englyn penfyr form—it is not as easy as it may seem. I have found that the form itself dictates the words you can use in order to express what you intend. Give it a try to understand what I mean. Here is one of the poems I wrote; it's not perfect, but I think it will provide a good enough example to get you started.

The Three Realms/Englynion Trioedd Tiroedd

Deft fingers work the loom she **weaves** in **time**
Hands of **Nine** unknot what **grieves**
Chaired in truth, the soul **believes**

A crash of tines cry out in **white** stag **wood**
Crow-black **hood** and feathered-**night**
Sovereign vessel heals the **blight**

Blood of ancients, hued in wis**dom's ochre**
Bones to **broker** songs to **come**
Awen's muse and apple'd **tongue**

After researching the art and process of using this type of poetic expression, choose a form and use it to create a poem of nine verses—one englyn for each of the Nine Paths; you can also create verses to open and close your poem if you so choose. Each verse should reflect the energy of the path it is written for and is best approached one at a time. I recommend writing them while immersed in the energy of the path and in presence of the Path Shrine you will be creating in the next chapter. Consider using a threshold tool to open yourself to the energy of Awen as part of this process; more details can be found on page 382.

Of course, englynion are traditionally written in the Welsh language, but if you are not a Welsh speaker, you can adapt the form to your native tongue. If you are a Welsh learner, try your hand at writing englynion as part of your language immersion.

If you find writing englynion to be too limiting or too difficult in a non-Welsh language, you can of course compose this Ninefold devotional work using a poetry form you prefer. However, continue to try your hand at writing englynion; it is a powerful skill to develop as a devotional practice because of its strong connection to Bardic tradition, as well as a way to honor and support Welsh culture.

Helpful Resources

Singing in Chains: Listening to Welsh Verse by Mererid Hopwood (2005, Gomer Press)

https://www.writersdigest.com/write-better-poetry/poetic-forms/welsh-poetic-forms

THE PATH OF THE LAWSPEAKER

The wheel—what is its nature?
Does it not speak from the Cauldron of Wisdom?
Does it not challenge the world with its truth—
Steering stars, testing hearts,
Ending harm?

The Triad of the Lawspeaker

Three Fair Balances of She who Seeks Justice: acknowledging ignorance of the greater pattern; living in right action; knowing her own heart.

Correspondences

Role: Judge/Mediator

Threshold Guardian: She Who Measures

Archetype: The Fate

Energy: Crystal Ray in the Realm of Sky

Moon phase: Full moon

Stone: Bone, acorn

Herb: Wood betony

Animals: Eagle, wren

On the Path of the Lawspeaker, discernment is the key that permits access to the threshold of integrity through which the Vessel of Truth can be accessed. The Vessel of Truth pours forth the aspect of Awen connected to morality, ethics, principles, oaths, contracts, law, justice, equity, order, balance, and impartiality. It is the power of keeping one's word.

The gifts of this vessel are poured out in priestess service to others when taking on the work and responsibility of creating order and equity within our spiritual communities. This can be accomplished by means of a transparent set of policies and procedures in order to establish guidance around community expectations and responsibilities. This service incorporates being an impartial mediator in instances of conflict, as well as having set up methods of remediation ahead of time so that resolution is followed by healing and reintegration in community.

The Path of the Lawspeaker Informed by Tradition

Reflecting on those from ancient times whose names we do not know, those whose sacred work aligned with the energies of the Lawspeaker served their people as mediators, judges, and champions of morality and order. They were involved in the making of contracts, the swearing of oaths, and the interpretation of omens deriving from the natural world.

In the mythic realm, they tested the worth of potential rulers, as is the practice of Sovereignty Goddesses; enforced the bonds of commitments and the integrity of contracts, as did the Lady of Llyn y Fan Fach, whose husband was prohibited from striking her thrice without cause; laid destinies and prohibitions on heroes and princelings, as did Arianrhod in the Fourth Branch; and challenged the mettle of those who would be knights and great warriors, in order to train those who were deemed worthy, as did the Witches of Caer Lowy with Peredur.

Inner Reflections on the Path of the Lawspeaker

Reflecting the Path of the Lawspeaker within calls us to remember the origins of the moral compass and unconsciously held perspectives that have guided our lives. As these perspectives are often taught to us directly in our families of origin or learned indirectly from experiences during our formative years, they may not be in alignment with our personal truths or accurate reflections of our Sovereignty. This self-evaluation assists us in forming an ethical framework that more completely reflects our understanding of who we truly are and is supported by a continually-developed sense of clarity that permits us to view ourselves and others with as much truth and honesty as possible.

It is equally important to remember that the beliefs, perspectives, and values of others arise from their own experiences and enculturation. If we want to understand the needs, biases, and challenges of others, we must step outside of our own personal contexts and listen. A dedication to equity recognizes that just as there are no universal experiences, there are no universal solutions. This will help us to establish or renew our dedication to being a force for justice, fairness, and equality in the world—even if our reach is limited to the spaces we inhabit, work in, or move through.

We are called to reclaim the power of our words by being as precise and clear as possible with our language. We must also reclaim the power of our words by truthfully evaluating our ability to follow through on what we commit to before we make those commitments. This will support an intention to live from a place of centered discernment, while continually striving to be guided by virtue, dedicated to equity, and acting with integrity in all that we do.

Dedicatory Project for the Path of the Lawspeaker:
The Ninefold Commitment

According to Geoffrey of Monmouth, one of the characteristics of the Island of Apples is that it is ruled by Nine Sisters who have established "a set of fair laws." This aligns with classical accounts of Gaulish Druids who served as the judges, arbitrators, and enforcers of oaths for their people. It also resonates with the tests of Sovereignty to determine the worthiness of a potential king.

This dedicatory project invites those who feel called to devote themselves to the work of the Lawspeaker's path to embrace a nine-month discipline that tests personal resolve, deepens one's commitment to the integrity of their word, and shines a light on the things that matter to us most.

For each of the Nine Paths, identify a promise and a prohibition related to the energies of that path. The promise will be something you commit to doing or completing during the month you are focused on that path, and the prohibition is something you commit to not doing or indulging in during the same month. Try to choose these promises and prohibitions with your personal growth in mind, ideally after spending some time in self-assessment. Think about aspects of yourself that could use some development, places where you could use some confidence, or areas where you would benefit from making some changes.

During the Lorekeeper's month, for example, if reading history isn't something you particularly enjoy or if you've not gotten around to studying the Four Branches of *Y Mabinogi*, you could promise to read a set amount of pages every night and then journal your thoughts. During that same month, you might choose a prohibition that bars you from engaging in negative self-talk and requiring you to instead reframe the story you tell about yourself. Try to set up your promises and prohibitions for each of the nine months ahead of time so that you have a clear sense of what your work will be. While you can be flexible enough to change future months, you must stick with the commitment you have made for that entire month (barring circumstances outside of your control).

At the beginning of each month, go before your altar, light your Law-speaker Candle and the Path Candle of the discipline you are focusing on for that month (discussed in chapter 13), and speak some heartfelt words of commitment and intention. You don't need to speak an oath to the gods—just make a commitment to yourself while in the presence of the energies of each path.

Do not beat yourself up if you falter or forget; this isn't an exercise intended to impose guilt or shame. It's important to forgive yourself and then move forward with a renewed dedication to your promise and your prohibition. There are no consequences for stumbling, but there are benefits for seeing these commitments through: you will learn a lot about yourself, feel good about living with intentionality, become invested in the power of keeping your word, and perhaps even establish positive new habits while leaving old patterns behind.

THE PATH OF
THE EMISSARY

The branch—what is its nature?
Does it not summon the worthy to questing?
Does it not span the abyss like a bridge—
Hearing well, speaking true,
Weaving peace?

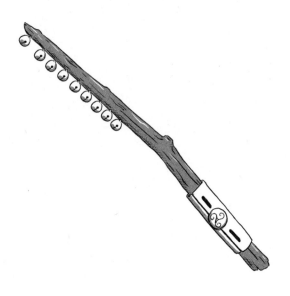

The Triad of the Emissary

Three Sharpened Senses of She who Seeks Understanding: clear sight, keen hearing, and true speech.

Correspondences

Role: Counselor/Diplomat

Threshold Guardian: She Who Connects

Archetype: The Messenger

Energy: Gold Ray in the Realm of Sky

Moon phase: Waxing gibbous

Stone: Sea glass, amber

Herb: St. John's wort

Animals: Raven, starling

On the Path of the Emissary, understanding is the key that permits access to the threshold of trust, through which the Vessel of Harmony can be accessed. The Vessel of Harmony pours forth the Awen connected to communication and eloquence, diplomacy, peace and harmony, guidance and counsel, relationships and social connections. It is the art of words.

The gifts of this vessel are poured out in priestess service to others when we take on the work and responsibilities of serving in advisory roles, forging connections between people or between different groups within a community, and being a clear-voiced representative of one's own community—spiritual or otherwise—out in the wider world. The art of clear communication and diplomatic speech in order to foster mutual trust and understanding between parties is enhanced by the eloquence gifted by the Awen.

The Path of the Emissary Informed by Tradition

Reflecting on those from ancient times whose names we do not know, those whose sacred work aligned with the energies of the Emissary served their people as diplomats, advisors, arbitrators, and messengers. They were involved in the making of treaties and the negotiation of conflicts, serving as couriers of news and spreaders of reputation.

In the mythic realm, they called upon heroes to undertake quests, such as the Otherworldly woman from *The Voyage of Bran*; they served as Peace Weavers who united warring nations through marriage, like Branwen; served as counselors and advisors at royal courts like Nimue; and recited poems that could change the hearts of all who heard them.

Inner Reflections on the Path of the Emissary

Reflecting the Path of the Emissary within can assist us in learning how to communicate from a place of authenticity and clarity, teach us how to be in right relationship with ourselves and others, and guide us as we seek to establish connections that foster harmony, prioritize understanding, and encourage growth beyond our already-established boundaries.

Our primary and most important relationship is the one we have with ourselves. As we walk a path of self-knowledge and work toward wholeness, it is important that we open lines of clear communication between all aspects of the self, building bridges of connection between what is conscious and what is unconscious; between our head and our heart; between the instincts of the body and the intuition of the spirit; between who we once were, who we now are, and who we are working to become.

Part of this building process requires that we reclaim the power of our voice to verbalize our needs once we acknowledge them; share our truths once we identify them; and speak our intentions into being once we have established them. Along with this is the reclamation of our power to hear with clarity, listen with compassion, and respond with integrity—all with the intention to build connection and reach understandings with others.

Dedicatory Project for the Path of the Emissary: The Ninefold Waves of Intention

The energies of the Ninefold have many correspondences with waves—the Otherworld lies beyond the Ninth Wave, Gwenhidwy tends a flock of nine sheeplike waves, and Germanic tradition speaks of the Nine Wave Sisters who are the daughters of Ran. Waves are our companions in journey, whether through the power of symbol or the power of the sea.

The Emissary likewise harnesses these waves of connection as they journey over the waters between nations, across the depths of the unconscious, and through the very air around us—as words become the vehicles of our intention. When spoken, they are carried by waves of sound; when written, they transmit on frequencies of light. Like a ripple across the surface of a pond, our words and their intentions can travel farther than we perceive and have long-reaching effects that we can only imagine.

Being both conscious and conscientious in the words we use—what we tell ourselves, what we say to others, what we communicate to the Universe—is an important component in the reclamation of our Sovereignty. Likewise, the words we take in—the opinions we accept, the information we ingest, the sounds and sights to which we consciously expose ourselves—ripple across our inner ponds as well, affecting how we think about ourselves and the world around us.

In this dedicatory working, spend some time in contemplation of the energies you transmit as well as the ones you receive. Think about the Ninth Wave Journey that we use to enter the mythic Otherworld (chapter 15); in *Mythic Moons of Avalon*, we talked about assigning time periods to each of the waves for our exploration of the realms of Avalon. Here we are journeying through our own energies, seeking to map out the different ways that we are in relationship with ourselves, others, and the world around us.

To begin, create a diagram of yourself surrounded by nine waves of intention—like a nesting doll, each layer is larger than the last, encompassing everything within it. These are nine layers of boundaries, nine levels of impact, nine ripples of connection between you and all that is. These nine waves represent the energies you are sending out as well as those that are coming in. There are several different ways to construct this map, and no right way of ordering the waves around you; as such, you may find it may take several tries before you are happy with your map or else find that you can construct different versions for different purposes.

For the sake of example, in creating mine, I started with the outermost layer and worked my way inward in order; I assigned that outer layer to the energies of Emissary, as that is my "agent" in the world—the way I navigate spaces that are unknown or uncomfortable; my most polite and formal self. So, if that is layer nine, I worked my way backward toward myself, with layer one being the most intimate.

Once I assigned paths to each of these nine waves, I now had a tool I could use for self-assessment as well as for personal empowerment. I came up with a list of questions to ask myself and meditate on about my communication methods in any given situation. Honest reflections gave me the answers I needed to understand what was going on and what I needed to improve. I have also found that when I know I'm going to have a specific kind of exchange with someone—for example, needing to have a difficult conversation with a coworker who does not take constructive criticism well—I could use this tool to determine the best way to communicate in that situation, and then to prepare myself by ahead of time by activating and harnessing the energies of a particular wave.

Using the framework presented here, I determined that I wanted to approach this situation by harnessing the energies of the Guardian wave. To do so, I would close my eyes and connect with the energy field around my body, envisioning the boundaries of the nine layers formed by the nine waves taking form around me. With my breath and intention, I would connect with my heart space—my energetic core—and then breathe energy out from my heart into my energy field. I would move the energy to pass through each of the waves in turn until I reached the sixth wave…my Guardian wave. Using the Ninefold Breath and focusing on the symbol and statement of the Path of the Guardian (beginning on page 335), I would fill the space from my heart through to the far edge of the sixth wave with clear heart energy…open, empowered, and activated. In this way, the frequency of the wave—the vibration of the Guardian path—is what will come through me during this discussion.

Ninth Wave: Emissary—Am I communicating authentically? Am I being passive aggressive? Am I holding something back or telling untruths? Am I am being honest or saying what I think others want me to say? Am I seeking understanding or do I just want to "win"?

Eighth Wave: Lawspeaker—Am I communicating fairly? Am I allowing my biases to color what I hear and say? Am I seeking resolution or have I already made up my mind? Am I being too trusting? Am I being too judgmental? Do I know how to come to a consensus?

Seventh Wave: Lorekeeper—Am I communicating knowledgeably? Do I have enough information to share an opinion? Am I making assumptions about what others know or do not know? Am I talking down to someone? Am I saying too much or too little? Am I dominating the conversation? Am I listening to what others have to say and share?

Sixth Wave: Guardian—Am I communicating bravely? Am I able to have authentic conversations about difficult subjects? Am I advocating for myself or others? Am I receiving the words of others in the spirit they are intended? Am I being aggressive in my tone or language? Am I talking over someone else? Am I being defensive?

Fifth Wave: Hearthtender—Am I communicating kindly? Am I speaking my needs? Am I responsive to the needs of others? Am I holding respectful space for myself and others? Am I being mindful of my available resources and my limitations? Am I a safe person to talk to? Do I keep confidences?

Fourth Wave: Artisan—Am I communicating nonverbally? Am I expressing myself through my actions, through my service, through my presence? Have I clarified this mode of expression with others in my life so they understand me? Do I pick up on the nonverbal communications of others?

Third Wave: Ritualist—Am I communicating lovingly? Am I speaking from my heart? Am I being reverent in what I say and how I receive what is being said to me? Do I respect the perspectives and opinions of others, even when we disagree? Do I regularly communicate my feelings of love and appreciation to others?

Second Wave: Healer—Am I communicating compassionately? Am I being too vulnerable? Am I offering unsolicited help? Am I giving the support have asked for in the way that they've asked for it? Am I asking for the support I need? Am I using my words to hurt or to heal?

First Wave: Seer—Am I communicating consciously? Am I considering the impact of my words, or lack thereof? Do I believe the words of others? Am I being empathetic? Am I aware that I have the power to speak my words into being—and, knowing this— do my words reflect the truth of the person I aspire to be, the me of my hopes and dreams?

I can use these nine waves of intention for any situation that requires me to communicate in a particular way for a specific purpose. Feel free to make use of this tool as well, customizing it to your own experiences and placements of the paths with these waves. I am sharing this as an example of what you can create, but it is still important for you to create your own tool, your own approach to this dedicatory project that connects to each of the nine on the Path of the Emissary.

THE PATH OF
THE ARTISAN

The spindle—what is its nature?
Does it not twist with the thread of tradition?
Does it not yield to the hand of the master—
Forging craft, casting skill,
Birthing soul?

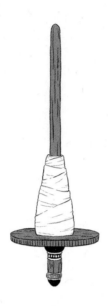

The Triad of the Artisan

Three Shining Truths of She who Seeks Awen: truth in vocation, that comes only from the heart; truth in manifestation, that comes only through the body; truth in inspiration, that comes only from the Mighty Ones.

Correspondences

Role: Artist/Craftsperson

Threshold Guardian: She Who Creates

Archetype: The Enchanter

Energy: Silver Ray in the Realm of Land

Moon phase: Third quarter

Stone: Chalk, clay bead

Herb: Flax

Animals: Bee, sheep

On the Path of the Artisan, discipline is the key that permits access to the threshold of mastery, through which the Vessel of Art can be accessed. The Vessel of Art pours forth the Awen connected to creativity, skill, crafts, trade, technology, alchemy, spellcraft, and charms. This aspect of Awen can be obtained by seeking innovation that arises from applying skill to meet a need as well as engaging with the apprenticeship model of learning a craft or a trade and the improvisational flow that moves through us when we obtain a degree of mastery in how we birth our creation.

The gifts of this vessel are poured out in priestess service to others when we take on the work and responsibility of committing ourselves to developing skills through practice and discipline, as well as when we pass along the tools and techniques that we have learned over time to others. Our inspired works may likewise serve to inspire others, such as with the creation of devotional art or music that functions to create bridges of connection between others and the Divine or the making of items that assist others in forging their own connections, such as with ritual tools and ceremonial garb.

The Path of the Artisan Informed by Tradition

Reflecting on those from ancient times whose names we do not know, those whose sacred work aligned with the energies of the Artisan served their people as creators, crafters, and makers of all kinds. They were expert textilers, clothiers, metallurgists, leatherworkers, potters, builders, woodworkers, and artists. They made beautiful and utilitarian items in service of their community, for both ritual purposes and trade. Alchemy and other magical arts were closely aligned with this path.

In the mythic realms, they were smiths like those who crafted Excalibur on the Island of Avalon; makers of exquisite shoes, shields, and saddles that inspired deep resentment and murderous envy in other crafters, like Rhiannon, Cigfa, and Pryderi under the tutelage of Manawydan in the Third Branch; and they were various charms and magical items, such as a cloak that would burst into flame once donned, created by renowned enchantresses like Morgan le Fay.

Inner Reflections on the Path of the Artisan

Reflecting the Path of the Artisan within calls us to remember the dreams of our youth; the creative impulses of our spirit; and the gifts of our head, heart, and hands as the sacred callings they truly are. Remember that the gifts we possess, the talents we develop, and the passions we pursue are present in our lives for a reason; they are sacred invitations to participate in the cocreation of the world around us. We may have been dissuaded from following our passions, did not possess the resources needed to develop our skills, or lacked the confidence to pursue our aspirations, but the potential that lies within us awaits us still—and we are worthy of tending this inner garden.

We can reclaim a sense of joy in the act of creation, without attachment to perfection, without investment in the final outcome, without concern for the praise or acceptance of others. The clearer we are in our intention, and the more present we are in our process, the more open we become to the flow of Awen. Let us also expand our definition of creativity to encompass acts of personal expression, innovative problem-solving, and birthing any vision into being.

While what we do to support ourselves does not define who we are, we may find that we possess a calling or multiple callings that bring meaning to our lives and add richness to the world. Acts of creativity and innovation transcend those they come through, serving to meet the needs of those who use or witness their end result—a full spectrum of experiences that benefit us emotionally, mentally, physically, and spiritually, and that affect us individually, communally, and collectively.

Dedicatory Project for the Path of the Artisan: The Ninefold Manifestations of Art

After engaging with some of the immersion work presented in the next chapter, create a piece of devotional art representing the energy of each of the Nine Paths and to be used as part of your priestess practice. These creations can take many forms, including an image, object, or tool that can be placed on or hung near each of the Nine Path shrines; a series of nine chants, a musical composition with nine movements, or a song with nine verses that can be used to connect with each path; nine articles of ritual garb or devotional jewelry specific to each of the paths to be worn when working with the energies of a specific path, and so on.

While there are many ways to approach this project, here are some suggestions. Consider the effect of the medium you will be working with. Using the same medium across all Nine Paths—say, creating nine clay statues, wood carvings, or precious metal clay talismans—centers the interpretation of the different Ninefold energies through that medium when they are observed as a set. Alternatively, one could allow the energy of each path to determine which medium is used to represent it; for example, perhaps one could create a musical theme for each of the Nine and then use nine different instruments to perform them.

Another approach is to choose widely different media for each path and allow the form it takes to be a part of the expression of energy. This could look like forging a harvesting knife for the Path of the Healer, a carved wooden staff for the Path of the Guardian, a stained glass ornament for the Path of the Seer, and so on.

Finally, consider learning a traditional craft or art form from Welsh, Breton, or other Celtic culture. These include music and dance, poetry and painting, weaving and costuming, carving and brewing. Not only is this learning a beautiful devotion in honor of the gods, but it is a powerful way to support and preserve today's living cultures—especially when we are taught by a native tradition holder.

THE PATH OF THE HEARTHTENDER

The horn—what is its nature?
Does it not fill from the Cauldron of Plenty?
Does it not pour out the sweetness of welcome—
Slaking thirst, warming hearts,
Feasting long?

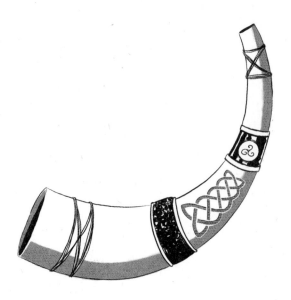

The Triad of the Hearthtender

Three Hearth Blessings of She who Seeks Center: fuel for the fire, bread for the oven, harmony in the home.

Correspondences

Role: Host/Benefactor

Threshold Guardian: She Who Sustains

Archetype: The Fosterer

Energy: Crystal Ray in the Realm of Land

Moon phase: Sovereign moon

Stone: Flint, coin

Herb: Heather

Animals: Dog, pig

On the Path of the Hearthtender, responsibility is the key that permits access to the threshold of generosity, through which the Vessel of Abundance can be accessed. The Vessel of Abundance pours forth the Awen connected to home, family, fosterage, community, hospitality, feasts, gatherings, agriculture, commerce, resources, nurturance, fertility, hearth, and home.

The gifts of this vessel are poured out in priestess service to others when we take on the work and responsibility of sacred hearth tending, which itself is both the act of creating and maintaining a shrine or sacred space in our homes or on our property as well as the act of reclaiming the inherent sacred nature of tending our home and family. Whether managing a household, a community space, a celebration, or an organization, the foundational work that needs to be done to support and maintain these spaces is critical to their ongoing existence and well-being.

The Path of the Hearthtender Informed by Tradition

Reflecting on those from ancient times whose names we do not know, those whose sacred work aligned with the energies of the Hearthtender served as guardians of the sacred center, nurturers of families, and benefactors of the greater community. Through systems of fosterage, caring for children and elders, strong ties with kin, hosting feasts, and providing hospitality to strangers, they maintained the holy flame of community and ensured the continuity of traditions around social status. They managed households and estates, dictated the wise use and distribution of resources, and were sponsors of the arts and benefactors of the poor.

Of course, the fire temple of Brigid and her eternal flame was maintained by a community of holy women in Ireland, an ancient practice with analogs around the world. Perhaps the most famous example is the eternal flame of Vesta, the sacred hearthfire of Rome—and, eventually, its empire—tended by six Vestal priestesses, who dedicated thirty years of their life to honored service as virgins in her temple.

In the mythic realms, they were the women dwelling on Otherworldly islands, who offered hospitality to shiploads of adventurers from the mortal world. They were Fairy Queens who fostered orphaned children, like Nimue, the Lady of the Lake who raised Lancelot from infancy when his father, King Ban, was killed. And they were the Well Maidens from "The Elucidation" who served travelers whatever food and beverages they desired out of their golden cups and silver platters.

Inner Reflections on the Path of the Hearthtender

Reflecting the Path of the Hearthtender within is a call to identify our foundational needs and evaluate how they are being met—physically, mentally, and emotionally. We have a right to create and dwell in a space where we know that we are safe, where we are secure in our access to the resources necessary to meet our needs, and which serves as a peaceful haven that remedies the challenges of the outside world. This safety extends to conditions of our environment—at home, at work, in community—as well as our relationships with the people with whom we share those spaces—partners, family, friends, and coworkers.

We must remember that the practice of generosity begins with the self, as we cannot serve others from an empty cup. It is critical that we periodically take an inner inventory to identify the parts of ourselves that are in deficit as well as those that possess a surplus. When we give from our places of abundance, and grant ourselves permission to care for ourselves in those spaces that need tending, we can then engage in a sustainable practice of generosity through a wise use of our resources.

It is likewise important to reclaim the sacred nature of tending hearth and home and recenter ourselves in an understanding of how critical this holy service truly is. This tending extends to being a good steward to our land and resources, raising and educating our children, ensuring the well-being of the elderly, sick, and vulnerable, and working to meet the needs of our communities. It can be empowering to reframe our perspectives on duties that come with maintaining our living spaces and tending to the needs of our family and community as the holy work of keeping the perpetual Hearthfire alight.

Dedicatory Project for the Path of the Hearthtender: The Ninefold Vigil

According to tradition, visitors to Glastonbury were required to spend a night in prayerful vigil at the shrine to St. Mary on Beckery before proceeding onto the island itself. Another form of vigil is the flame tending practice associated with both the saint and goddess Brigid of Kildare. There is a strong connection between Beckery—believed to mean "Little Ireland" or "Beekeeper's Island"—and Ireland; there seems to have been a settlement of Irish migrants in and around that area.

In the early twelfth century, William of Malmesbury wrote that St. Brigid herself visited Glastonbury in the fifth century, spending two years in contemplation at the shrine of St. Mary Magdalen at Beckery. She is said to have left several relics behind, including a bell, a necklace, and some embroidery tools. She is depicted milking a cow on the facade of St. Michael's Tower, which was built on the Tor in the fourteenth century.

The modern practice of flame tending—usually a collectively maintained eternal flame, lit from the renewed and constantly tended sacred flame of Brigid in Kildare—has enjoyed a revival in devotion in recent decades, with tenders all around the world. Whether Christian or Pagan, lovers of Brigid have taken up flame tending as a beautiful devotional practice, work traditionally shared among cells of nineteen women, each of whom take a night to spend time in vigil with Brigid's flame, leaving the last night for Brigid to tend for herself before starting the rotation over again. There are both traditional and modern variations of the flame tending practice, the best of which are mindful of how much this practice is a treasure of Irish culture.

While there is nothing that suggests that the overnight vigil of prayer and purification at Beckery that is described in Arthurian Tradition has anything to do with Brigid herself, it could potentially indicate an imported practice since there appears to have been both an Irish community as well as a Christian women's religious community in the area. That said, purification vigils of this sort were not uncommon in the medieval period and were particularly undergone the night before the rites of knighthood, as part of a man's preparation.

In *Trioedd Ynys Prydein*, Triad 90 lists the Three Perpetual Harmonies of the Island of Britain:

> *One was at the Island of Afallach,*
> *and the second at Caer Garadawg,*
> *and the third at Bangor.*
>
> *In each of these three places there were 2,400 religious men;*
> *and of these 100 in turn continued each hour of the twenty-four hours of the day and night in prayer and service to God,*
> *ceaselessly and without rest for ever.*[194]

The idea of a perpetual harmony maintained in three separate areas of Britain known to have been important religious centers in their day holds resonance with flame tending disciplines.

There is also a directed prayer practice (done to petition God for a specific blessing or outcome) in Catholicism and other Christian traditions that is performed for nine consecutive days; it is called a *novena*, from *novem*, the Latin word for "nine." This practice has its roots in the early church and is likely borrowing from pre-Christian Greek and Ro-

---

194   Bromwich, *Trioedd Ynys Prydein*, 232.

man traditions of mourning a death in the family for nine days, culminating in a feast in their honor. St. Augustine discouraged this practice in his writings, saying it was too Pagan and had no biblical standing.[195]

With this information as a foundation that puts the idea of vigils in a wider cultural context—while drawing some lines of connectivity between vigils, flame tending, Brigid, perpetual harmonies, and the Island of Afallach in Triad 90 (which scholars have concluded is specifically referencing Glastonbury)—begin to think about an approach to creating a Ninefold vigil practice that maintains the sacred center of the Hearthtender path while honoring the essence of the Ninefold. Perhaps you could incorporate the Path Candles from chapter 13, lighting one a night for nine nights, along with a meditation, journey, prayer, chant, or song verse of your creation that reflects the energies of each of the nine. It can have a desired outcome—such as purification, releasing, or manifesting—or simply be a means of establishing relationship with, and mindfulness of, the Ninefold in our lives.

---

195 Joseph Hilgers, "Novena" in *The Catholic Encyclopedia* vol. 11 (New York: Robert Appleton Company, 1911), accessed Aug. 25, 2022. http://www.newadvent.org /cathen/11141b.htm.

THE PATH OF THE GUARDIAN

The torch—what is its nature?
Does it not burnish the torc of the sovereign?
Does it not incite the brave into battle—
Holding strong, changing lives,
Risking all?

The Triad of the Guardian

Three Mighty Weapons for She who Seeks Change: strong boundaries; just causes; pure intentions.

Correspondences

Role: Champion/Advocate

Threshold Guardian: She Who Incites

Archetype: The Fury

Energy: Gold Ray in the Realm of Land

Moon phase: First quarter

Stone: Slate, tooth

Herb: Juniper

Animals: Horse, bear

On the Path of the Guardian, purpose is the key that brings us to the threshold of valor, through which the Vessel of Honor can be accessed. The Vessel of Honor pours forth the Awen connected to bravery, loyalty, duty, passion, and authority. This aspect of Awen can be obtained by dedicating ourselves to causes larger than ourselves, using our passions to embolden others to fight for change, and making a commitment to establishing and maintaining Sovereign boundaries.

The gifts of this vessel are poured out in priestess service to others when we take on the work and responsibility of being an agent for positive change in the world and have the courage to stand up for what is right. It is poured out when we are in service as an activist, challenging systems of oppression or injustice; a warrior, whose discipline of body and mind gives us the strength to safeguard boundaries of many kinds; and a protector, serving as a shield against tyranny, particularly in defense of the voiceless—such as animals, water, and the environment.

The Path of the Guardian Informed by Tradition

Reflecting on those from ancient times whose names we do not know, those whose sacred work aligned with the energies of the Guardian served their people as maintainers of sacred space, defenders of the land, and champions of causes. They ensured the integrity of their tribal borders and were willing to cross the border between life and death if that meant those they loved were safe. Accounts of the Greeks and Romans praise Gallic women for their strength, courage, and skill in battle—some saying they were even more fierce in a fight than the men. And when they didn't fight directly, women often accompanied the men of their tribes to the battlefields, calling to them from behind the lines to rally their courage and ensure they didn't dishonor themselves. Ruling queens like Boudica rallied her people to revolt against the Romans, while Cartimandua protected her people by allying with the Romans themselves—in defiance of all honorable expectations.

(Most Celts and even some Romans considered her a traitor for betraying the rebellious chieftain Caractacus to Rome.)

In the mythic realms, Otherworldly women like Scáthach and the Witches of Caer Lowy trained warriors who had proven themselves worthy of their tutelage. Irish heroines like Creidne became *banfénnid*, members of a *fianna* war band. Other women used their magic to create barriers of protection—and sometimes of imprisonment. In some versions of his story, Merlin falls in love with Niniane, his pupil in the magical arts, but his feelings are not returned. He is nevertheless ceaseless in his pursuit of her, and when she has learned everything from him, she creates an impenetrable prison of air to entrap Merlin forever in what he perceives to be a glass tower in the Brocéliande forest.

Inner Reflections on the Path of the Guardian

Reflecting the Path of the Guardian within is a call to remember that working toward Sovereignty includes the establishment and maintenance of personal boundaries that are strong, but not too rigid…self-contained, but not too isolating. This requires that we engage in mapping the contours of our inner topography so that we know ourselves well enough to understand where we end and others begin. The building and maintenance of appropriate boundaries for ourselves requires that we develop the ability to honor and respect the boundaries of others.

It is important for us to reclaim our personal power from the people, institutions, and self-limiting perspectives that require our conformity to their expectations. While boundaries function to keep us safe and secure, they also serve to give us definition. When we are empowered to define ourselves on our own terms, that identity increasingly becomes an authentic reflection of our whole and sovereign selves. This self-definition brings with it the need to honor and respect ourselves—both in terms of our strengths as well as our challenges.

We have the power to be an agent of change in the world. Making a commitment to advocate for the things that are important to us, and that will uplift and improve the lives of others, includes being willing to do the work that is necessary to bring about positive change while respecting the Sovereignty of others as we do so.

Dedicatory Project for the Path of the Guardian: Ninefold Embodiments

Create a physical embodiment devotion for each of the Nine Paths with the intention that they facilitate connection with, and expression of, these energies through the body. Some ideas for these embodiment devotions include:

Trance postures: Physical postures assumed by the body that emulate symbols, images, or landscape areas. When accompanied by rattling or drumming, they can unlock powerful journey experiences. Several examples of these are given in chapter 12. Creating a trance posture for each of the Nine Paths requires obtaining a symbol set of some kind which the body could then assume; seek out guidance for these postures as you engage with each Path and its Guardians, as detailed in the Ninefold Immersion process to follow. These postures can also be inspired by the Path Symbols, the Ninefold glyphs given in the devotional project for the Path of the Seer later in this chapter, or the correspondences given for each path (animals, trees, herbs, stones, etc.). When using these or other correspondences, it is best to draw from a consistent symbol set—that is, all nine postures are animals, trees, or glyphs, and so on. These postures can then be used as a means to journey into connection with the paths and explore their energies or meet with their Guardians.

Dance: Create a series of dances for each of the Nine Paths, perhaps drawing upon different dance styles or different energetic interpretations of the same dance. Learning traditional dances from Celtic lands can add another layer of connection to this devotion. Another approach is to create a series of steps or dance moves that can be used individually to evoke the energy of a specific path; these can then be combined in such a way that they flow together, in order to connect with all Nine Paths. These dances can be used in many ways, including as a means to evoke the energies of a path or paths within the practitioner for use in further work, and to raise these energies during ritual for the self or with others.

Flow arts: These are movement forms that draw upon a variety of physical disciplines, including martial arts, interpretive or traditional dances from around the world, and balance exercises that incorporate props, such as juggling or spinning. The flow and focus of these movements, once mastered, can induce shifts of consciousness; creating and performing flow forms for each of the Nine Paths with sacred intent can create powerful bridges of connection.

Hand positions: Creating hand, arm, or finger positions that are static or incorporate movement is another way to evoke and embody the energies of the Nine Paths. These can be used during meditation, to raise energy, or as an imperceptible method to connect with the essence of a particular path for support no matter where we are or what we are doing. A component in many magical and spiritual traditions, the use of sacred hand positions to shift consciousness is probably best known through the mudras of Hinduism. The Greeks and Romans made use of *chironomia*, a system of hand signals for use during oratory to convey unspoken meaning; these hand positions were also used in both Pagan and Christian iconography from these areas. Likewise, these cultures used hand gestures for apotropaic magic, such as the Italian *mano figa* for use against the evil eye. In Irish tradition, *In Lebor Ogaim* (*The Book of Ogams*) details systems of foot ogham and nose ogham wherein the fingers were used to sign ogham letters against the leg or the nose, ostensibly as a method of nonverbal communication, but it could have other applications as well.

THE PATH OF THE SEER

The mirror—what is its nature?
Does it not shimmer with patterns of prophecy?
Does it not open the pathways to wisdom—
Showing cause, cleaving lies,
Shining truth?

The Triad of the Seer

Three Sage Reflections of She who Seeks Wisdom: that which has come before—that the pattern may be revealed; that which is happening now—that changes may be made; that which is within—that potential may be realized.

Correspondences

Role: Oracle/Visionary

Threshold Guardian: She Who Reveals

Archetype: The Prophetess

Energy: Silver Ray in the Realm of Sea

Moon phase: Waning crescent

Stone: Hagstone, shell

Herb: Poppy

Animals: Salmon, owl

On the Path of the Seer, clarity is the key that brings us to the threshold of awareness, through which the Vessel of Wisdom can be accessed. The Vessel of Wisdom pours forth the Awen connected to prophecy, divination, intuition, foreknowledge, and the Sight. This aspect of Awen can be obtained by achieving the degree of self-knowledge necessary to differentiate between the truth of spirit and the voice of fear. It springs into the light of consciousness by following the path of clarity hewn over time by practice, clarified by commitment to a divinatory art, and smoothed by trust born of discernment.

The gifts of this vessel are poured out in priestess service to others when we take on the work and responsibility of clear and unbiased Seership, no matter what system or discipline we are called to use: reading omens, performing augury, consulting decks or other oracular systems, casting horoscopes, throwing ogham or runes, incubating visionary trance, using divinatory tools, or serving as a vessel of mediumship.

The Path of the Seer Informed by Tradition

Reflecting on those from ancient times whose names we do not know, those whose sacred work aligned with the energies of the Seer served their people as holy oracles, channels for prophecy, performers of augury, and interpreters of omens. They were the Awenyddion—the Inspired Ones—who fell into trance to utter mantic verses. Often dwelling in the margins of society, or high in a tower, or isolated on an island, they embraced their sacred wild nature and allowed the Otherworld to speak through them. Possessing the gifts of Sight, they could trace the threads of fate and destiny and read the patterns within and between them.

In the mythic realms, poets and seers—both of whom had powers of foreknowledge—are often consulted by queens and kings to obtain prophecies on concerns such as forthcoming battles, the destinies of children, and the inheritance of the throne. In *The Táin Bó Cuailnge*,

Queen Medb consults the *banfhili* Fedelm and asks her to use her *imbas* (divine inspiration) to predict the winner of an imminent battle. In the *Vita Merlini*, Merlin has gone mad with grief after a devastating war, living like a wild man beneath some apple trees; in this liminal place, he makes many prophecies. He is joined by his sister, Ganieda, who in earlier traditions may instead have been his lover. After much sorrow, she too renounces the world and gains the powers of prophecy as well. Merlin retires from his seership in deference to her power.

Inner Reflections on the Path of the Seer

Reflecting the Path of the Seer within is to remember that cultivating clarity and developing discernment is best obtained through the self-knowledge and integrative wholeness that comes from engaging with our Shadow. A commitment to self-evaluation is critical to the work of strengthening our trust in ourselves. It teaches us how to know the difference between the sound of our fears and the song of our truth. It allows us to discern the voice of our intuitive wisdom over the static of our self-doubt and enables us to hear—with increasing clarity—guidance received though a consciously developed relationship with our guides and our gods.

When our perspectives shift, the world around us changes—a mirror of our own internal changes. When we can see the people, circumstances, and events in our lives for what they are, rather than through the filter of our past hurts, future worries, and self-imposed restrictions, we hone our Sight—the ability to see beyond our limitations and the illusions they bring. The work of the Avalonian Cycle of Healing is specifically structured to assist with this ongoing process in a gentle and gradual way; however, it is important to seek support from a mental health professional should we require it

Another aim for the work of this path is to reclaim the power both to hold a vision of what we seek to manifest as well as to be open to the insight that is informed by intuition. That is, empowering ourselves to actively engage in envisioning the future we wish to bring into being, rather than just seeking a vision of a future we haven't been actively cocreating.

Dedicatory Project for the Path of the Seer: The Ninefold Oracle

After engaging in at least the first stage of the Ninefold Immersion process in chapter 13, develop an oracular system to help you connect with, and receive guidance from, the Ninefold. To do so, symbolic representations for each of the Nine Paths must be developed, a divinatory medium must be chosen and manifested, and then a process for receiving insight must be created using physical components and a ritual process of your choosing.

These representations can take any form; some ideas include symbols or sigils; paintings, collages, or photographs; a collection of crystals, feathers, or other small physical objects; herbs for each of the Nine that can be used as a loose tea for tasseomancy, and so on. Using a consistent medium for all representations is preferable (all sigils or all feathers, for example), but that is up to the practitioner.

Whatever form they take, however, I strongly recommend that you develop them with guidance—ideally that of the Threshold Guardians of each path, but also with one or more of the goddesses of Avalon, as well as your personal Avalonian guide. Engage with the symbols you receive through doorway work (from *Avalon Within*) to ensure that the energy they hold and the effect that they have are good reflections of their paths.

You may find that nine is too limiting a number of symbols for the divinatory process you are envisioning. Although I recommend starting there, one way of expanding this oracular system is to create representations of the Nine Paths through the three modes of service—service to self, service to others, and service to Source—for a total of twenty-seven components. An example of how this can be implemented is presented below.

Once these representations are developed to your satisfaction, they can then be expressed as a divinatory set in the medium of your choosing: images rendered on oracle cards, symbols carved into clay, sigil-painted river stones, pyrography on slices of applewood—whatever you feel called to create.

There are many approaches to using your Ninefold oracle for receiving insight once it has been created. You may conceive of the process before you even manifest the oracle; if that happens, let the process you have in mind determine what medium to use in making your oracle. Ways to obtain insight can include a daily singular draw from your deck or a pull from your pouch of stones; a casting of objects onto a grid or meaningful field (such as the cosmological map of the Avalonian Tradition from chapter 10); a personalized card layout to meet your specific needs; a tea leaf reading process; or a full oracular ritual incorporating one of the bridging tools discussed in chapter 12.

What follows is a Ninefold divinatory system I have developed. You are welcome to use, expand, or alter it as you see fit, or simply see it as an example of what is possible. If your intention is to make a dedicatory project for the Path of the Seer, it is still important for you to create your own system along with a ritual process with which to receive insight.

Ninefold Glyph System

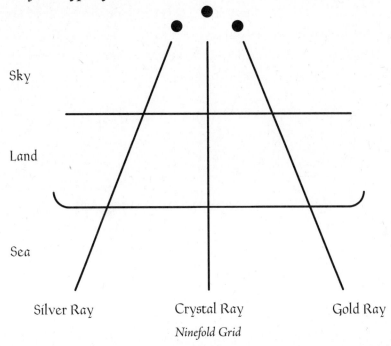

Sky

Land

Sea

Silver Ray   Crystal Ray   Gold Ray

Ninefold Grid

This glyph system is very straightforward and is based on the grid that I used as my guide to understand and explore the energies of the Ninefold. I took the Three Rays of Awen and overlaid them upon the Three Realms. I included the three circles at the top of the Awen that many Druid groups use; they represent many things, including a triune divine source and what has been called the Triad of the Sunrises, depicting the sunrise positions during the solstices (left and right) and the equinoxes (center). I also added a bit of a curl to the edges of the Realm of Sea, suggestive of the rim of a cauldron.

I then broke the grid up into nine parts, creating symbols representing each of the Nine Paths. The resulting glyphs visually describe the specific energetics of the Nine Paths in terms of the ray and realm that comprise each of them. Without the additions of the three dots to represent Source in the Realm of Sky and the rim for the Realm of Sea, the symmetry of the grid would make it difficult to differentiate a few of the glyphs. All that we need to remember is that the rim and the dots point up in their upright positions.

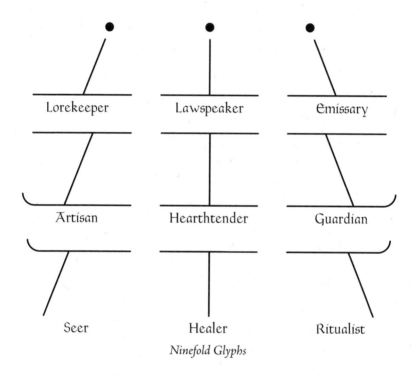

Ninefold Glyphs

Once the glyphs were sorted and I worked with their energies to ensure they did what I expected, I painted them on wooden craft disks about an inch and a half in diameter. I expanded the entire oracle system by making three sets of glyphs and rendering them in three different colors: white to represent service to Source, black to represent service to others, and red to represent service to self.

There are many ways to use this completed oracle system. How I wound up using it the most is by placing the twenty-seven disks in a pouch; at the beginning of my day, I pull two disks—one at a time, being sure to return the first to the bag before pulling the second. With the first, I ask what Shadow aspects I need to be mindful of for the day—challenges, illusions, or fears that might be triggered—and with the second, I ask which aspects of Sovereignty will best serve me as I face the day's challenges. In the evening, when journaling, I am always sure to write down my reflections on this guidance and how it played a part in my day.

Finally, I sometimes use the glyphs as symbols for the Nine Paths in non-oracular workings when I want to have those individual energies present in what I am doing; I incorporate them in talismans, inscribe them on objects, or draw them energetically in places where I want to bring their energies in support of what I'm doing. For example, I draw the glyph for the Lorekeeper on my laptop nine times when I sit down to write. There are many applications…let your intuition guide you!

THE PATH OF
THE HEALER

The sickle—what is its nature?
Does it not service the Cauldron of Healing?
Does it not flash in the light of the moon—
Reaping herbs, cutting cords,
Guiding souls?

The Triad of the Healer

Three Potent Medicines of She who Seeks Wholeness: seeking causality; taking responsibility; affecting change.

Correspondences

Role: Healer/Midwife

Threshold Guardian: She Who Restores

Archetype: The Psychopomp

Energy: Crystal Ray in the Realm of Sea

Moon phase: Dark moon

Stone: Ammonite, hematite

Herb: Mistletoe

Animals: Snake, crane

On the Path of the Healer, acceptance is the key that brings us to the threshold of compassion, through which the Vessel of Wholeness can be accessed. The Vessel of Wholeness pours forth the Awen connected to healing, restoration, integration, and spiritual renewal. This aspect of Awen can be obtained by accepting the truth of our limitations, both in terms of what can be healed and what must be carried, and by embracing patterns of being that are in alignment with maintaining and regaining physical, mental, and emotional wellness.

The gifts of this vessel are poured out in priestess service to others when we take on the work and responsibility of being a trained and qualified healer, no matter what modality we use: holistic or allopathic, physiological or psychological, complementary or alternative, herbal or pharmaceutical. It is poured out when we are in service as a psychopomp, guiding souls into the world through birth, helping to reintegrate parts of the soul in life, and facilitating the passage of souls out of the world through death.

The Path of the Healer Informed by Tradition

Reflecting on those from ancient times whose names we do not know, those whose sacred work aligned with the energies of the Healer served their people as wise ones, midwives, and tenders of the body, mind, and spirit. Through the use of many tools including plants, stones, heat, sound, water, and magic, these healers kept bodies whole, minds clear, and spirits centered.

In the mythic realms, Avalon was especially renowned for the healing abilities of those who dwelt there, and the Barge of the Holy Isle is an iconic representation of her service as a psychopomp. Morgen is said to be the first among her sisters in knowing the properties of plants for use in healing, and her earliest appearances in Arthurian tales very much shows her benevolence to Arthur and his court through her gifts of powerful salves and ointments, able to heal both body and mind.

The Physicians of Myddfai are an historical lineage with a mythic heritage; the founding physicians of this family line are said to have received their famed herbal formulary from their mother—the Lady of the Lake of Llyn y Fan Fach: an Otherworldly Lake Maiden or one of the Gwragedd Annwn.

Inner Reflections on the Path of the Healer

Reflecting the Path of the Healer within is to remember that our goal is not to achieve perfection, but rather to strive for wholeness. There will always be room for us to grow, things for us to change, and hurts for us to heal—but that doesn't mean that we cannot love and accept the totality of who we are in the here and now. Authentic wholeness allows us to have gratitude for our blessings, celebrate our achievements, honor our challenges, have compassion for our struggles, acknowledge our limitations, and work to understand our Shadow.

Assessing the degree of personal wholeness in the body, mind, and spirit allows us to see where work needs to be done. The first step to affecting deep and lasting healing is learning to recognize the symptoms of imbalance and then committing to address their causes. We cannot heal what we cannot see; covering up the symptoms or denying the reality of their existence—as with spiritual bypassing—only serves to perpetuate or worsen the imbalance. Committing ourselves to pursuing healing with the goal of wholeness—while striving to live in a way that creates and supports a balanced and healthy functioning of body, mind, and spirit—is key. It is seeking to live a life that finds joy in all that we are, even as we work to change what we can and learn to carry what we must

It is also helpful to remember that everyone we meet has wounds in need of healing, fears in need of soothing, and a Shadow in need of acknoweldgment. While this does not mean that we must condone damaging behaviors or put ourselves in harm's way, this understanding can help us meet others where they are with clarity and compassion.

Dedicatory Project for the Path of the Healer: Ninefold Formulary

The power of the number nine is evidenced in Welsh tradition in how it appears in famed herbal formulary of the Physicians of Myddfai—a hereditary lineage of healers that spanned five hundred years and claims descent from the Lady of the Lake of Llyn y Fan Fach. The numbers three and nine appear regularly in the medieval manuscript. One pattern of approach appears to have been to create remedies using three ingredients administered three times a day over a period of nine days. Likewise, this dedicatory project will draw upon the power of nine to potentiate our creations.

As there are many modalities of healing, there are a number of ways to approach this project. As with the other dedicatory projects, it is best to have spent some time getting familiar with the discrete energies of the Nine Paths before undertaking this work, and so having completed phase one and two of the Ninefold Immersion is recommended. Having done so, engage with the Ninefold through the energies of the Path of the Healer using the medium of your choice—such as gemstone elixirs, massage techniques, dietary protocols, exercise routines, aromatherapeutic blends, medicinal teas, healing ointments, and so on.

When choosing a modality, it is important that you are well versed in how to make and use these creations in ways that are safe and in keeping with the ethical requirements of your discipline, field, or profession. This is especially important if you are going to use any of these tools, techniques, or remedies in service to others. It is good practice to always write down the ingredients and proportions used in the making of any projects, and to be sure to clearly label all of your creations.

Once you have decided on the form your devotional project is going to take—for the sake of our discussion, let's use the example of therapeutic herbal bath soaks—consider how each of the Nine Paths can be represented by your chosen modality. Perhaps these creations can be guided by function—bath soaks that are clarifying, astringent, soothing, cooling, detoxing, relaxing, invigorating, and so on—and then determine which function corresponds with which path. Alternatively, perhaps they can be directly guided by the paths themselves—creating nine soaks made up of herbs that energetically connect with each of the paths. Or perhaps you can create nine oil blends or medicinal teas, each made of nine different oils or herbs. There are many different ways to approach this work, so let your creativity and your healing expertise be your guides.

Helpful Resources

The Physicians of Myddvai; Meddygon Myddfai, translated by John Pughe, 1861

https://archive.org/details/physiciansmyddv00willgoog

There are newer translations of the Myddfai materials available, but this can be accessed for free online as it is in public domain. This is a great resource for the study of Welsh Herbal Traditions. I don't recommend trying any of the formulas included without consulting a doctor or a trained and experienced herbalist.

THE PATH OF
THE RITUALIST

The drum—what is its nature?
Does it not knock on the door of the mysteries?
Does it not pulse with the heart of the grove—
Turning years, counting seeds,
Going home?

The Triad of the Ritualist

Three Inner Quests of She who Seeks Transformation: establishing rhythm; keeping balance; respecting process.

Correspondences

Role: Celebrant/Sacrificer

Threshold Guardian: She Who Transforms

Archetype: The Initiator

Energy: Gold Ray in the Realm of Sea

Moon phase: Waxing crescent

Stone: Antler, jet

Herb: Fern

Animals: Hare, deer

On the Path of the Ritualist, reverence is the key that brings us to the threshold of sanctity, through which the Vessel of Transformation can be accessed. The Vessel of Transformation pours forth the Awen connected to initiatory experiences, revelation of the mysteries, spiritual oneness, and transcendence. This aspect of Awen can be obtained by building authentic relationships with the divinities, guides, and guardians of our tradition, and with spirits of place. This can be accomplished through acts of devotion, the giving of offerings, and engaging in workings to forge connections with them.

The gifts of this vessel are poured out in priestess service to others when we facilitate rituals and rites of passage, when we invite their participation in festivals and celebrations, and by aligning our offerings and practices with the cycles of Earth, moon, and sun—allowing what is around us to empower that which flows through us.

The Path of the Ritualist Informed by Tradition

Reflecting on those from ancient times whose names we do not know, those whose sacred work aligned with the energies of the Ritualist served their people as keepers of the calendar, ceremonialists at seasonal festivals, facilitators of rites of passage, propitiation of the gods through offerings and sacrifices, givers of sacred teachings, and initiators into the mysteries.

In the mythic realms, shapeshifting is often a metaphor for spiritual transformation and initiation, such as with Ceridwen's pursuit of Gwion after he stole three drops of wisdom from her cauldron—the result of a yearlong magical operation. The pair each assumed the form of several animals—with Gwion as prey and Ceridwen as predator—before she finally consumed him and later birthed him anew. He was renamed Taliesin, "Radiant Brow," in recognition of the wisdom he now possessed. It is thought that this sequence referenced the process of initiation into the bardic mysteries; to become "enlightened," one's old self must die to be reborn of Ceridwen—Muse and Mother, and source of the Awen.

Inner Reflections on the Path of the Ritualist

Reflecting the Path of the Ritualist within us is to remember that the rhythms of nature that reveal themselves in the world around us can also be found in the world within us. There are times when we can flow and times when we must ebb. There are aspects of our inner landscape that are ripe and abundant and others that lie dormant. It is important for us to acknowledge the existence of these rhythms and allow ourselves to honor them with our choices.

Listening to the promptings of the spirit concerning the energetic tides within us is a powerful statement in support of our Sovereignty. Acknowledging and celebrating the seasons of our lives—the times of outward expansion as well as those of inward contraction—assists us in aligning our natures with nature and helps us reclaim our place within the universal All. There is an enormous perspective shift that comes when we start seeing ourselves as part of the fabric of the world around us and seeing the world as part of the fabric of the self.

Honoring the turning of the seasons, acknowledging the shifts in status within ourselves and for those in our communities, and initiating a deepening pursuit of spiritual mysteries are all components of the Path of the Ritualist. We are called to rekindle our sense of wonder at the mechanisms that underscore the workings of Universe, as well as to be moved by the sacred awe arising from the cultivation of a relationship with the Divine. All of these contribute to our spiritual evolution and bless us with a sense of joy and comforting peace arising from the knowledge that we are part of something larger than ourselves: we are a part of the All, and the All is part of us.

Dedicatory Project for the Path of the Ritualist: Ninefold Rites of Passage

One of the most common ways of priestessing in service to community is the facilitation of rites of passage. These are ceremonies that mark the stages and milestones in our lives, especially within the context of the communities in which we participate. Some rites are specifically spiritual, as with rituals of dedication or initiation within a religious tradition, while others can be more general and communal, as when we celebrate a marriage. Some rites are meant to help individuals transition to a new phase of their lives as in coming of age rituals, while others are meant to help the communities process the loss of a beloved member, as with funerals. Each type of ritual is triggered by a different event, and the purpose of each ritual may have a different goal, but all have the same foundational intention: to assist in the crossing of a threshold.

This dedicatory project is an invitation to create a body of liturgy that reflects the threshold energies represented by each of the Nine Paths. These can take any form we wish: for personal use, for use within our faith communities only, or as a ready resource on hand for participating in ceremonial service to our greater communities.

Whether choosing to create threshold crossing rites reflecting, for example, significant points within the cycles of spiritual work within the Avalonian Tradition or to create rituals that are more broadly applicable, we must first identify the thresholds we will be addressing. Then, we must assess these thresholds from the perspective of the Ninefold, to see with which paths they are primarily aligned. And finally, we must consider the nature of the threshold itself and what is needed from our priestess service. Is our work—and therefore the purpose and intention of the ritual—to facilitate a crossing, to assist those involved in preparing for a crossing, to celebrate a crossing, or to give support after a crossing? Once the intention and the need we are seeking to meet with the rite is clear, we can proceed with its creation.

Here is one approach on how to proceed. For the purpose of this discussion, we will consider major life milestones the theme for the cycle of rites we are creating. A list of milestones could include things such as: birth, baby blessings, starting school, menarche/puberty, graduation, living independently, starting a career, celebrating career goals, entering and exiting relationships, pregnancy, childbirth, loss of a loved one, menopause, elderhood, illness, and death. Next, we consider which of the Nine Paths best corresponds with the energies of each of these milestones. Although we will have more than one milestone per path, it's best to embark upon this project by narrowing the field down to nine rites, one for each path. Once these nine have been decided upon, take one at a time and spend time interacting with the energies and Guardians of that path to develop the rite. The incorporation of some of the path correspondences into rituals can be used to good effect.

Another way to approach this project is to start by establishing a framework for ritual that can be used to give all of the rites a consistent, effective form. Unsurprisingly, applying the structure of the Ninefold to this process can give us good guidance on how to proceed. We can also use the Ninefold as a way to evaluate the rites to ensure that we've accounted for all that may be needed for a safe, effective, and transformational ritual experience for everyone involved. What follows are a few suggestions; you can use them as a guide or take this process where you are drawn to go.

Ninefold Elements of Ritual

Lorekeeper: *Foundation and Tradition.* From which traditions, myths, and cultural connections will this rite draw inspiration? How will these be incorporated into the ritual, and how can they do so in ways that are respectful of the original cultural context? What do the participants need to know in order to be prepared for and open to this ritual? How and when will that information be given to them?

Lawspeaker: *Structure and Process.* What does this ritual intend to accomplish? How will it do so? What is the structure and flow of the ritual? What ritual roles need to be filled? What contingencies should be planned for ahead of time?

Emissary: *Communication and Connection.* How will the facilitator communicate and guide the ritual flow? Will there be participation from attendees? Are there speaking parts? Will the working require a script for participants or a program for attendees? What, if anything, needs to be communicated to people outside of the faith community about the ritual?

Artisan: *Energy and Intention.* What needs to be created in support of the ritual intention? What will be used to build and maintain the energetic tone? Will the flow of ritual need choreographing for best use of time and space? Are there any garb, altar dressing, environmental, or decorative needs? Will music, dancing, or chanting be incorporated in the working? How, where, and what are these intended to accomplish?

Hearthtender: *Center and Container.* What resources are required for the ritual, including magical tools and altar items? Are there other supplies needed? What mundane concerns are necessary to secure the ritual space—permits, insurance, pavilions, chairs, rental fees? Has accessibility been taken into account? Will food or drink be available?

Guardian: *Safe and Sacred Space.* Who maintains the integrity of the working space both physically and energetically? Who will ensure the safety of participants, and how will this be accomplished? What processes are in place to give assistance to those who fall ill, get injured, or feel emotionally or energetically imbalanced during or after the ritual?

Seer: *Guidance and Divination.* What intuitive guidance is necessary to create and facilitate this ritual? Will a divinatory working be part of the overall working? Will there be an opportunity for participants to reflect and ask for answers as well? If so, how will that occur? Will there be a request for the presence of divinities, ancestors, entities, or spirits during the rite? Have they been consulted ahead of time?

Healer: *Support and Wellness.* In what ways are the emotional needs of participants accounted for as part of the ritual itself, e.g., grounding energies that are raised, closing doors that were opened, thanking and releasing any beings whose presence was requested, bringing participants back to center after strong emotional releases as with rites of grief or catharsis, and so on. Will there be an opportunity to clear, cleanse, and center before and after the working? How will this be done?

Ritualist: *Spirit and Devotion.* What spiritual needs does this ritual seek to meet? Is it a rite or a celebration? Is it a request for change, a celebration or acknoweldgment of change, or a magical operation intended to trigger change? Does it require the shifting of consciousness, as with trance work? Is it intended to unify intentions toward a stated goal or purpose? Is it a community ritual meant to forge connections between people, or is it a seasonal celebration intended to honor and align with the cycles of nature? What magical processes or principles can be applied to best meet these needs?

THE NINEFOLD IMMERSION

Throughout this book, we have been engaging with the Avalonian Stream of Tradition, first by remembering all that has come before, and then reclaiming that information in a context that provides us with an understanding of the past and inspires us with a vision for the present. With this work as our foundation, we can now turn our attention to forging a renewed connection to the Holy Isle—one that is personal, dynamic, and alive.

What follows is a process through which a seeker can obtain direct experience of the interconnected nature of the Ninefold, as well as a deeper understanding of the Ninefold as it exists within us and around us. These, in turn, will provide opportunities to forge relationships with the Threshold Guardians of Avalon's Nine Pathways—the custodians of the Mysteries of Avalon. These Nine reveal themselves in many ways, and we have come to know them best as the Nine Morgens of the Holy Isle, the Nine Sisters of the Island of Apples, and the Nine Maidens of Annwn.

In the chapters that follow, I have laid out a process for engagement that is intended to guide you into an authentic relationship with the Holy Isle as well as those who hold it in their care. This map has been laid out in very structured fashion and has itself been constructed based on energetic correspondences and alignments with the lunar tides. Every seeker is different: some love structure as it keeps them on track, while others find it too restrictive. Some seekers enjoy the challenge of keeping up a particular pace, while others feel that missing a working or two requires starting over. No matter what kind of seeker you are, I ask that you take this structure as the offering it is—it is meant to be a guide, not a prison … an inspiration, not an exacting task-mistress.

Center yourself in your Sovereignty as you proceed with this work. While establishing a regular personal practice is a powerful discipline that catalyzes our growth, we must also remember to honor the rhythms of our life circumstances. Like the tides of moon and ocean, we ebb and flow. Sometimes other things in our lives must take precedence … other times, we need the rhythms set by developing a regular practice to overcome our inertia. Knowing the difference between a lack of personal resources and a lack of will is important—as is the ability to make a sovereign choice to honor the first or push through the second.

Either way, it is important that we do our best and not engage in feelings of guilt or inadequacy if our practice falls away for a time, if we aren't able to complete the work in a given time period, or if we do not meet our personal goals. We must cultivate a perspective of compassion and forgiveness for ourselves and then pick the work up where we left off. Whether you choose to follow the structure offered here or approach the work at your own pace, commit yourself to doing the best you can—*not* to being perfect. It is more important to proceed in order, rather than to adhere to a time frame. That said, undertaking the Ninefold Immersion is not done lightly. It requires you to make space in your life dedicated to this work; it is a commitment that you make to yourself and to the Holy Isle.

Read through this chapter completely before embarking upon this journey. Take some time to determine if the approach offered here fits with your process or if you would benefit from adjusting the suggested time frame. Consider the tools necessary and what you may need to do to obtain or create them.

This process has been broken down into phases, and a suggested time frame for completing each is included; however, the time frame is less important than the order of completion. The recommendations reflect an ongoing practice of immersion that builds magical momentum, but feel free to expand it over a longer period of time if necessary because of your life circumstances or because it is a more comfortable pace. Going at a faster pace or skipping steps in this process will not serve you in the long run. The goal is to establish authentic connections with the Ninefold, not to cross things off of a to-do list. More than that, each phase builds upon the ones before, so it is important to have done the work in order to proceed.

A recommended approach to the Ninefold Immersion looks like this:

Pre-Phase: Gathering the Tools

This phase concerns the defining of sacred space, the gathering of devotional items, and the use of various priestessing tools that will be used as part of this immersion to assist in connecting with and exploring the energies of the Nine Paths. As you gather the items you need for your shrines, use this time to practice the tools we will be using during this immersion: the Ninefold Breath, the Cauldron posture, the Awen posture, and the two threshold tools discussed on page 382. There is no time frame suggested for this preparatory portion.

Phase One: Illuminating the Pathways

We will begin our explorations of the Ninefold by establishing connections with each of the Nine Paths through the threshold of their corresponding moon phases.

Suggested time frame: Nine sessions of three nights each, in alignment with the phases of the moon. At minimum, one month.

Phase Two: Exploring the Currents

Diving deeply into the fractal nature of the Ninefold, we will immerse ourselves in the exploration of the nine composite currents of each of the Nine Paths.

> *Suggested time frame:* Nine sessions of eleven nights each, with at least three nights of integration time between them. At minimum, five months.

Phase Three: Awakening the Orchard

Undertaking a series of journeys beyond the Ninth Wave, we will forge a connection with Avalon in the Otherworld to activate and honor the sacred orchard at the heart of the Holy Isle.

> *Suggested time frame:* Nine sessions of nine nights each, with at least three nights of integration between them. At minimum, three months.

Phase Four: Meeting the Guardians

With all the work we have done thus far in this immersion as preparation, we will journey to meet the Threshold Guardians of each of the Nine Pathways.

> *Suggested time frame:* Nine sessions of four nights each, with at least one night of integration time between them. At minimum, a month and a half.

Phase Five: Kindling the Cauldron

In this final phase—actually the beginning of the next phase of your deepening priestessing journey—we will kindle the Vessel of Sovereignty at the heart of the Inner Avalon and meet the Holy Island's Once and Future Guardian.

Suggested time frame: Three consecutive nights.

Gathering the Tools

Undertaking this immersion will require a bit of preparation; there are physical tools to gather and/or create, detailed under the heading "Tools for Devotion" on page 382, as well as a few magical tools and techniques to learn and practice outlined here as "Tools for Mastery." Gathering supplies and working toward mastery of these tools can happen concurrently, and there is no time frame in which to complete this work. It is best to move to the first phase of this immersion only when you feel you are adequately prepared.

Tools For Mastery

The Ninefold Immersion is not about ticking accomplishments off of a list; the truth is that the more facility you have with these tools and the more discernment you've been able to build over time through the use of the different systems of Avalonian Tradition (the Cycles of Healing and Revealing, for example), the clearer and stronger your connection to the Holy Island and its Guardians will be. The following tools will be foundational to the immersion that follows.

The Ninefold Breath

The Ninefold Breath is a tool that can be used in many ways, but generally serves to activate our consciousness, align our energetic intentions, and bring us into an increased state of presence. Engaging the Ninefold Breath before and after any ritual or journeying work is an excellent centering tool. As part of a daily practice, it can be performed upon waking to help us bring our best selves to our day and then once more before bed to help us clear our energetic slate of the residue from our day. It is also a simple but effective tool to use whenever we need to take a moment to refocus and restore our inner balance.

For each path, you will engage a three-part breathing cycle called the *kindling breath*: a deep inhale and exhale, nine sharp inhales and a deep exhale, and then a deep inhale and exhale once more. Each cycle of breath is accompanied by an intention invocation connected to one of the Ninefold Paths; each line is intended to be held in your mind for each cycle. Once you have established a good rhythm with this tool, you may write your own intentions or engage the Ninefold Breath in silence instead.

You can also use the Ninefold Breath to fill yourself up with a singular energy, whether one of the Nine Paths or something else you are working with—the full moon, for example. In this case, switch out the symbols and intention to something appropriate, but maintain the breathing pattern.

The Process

1. Assume the Awen posture (page 376).

2. For each cycle of breath, envision one of the nine Path symbols (page 383) in the center of your forehead.

3. Once it's there, speak the line associated with that path with intention; this can be done silently or spoken out loud.

4. Inhale deeply "through" the symbol, envisioning the energy activated by your breath entering your energy field at that third eye point—and being held there.

5. Exhale deeply while envisioning the energy that has built up in your third eye to drop down from your brow and into the rest of your energy body. Feel it settle and integrate within and around you.

6. Focus again on your brow, and once more recite the line associated with the path.

7. Take nine quick, sharp inhalations through the symbol, holding the energy in the third eye center.

8. One again, exhale the energy down into and through you.

9. Bring your attention to the symbol on your brow once more, and speak the invocation for the third time.

10. Inhale deeply through the symbol, holding it in place.

11. Exhale deeply, and feel the energies become integrated with your own.

12. Connect with the next Path Symbol and visualize it over your third eye.

13. Repeat the steps in this process until you have activated the energies of all Nine Paths within you, switching out the Path Symbols accordingly.

The Intention Invocation

May I be:

Grounded in sacred memory (Lorekeeper)

Centered in balanced truth (Lawspeaker)

Committed to authentic expression (Emissary)

Dedicated to meaningful work (Artisan)

Devoted to sustainable service (Hearthtender)

Motivated to sovereign action (Guardian)

Opened to intuitive clarity (Seer)

Focused on attaining wholeness (Healer)

Transformed by divine presence (Ritualist)

Avalonian Trance Postures

Trance or ritual postures are embodiment exercises wherein we use our bodies to replicate the energies of a symbol, sacred image, or landscape feature and use this physical position as a means of entering into a trance state and undertaking a journey. I found this tool to be very much in alignment with the shapeshifting powers attributed to the Nine Sisters of Avalon and other Ninefold groups. The shift of consciousness that accompanies the induction of embodied trance is especially effective when accompanied by trance drumming or rattling at 200 to 210 beats per minute.

Inspired by the work of Anthropologist Felicitas D. Goodman (see her 1990 book *Where the Spirits Ride the Wind: Spirit Journeys and Other Ecstatic Experiences*, Indiana University Press), I developed an Avalonian Trance posture system, covered in greater detail in *Avalon Within*; five postures from the system are presented in that work. Although both have multiple applications, I share here two additional postures that are especially effective tools to assist us in connecting with the energies of the Ninefold: the Awen posture and the Cauldron posture.

Engaging with the essence of Awen and the functions of the cauldron directly is a powerful way to inform our understanding of both. One way to achieve this is through the use of trance postures. The Awen posture is powerful to use as part of a daily practice as it functions to clear and open our energetic channels in preparation for the receipt of Awen—a sacred gift and sacrament of the Cauldron. It can also be used to directly request a portion of its illumination to assist in a specific aspect of our work, as we shall see.

The Cauldron posture brings insight into the function and power of cauldrons in general; it can also be used with the intention to embody specific mythic cauldrons in order to experience and engage their differing properties. Finally, it can be used as an alternative scrying tool.

We will be using both of these postures as psycho-kinesthetic bridges of connection to the energies of the Ninefold Path. It is therefore important to spend a few weeks working these tools in order to become comfortable and experienced with using them in their direct forms before shifting their intentions for use as part of this Ninefold Immersion.

The Awen Trance Posture

The Awen Trance posture uses our bodies to emulate the symbol that has come to represent the energies of Awen; it is variously called the Three Rays symbol, the Three Illuminations, or the Tribann. While the first written instance of the word *Awen* appeared in 796 CE and is believed to be an even older concept, this symbol has its origin in the Druidic Revival movement of the eighteenth century and is believed to be the creation of Iolo Morganwg.

Many interpretations have been ascribed to the symbol; some have described it as representing the three drops of wisdom leaping from the Cauldron of Ceridwen, while others see it as the creative energies of the Divine streaming down through the Three Realms to find manifestation in the physical plane. Each of the Three Rays has various interpretations as well; I see them each as representing a specific energetic portion of the Awen that in turn has many correspondences. Generally speaking, the Silver Ray on the left represents receptive energies, the Gold Ray on the right represents expressive energies, and the Crystal Ray in the center represents integrative energies (see chapter 9).

This posture assists us in consciously opening ourselves up to, and preparing our energetic pathways for, receiving the wisdom, transformation, and illumination of the Awen.

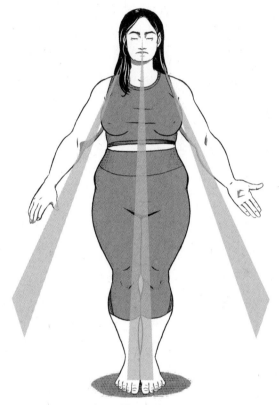

Awen Trance Posture

1. Stand with legs and feet together. Alternatively, sit on the edge of a chair, with legs together and feet flat on floor, if possible.

2. Back is straight, torso is upright, and head faces forward. If you need to support your back, consider standing up against a wall or using pillows or a bolster of some kind if you are doing this posture seated.

3. Arms are held at approximately thirty-degree angles from the body.

4. Hands are open with fingers together. The palm of the dominant hand faces forward, while the palm of the nondominant hand faces behind.

The Process

1. Using the Ninefold Breath, clear and center yourself in preparation for the trance journey.

2. Engage a steady rhythmic breathing pattern for fifteen minutes before assuming posture. Accompany working with fifteen-minutes of trance drumming, at a speed of 200 to 210 beats per minute. A track created specifically for this work can be found here: https://tinyurl.com/PostureDrum.

3. Assume the posture as described above and clear your mind of everything but the intention you have set for this working. When first using this posture, set your intention as being opened to the experience of the Awen. We will discuss the use of other intentions later.

4. When you are ready, visualize a point high above your head that connects you to the Divine via the Realm of Sky. If you have established a relationship with Ceridwen, you can envision this as a connection to her, the source of the Awen, or you can envision a more generalized idea of the universal Divine.

5. Once you feel that connection point, ask Ceridwen or the Divine for the gift of the Awen, identifying yourself as one who is seeking to walk the Ninefold Path. When it feels right and like you are being supported, envision a shaft of pure white light energy streaming down through the point from high above, moving down toward you.

6. Just as it touches the top of your head, it splits into three parts, moving through you and over you as the symbol of the Three Rays.

7. Continue with your rhythmic breath and allow the drumming to facilitate your journey.

8. Feel yourself merging with the energy flowing into and through you. You are a vessel filled with the Awen, emulating the Awen, embodying the Awen. Pay attention to how this process of embodiment makes you feel. What if anything has changed? Are there any areas of resistance? How can you resolve them so that the energy flows clear?

9. Be present in this experience and take note of any messages you may receive while standing in the abundant flow of this energy. Messages may come in the form of words or phrases, symbols or memories, or just a sense of knowing. Sometimes while in a posture, you may journey into a scene or meet someone. Engage with them; ask where you are and why, ask who they are and what you need most to know at this time in your life and in your work.

10. Go where the posture takes you, but use your discernment to ensure that you are not following a distraction. When in doubt, call your guide for assistance. Should your concentration break, bring your attention back to the drumming, back to your breath, and back to the streaming rays of divine light.

11. The drumming track includes a callback beat—a shift in rhythm to signal that the journey is coming to a close, and that you should start to wrap up your work. Be sure to thank your guide, and any other beings you've connected with during your trance journey.

12. When the drumming is complete, with your breath and your intention, envision the flow of the Three Rays ending, and the point of connection above you closing. Be sure to send gratitude to the Divine for the gift of this energy and the connections you've made. Allow the last of the streaming light to flow through you—exiting your energy field through your hands and your feet; use your breath to assist in this release, and envision it being received as an offering to the earth below you.

13. Be sure to ground and center. Should you feel imbalanced in any way, place the palms of your hands on the ground or use the bottoms of your feet to breathe any excess energies out and into the earth. Do this until you feel centered once more. Eating something grounding and taking some time to sit and process your experience can also be helpful.

14. Journal your experiences, being sure to include any symbols, messages, memories, or beings you may have encountered.

The Cauldron Trance Posture

The cauldron trance posture facilitates the embodiment of one of the most potent symbols in the Avalonian Tradition. We've discussed the powers and functions of the cauldron in British Celtic culture, explored its meanings in lore and legend, used it as a tool for ritual and journey work—and now we can use this trance posture to directly experience its transformative energies for ourselves. There are multiple applications for this posture that will be covered as we go; to begin, it is important to lay a foundation of facility with the posture and become experienced in embodying the cauldron.

Cauldron Trance Posture

1. Sit comfortably on the floor, couch, or bed. Create an open, rounded space like the bottom of a cauldron by bending your knees and crossing your lower legs in front of you. The leg of your dominant side should be crossed in front over the other. If you are able to do so, keep your feet flat on the floor, and keep your knees spread but high. Use pillows or rolled blankets to support your calves, knees, and hips if necessary.

2. Back is straight, torso is upright, shoulders are squared, and head faces forward. Consider supporting your back using a pillow or bolster, or the back of your couch or by sitting against a wall.

3. Arms are bent at the elbows and forearms rest comfortably on the knees.

4. Palms are open, facing inward, with the tips of your fingers touching. Your arms and hands create a rounded space like the rim of a cauldron, encircling the deep belly of the cauldron created by your legs and torso.

The Process

1. Follow the first three steps as outlined for the Awen posture above. When first using this posture, set your intention as being opened to the experience of embodying the cauldron. (The use of other intentions is discussed later.)

2. Unlike the Awen posture, which is unique in how it actively ties into a source of energy, this trance posture is one of pure embodiment; with each cycle of breath and each beat of the drum, you feel yourself more and more becoming the cauldron. Your body knows what to do—let go of any mental resistance, and lose yourself in the experience of being.

3. While performing this posture, take note of how the different energies feel in your body. What gifts does the energy of the cauldron hold for you? In what ways does this posture facilitate your opening to your inner source of wisdom? What does this posture illuminate about any challenges or energetic blockages that may affect your experience of this transformational force? How can you use this posture to work through these challenges? What is the highest expression of the cauldron in your life?

4. Be present in this experience and take note of any messages you may receive while embodying the cauldron. Messages may come in the form of words or phrases, symbols or memories, or just a sense of knowing. While in a posture, you may sometimes journey into a scene or meet someone. Engage with them; ask where you are and why, ask who they are and what you need most to know at this time in your life and in your work.

5. Go where the posture takes you, but use your discernment to ensure that you are not following a distraction. When in doubt, call your guide for assistance. Should your concentration break, bring your attention back to the drumming and breath, and reinforce your intention of embodying the cauldron.

6. As with the Awen posture above, the callback beat is your signal to wrap up your work and thank your guide and anyone you may have met during your experience.

7. When the drumming stops, be sure to ground any energies you may have brought back with you that make you feel imbalanced. This is also a good time to journal your experiences.

Tools for Devotion

As part of this immersion, we will spend time engaging with each of the Nine Paths in turn; in support of this, we will be establishing a shrine for each path to use as a focus of our work. These shrines can be as elaborate or simple as you like, but at the minimum you will need a candle, a representation of the path's symbol, a silver-tone sleigh or jingle bell, and an image of the Seren Afallon—all of which are covered in this section. In addition, you may choose to include items that hold energetic correspondences with the paths; some—such as stones and herbs—can be actively used as tools for connection, while the presence of others can serve to reinforce and help hold the energies of each pathway. These correspondences can be found in the discussions of the Nine Paths in chapter 11. The Ninefold Correspondence table later in this chapter gathers the major correspondences all in one place.

Path Symbol

To say that each of the Nine Paths has a symbol associated with it is an enormous simplification—there are many layers of symbolism for the paths, particularly when the Ninefold is viewed through specific energetic filters—as when we explore the individual currents of each path. Over time, you may come to make personal symbolic associations with each of the nine or find that using representations of their associated trees, or herbs, or animals makes a stronger connection. I encourage this kind of exploration and the development of a personalized symbol set to build your bridges.

However, it is important to begin your work with the following nine symbols used in the Avalonian Tradition, as they are based in associated lore and already keyed into the energetics of the Nine Paths. Doing so will allow you to harness the power of already well-established symbols to assist in the forging of connections.

In addition to using these symbols to create the nine Path Candles described here, you may consider creating or collecting these objects (or representations of them) as magical tools to use when working with the energies of a specific path and as things you can place on your Path Shrine or Ninefold altar. The symbols of the Nine Paths—images of which can also be found at the beginning of their individual sections in chapter 11—are:

Symbols of the Nine Paths

Lorekeeper	Lawspeaker	Emissary
Celtic Harp	Nine-Spoked Wheel	Silver Branch
Artisan	**Hearthtender**	**Guardian**
Drop Spindle	Mead Horn	Flaming Torch
Seer	**Healer**	**Ritualist**
Bronze Mirror	Crescent Sickle	Frame Drum

Path Candle

After its initial creation during the first phase of this immersion, the Path Candle will be an energy focus for each shrine and will be burning every time we connect with this aspect of the Ninefold. For these, I recommend purchasing ten white pillar candles in glass holders, ideally the refillable kind. You can also use votive candles or tea lights in clear glass holders, but opt for the largest that works for your space.

Using paint, permanent markers, specially made stickers, or another method of your choosing, affix the symbol for each of the Nine Paths to a glass candleholder; on the tenth, do the same using the Seren Afallon. If you cannot use lit candles for whatever reason, substitute electric candles; however, since the flame will be used as a means to connect energetically with the Ninefold, I recommend using another way to hold that energy. Methods using herbs, stones, and elixirs are described as part of the immersion where appropriate.

Path Correspondences

The foundational philosophy of the Ninefold Path of the priestess is that everyone seeking to walk in the way of Avalon can and should do so from a place of Sovereignty that honors their individual gifts and passions. There are many ways to be in service, many ways to build a bridge over the Otherworld and to the Divine, and many keys to open the door into relationship with the Holy Isle.

The Hermetic principle of correspondence teaches that like energies attract each other. When assembling our Path Shrines, it can therefore be helpful to include items such as stones, herbs, and representations of animal allies that hold corresponding energies for each of the nine. In addition to the Path Candle, a shrine can include as many correspondences as you desire. Alternatively, you may choose to focus on one or two types of correspondence—for example, working only with stones or with stones and herbs—for each of the nine, because you resonate most strongly with these tools or find that they help you connect more effectively than others. Whatever you choose, spend time working with the energies of these correspondences, research their traditional meanings, and seek out associations from legends and lore until you understand how and why they are resonant with each path.

A variety of correspondences for each of the Nine Paths are listed in the following chart. They are offered here to serve as energetic signposts to help you initiate connection and deepen your relationship with the nine. These correspondences were a result of direct work with each of the Nine Paths and are also informed by symbols found in myth, traditional lore, the archaeological record, and established folk practice.

As you grow in your relationship with the Ninefold, I encourage you to seek out additional correspondences. Not only will this provide you with additional tools for connection, but it is a practice that will expand your understanding of each individual path as well as how they function in relationship with each other. For example, what color is aligned with each of the Nine Paths? What musical note or instrument?

This is an especially fruitful exercise in the context of your primary path of priestessing as well as for your vocational or avocational services and passions. How does the Ninefold reveal itself in the practice of nursing? In the physiological processes of respiration? In the stages of wound healing? In the manifestation of an oil painting? In the baking of bread? There are so many ways to connect with the wholeness of the Ninefold in the things we do, the world we live in, and the lives we live.

	Ninefold Correspondence Table		
	Chord of Sky **Cauldron of Wisdom—White Spring**		
	Lorekeeper	**Lawspeaker**	**Emissary**
Symbol	Celtic Harp	Nine-spoked Wheel	Silver Branch
Role	Bard, Poet	Judge, Mediator	Counselor, Diplomat
Threshold Guardian	She Who Preserves	She Who Measures	She Who Connects
Archetype	The Muse	The Fate	The Messenger
Virtue	Knowledge	Fairness	Honesty
Disciplines	History and Literature	Government and Law	Politics and Diplomacy
Moon Phase	Waning Gibbous	Full Moon	Waxing Gibbous
Stone	Bluestone, hazelnut	Bone, acorn	Sea glass, amber
Animals	Swan, blackbird	Eagle, wren	Raven, starling
Tree	Hazel	Oak	Apple
Herb	Rosemary	Wood Betony	St. John's Wort
Bridging Tools	Repetitive chant, spell-songs, prophetic poetry, invocational verse, automatic writing	Magical operations, devotional contracts and oaths, omens, synchronicity	Mediumship, channeling, inspired speech, glossolalia, journeying, immrama

Ninefold Correspondence Table

	Chord of Land Cauldron of Abundance—Black Spring		
	Artisan	**Hearthtender**	**Guardian**
Symbol	Drop Spindle	Drinking Horn	Flaming Torch
Role	Artist, Craftsperson	Host, Benefactor	Champion, Advocate
Threshold Guardian	She Who Creates	She Who Sustains	She Who Incites
Archetype	The Enchanter	The Fosterer	The Fury
Virtue	Skill	Generosity	Courage
Disciplines	Art and Industry	Society and Economy	Military and Infrastructure
Moon Phase	Third Quarter	Sovereign Moon	First Quarter
Stone	Chalk, clay bead	Flint, coin	Slate, tooth
Animals	Sheep, bee	Dog, pig	Horse, bear
Tree	Willow	Ash	Alder
Herb	Flax	Heather	Juniper
Bridging Tools	Alchemy, creative flow, trance-crafting, inspired art, sympathetic magic	Fire scrying, ritual fasting, rites of mead intoxication, feasting and revelry, sexual rites	Embodiment practices, ecstatic dance, trance postures, flow meditations, battle frenzy, ritual incitement

Ninefold Correspondence Table

	Chord of Sea Cauldron of Regeneration—Red Spring		
	Seer	Healer	Ritualist
Symbol	Bronze Mirror	Crescent Sickle	Frame Drum
Role	Oracle, Visionary	Healer, Midwife	Celebrant, Sacrificer
Threshold Guardian	She Who Reveals	She Who Restores	She Who Transforms
Archetype	The Prophetess	The Psychopomp	The Initiator
Virtue	Wisdom	Compassion	Devotion
Disciplines	Psychology and Ethics	Science and Medicine	Philosophy and Religion
Moon Phase	Waning Crescent	Dark Moon	Waxing Crescent
Stone	Hagstone, shell	Ammonite, hematite	Antler, jet
Animals	Salmon, owl	Snake, crane	Hare, deer
Tree	Hawthorne	Elder	Yew
Herb	Poppy	Mistletoe	Fern
Bridging Tools	Prophecy, divination, scrying, oracular trance, dreamwork, mantic incubation	Psychopomp work, soul retrieval, ritual catharsis, plant ally journeys, fever dreams, purification rites	Initiation, shapeshifting, aspecting, rites of passage, devotional offerings

The Silver Branch

Like the magician's wand or the spirit walker's rattle, the Silver Branch is both an extension of will and a means through which we undertake the journey through the realms of spirit. As a symbol, the nine silver bells affixed to the branch reveal themselves as representing a reflective, lunar pathway; as the tool of the psychopomp who moves between the worlds, the Silver Branch is the key that initiates the inner voyage along the Stream of Tradition flowing from within. One way it is used in Avalonian ritual is as part of defining the sacred space within which the ritual occurs—ringing forth with the intention that begins the process of placing the working between the worlds. It is used to trace the boundary, the enclosing hedge, the shape of the vessel that carries us over the bridge that ritual builds. (See the solitary ritual in *Avalon Within* for more details.)

The crafting of the Silver Branch should therefore be imbued with intention and invested with meaning. As it is through the focused energies of this tool that we communicate our aim to the Universe, it is important to be deliberate as we create it as well, so that each shake of the branch carries with it the vibratory essence of our innermost selves. In many ways, the Silver Branch acts as our agent and reverberates our intention through each of the Three Realms.

> *The Silver Branch calls to the Realm of Sea* … It is, in and of itself, a tool of mythic memory, anchored in the wisdom tales of the past. It stirs us to remember the truth of who we are, and connects us to a spiritual lineage that empowers our strivings and elevates our work out of the realm of metaphor and symbol.

> *The Silver Branch calls to the Realm of Land* … Its physical components are made from the wood of an apple tree, the spun and woven fiber of ribbon, and smelted metals mined from the body of the planet herself. Its bells remind us to be present and fully inhabit the whole of our experience in this body and in this life.

The Silver Branch calls to the Realm of Sky ... It embodies the soul's journey to return to Source and creates an energetic bridge that brings us further and further into the wholeness of the divine presence. Its vibrations weave the ever-growing plait of our realized potential, as we look to live in greater harmony with the truth of our divine purpose.

There are many ways to undertake the creation of the Silver Branch, and one approach in the Avalonian Tradition is for it to reflect the energies of the Ninefold Sisterhood. Even if you have crafted a Silver Branch before, creating a new one that is connected to the work of this Ninefold Immersion yields a powerful priestessing tool, and its completion can be a way to mark the fulfillment of this phase of your spiritual journey.

To begin, you will first need to obtain nine silver bells. The bells you choose to use to craft your Silver Branch is completely up to you. Some seekers simply use silver-tone jingle bells, while others prefer the tone of sleigh bells or those used as percussion instruments. Others have sought out sterling silver bells that have been crafted to resemble apples. The size, shape, and sound of the bells is likewise a matter of personal choice.

Once you have gathered these nine bells, affix a tag to each and label them so that you have a bell associated with each of the Nine Paths. As you work through the Nine Pathways in turn, keep the individual Path's associated bell on the shrine so that it becomes infused with that Path's energies. Physically hold it as you journey, and breathe the essence of the path's energy into the bell in order to reinforce its connection to that path. It may be helpful to keep uncharged bells together in a little pouch; as they are charged and dedicated to a particular path, wrap them individually with a small piece of silk (I've purchased silk scarves from a thrift store and cut them into pieces for this purpose) and put them in a separate pouch. Once you have worked through each of the Nine Paths in the first phase of this immersion, you will be ready to use these nine bells to ritually assemble your Silver Branch, using the following additional components:

A *length of applewood*. If applewood is difficult to obtain where you live, the wood of any tree that is significant to you or to which you personally feel connected will do. It is better to use fallen wood gathered with intention than something cut from a living tree; when possible, leave an offering of gratitude to the tree from which it was obtained. The length and thickness of the wood is up to you, but it should be strong enough to hold the weight of the bells as well as able to be shaken without bending. You can peel the bark and sand the branch before affixing the bells, embellish it by carving or burning symbols onto the branch, or keep it wholly natural. This is a matter of personal choice and expression.

A *method of attachment*. There are several methods for affixing the bells onto the branch; these include tying them on with ribbons (black, white, and red are often used), crafting wire, or using nails or carpentry staples to permanently attach the bells to the wood. Each bell can be tied to the branch individually, or they can be all strung onto one ribbon and wrapped onto the branch. The bells can be attached along the length of the branch or concentrated at the end. The method is up to you: your branch should be as much of a reflection of who you are and what you like as possible.

Optional additional decoration. In addition to carving or painting the wood of the branch directly, you can decorate your Silver Branch in other ways. I have tied a spiral shell, a hagstone, and a crow feather—all of which I have found myself—to my personal branch to represent the Three Realms. Others have added symbols of Avalon or the five goddesses of the Avalonian Tradition to their branches. Again, it's up to you.

When you have gathered together all the components needed to create your branch and have planned out what it is going to look like and how you are going to attach the bells, take the time to put it together in as conscious and deliberate a way as possible. You may want to wait for an energetically auspicious time, a particular moon phase, or a significant holy day to craft your branch. Be sure to journal your insights and experiences around the crafting of your branch. Once you have created the Silver Branch, you can keep in on your altar for use in ritual or prior to any kind of deep working that involves embarking upon an inner journey—shaking it nine times to communicate the intention of your work on all of the realms.

Seren Afallon

While not a symbol of specifically Celtic provenance, a nine-pointed star (also called a nonagram or enneagram) is a geometric figure that can be used to represent the energies of the Ninefold as a wholeness. There are several manifestations of the nine-pointed star, but the version of the nonagram most commonly used in the Avalonian Tradition is comprised of three interlaced equilateral triangles—one white, one black, and one red—representing the three chords that comprise the Ninefold.

The star is often inscribed within a circle, making the nonagram more properly called a *nonacle*. However, within the context of this tradition and to differentiate this symbol from its other uses out in the world, we call it the *Seren Afallon*—the "Star of Avalon." It is used as part of this Ninefold Immersion, and you are encouraged to make one to use as a focus on your working altar. Each point on the star is associated with a specific path and is labeled here. Meditate upon the meaning and energy of this symbol using the doorway tool from *Avalon Within* or the kinesthetic scrying technique presented along with the Cauldron trance posture presented earlier in this chapter.

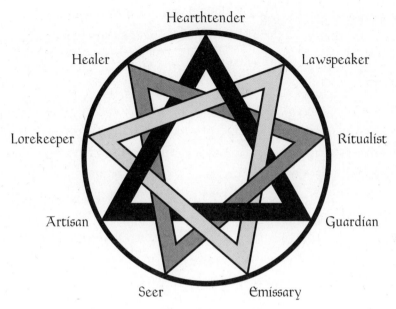

Hearthtender

Healer

Lawspeaker

Lorekeeper

Ritualist

Artisan

Guardian

Seer

Emissary

Seren Afallon—The Star of Avalon

We will be using an image of the Seren Afallon as part of this Nine-fold Immersion, and there are multiple ways to create it. Whether it is printed out and laminated, painted on a canvas, embroidered onto an altar cloth, burned onto a piece of wood, or made from ribbons or yarn wound around and affixed to an embroidery hoop, create a tricolor representation of the Seren Afallon to place on your Ninefold altar. However you do so, aim to make it large enough that you can place tea lights or stones within or on each of the nine points of the star.

It is important to work with the image of the Seren Afallon to become grounded in its meaning and develop an understanding of everything the symbol holds. A good way to do this is to meditate on the symbol itself, using it as a visual focus for exploration. The doorway tool presented in *Avalon Within* provides a good technique for working with this and other symbols; if you have not already added it to your magical toolbox, I highly recommend doing so; this tool will also be used to connect with the nine Path Symbols.

Journal

Finally, I recommend using a dedicated journal to record the details of each working: the date, time, lunar phase, your altar or shrine setup, and the intention of your working. Also include words about your experiences: insights, answers, emotions, connections with guides or other entities, and any symbols you received during your session. Even if you don't understand the meanings of everything you received, it's important to make note of the information; understanding often comes over time. This journal is a powerful archive of your process and progress along this journey … and a sovereign gift to yourself.

When you feel comfortable with the techniques presented in this chapter and all the necessary tools have been gathered and created with intention, you are ready to embark upon the work of phase one: Illuminating the Pathways.

PHASE ONE: ILLUMINATING THE PATHS

The first phase of this Ninefold Immersion sets us on the path for the journey to come. During this time, we gather together our physical materials, set up our sacred space, and begin to forge a relationship with the energies of the Ninefold. It is said that anything done daily over the course of a month can establish a new habit or release an old one. By committing to engage in a daily practice for this first month of work, we are laying down new energetic pathways within ourselves and fostering a spiritual discipline that will serve us both for the rest of this immersion and the rest of our lives.

Preparation

I want to acknowledge that not everyone has the ability to maintain a daily practice due to energetic limitations of various kinds. It is important to discern the approach to this work that works best for you from a place of clarity and honesty. While it is always good to test our limitations to see if they are related to Shadow issues—for example, not having time to spend fifteen minutes at our altar because we've chosen to scroll through social media—or if they are a reflection of where we are with our health or living situations. While learning how to prioritize our time may be part of the work required to move past our limitations of habit, pushing ourselves beyond what we are able to accomplish because we struggle with chronic health issues, for example, will only lead to burnout. This is part of the discernment process.

All that said and all else being equal and as you are able, try to dedicate at least fifteen minutes a day to this practice. It can be a powerful statement of commitment to yourself and your work as you begin the process of illuminating the inner pathways that are part of this Nine-fold Immersion journey of the Avalonian priestess.

Needed Tools

+ Seren Afallon

+ Nine small white taper candles and candleholders

+ Journal

+ Nine labeled bells for the Silver Branch

Optional Tools

+ Corresponding stones for each of the Nine Paths

+ Corresponding herbs for each of the Nine Paths

+ Cauldron with charcoal for burning the herbs

+ Reference images of the nine Path Symbols (drawn or printed)

+ Reference images for each of the phases of the moon (drawn or printed)

+ Materials required for making path elixirs, if you elect to do so. Detailed instructions are found in chapter 2 of *The Mythic Moons of Avalon.*

Recommended time frame: One month, in alignment with the phases of the moon. Alternatively, you can spread these workings over several months, so long as you begin the three days of work for each path on the night before the moon phase that corresponds to it.

Planning the Work

We begin our work by using the moon as a guide to help us navigate the deep waters of the Ninefold Mysteries. We will do this by connecting with the energies of each of the Nine Paths during its corresponding moon phase, beginning with the full moon and working our way through the entire lunar cycle. Not only does this process of using the lunar tides as thresholds permit us to directly experience the specific energies of each of the Ninefold Pathways, it also directs the focus of our explorations along an established, accessible, and potent energetic template. These lunar correspondences are summed up in the following chart:

Ninefold Correspondences—Moon Phases

Lorekeeper Waning Gibbous	Lawspeaker Full Moon	Emissary Waxing Gibbous
Artisan Third Quarter	Hearthtender Sovereign Moon	Guardian First Quarter
Seer Waxing Crescent	Healer Dark Moon	Ritualist Waning Crescent

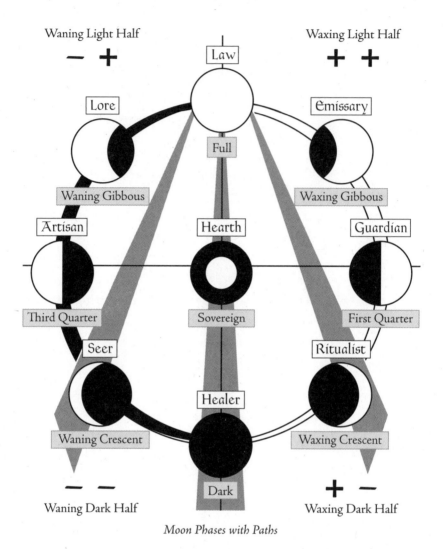

Moon Phases with Paths

The *Mythic Moons of Avalon* explores the energies of each moon phase in great detail and introduces the concept of the Sovereign moon as the ninth "phase"—acknowledging the essence of the moon as it is, independent of the light and darkness that gives it the appearance of phases. Briefly stated, the phases of the moon are caused by the position of the moon as it orbits Earth and the angles it makes with the sun relative to our perspective. As the angle between the moon and the sun increases, more of the illuminated side of the moon is visible from Earth; as the angle decreases, less of the illuminated side is visible.

However, the moon itself does not change; it remains the same regardless of how it looks from our vantage point here on Earth. This is the Sovereign moon—and it is our practice to meditate upon and connect with its authentic essence, removing it from the way it is perceived relative to a specific, external viewpoint or in context of its relationship with other heavenly bodies. A working related to this practice can be found in chapter 2 of *The Mythic Moons of Avalon*.

Synchronizing our first month's work with the phases of the moon requires a bit of preplanning. I suggest using a lunar calendar to determine the dates of the eight moon phases, starting with the full moon and ending with the next full moon. The last full moon will be the phase we use to connect with the Path of the Hearthtender, as the Sovereign moon is always present as the canvas upon which the other phases are cast; just be sure to envision this moon as the essence of the moon itself rather than the light being reflected from it. Again, see *The Mythic Moons of Avalon* for more details.

Once the dates for the nine moon phases are established, set up a schedule that dedicates three nights to working with each of the Nine Paths, beginning with the night *before* the night closest to when the full moon is at 100 percent illumination. The following is an example schedule; keep in mind that there may be a day or two between a three-day working session here and there, depending on the moon's movement.

Path of the Lawspeaker—full moon—day 1, 2, 3

Path of the Lorekeeper—waning gibbous moon—days 4, 5, 6

Path of the Artisan—third quarter moon—days 7, 8, 9

Path of the Seer—waning crescent moon—days 10, 11, 12

Path of the Healer—dark moon—days 13, 14, 15

Path of the Ritualist—waxing crescent moon—days 16, 17, 18

Path of the Guardian—first quarter moon—days 19, 20, 21

Path of the Emissary—waxing gibbous moon—days 22, 23, 24

Path of the Hearthtender—Sovereign moon/next full moon—days 25, 26, 27

Again, remember that you can spread these workings over several months, so long as you begin the three days of work for each path on the moon phase that corresponds to it.

The Ninefold Altar

Your working altar for phase one will consist of the Seren Afallon, with the nine white taper candles arranged around the star—either within the points or just outside but touching them, depending on the size of your Seren Afallon. Using a stylus of some kind (I use a tool meant for working with clay), carve one Path Symbol on each taper so that you have a complete set of nine. Using the Seren Afallon image in chapter 12 as a guide, place each labeled candle on its corresponding point. These will be used in the creation of path flames and will not be lit other than during those times.

If you are incorporating the nine path stones on the altar—optional unless your personal circumstance prevents you from using candles— place them on or next to the points of their corresponding path. If you are only using stones, place them in or on the corresponding points themselves. The stone correspondence chart gives two "stones" for each path; the second one is provided for those who may not have easy access to some of the stones and as an alternative for those who do not wish to use animal parts in their work.

Ninefold Stone Correspondences

Lorekeeper	*Lawspeaker*	*Emissary*
Bluestone	Bone	Sea glass
Hazelnut	Acorn	Amber
Artisan	*Hearthtender*	*Guardian*
Chalk	Flint	Slate
Clay bead	Coin	Tooth
Seer	*Healer*	*Ritualist*
Hagstone	Ammonite	Antler
Shell	Hematite	Jet

Integrating Herbal Allies

For those who have strong connections to herbal allies or want to include an additional component to this immersion work, creating lunar elixirs for each of the Nine Paths is highly recommended. The herbal correspondences are listed in the Ninefold Correspondence table in chapter 12. The process of crafting lunar elixirs is outlined in chapter 4 of *The Mythic Moons of Avalon*. What differs here is that the elixir empowerment process occurs on the night of each herb's corresponding lunar phase rather than on the full moon only. I recommend placing the Path Symbol on the bottle labels for both the Mother and Daughter elixirs.

There are two ways to approach the creation of these lunar elixirs. You can create them alongside the other work outlined for phase one, giving you the advantage of being able to use them as part of the Path Immersions in phase two. Alternatively, you can create them as part of those Path Immersions, being mindful to always create the elixirs on the night of its corresponding moon phase. Finally, if you cannot use candles and prefer to work with herbs over stones or are unable to obtain the stones, you can craft the path elixir on the second night of each path's three nights of working—the night closest to the moon's fullest embodiment of the phase and when we will integrate the moon in our work—and use it as your energetic focus.

Ninefold Correspondences—Lunar Path Elixirs

Lorekeeper Waning gibbous Rosemary	*Lawspeaker* Full moon Wood betony	*Emissary* Waxing gibbous St. John's wort
Artisan Third quarter Flax	*Hearthtender* Sovereign moon Heather	*Guardian* First quarter Juniper
Seer Waxing crescent Poppy	*Healer* Dark moon Mistletoe	*Ritualist* Waning crescent Fern

Another way to integrate the use of herbal energies in this work is to burn the herb associated with each Path as incense during the three nights with that path. You can also create a talisman for each of the Nine Paths—a pouch containing the corresponding herb and stone— to wear on your person during each immersion period. Becoming familiar with these energies and how they make you feel is an important aspect of this immersion process. This is a completely optional component but is highly recommended.

Engaging the Work

Once you have set up a working schedule for phase one of this immersion and gathered everything you need to set up your Ninefold altar, you are ready to begin. Throughout this month, we are going to use the Awen trance posture as a bridging tool to make a direct energetic connection with each of the Nine Paths. This is possible because the energies of Awen are what empower the whole of the system; as discussed in chapter 9, the Nine Paths are formed by the Three Rays of Awen manifesting in each of the Three Realms. The nine phases of the moon also hold resonance with each of the Nine Paths, so we will establish a link through them as well.

Night one: Connect with the path using the Awen posture.

Night two: Connect with the path using the Awen posture and the moon phase. If you are creating path elixirs at each of the phases, this is the optimum night to do so.

Night three: Connect with the path using the Awen posture, and create the Path Candle. The work of this month will lay the foundation for the deep immersion of the year to come.

Begin each working in the following manner:

1. Set up your altar with the Seren Afallon at the center. Place the nine inscribed candles (and/or stones) around the star, either in or touching the point that corresponds to their paths.

2. Place an image of the Path Symbol on the right side of your altar and an image of the corresponding moon phase on the left side of your altar.

3. With mindful intention, prepare and clear your working space. One way of doing this is burning poplar buds, juniper, or mugwort on a charcoal disk in a small cauldron.

4. Perform the Ninefold Breath presented in the last chapter to come to a place of centered clarity and receptivity.

5. Center yourself in the intention to connect with the energy of the path you are focusing on in this working.

6. If you wish, call your guide to assist you in this work. (A working to meet your Avalonian guide is found in *Avalon Within*.)

7. Engage in the work of the night, as outlined below.

Night One: The Awen and the Path

After you have set up your Path Shrine and have all of your tools present, perform the Awen trance posture as described in the last chapter, with the following modifications in place of steps 5 through 8:

5. Visualize the point of connection with Ceridwen or the Divine shining high above you. Once you feel that connection point, identify yourself as one who is seeking to walk the Ninefold Path, and ask for the gift of experiencing the Awen as it reveals itself through the Path of the [name of Path of Immersion for this working]. When it feels right and you feel supported, envision a shaft of pure while light energy streaming down through the point from high above, moving down toward you.

6. About halfway between the source point and the top of your head, and before the energy splits into the Three Rays, envision a translucent symbol of the Path of Immersion between you and the beam. Be sure that you can see the Path Symbol very clearly before proceeding; the symbol should be wider than the stream of light. Once it is strongly present, allow the light to continue down toward you, passing completely through the symbol. Make note of any changes in color, temperature, brightness, or feeling as this occurs.

7. As in past workings, just as it touches the top of your head, the symbol-modified path of energy splits into the Three Rays. Continue with your rhythmic breath and allow the drumming to facilitate your journey.

8. Pay attention to how this process of embodiment makes you feel. While you are experiencing the energies of the Path, make note of the ways in which this Path experience differs from your experiences of working with this posture solely to experience the Awen. If you've already used this posture to connect

with others of the Nine Paths, how does it compare from the embodiment experiences you've had with them? What is the same? What is different? As you journey with this posture, set your intention to discover the connection between this Path Symbol and its corresponding Path of the Ninefold. Ask what you need most to learn from this path at this point in your life's journey. Be open to any and all experiences as you journey.

Continue with the rest of the posture experience as you have before, including grounding and centering when you have finished and making sure to journal your experiences. Be sure to write everything you saw, heard, and felt during the posture, even if it doesn't make sense to you right now.

Night Two: Awen, Path and Moon

On this second night, the night closest to the fullest expression of whatever moon phase is associated with this path, we are going to make one additional modification of the trance posture. If you are making lunar elixirs for the Nine Paths, this is the night it should be set out.

After you have set up your Path Shrine and your tools are present, perform the Awen trance posture, with the following modifications in place of steps 5 and 6:

5. Visualize the point of connection with Ceridwen or the Divine, shining high above you. Once you feel that connection point, identify yourself as one who is seeking to walk the Ninefold Path, and ask for the gift of experiencing the Awen as it reveals itself through the Path of the [name of Path of Immersion for this working] and the [phase of the moon]. When it feels right and you feel supported, envision a shaft of pure while light energy streaming down through the point from high above moving down toward you.

6. About a quarter of the way between the source point and the top of your head, envision the moon in its current phase corresponding to that of this path. Spend a moment to really see the moon clearly, making sure that it is larger than the beam of light. Then, will the image to become infused with divine energy. When the moon feels charged and ready, envision the beam continuing its descent through it until it reaches the halfway point between you and the point of origin. As before, envision a translucent symbol of the Path of Immersion between you and the beam. Once it is strongly present, allow the light to continue down to you, passing completely through the symbol. Make note of any changes in color, temperature, brightness, or feeling as this occurs.

Continue with the posture as before, allowing the moon phase and path-symbol-modified energies of the Awen to pass into and through you. Journey where it takes you. Reflect on how this energy feels compared to the encounter without the moon phase energy. What is the significance of any differences you may be feeling? Ask to understand the nature of the relationship between the moon phase and the path, as well as between the moon phase and the Path Symbol.

When you've been called back by the drum and are no longer holding the posture, be sure to ground and center. Journal your experiences, being sure to record everything you saw, heard, and felt during the posture, even if it doesn't make sense to you right now. Bring your elixir in and complete the process of making the Mother elixir, being sure to label and date the bottle.

Night Three: Kindling the Path Flame

On this third night when you set up your Path Shrine, be sure to have the unused white candle you have labeled for use with this path at hand along with a way to light it. If you are going to be using a stone instead of a candle, be sure it is present and accessible. When you are ready, perform the Awen trance posture using the same modifications as you did the first night—that is, the beam of light descending from Source and passing through the Path Symbol before splitting into the Three Rays.

The modification for this stage occurs toward the end of the posture, after you've spent some time immersed in the energies of this path—being sure to reflect at some point on the ways in which the addition of the lunar energies in stage two differs from the experience of the path energies without it. As you draw close to the end of the experience, instead of allowing the energies of the Three Rays to pass through you, close off their exit points so that you become filled with the energies instead.

When the drumming ends, bring your attention to your unlit candle and visualize the symbol for this path overlaying it. Spend as much time as you need to really feel and see the symbol on the candle. Maintaining the Path Symbol as your visual focus, light the candle with intention, and say these words (or something similar from your heart) three times:

> I am (your name), and I seek to learn the ways of the Ninefold.
> Today I kindle this flame to illuminate my journey as I connect
> with the Path of the (name of path you are focusing on).

With your breath and intention, charge the candle. Begin by placing your hands a safe distance above it, palms open and angled toward the flame. As you inhale, gather into your hands the path energies built up in your energy field during during the trance posture. As you exhale, breathe those energies out of your hands and into the candle flame, charging it and the wick with the essence of the path. Perform this step three times or until all of the energies you've collected are now in the flame. Use this same technique to charge your path stone.

When you are ready, scry into the charged candle flame. This is best accomplished by softening your gaze as you look past it, shifting the focus of your eyes so that you look into the flame using your peripheral vision only; do not stare into it if it causes pain or for a long period of time—you don't want to hurt your eyes. Open yourself to any imagery or information that may arise for you while seeking answers to the following questions:

1. What steps can I take to keep the flame of this path alive in my life?

2. What parts of my life and my service will this path illuminate for me?

3. What do I most need to know as I engage with the energies of this path?

Take what time you need to receive your answers, in whatever form they come—images, words, symbols, scenes, a sense of knowing, and so on. When you are done scrying, speak some words of gratitude from your heart for the insights you have received, and then take three deep, centering breaths to bring you back to the here and now. Be sure to ground any additional energies that may make you feel imbalanced. If you wish, take up your journal and record your experiences and insights while still in the presence of this charged path flame.

When you are done, it is time to complete the creation of the Path Candle using a process called *candle smooring*—a modification of a traditional practice for settling the hearth fire at night. Smooring is a technique I learned when I received Brigid's Flame kindled from her perpetual flame at Kildare; it is how the flame has been able to travel all around the world. Smooring the flame is a way of extinguishing the fire while infusing its energy into the wick of the candle itself. Once you have done so, every time you light this candle afterward, it is a continuation of the charged energy the fire now holds. Every candle you light from this candle will have that energy transferred into it.

To smoor the candle, first set the intention that this act will lock the energies of this candle's charge into its wick so that all flames lit from this candle will carry that same energy. You can hold this intention in your mind or say something out loud in support of it. Then, with all focused purpose, put out the candle either by wetting your thumb and forefinger before quickly snapping them together around the flame to snuff it out or using a metal candlesnuffer/the bottom of a spoon to smother it quickly. Either way, be careful not to get burned, and be sure to visualize the energy of the flame entering the wick as it goes out.

Creating the Path Candles

By the end of this monthlong working, you will have a full set of nine Path Candles that will hold the energy and intent of each path. These first nine will serve as the mother flames from which you can light any number of daughter candles; when these first nine have burned down, they can then be replaced with any candle lit from this one that you can designate as the mother flame.

You will want to transfer these flames to a larger Path Candle for use in subsequent portions of this immersion. I made my Path Candles using ten white seven-day candles in their own glass holder. Each of mine has a transparent sticker with one of the nine Path Symbols on it, made and offered by one of my SOA Sisters; you also can paint the symbols on or affix them in other ways. Place an image of the Seren Afallon on the tenth candle; it has its own process for creation. To make it, you will also need an additional unused white taper candle with the Seren Afallon carved into it.

Once you have all the mother flames, your ten labeled candles, the new taper, and time set aside to create these tools in a sacred manner, you are ready to begin. Place your Seren Afallon in the center of your working altar, and line up the large candles in a row behind it in a way that is safe and accessible; be sure that the Path Symbols on them are facing forward. Create the Path Candles one at a time by doing the following:

1. Making sure you use the correct mother flame and Path Candle pair, place the new and unlit Path Candle in the center of the Seren Afallon. Then, light the mother flame while holding the intention that you are reawakening the charge of the path in the wick.

2. Use the Ninefold Breath to fill yourself up with the energies of that Path through its mother flame.

3. With the intention of passing along the sacred spark from one candle to the other, light the wick of the Path Candle.

4. Smoor the mother flame and set it aside.

5. Charge the Path Candle with almost all of the energy you filled yourself up with from the mother flame; retain a bit for use in a moment.

6. Spend as much time as you wish in contemplation and meditation.

7. Pick up the taper candle with the Seren Afallon carved into it. With intention to pass the spark of the path to its wick, light the taper from the Path Candle. Using your breath and intention, charge the taper with the remainder of the energy you filled yourself up with from the mother flame. Once you feel the taper is well charged, smoor it with intention; put this aside in a place where you won't confuse it with any of the other mother flame tapers.

8. When you are ready to move on, place the still-lit Path Candle back in its place on your working altar.

9. Repeat this process until all nine Path Candles have been lit and arranged around the Seren Afallon.

10. *Optional:* As you create each candle, place a pinch of the herb associated with each path on some lit charcoal to support the working.

11. To create the Seren Afallon candle, place it in the center of the Seren Afallon. With intention, light your Seren Afallon mother flame, which now holds the energies of all Nine Paths. Use the Ninefold Breath to fill yourself with the energies of all Nine Paths from its mother flame and, when ready, use it to light the candle in the center. Smoor the taper and put it aside. Use the energy you've filled yourself up with to charge the Seren Afallon candle.

12. If possible, circle the other candles around the Seren Afallon, with its Path Candle in the center. Take some time to feel the energies of this configuration and know that you now have a full toolbox of support for working with these energies and bringing them into your life as you need them.

13. When you are ready, being as present and as careful as you can (and perhaps opting to use a snuffer rather than your fingers), smoor each candle one by one, leaving the Seren Afallon for last.

14. Close down the space, center yourself, and journal your experiences. Be sure to store the Mother Flames in such a way that you will be able to identify them in the future.

There is a special connection between the transformational and illuminating properties of fire and the Awen. The poetic notion of the fire in the head or possessing a radiant brow like Taliesin is related to having received the gifts of the Awen. We will be using these Path Candles elsewhere in this immersion, but they are also excellent to light whenever you are working with a particular path or want to bring the energies of that path into your environment.

14

PHASE TWO:
EXPLORING THE CURRENTS

The goal of the next phase of this immersion is to engage in a deep exploration of the Nine Paths of the Avalonian Tradition. We will be using the Cauldron posture to journey up the Avalonian Stream of Tradition using the energies of each of the Nine Paths in turn, seeking their source—the place where they bubble up from the Otherworld. We will also seek direct experience of the fractal nature of the Ninefold by immersing ourselves in the nine component currents that comprise each of the Nine Paths.

Each session gives us an opportunity to experience the energies of the Nine Paths and their Nine Currents for what they are. We will also be able to reflect on how these energies show up in our own lives, as well as the ways in which they can have an impact on our growth and priestess service. It is therefore important for us to journal our experiences after each session so that we may have a record of our insights and a comprehensive energetic inventory of the Ninefold we can use in our future work.

Ultimately, completing this immersion will serve us in obtaining a deeper understanding of ourselves and a more direct understanding of the energies of the Ninefold. It will also provide us with a uniquely

Avalonian magical practice that will empower us as we work toward lasting change and profound transformation in our lives. Once we understand the Nine Paths and the Nine Currents that compose their streams of tradition, we can use them to empower our priestessing service to self, others, and Source.

How to Proceed

For this immersion, we will engage with each of the Nine Paths in turn, for a period of eleven days each. On the first day, we will use the Cauldron posture form to journey to the source of this Path's Stream of Tradition as a whole. On days two through ten, we will focus on one of the Nine Currents that make up the path, and then on the last day, we will journey back to the source of the path as a whole in order to evaluate how our understanding of the whole has changed by exploring its component parts.

Our working altars will reflect the energies we are working with by our placing the appropriate Path Candles, Path Symbols, and corresponding herbs and stones for each session. We will follow the same process for each of the Nine Paths. It can help to begin each of the nine eleven-day immersions on the night of that path's corresponding moon phase, but it is not required. This entire process will be repeated for each of the Nine Paths, but while it is best for the eleven sessions of each path immersion be consecutive if possible, it is recommended to have some integration time between the immersions themselves. If you choose to begin each immersion on the night of that path's corresponding moon phase, a natural spacing between immersions will occur accordingly.

Because this working is comprised of multiple steps, I have provided subheadings for clarity.

Needed Tools

+ Seren Afallon

+ Path candles

+ Dedicated cauldron or scrying bowl filled with water that will fit in the center of the Seren Afallon

+ Any pillows or cushions you might need for support while doing the Cauldron trance posture

+ Journal

Optional Tools

+ Corresponding stones for each of the Nine Paths

+ Corresponding herbs for each of the Nine Paths

+ A silver apple, to represent the energies of Avalon

+ Cauldron with charcoal for burning the herbs

Planning the Sessions

Here is what the eleven-day schedule looks like, along with the altar setup for each session.

Session 1: The Path as a Whole

ALTAR SETUP

Place the Seren Afallon in the middle of the working altar.

Place the scrying cauldron (two-thirds filled with water) in the center of the Seren Afallon.

Place the Path Candle for the Path of Immersion on its associated point on the Seren Afallon.

If you are using stones, place the stone for the Path of Immersion on its associated point on the Seren Afallon.

If you are using herbs, burn only the herb associated with the Path of Immersion.

Sessions 2 through 10: The Nine Currents of the Path

ALTAR SETUP

Place the Seren Afallon in the middle of the working altar.

Place the scrying cauldron (two-thirds filled with water) in the center of the Seren Afallon.

Place the Path Candle for the Path of Immersion on its associated point on the Seren Afallon.

For each consecutive session, place the Path Candle for a different current on its associated point of the Seren Afallon; in this way, you'll have two candles burning for each session. The Path of Immersion candle will remain the same, but the Path of Current Candle will rotate through the rest of the Ninefold in this order, changing each session in turn: session 2: Lorekeeper, session 3: Lawspeaker, session 4: Emissary, session 5: Artisan, session 6: Hearthtender, session 7: Guardian, session 8: Seer, session 9: Healer, and session 10: Ritualist.*

If you are using stones, place the corresponding stones in or near their appropriate points.

If you are using herbs, burn the herb associated with the Path of Immersion along with the herb associated with the current for that session. I suggest a blend of one part path herb, one part current herb. You don't need a lot, as you are using this blend to set the energetic tone for the working.

Note: One session will have the Path of Immersion and the Path of Current be the same (for example, the Current of the Lawspeaker on the Path of the Lawspeaker). When this occurs, place the Seren Afallon candle together with the Path of Immersion candle at the associated point of the star. The Path of Immersion candle should be on the point with the Seren Afallon Candle behind it. Remember that glass holders tend to get hot, so don't allow them to touch each other while they are next to each other.

Session 11: The Path as a Whole

The altar setup is the same as that for session 1.

The Working

After setting up your altar space as directed above, clear and center yourself using the methods of your choosing—I recommend burning a cleansing herb such as poplar buds or juniper and doing a centering exercise like the Ninefold Breath. If you are going to be supporting your work with burning herbs, place some on the charcoal as you begin, and add more as you feel called throughout the working.

Note: For the sake of clarity in the directions that follow, "Path of Immersion" refers to the path that is the present focus of the eleven-session immersion; that candle and symbol will be used every day of the eleven days. The "Path of Current" refers to the Nine Currents that comprise each path; that candle will change every day during the eleven days. Energetically speaking, each path is made up of nine constituent subalignments.

Opening the Space

1. Set up the working altar with the tools appropriate for the session.

2. Cleanse and center.

3. Call your guide to accompany you on your journey.

4. With the intention of welcoming its energies into your space, light the candle for the Path of Immersion.

5. Likewise, light the candle for the Path of Current (if there is one for this session), allowing its presence to mediate the energies of the Path of Immersion.

Awen Trance Posture

1. With the intention of filling yourself with the energies of Awen through the lens of a specific current from the Ninefold Paths, perform the Awen posture, accompanied by drumming.

   + For the first and last sessions, just as you did in the previous phase of this immersion process, use the symbol for the Path of Immersion as the filter through which you invite the energies of the Awen down and into your energy field.

   + For sessions two through ten, much as you did when you used the moon phase along with the Path Symbol, you will double up the symbols though which you invite the energies of Awen down and into your energy field. The first filter is the Path of Immersion symbol; once the beam of light passes through that, then add the second filter—the symbol for the Path of Current. Once the energy from source passes through both symbols, it will split into Three Rays just before entering your energy field as before.

   + Use the posture to fill yourself up with the energies of the path. Be as present with these energies as you can, making note of anything you may feel, see, or experience. However, stay focused on the intention to use this posture to build and collect the Path-specific essence of Awen within you.

Charging the Cauldron

1. When the drumming ends, place your hands palm-down over the scrying cauldron at the center of the Seren Afallon. As you did when making the Path Candles, use your breath and intention to gather the Awen you've built up within you to charge the cauldron and the water it contains. (Be mindful of the candles' heat.)

2. You have two options for scrying the streams: Option 1 is to use visual scrying with the charged cauldron as the portal. Option 2 is to use kinesthetic scrying, using the Cauldron posture as a portal. I recommend practicing both options before undertaking this phase of the immersion to see which you prefer. The details for each are given on the following pages.

3. Before beginning either journey, take a moment to center yourself in this very specific energy that you have built through and around you. Dip your finger into the charged cauldron and use the charged water to draw the Path of Immersion symbol on the center of your forehead nine times with the intention of activating and opening the threshold of the Sight. Dip your finger again, and then draw the Path of Current or the Seren Afallon in the same place nine times. Finally, dip once more and redraw the Path of Immersion symbol nine times.

4. Check in with your aims and intentions for this working session (see the end of this chapter for a list of directed threshold intentions for each current), being sure to keep them at the forefront of your mind as you begin.

Option 1: Scrying the Stream Visually

1A. When you are ready, drop into a steady, even breathing pattern. Position yourself in such a way that you can look down upon the Seren Afallon from above while maintaining a distance from it that allows you to see the form in its entirety.

1B. From this vantage point, look down into the cauldron. Reaffirm your intention for the work, by saying or thinking something like:

1C. *"My name is [name], and I seek to learn the ways of the Ninefold. Today I journey to seek the source of the Path of the [name of Path of Immersion] through the current of the [name of Path of Current.]"*

1D. Continue looking at the surface of the water in the cauldron, but soften your gaze in such a way that you are using your peripheral vision to focus on the shape of the Seren Afallon. With your peripheral vision engaged in this way, you are creating a space of liminal reception in the center of the cauldron, allowing your third eye to be stimulated with the area of central vision out of focus.

1E. While that is happening in the periphery, hold your intention in your mind as you project your consciousness down into the waters of the charged cauldron in search of the Stream of Tradition for this path. You may journey deep, or you may see images or scenes start to play on the surface of the water. Either way, allow yourself to be taken where you need to go.

Option 2: Scrying the Stream Kinesthetically

2A. When you are ready, take on the posture position. Depending on what works best for you, you can hold the charged scrying cauldron in your hands while supporting your forearms on your knees, or you can place the cauldron on the ground in the center of the space made by your body, specifically between your feet and your groin. Either way, the charged cauldron will be used as an energetic power supply that will fuel our journey.

2B. Start the drumming track and then reaffirm your intention for the work, as shown in item C on the previous page.

2C. Close your eyes and attune with the energies of the posture for a few moments. Project your consciousness down into the waters of the cauldron, seeking the Stream of Tradition for this path. Take some time journeying up the waters, then ask for the answers and insights you are seeking to come to the surface of your consciousness in the same way they would appear on the surface of the water in the scrying cauldron. Here and now, *you* are the Vessel of Sight. Ask to be shown the source of the stream and given the insights of the current. Allow the posture to take you where you need to go. From this point forward, the work is the same no matter the scrying technique you've chosen … except to be mindful of the callback drum beat, and being sure to wrap up your work and begin to express your gratitude when you hear it.

Receive Insight

6. However you choose to scry, ask the directed questions provided, along with any others you may have. Be open to the answers, and keep in mind that you may receive information through other senses as well: you may hear words or music, enter into a discussion, or start to see things in your mind's eye rather than physically in the water before you. Be gentle with yourself. This practice incorporates several magical skills at once, so it may take time and practice to begin to get the results

you'd like. You can always call upon your guide to help you with this process.

7. Take note of everything you experience so that you can remember and write them down, even if you don't understand them in the moment. Spend as much time as you can in the journey, going as far as you can and getting the answers you need. If you can, pay attention to the state of the water you are journeying on, the landscapes you pass through, the sounds and sights, and as many details as you can about the source of the stream. You will be returning here via different currents for the eleven sessions of this immersion, so you'll have many opportunities for exploration.

8. When you are ready to return or when you hear the callback beat if you are using the Cauldron posture, thank your guide and anyone else you may have encountered along the way. Leave an offering at the source of the stream or pour a libation into the water, and close anything you may have opened.

9. Envision yourself returning up from the depths of the waters, back to the vessel, returning to its place in the center of the Seren Afallon, to where you are in the here and now.

Releasing, Centering, and Archiving

1. When you have finished scrying and journeying, be sure to ground any residual energies that may cause you to feel imbalanced; place your hands on the ground and breath the energies out from the palms of your hands.

2. Be sure to shut down the threshold form and close the cauldron portal. I dissipate the energy by holding my crossed hands—palms down—over the active altar space. I inhale deeply through my nose, feeling the energies rise up from the

vessel to touch my palms—but I do not take the energies in.
Instead, as I exhale I pass my facedown hands over and parallel
to the altar in a strong but deliberate banishing motion, un-
crossing my hands as they move from the center to the opposite
sides of the altar, dissipating the energies of the portal as they
go. Hands outstretched but still facing down, I end my exhale
with a simultaneous flick of my hands and flaring of my fingers,
sending the energies out and down to be absorbed in the earth.
I do this at least three times or until I feel like the cauldron and
the space have returned to a neutral charge.

3. To complete shutting down the cauldron portal, I bring it
   outside to pour out the charged water as a libation to the land,
   visualizing the vessel becoming inert as I do so. I then dry it,
   wrap it in black silk, and store it away. If I cannot make it outside until the next morning, I cover the mouth of the cauldron
   with a piece of silk—a temporary way to keep any residual
   energies within the cauldron. When using a cast-iron cauldron,
   it is best to pour the water into a glass and to dry the inner
   surface of the cauldron so that it doesn't rust overnight. I place
   the glass in the cauldron and cover them both with silk until I
   can pour out my libation in the morning.

4. When you are completely done and your space feels clear and
   properly secure, smoor the Path Candles with intention, to
   signal the completion of the working.

5. Be sure to record everything you did, saw, and experienced in a
   journal. This will serve as a vital resource later on in your work.

Condensed Outline

This working may seem complicated because of the detailed description of the process, but it really just breaks down into the following:

1. Undertake an immersion into each of the Nine Paths as well as their component Nine Currents. Each immersion is made up of eleven sessions performed on eleven consecutive nights:

    - *Session 1:* The path as whole, to set a baseline experience of its energy

    - *Sessions 2–10:* The path through each current, nine sessions in all

    - *Session 11:* The path as a whole, put in context after having experienced its separate parts

2. Each session has a working altar setup using the Path Candles, the Seren Afallon, and optional tools of correspondence (herbs, stones, images, and so on).

3. Clear and center, using Ninefold Breath and optional incense. Call your guide.

4. Use the Awen trance posture to draw down the essence of Awen through the filter of each path and then each path's Nine Currents.

5. Charge the scrying cauldron with the energies received though the posture.

6. Use the charged cauldron to scry the stream. This can be done visually, using the waters of the cauldron, or kinesthetically, using the Cauldron trance posture.

7. Scrying the stream means to undertake a vision journey up the path's Stream of Tradition to its source, seeking specific information about the path through the lens of its component currents.

8. When done, return back down the flow to the here and now. Give offerings of gratitude, close everything that's been opened,

and clear and ground the energy both of self and of working tools.

9. Journal all of your experiences and insights.

Repeat this process for each of the eleven sessions that comprise the immersion into each path; it is best if these sessions are daily and consecutive. Aside from swapping out the Path Candles and intentions for each of the currents (and stones and herbs if you are using them), these working will be performed exactly the same way each time. What will differ are the intentions and reflections for each working and whatever guidance and insights that come to you.

Understanding the Currents of Each Path

One way to understand the currents of each path is to explore that path through the filter of the Ninefold. Through this process, the fractal nature of the Ninefold is revealed. The wholeness inherent in each path by virtue of the Ninefold is what underscores our ability to achieve personal wholeness, engage in priestess service, and build divine relationship through a devotion to one of the Nine Paths.

What follows is a list of questions to ask yourself while immersed in the specific current during the eleven-day path immersion. There are focuses for the path as a whole (day 1) as well as for each of the Nine Currents. For the last day, after journeying with the whole and each of the nine parts, I recommend coming up with a list of your own threshold intentions to focus on.

1. **The Path:** What is the overall lesson that this path holds for me in my life? What do I need most to heal in relation to this path? What do I need most to reveal about my strengths and gifts in relation to this path? What can this aspect of the Ninefold teach me about wholeness?

2. **Current of the Lorekeeper:** What is the meaning and nature of this path? What part of my personal history is mirrored in its waters? What do I need most to know about the source of this Stream of Tradition? What does this path call me to learn?

3. **Current of the Lawspeaker:** What is the primary function of this path? What biases do I hold related to the energies of this path? How can I shift my thinking around these perspectives to see with greater clarity? What does this path call on me to clarify?

4. **Current of the Emissary:** What is my relationship with the energies of this Path? How will I know that the energies of this Path are trying to make itself known to me? How can I best call upon its guidance and connect with its Guardians? What does this Path call on me to say?

5. **Current of the Artisan:** What is the manifestation of this path within my life? What does this path reveal about my work in the world? What does this path have to teach me about developing my skills and abilities at this point in my journey? What does this path call on me to create?

6. **Current of the Hearthtender:** What resources does this path hold for me? What aspects of myself are nourished and supported by its waters? How can I best be in service to others through the energies of this path? What does this path call on me to share?

7. **Current of the Guardian:** What challenges does this path hold for me? How have those challenges defined me, and how can I best overcome them? In what ways can this path be a source of strength for me? What does this path call on me to change?

8. **Current of the Seer:** What insights and wisdom does this path hold for me? What does it reveal about the truth of my Shadow and Sovereignty? How can this path help me to hone my Sight? What does this path call on me to see?

9. **Current of the Healer:** What potential for renewal does this path hold for me? What are the healing properties of its waters? In what ways does this path contribute to my quest for wholeness? What does this path call on me to accept?

10. **Current of the Ritualist:** What impact or influence does this path have on my spiritual practice? How does this path facilitate my connection to the Divine? What does this path teach me about honoring the goddesses and guardians of Avalon? What does this path call on me to transform?

While your explorations of these streams and currents need not be limited to answering these questions, it is important to seek these answers as you undertake this immersion process; you will ask the same questions of each path and then compare what you've learned for each. Not only does doing this work bring us firsthand experience and knowledge of each of these streams, but understanding the properties and energies of each fractal portion of the Ninefold helps us to discern which energies to use when we are seeking to manifest change in our lives or to correct an imbalance. This process gives us insight on where to go when we need guidance about particular aspects of our lives and serves as a potent tool for self-evaluation and reflection.

15

PHASE THREE:
AWAKENING THE ORCHARD

What follows is a journey that will take you over the Ninth Wave of the inner sea—a threshold into the Otherworld—where you will find a reflection of the Holy Island of Avalon within you. It is a small island, a blank slate awaiting your will and intention to build bridges of connection to the Otherworldly Avalon and her nine Guardians. This is a journey you will embark upon many times as you do the work of establishing a personal connection with the realms of Avalon as they have manifested through the currents of myth, legend, and history.

To undertake this working, first read it through a few times to create a mental map of the journey and understand the work you will be doing along the way. While the written journey has been broken into several parts, you are meant to work through all of them in the same session. The subheadings are intended as prompts to assist in keeping the flow of the working in order; it may be helpful for you to write the headings down on an index card to keep with you to reference as you journey.

As with any new endeavor, this may seem complicated at first. However, over time and with consistent practice, this working will become second nature to you as the intention and energy you expend in doing this work lays down an energetic pathway that builds a bridge to the

Priestess Isle within you. Trust the process. That said, everyone is different; you may find that breaking this journey down into stages works better for you.

Once you have accomplished the work of the next three phases of the Ninefold Immersion, this inner Avalon can serve as the sacred center from which your service as priestess will flow. It is a place to receive guidance from any (or all) of the Nine, to connect with the goddesses of Avalon, and to continue the work of the Avalonian priestess in service to self, service to others, and service to Source.

The Process

Awakening the Orchard is a three-month concentration that should take no less than ninety days. Starting with Lorekeeper, we will undertake this journey for each path nine nights in a row:

First three nights: Visit the Realm of Sea through the tree associated with the path currently being explored.

Second three nights: Visit the Realm of Land through the tree associated with the path currently being explored.

Last three nights: Visit the Realm of Sky through the tree associated with the path currently being explored.

Take three days to integrate and reflect, before starting the process again with the next path. Repeat this process until all Nine Paths have been explored.

Needed Tools
+ The Path Candle
+ The Seren Afallon
+ Bell for the Silver Branch for this path (to sit and charge on altar)

- A comfortable place to sit for the journey
- Journal

Optional Tools

- Any desired correspondences for the Path Shrine—stones, herbs, images
- A silver apple to represent the energies of Avalon
- Path elixir—take three drops under the tongue before beginning the working
- Cauldron, charcoal, and path herb, to support working by burning incense
- An index card with the journey steps, should you desire

Set up your altar with the Seren Afallon in the center and the Path Candle in the center of that. The rest of the working space can be set up however you wish.

A. Preparing the Self and the Space

1. Set up the working altar with the tools appropriate for the session.
2. Prepare and clear your working space.
3. Cleanse and center.
4. Call your guide to accompany you on your journey.
5. With the intention of welcoming its energies into your space, light the Path Candle.
6. Use the Ninefold Breath to fill yourself with the energies of the Path Candle, in preparation of the work to come.
7. When you are ready, undertake the Journey over the Nine Waves to reach the Otherworldly Avalon.

B. Undertaking the Journey

1. When you are ready, undertake the Journey over the Nine Waves (next page), to reach the Otherworldly Avalon. Note: it is best to record all the journeys in this book and play them back as a guide until you know the way.

2. When you arrive on the island, proceed to the orchard by following the process beginning on page 430.

3. Once you have identified your Path Tree for this set of nine workings, the work will unfold as follows:

   - The first three nights, you will work with the Realm of Sea (page 440)

   - The second three nights, you will work with the Realm of Land (page 441)

   - The last three nights, you will work with the Realm of Sky (page 443)

4. When your work with the Path Tree is complete, do the work in the section called "The Departure" (page 444).

C. The Return Journey

1. When you are ready, undertake the Return Journey to arrive back in the here and now.

2. When you have returned, be sure to release any residual energies that may cause you to feel imbalanced; place your hands on the ground and breath the energies out from the palms of your hands.

3. Thank and release your guide.

4. Smoor your candle and close down the energies of your working space.

5. Be sure to record your insights and experiences in your journal.

Journey over Nine Waves

This is the induction to be performed at the beginning of each journey into the Otherworld. The return journey is likewise given below. This frame will be used for the next three phases of this immersion: Awakening the Orchard, Meeting the Guardians, and Kindling the Cauldron.

———————

Envision yourself standing on a rocky shoreline, looking west over the cold waters of the Atlantic Ocean. The sky is grey and the waters tumultuous; the waves hiss at you as they strike at the shore, over and over again. Match the rhythm of your breath with the rhythm of the tides, and feel all resistance to this journey and the work you will be doing simply fall away.

You become aware that to the left of you, glinting and wet on a large stone boulder is a branch with nine cleverly-wrought bells in the shape of small apples. You have a sense that you are being awaited. With confidence you reach down to pick up the Silver Branch. State your intention: Why do you wish to visit the Otherworldly island of Avalon? Keep your intention clear in your mind as you begin to shake the branch; nine times you ring it, and with each shake, you feel the bells take on a greater and deeper resonance. When the last bell has rung, you place the branch back on the boulder, and fix your eyes on the horizon and wait.

It does not take long for your call to be answered; moving more quickly than you could ever think is possible, an enchanted boat comes into view. Within the space of three heartbeats, it comes to rest on the beach before you in that place where the waves meet the sand. When you are ready, enter the craft and take the place in the boat that is waiting for you. As soon as you are settled, the boat begins to move again, this time out to sea. Become aware of the waves over which the small craft is sailing, and with your mind focused on your destination, begin to count down the nine waves that, when crested, will see you firmly in the Otherworld.

And so you sail over the first wave.

And now the second. All resistance falling away.

Smoothly you move, without hesitation, over the third wave.

And now the fourth. You breathe into this journey, feeling yourself move deeper and deeper in.

Cresting the fifth wave. Feeling clear, feeling present, feeling safe.

Farther and farther away from the shore, you move over the sixth wave. The shore from which you departed is no longer in sight.

And now the seventh wave. Breathing deeply, you feel yourself getting lighter, moving farther.

You are completely surrounded by ocean as you go over the eighth wave.

And finally the ninth wave.

You crest over the ninth wave.

And passing over the ninth wave, you feel yourself someplace altogether different.

Take three deep, anchoring breaths. Feeling yourself fully centered, fully present, and fully open.

The boat slides upon a distant shore and comes to a full stop once more.

The Return Journey

To be performed at the end of the working to journey back to this world.

Take three deep centering breaths. Remember all that you have seen, and received, and committed to in this moment. When you are ready, follow the thread that connects you to the vessel that brought you to this land beyond wave, taking your place in the boat once more, to begin the journey back over the Nine Waves.

And so you sail over the ninth wave.

And now the eighth. Remembering everything you experienced.

It's easy to pass over the seventh wave, releasing any excess energy as you go.

And now you crest over the sixth. You breathe into this journey, feeling yourself moving further and further out.

Cresting the fifth wave. Feeling clear, feeling present, feeling safe.

Closer and closer, you can make out the outline of the shore in the distance as you move over the fourth wave.

And now the third wave. Breathing deeply, you feel yourself getting lighter, returning home now...

The shore where this journey began is so close now.

The whole beach is clearly in view as you pass over the second wave.

And finally the first wave.

You crest over the first wave.

And passing over the first wave, you feel like you are back in familiar territory, with your mind and heart at ease.

The boat pulls up to the shore, almost as if by magic. It comes to a full stop once more.

Take three, deep, anchoring breaths. Feel yourself fully centered, fully present, and fully open.

When you are ready, open your eyes... and return to the place that is here, and the time that is now.

———————

Awakening the Orchard

The Arrival

Your vessel comes to a halt, gently landing on the shore of a small island. Looking down, you notice a fabric bag on the bottom of the boat near your feet. You peer inside and find it contains a skin of mead and a wooden bowl. You put it on so that the strap crosses your body and the bag hangs at your hip, knowing it was meant for you to bring along.

Connect with the Energy of Place

Disembark and plant your feet firmly on the ground where the sea meets the shore. With your breath, connect yourself with the essence of this Holy Island. Inhale the energy of place up through the bottom of your feet, through your body to the top of your head. Then exhale the energy through the top of your head, allowing it to fountain up, out, and around you. Do this nine times and feel yourself centered, connected, and ready to move more deeply into the work.

The Hedge of Mist

You walk toward the center of this small island and are met by a huge, impenetrable hedge of mist; you cannot see through it, and any attempt to enter is repelled by an unseen force. Turning to your right, you walk along it for a while and see the wall of mist continues unbroken, slightly curving in a way that lets you know that it completely encircles the center of the island.

You stop, remembering the skin of mead in your bag. You pour a portion of it into the wooden bowl. Holding the bowl between your hands, connect with a feeling of gratitude for being welcomed into this sacred place. With your breath, feel the energies of that intention move through your hands and into the bowl, charging the sweet-scented mead with your appreciation. When you are ready, say the following in a clear, strong voice or with a similar feeling from your heart three times:

> I am [name], and I seek to learn the ways of the Ninefold. Today I journey to connect with the Path of the (name of path you are focusing on).

When you have done so, approach the hedge of mist and pour out the libation about three paces in front of it. The offered mead sparkles for a moment before it gets absorbed into the ground. In its place, a line of energy moves across the ground toward the mist.

Crossing the Threshold

The moment the line of energy touches it, the once-solid barrier of mist begins to shift and swirl, and the whole of it starts to turn in a moon-wise direction. The rotating mists pick up speed until suddenly, a gap in the hedge rotates into view and stops directly in alignment with the energy line radiating out from the ground in front of you. Following the line, approach the opening and stand before it, noting that this gateway is sized perfectly for you to pass through.

Take nine centering breaths. When you are ready, take a deep breath in and hold it while you step through. As you cross the threshold, your eyes are filled with a blinding light, and your ears are filled with a deafening sound—until you exhale and find yourself on the other side of the hedge.

Entering the Circle

Once through, take several steps into the space; before you is a circular grove of ancient apple trees—silent, timeless, waiting. These are no ordinary trees; growing from each of them are branches sweet with blossoms, boughs heavy with ripened fruit, and bone-bare, twisted limbs— all at the same time. A sudden croaking sound pierces the silence. In the branches of the tree directly in front of you is a large raven who stares down at you intensely. It calls twice more before flapping its wings and flying off, deeper into the grove. You have been invited to follow—and you do.

Respectfully passing through a gap between two of the enormous apple trees, you find yourself in a clearing. Walk to the center of the space—also the center of the island. You are surrounded by a perfect ring of nine ancient apple trees. Silhouetted against the hedge of mists that completely encircles the grove, they look like giant dancing women frozen mid-step, their spindly limbs suspended in a variety of forms. Take nine deep, centering breaths—once more breathing the energies of place up through and around you. Take note of how this makes you feel.

Awakening the Grove

When ready, reach into your pouch and gather what you need in order to pour some of the mead into the bowl again. Hold the bowl between your hands, and once again fill it with your appreciation. When it feels charged, lift the bowl before you and bow your head in a gesture of respectful gratitude toward the space. With mindful intention, pour the libation of charged mead onto the ground in the middle of the circle, and return the bowl to your pouch. As the honeyed liquid is absorbed, the lushly green earth begins to glow… and grow. Starting from the place you poured the libation, nine lines of sparkling energy extend outward, flowing toward the apple trees. When the energy touches the trees, a wave of light races down into their roots, up through their trunk, and splays out to illuminate every last branch, leaf, flower, and fruit on every tree. Bright and shining, the grove has been awakened.

Requesting Connection

You now stand in the center of the awakened grove, at the hub of an illuminated wheel with nine shimmering spokes. Connect with the intention that has brought you here, and when ready, speak your need into the expectant silence of the grove. As before, in a clear strong voice, say the following (or something similar from your heart) three times:

I am [name], and I seek to learn the ways of the Ninefold. Today I journey to connect with the Path of the (name of path you are focusing on).

Just as your libation was received into the earth, so have your words been received in the air—and it shifts and shimmers around you. Like a pebble cast into a pond, the energy extends outward in a ring, expanding and moving through and past the circle of trees. As the wave of energy washes over them, one of the nine apple trees begins to shine brighter than the rest, pulsing in a way that calls to you.

Walk toward the tree until you are standing a respectful distance in front of it. Use the Ninefold Breath to connect your energy to that of the ancient and venerable being before you. When you are ready, take the mead from your pouch once more. Hold the skin in your hands and charge it with your gratitude and intention to make a connection. Step forward and reverently pour the rest of the mead over the roots of the tree as an offering. Take nine steps back.

The energy from your libation begins to course up the tree's trunk, illuminating the patterns created by the bark until it stops at the height of your heart in front of you. The energies swirl and coalesce, forming a symbol of light—the symbol of the path you have come seeking. Take note of any other symbols that may form in the tree bark.

Being the Bridge

Respectfully approach the apple tree. Place your nondominant hand on the illuminated Path Symbol. As you inhale, feel the energies of the Path flow from the tree through your hand and into your energy field. As you exhale, feel these energies become integrated and settled within you. Do this for nine cycles of breath until you feel that your energy has vibrationally matched that of the Path Tree. Once you have made this energetic match, it is a simple thing to take a deep breath, step into the tree, and then exhale once you are inside—allowing the energies to settle around and within you.

Take a moment to embody the totality of the Path Tree. Your legs and feet follow the undulations of its roots, reaching deep into the earth...energetically anchored in the Realm of Sea. Your torso matches the twisted solidity of its bark-armored trunk...energetically supported in the Realm of Land. Your arms and fingers splay into myriad boughs and branches...energetically connected to the Realm of Sky. Breathe these experiences and connections into being around you; become one with this Path Tree that bridges the Three Realms.

Visiting the Realm of Sea: First Three Nights

Once you feel fully immersed in the Path Tree as it bridges the Three Realms, drop your awareness down into the roots of the tree. Follow them as they expand and grow ever downward, seeking the nurturing waters of the Realm of Sea.

As you connect with these waters, push yourself to see the unspeakably wide and endlessly deep Cauldron of Regeneration directly below you, filled to its brim with the red-tinged waters of the Realm of Sea.

Using the symbol of the Path you are currently working with as your focus for each breath, engage in three cycles of the Ninefold Breath to match your energy with that of the Realm of Sea—accessed through the path of focus.

Fill yourself up with the essence of these maternal waters, here in this realm beyond memory that holds the resonance of all that has passed. This is the dwelling place of the ancestors and the space that cradles your personal unconscious relationship with yourself.

Once you are filled and connected, seek the answers to the following questions by scrying on the surface of the water.

What is the work of this path in service to self?

What do I need most to know about this path from the perspective of the Realm of Sea?

What is the nature of my relationship with the path from the perspective of the Realm of Sea?

What is most in need of acknowledgment? Of healing? Of celebrating?

Spend some time in this energy, open to any insights, visions, memories, and symbols that may arise for you. When you are ready, speak some words of thanks for all that you have received, and pour out the bowl of cider that magically appears in your hands as a libation of gratitude to the waters.

Begin the process of releasing the energies of the Realm of Sea, breathing them out of you and back into the vast cauldron of their origin. As you let the energies go, feel yourself begin to rise up…back through the roots, back to the tree until you feel yourself straddling all Three Realms once more.

Take three deep, centering breaths, and bring back the memory of all that you have seen and experienced, step through the tree, and find yourself standing in the circle of apple trees at the center of the Holy Isle once more. (Proceed to "The Departure" on page 444.)

Visiting the Realm of Land: Second Three Nights

Once you feel fully immersed in the Path Tree as it bridges the Three Realms, center your awareness on the trunk of the tree. Feel yourself expand to fill that place between, as you connect with the rich, vitalistic energies of the Realm of Land.

As you connect with these energies, push yourself to feel the expansive rim of the Cauldron of Abundance directly around you, expanding beyond vision to encompass the whole of the Realm of Land.

Using the symbol of the Path you are currently working with as your focus for each breath, engage in three cycles of the Ninefold Breath to match your energy with that of the Realm of Land—accessed through the path of focus.

Fill yourself up with the essence of this abundant planet, here in this this realm of the present that holds the essence of all who live. This is the dwelling place of plants, animals, and mycelium... of nature spirits and genus loci, and it is the space that supports your conscious relationship with the world.

Once you are filled and connected, seek the answers to the following questions by opening yourself up to the signs and symbols forming in this landscape of augury:

> What is the work of this path in service to others and to the world?
>
> What do I need most to know about this path from the perspective of the Realm of Land?
>
> What is the nature of my relationship with the path from the perspective of the Realm of Land?
>
> What is most in need of manifesting? Of supporting? Of defending?

Spend some time in this energy, open to any insights, visions, memories, and symbols that may arise for you. When you are ready, speak some words of thanks for all that you have received, and gift the golden apple that magically appears in your hands as an offering of gratitude to the landscape around you.

Begin the process of releasing the energies of the Realm of Land, breathing them out of you and back into the wide vessel of their origin. As you let the energies go, feel yourself begin to gather your energies back to the center, consolidating ... back to the trunk, back to the tree until you feel yourself straddling all Three Realms once more.

Take three deep, centering breaths ... and bringing back the memory of all that you have seen and experienced ... step through the tree, and find yourself standing in the circle of apple trees at the center of the Holy Isle once more. (Proceed to "The Departure" on the next page.)

Visiting the Realm of Sky: Last Three Nights

Once you feel fully immersed in the Path Tree as it bridges the Three Realms, raise your awareness up and into the branches of the tree. Follow them as they splay out and grow ever higher, new green leaves trembling in the breeze as they reach toward the infinite illumination of the Realm of Sky.

As you connect with these energies, push yourself to see the incomprehensibly vast and expansive Cauldron of Wisdom arching above you, its translucent dome a mere suggestion of form encompassing the possibilities of the Realm of Sky.

Using the symbol of the Path you are currently working with as your focus for each breath, engage in three cycles of the Ninefold Breath to match your energy with that of the Realm of Sky—accessed through the path of focus.

Fill yourself up with the essence of this expansive cosmos, here in this realm that holds the potential of all that may yet be. This is the abode of the gods, the patterns of the Universe, and the space that inspires your transpersonal relationship with the All.

Once you are filled and connected, seek the answers to the following questions by opening yourself up to the guidance of the Mighty Ones:

What is the work of this path in service to Source?

What do I need most to know about this path from the perspective of the Realm of Sky?

What is the nature of my relationship with the path from the perspective of the Realm of Sky?

What is most in need of learning? Of discerning? Of expressing?

Spend some time in this energy and remain open to any insights, visions, memories, and symbols that may appear. When you are ready, speak some words of thanks for all that you have received, and release the newly budded apple blossoms that magically appear in your hands as an offering of gratitude to the currents of the solar winds around you.

Begin the process of releasing the energies of the Realm of Sky, breathing them out of you and back up into the vastness of their origin. As you let the energies go, feel yourself begin to sink down … back through the stems of the leaves, back through the branches until you feel yourself straddling all Three Realms once more.

Take three deep, centering breaths … and bringing back the memory of all that you have seen and experienced … step through the tree, and find yourself standing in the circle of apple trees at the center of the Holy Isle once more.

The Departure

When you are ready, return to the center of the grove. Take nine deep, centering breaths to integrate all that you have seen and experienced. When you have done so, state your intention to return home and ask that the way be shown to you. Almost immediately, the hedge of mist beyond the trees begins to circle once more. When it comes to a stop, you can see a space in the hedge between two of the trees, and you head toward it. Before passing between the trees, turn toward the grove once more and speak some heartfelt words of gratitude for all that you have experienced in this safe and supportive space.

When you are ready, pass out of the circle of trees, and stand before the gap in the mists. Take a deep breath in and step through. As you cross the threshold, your eyes are filled with a blinding light, and your ears are filled with a deafening sound—until you exhale and find yourself on the other side of the hedge... standing on the shore where the vessel that brought you to the island awaits you.

Know that you can return to this island and work in this sacred grove whenever you have need of further guidance or insight from the Guardians you have met here. After once more speaking words of gratitude to your guides and the Guardians of this place, take your seat in the vessel and begin the journey across the nine waves to the place where you began.

16

PHASE FOUR:
MEETING THE GUARDIANS

The next phase in this immersion process invites us to seek out connections with the Threshold Guardians of the Avalonian Ninefold Path. This is the beginning of the deeper work with these Paths,
as these are the keepers of the Avalonian Mysteries—the literal Guardians at the gate. They and they alone determine who passes through the
threshold over which they preside. Like the Goddesses of Sovereignty,
like the Vessels of Testing, we must prove our worth. This is why all the
steps before this—and not just this immersion but all the inner work of
the Avalonian Cycles of Healing and Revealing in addition to the various kinds of Shadow work we have engaged in—are so critical.

We must arrive in a space of Sovereignty that is nevertheless committed to service, of positive self-regard without the delusions of con-
ceit. Of awe and respect, without the illusions of fear. It is a challenging
road that brings us here, requiring growth and transformation that is
often hard-won. But fear not—these Guardians will help us discover
the keys necessary to unlock those potentials within us, thus opening
the doors to the mysteries we seek. In turn, we must be patient and dili-
gent. We must be centered in our desire to be in right relationship with
Avalon and all she represents within us and in the Otherworld.

This is not an easy path, nor is access to the deep mysteries quickly attained, if ever. There is no guarantee that we will pass the tests of these Threshold Guardians; some doors may never open to us. This is not a failure on our part, nor should it be a source for hurt or a bruised ego. Instead, it serves to validate the achievement of the thresholds that we *are* able to cross and reinforce the authenticity of our work.

To begin, we are here to establish relationships with these Threshold Guardians in the three forms in which they typically appear in association with Avalon: the Nine Morgens of the Holy Isle, the Nine Sisters of the Island of Apples, and the Nine Maidens of Annwn. We call to them by their Threshold Guardian names, provided here; be sure about whom you will be connecting with before starting that night's journey.

Nine Threshold Guardians

Lorekeeper	*Lawspeaker*	*Emissary*
She Who Preserves	She Who Measures	She Who Connects
Artisan	*Hearthtender*	*Guardian*
She Who Creates	She Who Sustains	She Who Incites
Seer	*Healer*	*Ritualist*
She Who Reveals	She Who Restores	She Who Transforms

The Process

Meeting the Guardians is a month-and-a-half-long concentration, approximately forty-five days. Starting with Lorekeeper, for each Path we will undertake this journey four nights in a row, with at least one night of integration and reflection time between each Path.

First night: Meet all three Guardians of the Path

Second night: Connect with the Morgen of the Path

Third night: Connect with the Maiden of the Path

Fourth night: Connect with the Sister of the Path

Take a night off to integrate. Repeat this process until all nine Paths have been explored.

Needed Tools

- The Path Candle
- The Seren Afallon
- Bell for the Silver Branch for this Path (to sit and charge on altar)
- A comfortable place to sit for the journey
- Journal

Optional Tools

- Any desired correspondences for the Path Shrine: stones, herbs, images
- A silver apple, to represent the energies of Avalon
- Path elixir: take three drops under the tongue before beginning the working
- Cauldron, charcoal, and path herb to support working by burning incense
- An index card with the journey steps

Set up your altar with the Seren Afallon in the center and the Path Candle in its center. The rest of the working space can be set up however you wish. Prepare yourself and your working space in the same manner as the last phase of the immersion. When you are ready, undertake the journey over the Nine Waves to reach the Otherworldly Avalon.

The Journey

As before, perform the Ninth Wave Journey to the Holy Isle. Following the now-familiar path that brings you to the circle of apple trees, enter the grove, and walk to its very center. Once there, charge and pour out your libation of mead, watching as it is absorbed into the ground, sending shafts of energy to each of the nine trees, illuminating and awakening them.

Requesting Connection

You now stand in the center of the awakened grove, at the hub of an illuminated wheel with nine shimmering spokes. Connect with the intention that has brought you here, and when you are ready, speak your need into the expectant silence of the grove. Again in a clear, strong voice, say the following or something similar from your heart three times:

"I am (your name), and I seek She Who _____."

Just as your libation was received into the earth, so have your words been received into the air that now shifts and shimmers around you. Like a pebble cast into a pond, the energy extends outward in a ring, expanding and moving through and past the circle of trees. As the wave of energy washes over them, one of the nine apple trees begins to shine brighter than the rest, pulsing in a way that calls to you.

Walk toward the tree until you are standing a respectful distance in front of it. Take nine connecting breaths to match your energy to that of the ancient and venerable being before you. When you are ready, take the mead from your pouch once more. Hold the skin in your hands and charge it with your gratitude and intention to make a connection. Reverently pour the rest of the mead over the roots of the tree as an offering, and then take nine steps back. The energy from your libation begins to course up along the trunk of the tree, illuminating the patterns created by the growth of the bark until it stops at the height of your heart, in front of you. The energies swirl and coalesce, forming a symbol of light—the symbol of the path you have come seeking. Take note of any other symbols that may form in the tree bark.

Meeting the Guardians

As you stand before this ancient being, you hear a gentle burbling sound as a pearly vapor arises from the ground between its roots, pooling on the left side of the tree. Fluid and shifting, it swirls and grows into a glistening figure, formed by eddying waters and draped in a veil of silver mist. She is a Lady of the Lake, one of the Nine Morgens of the Holy Isle.

A sudden breeze becomes tangled in the branches of the tree, weaving a song of golden light that flows and sighs its way down along the right side of the venerable elder apple. A glowing whirlwind as gentle as a breath and as powerful as a cyclone condenses into a golden-veiled form. She is a Cauldron tender, one of the Nine Maidens of Annwn.

The whole of the tree now begins to shift, its sinuously twisting form shuddering and shaking loose a cloud of blossoms that form a body, a swirling of leaves that settle around her like a mantle, and a thudding of fruit heralding her footfalls as a fully embodied woman steps out of its core. She is a black-robed priestess, one of the Nine Sisters of the Island of Apples.

The three figures stand side by side before you—the Silver Misted Morgen, the Dark Hooded Sister, and the Golden Breathed Maiden. Take note of everything you can about them. Speaking as one, they address you, saying, "I am She Who _____. Who are you, what do you seek?" Respond to them with your name and your intention, with words from your heart.

The Vessel of the Self

The Sister steps forward and opens her hands before her, expectantly. She closes her eyes for a moment, and when she opens them again, an energy flows out from your center and fills her outstretched hands. At her touch, it solidifies into the form of a vessel she then hands to you, before stepping back to stand with the others. Take the vessel and make note of everything you can about it—its shape, size, material, color, state, and so on.

The Challenge of the Morgen: What Must Be Released?

The Morgen moves closer to you, her undulating form flowing to create two arms, stretched out toward you. You offer the vessel to her, and she places her shimmering hands above its rim. Waters flow out from her, filling the vessel.

She says, "These are the Waters of the Stream of Tradition, reflecting that which has come before. What do you bring with you from your past that will challenge you on this path? What must you release? What must you learn in order to pass over this threshold?"

Scry into the waters seeking the answers to her questions. Take note of any symbols, memories, insights, words, or phrases you may experience while gazing into the vessel filled with the waters of Avalon's Stream of Tradition. Once you have received the guidance you seek, should you have any questions for the Morgen of the Holy Isle about her, this path, or what you have just experienced, ask now. When you have done so and are ready to move on, bow or incline your head as a sign of respect for the Morgen. She moves away to join the others.

The Inspiration of the Maiden: What Must Be Created?

The Maiden of Annwn moves closer to you, the airy vortex of her shining nature solidifying enough to form a bright visage. You offer the vessel to her, and she breathes upon it—kindling a magical, glowing light that surrounds and activates it. Although you feel no heat, the waters within begin to roil and boil until a steam begins to rise from the depths of the vessel.

She says, "This is the Breath that tends the Cauldron of Annwn, kindling that which may yet be. What actions can you take to unlock your highest potential on this path? What must you create? What must you change in order to pass over this threshold?"

Breathe deeply of the vapors that arise from the vessel, and seek the answers to her questions. Take note of any symbols, memories, insights, words, or phrases you may experience while gazing into the shifting billows of steam. Once you have received the guidance you seek, if you have any questions for the Maiden of Annwn about her, this path, or what you have just experienced, ask her now. When you have done so and are ready to move on, bow or incline your head as a sign of respect. She moves away to join the others, and the last tendril of steam dissipates—clearing your sight and leaving the vessel empty once again.

The Gift of the Sister: What Is Most Needed?

The dark-robed Sister of the Island of Apples steps toward you once more. Although her face is shadowed by the depths of her hood, you are able to catch the faintest glint from her brow. You offer the vessel to her, and she covers its opening with her outstretched hands. As she does so, feel yourself become enveloped in the folds of her cloak as it expands to embrace you. You are safe, held, and whole.

She says, "This is the Bounty of the Fortunate Isle, providing all that is needed in the here and now. What is it that you most need to fortify yourself as you undertake both the challenge and the potential of this path? What will build the bridge that will allow you to pass over this threshold?"

In the warmth and security of this sacred darkness, reflect upon her questions, taking note of any symbols, memories, insights, words, or phrases you may experience. Take as long as you need. Should you have any questions for this Sister of the Island of Apples—about her, this path, or what you have just experienced—ask her now. When you are ready to move on, bow or incline your head as a sign of respect.

When you have done so, something shifts in the vessel you are holding, and you know that it is no longer empty. The Sister removes her hands from the mouth of the vessel, and your vision returns as her cloak gently falls away from you as she steps back to stand with the others.

Bring the vessel closer to your face to see what now lies within it. It is a gift that will sustain and support you as you engage with the work of this path, and you are meant to use it. Take note of everything you can about this gift: details about its shape, size, color, material, taste, smell, and so on, as well as how it makes you feel to use it. If it is an object, take it out; if it is liquid, drink it; if it is food, eat it; if it is a garment, wear it, and so on. If you have any questions about this gift, ask them now.

Reclaiming the Vessel

When you have completed your communion and are ready to move on, thank the three figures standing before you with a gesture of respect and words from your heart. As one, they reach toward the vessel in your hands. As you watch, the vessel transforms in a flash of light, becoming its most whole and sovereign form. Take note of the changes— what it looks like and how it feels. Once you have done so, it reverts to its purely energetic form, becoming a pool of pure light in your hands. When you are ready, bring your hands to your center. With nine deep, integrating breaths, return the energetic vessel to its place within you. Take note of everything you feel once the vessel has been reintegrated. What has shifted? What remains the same?

The three figures merge into one and step back to join with the tree once more. Silver shimmers illuminate its roots, golden light plays along its branches, and a velvety darkness wraps around its trunk like a cloak until all three energies fade away. Standing there alone, speak some words of gratitude for facilitating your experience and make a heartfelt gesture of respect for the venerable apple tree tree, and manifest an offering of your choosing to to leave as a gift of thanks.

Returning Home

When you are ready, return to the center of the grove. Take nine deep, centering breaths to integrate all you have seen and experienced. When you have done so, state your intention to return home and ask that the way be shown to you. Almost immediately, the hedge of mist beyond the trees begins to circle once more. When it comes to a stop, you can see a space in the hedge between two of the trees. You head toward it. Before passing between the trees, turn to the grove once more and speak some heartfelt words of gratitude for all that you have experienced in this safe and supportive space.

When you are ready, pass through the circle of trees and stand before the gap in the mists. Take a deep breath in and step through. As you cross the threshold, your eyes are filled with a blinding light, and your ears are filled with a deafening sound—until you exhale and find yourself on the other side of the hedge...standing on the shore where the vessel that brought you to the island awaits you.

Know that you can return to this island and work in this sacred grove whenever you have need of further guidance or insight from the Guardians you have met here. After once more speaking words of gratitude to your guides and the Guardians of this place, take your seat in the vessel and begin the journey across the nine waves to the place where you began.

Perform the Ninth Wave Journey home.

Nights Two through Four

After making the initial connection with all three Guardians on the first night, perform the journey the same way with the intention of meeting them again one at a time for the next three nights: Morgen of the Path, then Maiden of the Path, then Sister of the Path. Spend more time exploring those aspects of the Path with them, perhaps receiving clarification about what must be released, what must be created, and what is most needed.

Once you have made these initial connections with all Nine Paths—making sure to journal everything you've seen, heard, and experienced—this journey structure can be used whenever you wish to connect with the Guardians of a particular Path to receive insight and guidance.

ᴘʜᴀsᴇ ꜰɪᴠᴇ:
ᴋɪɴᴅʟɪɴɢ ᴛʜᴇ ᴄᴀᴜʟᴅʀᴏɴ

In the final phase of this immersion process—actually the beginning of the next chapter of your deepening priestessing journey—we will kindle the Vessel of Sovereignty at the heart of the Inner Avalon and meet the Holy Island's Once and Always Guardian.

The Process

Kindling the Cauldron is the culmination of this Ninefold Immersion process. It is recommended that this journey be performed three nights in a row to have the experience, lay down the new energetic pathways it stimulates, and integrate the insights, revelations, and shifts in energy it may bring.

Before engaging with this phase, complete the construction of the Silver Branch if you have not done so already. Use it every time you perform the Ninth Wave Journey or any other immram.

Suggested time frame: Three consecutive nights

Needed Tools

- The Seren Afallon Path Candle
- The Seren Afallon
- The Silver Branch
- A comfortable place to sit for the journey
- Journal

Optional Tools

- Any desired correspondences for the Path Shrine—all nine stones, herbs, images
- A silver apple, to represent the energies of Avalon
- Seren Afallon Path elixir—Create a new Seren Afallon Daughter Elixir, following the directions in *The Mythic Moons of Avalon*, using three drops from all nine Path Elixirs. Once complete, take three drops under the tongue before beginning the working
- Cauldron, charcoal, and blend of nine path herbs, to support working by burning incense
- An index card with the journey steps

Set up your altar with the Seren Afallon in the center and the Seren Afallon Path Candle in its center. The rest of the working space can be set up however you wish; keep in mind that these three workings will call for all Nine Paths at once, so set up your working altar accordingly. Prepare yourself and your working space in the same manner you did for the last phase of the immersion. When you are ready, undertake the Journey over the Nine Waves, to reach the Otherworldly Avalon.

The Journey

Once you have connected with the Threshold Guardians of all Nine Paths and feel ready to take the next step, perform the Ninth Wave Journey to the mythic Otherworldly Island of Avalon, as you have many times before.

Follow the now-familiar path that brings you to the circle of apple trees, and enter the grove. You immediately sense that something is different. From the very first step you take as you make your way toward the center of the sacred grove, you can see that it is no longer empty. At the very spot where you have been pouring libations—the center of the circle which is also the center of the island—now stands an enormous tripod made of metal poles that have been driven into the ground. The peak of the tripod is at least twice your height; hanging from a heavy metal chain attached to the place where the three poles meet is a large cauldron.

It is made of burnished copper with an iron rim; two iron ring handles attach to the rim on either side, allowing the cauldron to hang from iron hooks that in turn attach to the chain that suspends the cauldron. Beneath the cauldron is a fire circle of unblemished stones; no fire has yet burned within them, and there is no wood or kindling to be seen.

Take a moment to examine the scene before you, taking note of any details you may discern about the shape and ornament of the cauldron, if any. There is no indication of who may have set this up or why they may have done so. You look into the vessel as best as you can and see that it is filled with a liquid of some kind. Everything is cold—dormant and still, just like the grove.

You realize that you have not yet given your offering to the area and get the sense that pouring it under the cauldron is not the correct thing to do. Instead, you feel called to walk back over to the circle of trees and pour a small offering to each of them one by one. Remove the skin of mead from your bag, and walk to stand in front of the tree you recognize as the being connected to the Path of the Lorekeeper.

Using words that come from your heart, say something to honor and express gratitude to the Path Tree of the Lorekeeper, and then pour a libation over some of its roots. Almost immediately, the energy of the tree shifts—sparking into illumination. You step back and see the Path Symbol take energetic form at the center of the tree, and when it is in full focus, a shaft of light emerges from the tree, running along the ground toward the center of the clearing, where it stops directly below the cauldron.

You understand now what you are meant to do. You turn to the tree once more and make a gesture of respect. Before you move on, you see a tree branch about the length of your forearm leaning against the tree. You sense you are meant to take it and do so.

Lawspeaker. Emissary.

You continue around the circle, speaking words of gratitude and pouring libations.

Artisan. Hearthtender.

Watching as your offerings are accepted and each tree becomes illuminated.

Guardian. Seer.

Each tree revealing its symbol and sending a spoke of energy to the center of the orchard.

Healer. Ritualist.

Each tree gifts you with a tree branch. Strangely, you note that each of them is different...and none of them are apple. Nevertheless, you gather them up, and when all nine trees have been honored and awoken...when all nine trees have sent a shaft of radiance to the center, creating a nine-spoked wheel of purest light...you then make your way back to the center to stand in front of the cauldron.

Once there, you see that the nine energy lines meet at a point directly below the hanging vessel...illuminating it from below with its living light. Although they have not revealed themselves to you, you can sense that the Threshold Guardians of each path are watching...

the Morgens of the Holy Isle, the Sisters of the Island of Apples, and the Maidens of Annwn.

Feel into this moment. Ground yourself in it. Connect yourself to it with nine deep, anchoring breaths.

When you are ready, take up the bundle of tree branches you gathered. One by one—with presence, intention, and a sense of sacred purpose—arrange them beneath the cauldron. Allow yourself to be guided in this task; you know exactly how to lay them down.

When you are done, stand before the cauldron once more. Feel yourself there...at the center of the clearing, surrounded by a circle of apple trees, bordered by a hedge of mist, on an Otherworldly island beyond the Ninth Wave of the sea...you are held here, in the center of the world, in this eternally present moment, surrounded by expectant silence. And then, you know what you need to do next.

But you have no way to make a fire. No matches. No flint and iron. No sticks to rub together, in hopes of eliciting a spark.

A spark...

Kneel before the cauldron once more.

Reach down inside of yourself. Reflect on this journey you have taken. The dedication, the challenge, the growth, the change. The trust in yourself and in your process. Connect with your work, with your will, with your desire to be in priestess service...

Service to yourself, that you may live in peace and wholeness.

Service to the world, that you may act with sovereign purpose.

Service to the Holy Isle of Avalon—to her goddesses, guardians, and all who seek the haven of her shores—that you may love with joyful reverence.

And there, within that center of yourself, you find it. The spark of holy inspiration.

Connect with that spark, with presence and intention...

Bring your face as near as you can to the fire that you created...

When you are ready, begin the Ninefold Breath, as you have so many times before.

But this time, here in the sacred center of the Holy Island, the self-sufficient and abundant paradise of Avalon within, use your Ninefold Breath to kindle the Cauldron of the Chief of the Otherworld…

And when you've cycled through each of the nine breaths, you see that the nine branches of the nine woods burst into a magical flame of light, born of the nine bridges to the center wrought by each of the Nine Paths, kindled into life by your Ninefold Breath.

Stand again before the cauldron, and watch as it stirs into life. The magical fire beneath it brings warmth and light, but the wood does not diminish. The vessel begins to heat. More quickly than you could have imagined, tendrils of steam begin to form, curling above the activated cauldron, shifting, changing…

The water starts to boil in earnest, and you take a few steps back. You gaze into the thickly rising steam spiraling above the mouth of the cauldron, from which comes prophecy and poetry…and notice that you can almost make out images forming within the steam's movement.

Take this moment to ask to be shown an image of your fully-realized, whole and sovereign priestess self. Allow the image to form in the expanding steam. After it does, ask that image to reflect what it looks and feels like when you are engaged in your deepest and most actualized form of priestess service. Again, allow space for that to be shown to you. Finally, when you are ready, ask for a symbol and some guidance that will help you to build a bridge between where you are in your process right now and the self you have been shown, the whole and sovereign self you are working to reveal. Allow yourself time and space to receive the guidance you've asked for. When you are done, speak some words of gratitude from your heart for these insights and answers.

The energy within the cauldron begins to build. An enormous cone of vapor rises above the mouth of the vessel, but the liquid within it never diminishes, no matter how much steam roils out of it. As it spirals higher and higher, you become aware of something shifting within the grove. You take several steps back to take in everything you hear, see, feel, smell, and experience.

Your attention is drawn to the circle of apple trees around you and the nine-spoked wheel they form. The light around the trees seems to grow brighter ... and a pulse of energy emerges from all of them simultaneously, traveling along their bridges of energy on the ground like a wave before meeting in the center of the circle. Another pulse goes out ... and then another ... each one bringing more and more energy to the center. There are nine waves of energy in all.

The last wave rolls its way inward. When it joins the energies that have pooled in the center, a shaft of energy erupts from the ground— shooting up and through the rounded bottom of the cauldron, its essence further activating the liquid within. Surrounded by swirling vapors, the energies fountain high into the air reaching at least twice the height of the tripod, before it reaches its peak and begins to tumble down around itself, like a cascading geyser of living light.

It fountains there for a moment, drawing power through the cauldron from the Nine Paths ... and then the pillar of thermal waters begins to shift, changing its shape before your eyes, taking on the form of an enormous, luminous, female figure. Her energies seem to arise from the whole of the island itself. Ancient and enduring and complete unto herself ... you gaze upon her and know her for who she is.

She is the Queen Beyond the Waves.

She is the Lady of the Orchard.

She is the Sovereignty of Avalon.

Her features shift ... her form undulates, almost as if she were dancing while standing still. A crown of apple blossoms on her brow becomes a golden torc around her neck. A sharp-tipped spear held with power becomes a hammer, swung with purpose. She stands in the prow of a barge ... she sits on the bench of a judge ... she bends to take bread from an oven. In her hands, a golden cup ... an augur's bowl ... a pot of healing ointment. You hear the strum of a harp, the calling of crows, the rhythm of hoofbeats ... the laughter of children, the cries of the wounded, the wails of the grieving.

And then, there is silence. And then there is stillness.

And you sense she is waiting for you.

You stand before the Goddess of Sovereignty, the divine embodiment of the Holy Isle. Spend some time in her presence. Ask your questions. Share your heart. Ask how you can best be in her service, if that is what you will.

When you have completed your communion with her, speak some words of gratitude from your heart. Manifest an offering of thanks in your hands to set on the ground before her, in whatever form you wish. After you do so, step back and again signal your gratitude in some way.

Take nine deep, integrating breaths, and commit to remember everything you can about this experience.

Almost immediately, the form of the Goddess shifts, losing its human shape to become a fountain of energy once more. Take several more steps back, making sure that you are not standing on any of the nine spokes of light. The energy in the center continues to change and seems to be reversing its course, moving downward to the ground, backward toward the trees. The light begins to dim and the temperature starts to cool. As the column of energy continues to recede, you note that the tripod and cauldron have disappeared.

In its place, a mirror of the fountaining energy of the Goddess bubbles forth from out of the earth—a spring of pure water. There, in the center of the orchard, instead of the flames of a magical fire, a small spring-fed pool begins to form, with boundaries set by earth and by stone. As you watch, the lines of energy between the center and the trees are replaced by nine streams of water ... splaying from their source at the center of the Holy Isle to form nine smaller pools in front of each of the nine apple trees—sustaining them.

Take a few moments to set this vision into your memory and into your heart. This is your sacred orchard. Your sanctuary. Your grove. It is a place for you to continue to work with the Ninefold, the Threshold Guardians, and the Sovereignty of Avalon. The sacred spring before you is a resonance of the source of the Avalonian Stream of Tradition—and you have just now met its manifestation. You have laid the foundation and created the bridge to this... your inner Avalon.

You notice something on the edge of the pool. You walk over and see a cup has been left there for you. Pick it up and note everything you can—its shape and size, material and condition, markings, and ornaments. Dip it into the pool fed by the sacred spring. Take a sip of the water and take note of its taste, temperature, and how it makes you feel.

The cup you hold is your vessel of priestess service, meant to remain here beside the spring, but meant to be used... to be poured out in service. In three steps, then, drink the water in your cup... the first, in service to yourself. The second in service to others. The last in service to Avalon and her goddesses and guardians. Take note of how all three feel. Know that you can return here to drink deeply of this sacred spring whenever you need to replenish your resources.

When you are ready, take nine deep centering breaths, filling yourself with the energies of place so that you may bring its blessings back with you.

Speak some parting words of gratitude from your heart, and then proceed along the well-laid path that leads you back over the nine waves to the here and now.

Integration

By embarking upon and completing the work of this immersion, you have established, awakened, and empowered this sacred island within you. It is a bridge to the Otherworldly Avalon—a bridge that can only be built through dedication, diligence, and commitment—to yourself, to your work and those you serve, and to the Guardians and Divinities of Avalon. This path of priestessing is an authentic expression of who you are and what you are called to do. It cannot be purchased or given ... only walked, step by increasingly-conscious step.

The more you work with the sacred spring at the heart of your inner Avalon, the more activated it will become, and the easier it will be to connect with the wisdoms it holds. The more discernment you build, Sovereignty you obtain, and wholeness you achieve, the more this space will be a power center for you—both the heart and the foundation for your service as an Avalonian priestess. It is a self-sustaining resource that yields what is needed of its own accord. It is an island truly in and of the Otherworld.

It is an Avalon within.

CONCLUSION:
LIVING AVALON

Although so much of this work has focused on Avalon as she used to be, engaging with Avalon as a living entity frees her from the static conception of merely existing as a relic of bygone days—a truth irretrievably lost in the mists of legend and pseudohistory, blurred by the hazy memories of an elusive Celtic Pagan past. Certainly she can still inspire us in this form…but entering into relationship with the living Avalon opens doorways to so much more.

As the Island of Healing, she provides us with hope for restoration and the promise of peace that would mark King Arthur's return in our time of greatest need—while the living Avalon also contains the prospect of achieving a state of wholeness through the reclamation of our own Sovereignty, while teaching us to maintain strong boundaries in support of our personal realms.

As the Fortunate Island that provides whatever is needed of its own accord, connecting with the living Avalon gifts us with a limitless source of spiritual abundance that teaches us how to meet our own needs, and provides inner nourishment to assist us in furthering our aspirations and actualizing our greatest potentials.

As the Priestess Isle, Avalon provides a template for how to be in sacred community, especially of and with women, while engaging with the living Avalon reveals a process for walking the path of the Avalonian priestess in this day and age—a Sovereign path guided by an ethos of personal integrity, collective responsibility, and devotional service.

And finally, the living Avalon of the Mythic Otherworld can be perceived as a cosmological map that helps us identify our place in the Universe, our work in the world, and the sparks of wisdom in ourselves. She can teach us how to harness the energies of wholeness represented by the Ninefold in our own lives—within and around us—and in doing so, can bring us into balanced relationship with what is beyond us: the divine mysteries that are the source of the Stream of Tradition that has come to be expressed as and through Avalon.

BIBLIOGRAPHY

"Abracadabra." Oxford English Dictionary. Accessed February 28, 2022. http://www.oed.com/view/Entry/539.

Aldhouse-Green, Miranda J. *Boudica Britannia: Rebel, War-Leader, and Queen*. Harlow, UK: Pearson Longman, 2006.

———. *The Gods of the Celts*. New York: The History Press, 2011.

Allison, Sarah. "Morgan Le Fay and Her Sisters." *Writing in Margins* (blog). January, 2021. https://writinginmargins.weebly.com/home/morgan-le-fay-and-hersisters.

Anczyk, Adam. "Druids and Druidesses: Gender Issues in Druidry." *Pantheon. Journal for the Study of Religions* 10, no. 2 (2015): 21–33. https://www.academia.edu/22186011/Druids_and_Druidesses_Gender_Issues_in_Druidry.

Anonymous. "The Burial of Arthur | Claddedigaeth Arthur." Translated by Georgia Henley. Global Medieval Sourcebook. Accessed June 26, 2022. http://sourcebook.stanford.edu/text/burial-arthur.

Arthurian Studies. Cambridge, UK: D. S. Brewer, 2008.

Ashe, Geoffrey. *The Discovery of King Arthur*. Stroud, Gloucestershire, UK: The History Press, 2017.

Barber, Richard, "'The Vera Historia De Morte Arthuri' and Its Place in Arthurian Tradition." In *Arthurian Literature, Volume I*. Woodbridge, Suffolk: D. S. Brewer, 1999.

Baring-Gould, Sabine. *Brittany*. London: Methuen & Co. Ltd., 1902. https://www.gutenberg.org/files/51022/51022-h/51022-h.htm.

Barney, Stephen A., Oliver Berghof, J. A. Beach, and W. J. Lewis. *The Etymologies of Isidore of Seville*. Cambridge, UK: Cambridge University Press, 2006.

Bartrum, P. C. "G." In *A Welsh Classical Dictionary: People in History and Legend up to about A.D. 1000*. Aberystwyth: National Library of Wales, 1993.

Baudet, Louis. *Géographie De Pomponius Mela*. Paris: C.-L.-F. Panckoucke, 1843.

Beck, Noémie. "Goddesses in Celtic Religion: Goddesses of Intoxication." *Brewminate* (blog). February 10, 2018. https://brewminate.com/goddesses-in-celtic-religion-goddesses-of-intoxication/.

Bidwell, Paul T., R. Bridgwater, and R. J. Silvester. "The Roman Fort at Okehampton, Devon." *Britannia* 10 (1979): 255–58. https://doi.org/10.2307/526061.

Bollard, John K., and Anthony Griffiths. *Englynion y Beddau: The Stanzas of the Graves*. Llanwrst, UK: Gwasg Carreg Gwalch, 2015.

Borsje, Jacqueline. "Druids, Deer and 'Words of Power': Coming to Terms with Evil in Medieval Ireland." In *Approaches to Religion and Mythology in Celtic Studies*, edited by Katja Ritari and Alexandra

Bergholm, 122–49. Newcastle-upon-Tyne, UK: Cambridge Scholars Publishing, 2009.

Bowen, Charles. "Great-Bladdered Medb: Mythology and Invention in the Táin Bó Cuailnge." *Éire-Ireland: A(n Interdisciplinary) Journal of Irish Studies* 10, no. 4 (1975): 14–34.

Bromwich, Rachel. *Trioedd Ynys Prydein: The Triads of the Island of Britain.* Cardiff, UK: University of Wales Press, 2006.

Brunaux, Jean-Louis. *Les Druides: Des Philosophes Chez Les Barbares.* Paris: Points, 2015.

Bryant, Nigel. *The Complete Story of the Grail. Chretien De Troyes' "Perceval" and Its Continuations.* Cambridge, UK: D. S. Brewer, 2015.

Cambrensis, Geraldus, and Llewelyn Williams. *The Itinerary through Wales and the Description of Wales.* London: J. M. Dent & Company, 1908.

Cambrensis, Giraldus. "The Discovery of the Tomb of King Arthur from Speculum Ecclesiae." Translated by John William Sutton. The Tomb of King Arthur | Robbins Library Digital Projects, 2001. https://d.lib.rochester.edu/camelot/text/gerald-of-wales-arthurs-tomb.

———. *The Journey through Wales and the Description of Wales.* Translated by Lewis Thorpe. Harmondsworth, UK: Penguin Books, 1978.

———. "The Topography of Ireland." In *The Historical Works of Giraldus Cambrensis,* edited by Thomas Wright, translated by Thomas Forester. London: George Bell and Sons, 1849.

Campbell, Joseph. *Goddesses: Mysteries of the Feminine Divine.* Edited by Safron Rossi. Novato, CA: New World Library, 2013.

Carley, James P. *Glastonbury Abbey and the Arthurian Tradition.*
Cambridge, UK: D. S. Brewer, 2001.

Clarke, Basil. *Vita Merlini.* Cardiff: University of Wales, 1973.

Coe, Jon B., and Simon Young. *The Celtic Sources for Arthurian Legend.*
Felinfach, UK: Llanerch Publishers, 1995.

Cross, Tom Peete, and Clark Harris Slover. *Ancient Irish Tales.* New
York: Henry Holt and Co., 1936.

Davies, J. H. "Arthur a Kaledvwlch: a Welsh Version of the Birth of
Arthur (From a Fifteenth Century M.S., with Translation)." *Y
Cymmrodor: Transactions of the Honourable Society of Cymmrodorion*
24 (1913). http://www.maryjones.us/ctexts/kaledvwlch.html.

Davies, Sioned, trans. "How Culhwch Won Olwen." In *The
Mabinogion.* Oxford, UK: Oxford University Press, 2018.

De Boron, Robert. *Joseph of Arimathea: A Romance of the Grail.*
Translated by Jean Rogers. London: Steiner, 1990.

De La Villemarqué, Theodore Hersart. *Barzaz-Breiz. Chants
Populaires De La Bretagne, Recueillis Et publiés Avec Une Traduction
française, Des Arguments, Des Notes Et Les mélodies Originales.*
Wikisource 1. Vol. 1. Paris: A. Franck, 1846. https://fr.wikisource.
org/wiki/Barzaz_Breiz/1846/Les_Séries,_ou_le_Druide
_et_l'enfant.

Dio, Cassisus. *Roman History.* Translated by Earnest Cary. Loeb
Classical Library. Cambridge, MA: Harvard University Press, 1925.

Doble, G. H. "Hagiography and Folklore (Read before the Society
at a Meeting Held at Exeter College, Oxford, on November 11th,
1942)." *Folklore* 54, no. 3 (1943): 321–33. https://doi.org/10.1080
/0015587x.1943.9717685.

Dodds, Jeramy, trans. *The Poetic Edda*. Toronto: Coach House Books, 2014.

Eberhart, Lawrence. "Englyn Penfyr." Poetry Forms, June 7, 2020. https://poetscollective.org/poetryforms/englyn-penfyr/.

Echard Siân. *The Encyclopedia of Medieval Literature in Britain*. Hoboken, NJ: Wiley Blackwell, 2017.

Edwards, H. J. *Caesar: The Gallic War*. (Loeb Classical Library). New York: G.P. Putnam's Sons, 1917.

Enez, Kristin. "L'île d'Aval conte l'histoire." Ile-Grande Passion, January 16, 2016. https://www.ile-grande.bzh/aval-pommes-arthur/.

Evans-Wentz, W. Y. *The Fairy-Faith in Celtic Countries*. London, UK: H. Froude, 1911.

Fletcher, Paul, Nicholas Mann, Caroline Sherwood, and Natasha Wardle. *Chalice Well: The Story of a Living Sanctuary*. Glastonbury, UK: Chalice Well Press, 2009.

Flood, Victoria. "Arthur's Return from Avalon: Geoffrey of Monmouth and the Development of the Legend." *Arthuriana* 25, no. 2 (2015): 84–110. https://doi.org/10.1353/art.2015.0022.

Floyde, Marilyn. *King Arthur's French Odyssey: Avallon in Burgundy*. (Cambridge, UK: Vanguard Press, 2009).

Forester, Thomas. *The Historical Works of Giraldus Cambrensis*. London: George Bell and Sons, 1894.

Giles, J. A. *British History by Geoffrey of Monmouth, Six Old English Chronicles*. London: H. G. Bohn, 1848.

Goetinck, Glenys Witchard. "The Quest for Origins." In *The Grail: A Casebook*, edited by Dhira B. Mahoney, 117–48. London: Routledge, 2015.

Gould, S. Baring. "Brittany." Project Gutenberg. Accessed July 15, 2022. https://www.gutenberg.org/files/51022/51022-h/51022-h.htm.

Green, Miranda J. *Celtic Goddesses: Warriors, Virgins and Mothers.* London: British Museum Press, 1995.

Harper, Douglas. "Etymology of Nine." Online Etymology Dictionary, 2019. https://www.etymonline.com/word/nines.

Haycock, Marged. *Legendary Poems from The Book of Taliesin.* Aberystwyth, UK: CMCS Publications, 2007.

Henderson, George. *Fled Bricrend: The Feast of Bricriu.* London: Published for the Irish Texts Society by David Nutt, 1899.

Higley, Sarah. "Preiddeu Annwn: The Spoils of Annwn." Robbins Library Digital Projects. The Camelot Project, 2007. https://d.lib.rochester.edu/camelot/text/preiddeu-annwn.

Higley, Sarah Lynn. "The Spoils of Annwn: Taliesin and Material Poetry." In *A Celtic Florilegium: Studies in Memory of Brendan O'Hehir*, edited by Brendan O. Hehir, Kathryn Klar, Eve Sweetser, and Claire Thomas, 43–53. Lawrence, MA: Celtic Studies Publications, 1997.

Homer. *The Odyssey, with an English Translation by A. T. Murray, PhD in Two Volumes.* Translated by A. T. Murray. *Perseus Digital Library.* Cambridge, MA: Harvard University Press, 1919. http://data.perseus.org/citations/urn:cts:greekLit:tlg0012.tlg002.perseus-eng1:11.

Hopwood, Mererid. *Singing in Chains: Listening to Welsh Verse.* Llandysul, UK: Gomer Press, 2016.

Hunt, August. *The Mysteries of Avalon: A Primer on Arthurian Druidism.* CreateSpace Independent Publishing Platform, 2012.

Hutton, Ronald. *Blood and Mistletoe: The History of the Druids in Britain*. New Haven, CT: Yale University Press, 2009.

"Inspiration (n.)." Etymology. Accessed August 28, 2022. https://www.etymonline.com/word/inspiration#etymonline_v_9343.

Irslinger, Britta. "Medb 'the Intoxicating One'? (Re-)Constructing the Past through Etymology," in *Ulidia 4: Proceedings of the Fourth International Conference on the Ulster Cycle of Tales, Queen's University, Belfast, 27–9 June 2013*, ed. Mícheál B. Ó Mainnín and Gregory Toner (Dublin, Ireland: Four Courts Press, 2017), 38–94.

Jacobs, Joseph, ed. *The Book of Wonder Voyages*. *The Book of Wonder Voyages/The Voyage of Maelduin*. New York: The Knickerbocker Press, 1919. https://en.wikisource.org/wiki/The_Book_of_Wonder_Voyages/The_Voyage_of_Maelduin.

Johnson, Flint. *Origins of Arthurian Romances Early Sources for the Legends of Tristan, the Grail and the Abduction of the Queen*. Jefferson, NC: McFarland, 2012.

Jones, H. L. "The Geography of Strabo Book IV Chapter 4." In *The Loeb Classical Library, Vol. II*. Cambridge, MA: Harvard University Press, 1923.

Jones, Mary, "The Chair of Taliesin, Book of Taliesin XIII." Celtic Literature Collective. Accessed February 28, 2022. https://www.ancienttexts.org/library/celtic/ctexts/t13.html.

———. "Echtra mac nEchach," Leabhar Buidhe Lecain, Celtic Literature Collective. Accessed 10 June, 2014. Available at http://www.maryjones.us/ctexts/eochaid.html.

———. "Gwyn Ap Nudd and St. Collen." Celtic Literature Collective. Accessed August 2, 2022. https://www.maryjones.us/ctexts/collen.html.

Jones, Mary. "The Stanzas of the Graves." Celtic Literature Collective. Accessed August 26, 2022. http://www.maryjones.us/ctexts/ bbc19.html.

Jones, T. Gwyn. *Welsh Folklore and Folk-Custom*. UK: Folcroft Library Editions, 1977.

Keith, W. J. *John Cowper Powys's A Glastonbury Romance: A Reader's Companion—Updated and Expanded Edition*. Toronto, 2010. http://www.powys-lannion.net/Powys/Keith/Gcompanion.pdf.

Kessler, L. P., and Edward Dawson. "Mediomatrici/Mednomatrici (Belgae)." The History Files: European Kingdoms–Celtic Tribes, May 5, 2011. https://www.historyfiles.co.uk/KingListsEurope /BarbarianMediomatrici.htm.

Klar, Katrhyn A. *A Celtic Florilegium: Studies in Memory of Brendan O Hehir*. Lawrence, MA: Celtic Studies Publications, 1966.

Koch, John T. *Celtic Culture: A Historical Encyclopedia*. Santa Barbara, CA: ABC-CLIO, 2006.

———. *The Celtic Heroic Age: Literary Sources for Ancient Celtic Europe & Early Ireland & Wales*. Oakville, CT: Celtic Studies Publications, 2003.

Kunz, Keneva. "Eirik the Red's Saga." In *The Sagas of Icelanders: A Selection*, 653–74. New York: Viking, 2010.

Lacy, Norris J. *The Spoils of Annwfn (Preiddeu Annwfn)*. Garland, NY: The New Arthurian Encyclopedia, 1991.

Lacy, Norris J. "The Spoils of Annwfn (Preiddeu Annwfn)." In *The New Arthurian Encyclopedia*. New York: Garland, 1991.

Lagorio, Valerie M. "The Evolving Legend of St. Joseph of Glastonbury." *Speculum* 46, no. 2 (1971): 209–31. https://doi .org/10.2307/2854852.

Larrington, Carolyne, trans. *The Poetic Edda*. Oxford, UK: Oxford University Press, 1999.

Lewis, Timothy, and J. Douglas Bruce, trans. "The Pretended Exhumation of Arthur and Guinevere: An Unpublished Welsh Account Based on Giraldus Cambrensis." *Review Celtique* 33 (1912): 423–51. https://archive.org/details/revueceltique33pari /page/432/mode/2up.

Loomis, Roger Sherman. *The Grail: From Celtic Myth to Christian Symbol*. London: Princeton, 1991.

———. *Wales and the Arthurian Legend*. Cardiff, UK: University of Wales Press, 1956.

MacKillop, James. *Dictionary of Celtic Mythology*. Oxford, UK: Oxford University Press, 2017.

Mackinlay, J. "Traces of Cultus of the Nine Maidens in Scotland." *Proceedings of the Society of Antiquaries of Scotland* 40, no. (November, 1906): 255–65. https://doi.org/http://journals .socantscot.org/index.php/psas/article/view/7059.

Madden, Frederic, and Laymon Madden. *Layamon's Brut, Or Chronicle of Britain: A Poetical Semi-Saxon Paraphrase of the Brut of Wace. Now First Published from the Cottonian Manuscripts in the British Museum, Accompanied by a Literal Translation, Notes, and a Grammatical Glossary*. London: Society of Antiquaries of London, 1847.

Magie, David. *Historia Augusta*. Cambridge, MA: Harvard University Press, 1921.

Malmesbury, William of, and John Scott. *The Early History of Glastonbury: An Edition, Translation, and Study of William of Malmesbury's De Antiquitate Glastonie Ecclesie*. Woodbridge, UK: Boydell Press, 1981.

Malory, Thomas. *Le Morte D'Arthur vol. 2.* London: J. M. Dent and Sons, Ltd., 1915.

Matasović Ranko. *Etymological Dictionary of Proto-Celtic.* Leiden, Netherlands: Brill, 2009.

McHardy, Stuart. *The Quest for the Nine Maidens.* Edinburgh, UK: Luath Press, 2003.

Mela, Pomponius. *Pomponius Mela's Description of the World.* Edited by Frank E. Romer. Ann Arbor, MI: The University of Michigan Press, 1998.

Meyer, Kuno, trans. "The Voyage of Bran Mac Febal." Celtic Literature Collective. London: David Nutt, 1895. Accessed June 16, 2022. https://www.maryjones.us/ctexts/branvoyage.html.

Monmouth, Geoffrey of. *The History of the Kings of Britain.* Translated by Lewis Thorpe. London: Penguin Classics, 2015.

Monmouth, Geoffrey of. *Life of Merlin. Vita Merlini.* Edited by Basil Clarke. Cardiff, UK: University of Wales Press, 1973.

Monmouth, Geoffrey of. "The Life of Merlin." Translated by John Jay Parry. Vita Merlini: The Life of Merlin. Sacred Texts. Accessed August 26, 2022. https://www.sacred-texts.com/neu/eng/vm/index.htm.

Myers, Ernest. *The Extant Odes of Pindar.* London: Macmillan and Co., 1874.

Owen, Aneurin. *Ancient Laws and Institutes of Wales.* London: Printed by G.E. Eyre and A. Spottiswoode, Printers to the Queen's most Excellent Majesty, 1841.

Oxford English Dictionary. Oxford: Oxford University Press, 2018.

Parry, John Jay. *The Vita Merlini.* Urbana: The University of Illinois, 1925.

Paton, Lucy Allen. *Studies in the Fairy Mythology of Arthurian Romance*. Boston: The Athenaeum Press, 1903.

Pausanias, *Description of Greece with an English Translation by W. H. S. Jones, and H. A. Ormerod, in 4 Volumes*. (Cambridge, MA: Harvard University Press, 1918), http://data.perseus.org/citations/ .urn:cts:greekLit:tlg0525.tlg001.perseus-eng1:9.29.2.

Perrin, Bernadotte. *Plutarch's Lives*. Cambridge, MA: Harvard University Press, 1919.

Pindar. "Pythian Ode X." In *The Extant Odes of Pindar*, translated by Ernest Myers. London: Macmillan and Co., 1874.

Plutarch. "Bravery of Women." In *Moralia*, translated by Frank Cole Babbitt. Cambridge, MA: Harvard University Press, 1927. http://data.perseus.org/citations/urn:cts:greekLit:tlg0007.tlg083.perseus-eng1:20.

Plutarch. *Plutarch's Morals: Translated from the Greek by Several Hands*. Translated by William Watson Goodwin. Cambridge, MA: Little, Brown, and Company, 1874. http://data.perseus.org/citations/urn:cts:greekLit:tlg0007.tlg083.perseus-eng2:6.

Plutarch, and Bernadotte Perrin. "Sertorius." In *Plutarch's Lives*. Cambridge, MA: Harvard University Press, 1919.

Polyaenus. *Strategems of War; Translated from the Original Greek by R. Shepherd*. Translated by Richard Shepherd. London: Printed for G. Nicol, 1793.

Rees, Alwyn D., and B. R. Rees. *Celtic Heritage: Ancient Tradition in Ireland and Wales*. New York: Thames and Hudson, 1974.

Reno, Frank D. *The Historic King Arthur: Authenticating the Celtic Hero of Post-Roman Britain*. Jefferson, NC: McFarland & Co., 2007.

Rhys, John. *Celtic Folklore: Welsh and Manx*. Oxford, UK: Clarendon Press, 1901.

———. *Studies in the Arthurian Legend*. Oxford, UK: Clarendon Press, 1891.

Rohrbacher, David, David Magie, and Lampridius. "The Life of Severus Alexander, Part 3." In *Historia Augusta*. Loeb Classical Library. Cambridge, MA: Harvard University Press, 1921. https://penelope.uchicago.edu/Thayer/E/Roman/Texts/Historia_Augusta/Severus_Alexander/3*.html#60.6.

Rushton, C. J. "Avalon." In *The Encyclopedia of Medieval Literature in Britain*, edited by R. Rouse and S. Echard. Oxford, 2017. DOI: 10.1002/9781118396957.wbemlb507.

Saltzman, Benjamin A. "Glastonbury Abbey." In *The Encyclopedia of Medieval Literature in Britain*. Hoboken, NJ: Wiley Blackwell, 2017.

Savage, John J. "Insula Avallonia." *Transactions and Proceedings of the American Philological Association* 73 (1942): 405–15. https://doi.org/10.2307/283559.

Shepherd, Richard. *Polyaenus's Strategems of War*. London: Printed for George Nicol, 1793.

Siculus, Diodorus. *The Library of History*. Translated by C. H. Oldfather. Loeb Classical Library. Cambridge, MA: Harvard University Press, 1939. https://penelope.uchicago.edu/Thayer/E/Roman/Texts/Diodorus_Siculus/5B*.html.

Sims-Williams, Patrick. "Early Welsh Arthurian Poems." In *The Arthur of the Welsh: The Arthurian Legend in Medieval Welsh Literature*, edited by Rachel Bromwich, AOH Jarman, and Brynley F. Roberts, 33–71. Cardiff, UK: University of Wales Press, 1991.

Sowerby, Richard. "A Family and Its Saint in the Vita Prima
Samsonis." In *St Samson of Dol and the Earliest History of Brittany,
Cornwall and Wales*, edited by Lynette Olson. Suffolk, UK: Boydell
& Brewer, 2017.

Spence, Lewis. *Legends & Romances of Brittany*. Project Gutenberg.
Project Gutenberg, 1917. https://www.gutenberg.org/files
/30871/30871-h/30871-h.htm.

"Spirit (n.)." Etymology. Accessed August 28, 2022. https://www
.etymonline.com/word/spirit#etymonline_v_24031.

Spooner, B. C. "The Stone Circles of Cornwall." *Folklore* 64, no. 4
(1953): 484–87. https://doi.org/ http://www.jstor.org
/stable/1257874.

St. Leger-Gordon, Ruth E. *The Witchcraft and Folklore of Dartmoor*.
Newton Abbot, UK: Peninsula Press, 1994.

Stanciu, Radu Razvan. "Attitudes towards Paganism in Medieval Irish
and Old Norse Texts of the Trojan War." *Apollo*. Dissertation,
Cambridge University, 2016. https://www.repository.cam.ac.uk
/handle/1810/290141.

Stokes, Whitley, ed. "The Prose Tales in the Rennes Dindshenchas:
Inber n-Ailbine, Poem 4." *The Celtic Review* 15, no. 3 (1894):
277–336. https://doi.org/10.2307/30069819.

Strabo. *The Geography of Strabo*. Edited by Horace Leonard Jones.
Cambridge, MA: Harvard University Press, 1917. https://www
.perseus.tufts.edu/hopper/text?doc=Perseus:abo:tlg,0099
,001:7:2:3.

Strabo. *The Geography of Strabo. Literally Translated, with Notes, in
Three Volumes*. Translated by W. Falconer and H. C. Hamilton.
Perseus Digital Library. London, UK: George Bell & Sons, 1903.

http://data.perseus.org/citations/urn:cts:greekLit:tlg0099.tlg001.
perseus-eng2:4.4.4.

Sturluson, Snorri. *The Prose Edda: By Snorri Sturluson. Translated from
the Icelandic, with an Introd. by Arthur Gilchrist Brodeur.* Translated
by Arthur Gilchrist Brodeur. *Sacred Texts.* New York: American-
Scandinavian Foundation, 1916. https://www.sacred-texts.com
/neu/pre/pre00.htm.

Suetonius. *The Lives of the Twelve Caesars.* Edited by J. Eugene Reed.
Perseus Digital Library. Philadelphia: Gebbie and Co., 1889. http://
www.perseus.tufts.edu/hopper/text?doc=urn:cts:latinLit
:phi1348.abo015.perseus-eng1:25.

Tacitus, Cornelius. *The Complete Works of Tacitus.* Edited by Alfred
John Church, William Jackson Brodribb, and Lisa Cerrato. New
York: Random House, Inc, 1942. http://www.perseus.tufts.edu/
hopper/text?doc=Perseus%3Atext%3A1999.02.0083%3Achapter
%3D8.

Tacitus. "The Annals" In *Tacitus—The Annals vol. V,* edited by
John Jackson, Loeb Classical Library. Cambridge, MA: Harvard
University Press, 1937. https://penelope.uchicago.edu/Thayer/e
/roman/texts/tacitus/annals/14b*.html.

Telyndru, Jhenah. *The Mythic Moons of Avalon: Lunar & Herbal
Wisdom from the Isle of Healing.* Woodbury, MN: Llewellyn
Publications, 2019.

———. *Avalon Within: A Sacred Journey of Myth, Mystery, and Inner
Wisdom.* Woodbury, MN: Llewellyn Publications, 2010.

Thompson, Albert Wilder. *The Elucidation: A Prologue to the Conte Del
Graal.* Genève, Swizterland: Slatkine, 1982.

Velde, François. "The Nine Worthies." *Heraldica.* December 6, 2006.
https://www.heraldica.org/topics/worthies.htm.

Vopiscus. "The Life of Aurelian, Part 3." In *Historia Augusta* III, translated by David Magie. Loeb Classical Library. Cambridge, MA: Harvard University Press, 1921. https://penelope.uchicago.edu /Thayer/E/Roman/Texts/Historia_Augusta/Aurelian/3*.html.

———. "The Lives of Carus, Carinus and Numerian." In *Historia Augusta* III, translated by David Magie. Loeb Classical Library. Cambridge, MA: Harvard University Press, 1921. https:// penelope.uchicago.edu/Thayer/E/Roman/Texts/Historia _Augusta/Carus_et_al*.html#14.3.

"Votive Inscription from Divodurum—Metz (Belgica)." EDH: Inscription Database—Heidelberg University. Accessed August 26, 2022. https://edh.ub.uni-heidelberg.de/edh/inschrift/HD000334.

Wace. *Arthurian Chronicles: Roman De Brut*. Translated by Eugene Mason. *Arthurian Chronicles: Roman De Brut by Wace*. Project Gutenberg, 2003. https://www.gutenberg.org/ebooks/10472.

Wagner, Charles, Jillian De Gezelle, and Slavko Komarnytsky. "Celtic Provenance in Traditional Herbal Medicine of Medieval Wales and Classical Antiquity." *Frontiers in Pharmacology* 11 (2020). https:// doi.org/10.3389/fphar.2020.00105.

Wales, Gerald of. *The History and Topography of Ireland*. London: Penguin Books, 1982.

Webster, Jane. "At the End of the World: Druidic and Other Revitalization Movements in Post-Conquest Gaul and Britain." *Britannia* 30 (1999): 1. https://doi.org/10.2307/526671.

Weekley, Ernest. *An Etymological Dictionary of Modern English*. London, UK: John Murray, 1921.

Wood-Martin, W. G. *Pagan Ireland; an Archaeological Sketch a Handbook of Irish Pre-Christian Antiquities*. London: Longmans, Green, and Co., 1895.

"Ymddiriedolaeth Ynys Enlli / Bardsey Island Trust." Accessed August 27, 2022. https://www.bardsey.org/.

"Ynys Enlli." Pomiferous.com. Accessed May 16, 2022. https://pomiferous.com/applebyname/ynys-enlli-id-496.

INDEX

A

H

I

J

K

N

O

P

Pair Pen Annwn, 112, 227

Path Candle, 312, 333, 382–384, 403,
407–411, 414–419, 423–425, 430,
431, 449, 458

Path Shrine, 304, 325, 382–384,
404–406, 431, 449, 458

Peredur, 102–109, 171, 309

Physicians of Myddfai, 80, 157, 232,
356–358

Plutarch, 23, 120, 121, 133–135

Poetry, 17, 62, 88, 98, 104, 110, 112,
113, 152, 159, 180, 196, 208, 227,
229, 233–239, 241, 243, 245, 246,
262, 281, 284, 286, 287, 301, 303,
305, 325, 386, 462

Pomponius Mela, 83, 84

Posidonius, 85, 86, 134

Preiddeu Annwn, 57, 62, 63, 102, 108,
110–112, 150, 160, 233–235, 239,
285, 286, 290

Priestess, 3, 4, 16, 74, 77, 114, 115, 117,
119–121, 129–132, 156, 179, 182,
190, 191, 212, 214, 218, 220–222,
226, 231, 260, 261, 264, 267, 269,
270, 272, 278, 279, 284, 289, 290,
292–294, 296, 297, 301, 309, 315,
323, 325, 329, 337, 345, 355, 361,
363, 384, 396, 413, 425, 430, 451,
461, 462, 465, 466, 468

Priestessing, 4, 115, 209, 211, 212, 216,
218, 223, 245, 266–269, 271, 273,
363, 369, 370, 385, 390, 414, 457,
466

Prophecy, 15, 26, 27, 38, 56, 64, 87, 89,
101, 112, 117, 137, 140, 143, 152,
156, 159, 168, 169, 207, 216, 217,
227, 232, 235–237, 241, 243, 246,
261, 268, 277, 287, 289, 301, 302,
343, 345, 346, 388, 462

Prydwen, 290

R

Realm of Land, 151, 227, 231, 249,
256, 257, 280, 281, 284, 322, 328,
336, 389, 430, 432, 440–442

Realm of Sea, 227, 231, 249, 256, 257,
280, 281, 283, 284, 344, 349, 350,
354, 360, 389, 430, 432, 440, 441

Realm of Sky, 228, 232, 249–250,
255–259, 280, 281–282, 283, 290,
(*Realm of Sky, cont'd*) 300, 308,

314, 350, 377, 390, 430, 432, 440,
443–444

Rhiannon, 53, 192, 201, 222, 288, 323

Ritualist, 261, 263, 266, 277, 320,
359–363, 366, 373, 383, 388, 397,
400–402, 416, 427, 448, 460

Robert de Boron, 40

S

T

To Write to the Author

If you wish to contact the author or would like more information about this book, please write to the author in care of Llewellyn Worldwide and we will forward your request. Both the author and publisher appreciate hearing from you and learning of your enjoyment of this book and how it has helped you. Llewellyn Worldwide cannot guarantee that every letter written to the author can be answered, but all will be forwarded. Please write to:

Jhenah Telyndru
c/o Llewellyn Worldwide
2143 Wooddale Drive
Woodbury, MN 55125-2989
Please enclose a self-addressed stamped envelope for reply,
or $1.00 to cover costs. If outside the U.S.A., enclose
an international postal reply coupon.

Many of Llewellyn's authors have websites with additional information and resources. For more information, please visit our website at

www.llewellyn.com